From Poverty, To Prison, To Prosperity.

God's Making of Tekur Dalga Anbessa

(2022)

Tekur Anbessa

I dedicate this writing to my Mother, Evelyn Miles.

"Honour thy father and thy mother: that thy days may be long upon the land which Yahweh thy Elohim giveth thee." Exodus 20: 12.

The Kingdom of Yahshua The Christ Presents.:

From POVERTY,

To PRISON,

To PROSPERITY.:

God's Making of Tekur Dalga Anbessa

Chapter 1.

From Poverty,

"Poverty and shame shall be to him that refuseth instruction: but he that regardeth reproof shall be honored." Proverbs 13: 18.

~

Hello my Jewish and Church friends. I am The Holy Priest, Prophet, and Minister of Justice of Yud- Heh- Vav- Heh, Tekur (T- coor Dalga (Dalga) Anbessa (Ahn- bes- sa), but I didn't start out that way. I was born as Jamie Lamont Miles on a Wednesday, February 19, 1975 to a 27-year-old happy and aspiring Holiness pastor, named Elder Larry J Miles, and a 25 year old teacher. Her name is Evelyn Miles. But at church, the Saints all call her Sister Miles.

My parents first met through one of my father's friends, all the back in 1969. My father's friend, Butch had been dating my mother's sister, named Audrey. Butch told my father, "she gotta lotta sisters." And when my father went on around there, that's how he met my future mother.

My parents became married on February 8, 1971, and my mother would join and attend the Gospel Spreading Church of God, with her husband, that was founded by the Elder Lightfoot Solomon Micheaux, all the way back in 1919. That was 102 years ago from now, when we was just 54 years removed from crude negro slavery.

My Dad is a high school graduate of the 1966 Class of Huntington High School. He endured a rough childhood life himself. He was virtually raised in a single- parent household after his parents had divorced. He grew getting shuffled around between living with his mother, to living with his father, to living with his grandfather and grandmother, just so he could eat and survive.

Sometime in 1969 he joined the 3rd Marine Battalion of the United States Marine Corps, just as a means of supporting himself as a man. During the time of his enlistment America was also engulfed in a bloody raging war in Vietnam. That was the war that the Americans thrusted themselves in as an attempt to support the French against the Vietnamese's 30- year struggle for independence.

It was on the battlefields of Vietnam that my father first encountered the experience of having the Holy Spirit of God work in his life.: there was one time he was taking cover out near a field. And The Holy Spirit of God spoke to him saying.: "MOVE NOW."
And he moved.

When he went back to the spot that he perceived as "safe," that was out near the field-- there was scrapnell everywhere; all over the ground. My father realized that if he hadn't listened to The Lord, if he hadn't "MOVED;" he woulda been a Deadman.

At least a second time, my father was with his company, down in a bunker. Another perceived "safe" place, designed to prevent gunfire and a bomb attack from their Vietnamese opposition, when the Lord said to him, "MOVE NOW."

My father listened to THE VOICE that had been speaking to him, and he exited from out of the bunker. When he came back.: the bunker had been decimated in a bomb attack. Again, had my father not listened to the Lord, had he not "MOVED," he would've been a Deadman.

My Dad survived multiple skirmishes with death and quickly discovered that perhaps this military culture was not going to be the ultimate calling for his life. The Lord returned my father home. Home to his friends. Home to his family. And home to his future wife. During which time he still enjoyed cigarette smoking and his daily consumption of alcohol. Until one day, while he was relaxing with a drink of beer and catching a smoke, that the Spirit of Lord swept through the room, and frightened him. He heard a noise, that he ran from the room so fast, he ran straight to the trash to throw his beer and all of cigarettes away, including the one he was smoking. He never smoked or drank since.

The Lord say in HIS Word.: "THE FEAR of Adonai is the beginning of wisdom." Mishlei (Proverbs) 9: 10. Complete Jewish Bible. emphasis added.

Not only did my father not regress back to smoking and drinking, but he went straight into his ministry.

By 1974, while my mother was pregnant, Elder Micheaux had missed my generation. Even though I never had the physical opportunity to meet Elder Lightfoot Solomon Micheaux, never the less, the rest of my life would be forever affected by his doctrine and his very unorthodox brand of religion, and the way he taught and influenced the Bible. His attitude and charisma became a behavior that would be inculcated into each of his successors and congregation alike, including decades after his death. When my father would spill over into his own wonderful insombering sermons from the Gospel Spreading's pulpit, my Best Momma (my Father's mother), would later say that I was "rejoicing in the womb."

As I developed into the youth of my childhood, I witnessed astounding Elders who preached and taught the Word of God. They were men like Elder Willie Edwards Sr, Elder Jehu Riddick, Elder Walter Roman, Elder Tony Hurst, Elder Peter Smith, Elders' Jenkins and Rust, Elder James Johnson, and later Elder David Green.

But my father was my first inspiration. It is because of me hearing him preach, that made me want to learn how to read. The solid soul eloquence in how my father would say words and pronounce the names in the Bible, that made me want to learn how to read. I wanted to learn how to read like my father.

But church was confusing for me. Because in the midst of the ministry and all these sweet southern hymns teeming from the choir, and the babel of testimonies, and prayers, and the crying, and the screaming out of, "Thank you LORD!;" "Thank you Jesus!;" and of course the ever- popular Church famous of, "HALLELUJAH!!"

My question in all of this was.: "What is this

4

God? Who is this God? And is HE even real?" I was grappling with the concept of praising and praying to something that was invisible.
I would be told that the Holy Spirit would be, "where two or three are gathered together in my name..." Matthew 18: 20.

But was God's Holy Spirit truly even there?

We are not who we are by information. We are who we are by experience. Experience is more superior than information. And people will tell you, in information, that it's sin to doubt. But I will tell you from my experience that that's not absolutely true. As the scripture says in Matthew 7: 5.: "Ask, and it shall be given you; seek, and ye shall find; knock, and it shall be opened to you."

The problem is, that I was never actually "seeking" anything. More than half the time, I didn't even want to be in Church. I wanted to be with my friends. I wanted to be playing basketball, running football, rapping and listening to hip- hop and r&b music, and talking to girls.

But little would I know that my "doubt" in God, is what caused HIM to "seek" after me. I had my doubt, but it was young and unpretentious doubt.

Let's just take a second to rewind back to my early childhood.:

I was the only child. I had no brothers or sisters to play with. Outside of school I didn't have any acquaintances of many friends. I spent a lot of time, in the house, alone. And that's how my pillows and stuffed animals became more than my

5

friends, they became my congregation.

I started to preach to them.

I couldn't even read yet. The only words I knew were "the," "and," "Amen," and "Hallelujah!" The last one won't even in the Bible.

I would stay at my Best Momma's house. She has two daughters, Mottie and Esther. But that were both older than me. To them, I am a baby. I would even make time to break away from them, so I could go preach to some pillows. I found greater conversation in the pillow's conversation.

Sometimes I had a Bible. It was usually a little small green pocket- sized New Testament. Sometimes I didn't have any book at all. But one day my Best Momma caught me when she came to check up on me. The first time she didn't say anything.

So I went back.

Eventually Mottie and Esther would catch me. And they would laugh at me. But my Best Momma would come and push them out of the room. Then, my Best Momma had informed my father and mother what I was doing. But my parents didn't address it, so periodically I kept going. Let me take the minutes to explain to you the dynamic impact of my Best Momma.

At 5 feet 4 inches tall, she is The Queen. My Grandmother. The Matriarch. It is she, not my father, that is the Spiritual Leader of our family. Because it was her who first got introduced to Elder

Micheaux, while he was still alive, and introduced my whole paternal side of my family into the Gospel Spreading Church.

Her testimony always began from Matthew 1: 21.: "And she shall bring forth a son, and thou shalt call his name JESUS: for he shall save his people from their sins..."

At the alter, Deacon Rainey would cross his legs and rest his eyes into the meditation of her voice, and she would roll.: "... I wanna thank God for God. I wanna thank God for HIS son Jesus, that died on the cross. I wanna thank God for Elder and Sister Micheaux for showing us this beautiful way. I wanna thank God for the Saints. I wanna thank God for gettin me up this mornin! I wanna thank God for..."

I was good. Because if I was good, I might make her great list of long spiritual shout outs. So I always like to be good around her. It's because of her impact that my father would become a minister in the Gospel Spreading Church, to begin with. My Best Momma has 5 children altogether.: she has my Father, my aunts Novie, Esther, Mottie; my uncle Bobby...

And she got 'a husband she call, Pee- Wee. That's Mottie and Esther's daddy.

My momma on my momma's side, she has 8 girls and 5 sons. My mother is her 3rd oldest child. My mother was born April 1, 1950 to a World War II US Army Veteran and a full-time wife and mother. My mother was born and raised in Newport News just like my Dad. She lived for one year in Philly, but came back to be apart of the 1968 Graduating Class of Huntington High School.

    My first reminiscences of my mother is of a very strong woman who showed very little weaknesses, even during times of humor. She remains even with that same sense of humor even up to this day. Back then.: I do not recall living out Seven Oak Apartments, I was too young to remember the episode where my Dad went to church one night and my mother nurtured me at home, until she saw a mouse jotting cross the floor, and she jumped up on top of a kitchen table, holding on to my baby body in her arms, all the way up until my father returned back home.

    But I do remember living on 16th Street, in a small house that was joined onto a bigger house. The bigger house was my Best Momma's house, my father and mother raised me in the smaller one. It was only one bedroom, one dining room, but that was really my bedroom. It had a bed up in there only for me. One and a half bedrooms, and a living room, so my momma could entertain her sisters and girlfriends.

    My mother taught kindergarten and summer school all year long at Buckroe Baptist Child Care Center, out Hampton. So I think. My mother doesn't drive. There's an incident where she was trying to drive to get her license, and she pushed the brakes, and my head flew and hit the windshield. They didn't have oppressive seat belt laws back then. "Yeah mommy," I cheered for her after smacking my head against the glass. I was going to be supportive of my mother no matter

8

what. But she was so saddened that she almost hurt her beautiful little son, that she never got behind the wheel to drive a car ever again. She never even got her license. So many of the times, starting from on 16th Street, my mother would catch (3) buses in the morning to get to work. So I think.

I said that my mother was strong as I will began to tell you now and reveal more later; she would awake early in the morning, probably around 4 am, go to the bathroom to get herself together, get herself dressed, iron my clothes and set everything out for me to go to school, fix breakfast, write me a note of the day's instructions, and get her bags together. I say about 4am, because me myself, I was still in the bed sleep. All I know, she would be to work by 6 in the morning; and she had to catch (3) buses; so she had to be up early enough to do all that. All I know.: by the time I get up, my momma be gone!!!

All I knew she was there last night.

Before I knew she had a job-- I had to find out where she be going before I get up. So I lay back in the bed; you know.: like I'm sleep. I see her moving round in the house. She tryin to tip- toe, like she some kinda Santa Claus or somebody. Then, before she fly out the house, she be trying to turn the knob, and close the door all quiet, so I don't get up. But I was on to it. I jump up and zoom up out the house right behind her.

I don't know where she think she was going-- leaving me and my daddy, by ourself. And she got 3 bags in her hand and her purse. She dressed like she packin, and ain't coming back. I'm running down behind her, hollering and crying.

"Jamie! Get back in that house."

"NOOOOOO!!!"

"Jamie, get back in that house. You gon make me late for work."

HUNH! That's how I learned she had a job. She out here working- - somewhere...

I'd be wrapped around her legs. That's as far as I could stand up.

"LARRY! LARRY! Get up," she'd drag me all the way back to the house.
"Get up and get Jamie. I gotta go to work. I'm gon be late. He gon make me late!"

But, I still didn't know she was catching (3) buses. Hunh. I didn't find that out til the summer.

If I missed my momma; it was still some mornings she would get past me, then I had to be humiliated by my Dad's version of waking me up.:

"Get outta that bed and wash yo face and hands," he'd annoy me singing that stupid song, and at the same time he'd be standing there flicking my light on and off, and on.

"UUGGHHHH!!" I'd make for him to just go away.

I'd cover my head in the blanket for him and that light to leave me alone. But it ain't work...

"It's time to roll like 'a big wheel," he'd say while reaching down to lift me out the bed.

"UUGGHHHH!! UUGGHHHH!! UUGGHHHH!!" I would holler, scream, kick, and punch.

"Yap, yap, yap, yap," he would silence my violence.

I would hate him waking me up. But by the time I got my bath and put on my clothes, I was alright. By the time I get to the table, my mother had already left breakfast. And one of her Day's Instruction Notes. That's not what it was called. It ain't got no name. That's just what I call it for the sake of doing this book.

Jamie,

The note would start. That's how I knew it was for me.

Different notes said different things. It's all according to what she want me to do. I couldn't read. I just know all my life she wrote in cursive. So I'd sit up doing breakfast, while my Daddy read it to me.

Then after he read me mine...

Larry,

He won't exempt. She had one for him to. Erry day she wanted us to do something. Even when she ain't there. My dad would drive me to

school, at the time, I was going to Zion Baptist
Child Care Center in downtown Newport News.
After he'd drop me off, he'd drive himself to work- -
I'm just guessing...

When the summer times came, my mother would
take me with her to school, where she worked.
These were the mornings I had to be up earlier than
usual.

When she was ready to get me up, she'd just stand
there, "Jamie, Jamie, Jamie, Jamie, Jamie." I'd look
at her to see she was just there calling me over,
over, over, and over.

Sometimes, she too would flick the light.

"Get up!" she would demand.

"UUGGHHHH!!" I did my usual on her.

Then she'd come to snatch me up, and I'd get to
hollering, screaming, kicking, but I wouldn't punch
momma.

And she'd say, "Boy, stop!! before you make me
break 'a nail."

Boy, that's the last thing you ever wanna do
as a child, is make yo momma break her nail. That's
when I knew it was time to chill out. With her, this
was the only time I ain't have no kite sitting up
waiting on me, when I get up out the bathroom.
And she used to buck on my breakfast.

"Come on. You can eat when you get to
school."

Man, when she used to go to work.: that was the longest walk in my life.: "Sonny, when I used to walk with my mother to school, I used to walk fo 20 miles..."

Naw, it won't that bad.

"Jamie, hurry up! Stop walking so slow! We gon miss the bus," she scolded my lack of urgency.

For #1.: My legs ain't nowhere as long as yours.

Despite the fact, she got about 40 pounds in her hands and a purse. If I was moving to slow, she'd even lift me up, to carry me, 40 pounds, plus 'a purse. She won't ordinarily gon miss that bus. We had to walk straight down 16th Street, past Wickham, past that lil wrap around street after you pass Wickham, past Marshall, all the way past Madison, past where Lassiter used to be, all the way past the school that sit out in front of Lassiter, just to stop at 6th and Ivy.

Once we catch the 6th and Ivy bus, that take us over a bridge cross town, over on Washington Avenue. Washington Avenue won't the ghost town it is now. It was lit with Woolworths, banks, and department stores, and restaurants all up and down the strip back then. This was way, way back-- before they started Wal- Marts.

Yeah, but Washington Avenue was really a strip. And the bus station was over there, and that's where me and momma would transfer buses. My mother would let me put my change in the machine or hand the driver my transfer ticket.

When I was riding with my momma on the bus, I couldn't make unnecessary noise. I couldn't kick the back of other people's chairs. I couldn't try to fight the other kids on the bus. I couldn't pop my gum. In other words.: I couldn't be bad.

We'd ride that bus all the way out to Hampton, to a bus stop out Settlers Landing. They had a strip mall up out there. That's where Miller and Rhodes was at. But that's where we used to get up on a very very little, small bus, called a shuttle bus. And the shuttle bus would drop us off right in front of Buckroe. All we gotta do is walk right cross the parking lot. AND THERE IT WAS.:

Buckroe was broke down to four major parts. Before we would go to where my momma worked at-- she would show me off to all her co-working staff. She made sure everybody "at work" see me with her. First.: we'd go through the nursery. That's where Ms. Jean, Ms. Meredith, a few other babysitters, sometimes Ms. Lewis, and sometimes her boss, Ms. Bailey.

"This is my son, Jamie," she would always be grinning all the way from ear- to- ear.

The nursery always smelled like doo- doo, and like somebody tried to cover it up with baby powder. Then the second major part, which actually is the first major part, but when you walk across the parking lot, you get to the nursery First. So, for the sake of finishing this book, we just gon say the second part was where Ms. Bailey's office was, Ms. Bailey's assistant, Ms. Lewis' office was, the cafeteria (where I would eat breakfast... and lunch), and my momma's classroom. All her students and their parents loved to see "Mrs. Miles." I saw so many other people show so much love and admiration for my mother. And she would introduce me until everyone became familiar.

It was (3) classrooms in her building. But only (2) teachers.: my momma and an older black lady named Ms. Wilson.

My mother, Ms. Wilson, and Ms. Meredith were the only (3) black teachers. Well, Ms. Meredith was a babysitter... but umm... don't mess up this story.

The other major part was about a three-story white building. But for the most part it was empty. They only had (1) teacher over there.: Ms. Lewis' daughter named Ms. Penny. Umm, umm, umm, umm, umm, umm.

And they had a Chapel.

I would spend my early years in class with my mother. Despite the fact my momma taught the class, she ain't cut me no breaks. If I got to acting up, she gon pull me out her class, and she gon pop me. Sometimes she had to pop me more than two times a day. I stayed up in the bathroom getting straightened out, more than I was in the classroom. If I cut up, and my momma won't around, Ms. Bailey or one of the other teachers, would just let my momma handle me.

When the other parents would come bring in they kids, or come pick them up-- I better be on my best behavior, just so she could say, "That's my son, Jamie," and flash that big pretty smile God had put on her face.

But I loved going "to work" with my momma. I
hated when our summers would be over.

My early schooling was primarily at Zion
Baptist Child Care Center in downtown Newport
News. That is where my mother wanted me to go
despite most family refuting that she take me with
her to Buckroe year around. My mother remained
objected to it. Perhaps part of the reason is that she
didn't need me to slow her down all year around.

My dad would drive me up to Zion, and the
school's van would drop me back off. My Principal's
name was Ms. Daye. She was very nice and she was
fair, as far how she applied her administrative
policies. Zion also had a Chapel to it. I was
definitely getting used to seeing the Church as some
institution of righteousness, everywhere I go. But of
course my favorite time was being on the
playground. By the time I would get back home,
neither one of my parents or my Best Momma
would be home from working at Hampton Institute.

Mottie generally would watch me until
everybody else get home. I spent a lot of my early
childhood being around Mottie. The whole time I
was trying to figure out why she wasn't my sister.
Everybody else had sisters. I was trying to figure
out why I didn't have one.

Sometimes Mottie caught a break from
having to look after me. And the Zion van would
drop me off at my Grandmomma's house.
Everything was in downtown Newport News. I went
to church at 19th and Jefferson. I went to school on

19th, in between Jefferson and Ivy. I lived on 16th, between Wickham and before you get to Chestnut. And my grandmomma's house was on 30th and Orcutt, just diagonal from Huntington, and right behind Doris Miller; the hood rec center. Converse was the sneakers back then, and niggas couldn't wait to run scuff in a fresh pair of Dr Js out on the basketball court.

At this stage, I was still stuck in my church zone, because that was the dominant influence in my life.

One day, I traveled my ministry on the road... all the way up into my momma's momma house. My Grandfather lives there too. He even built the house himself. He did all the carpentry and maybe the brick work. He changed a former local corner store into a whole home for his family. But somehow, they only call it her house. Probably cause she gave him 13 children. She has 8 girls.: Dottie, Audrey, Evelyn, Paulette, Barbara Ann, Woodrina, Vivian (who we call Theresa), and Shanda. And 5 sons.: Ike, Charles, Pernell, Curtis (But we call him Ronnie), and Johnnie.

And her name is Pauline Jones. But I just call her "Grandma" for short. My Grandma is an Original Georgia Peach. She was born on August 8th in 1926, on a hog farm in Millen, Georgia. She got married to my Grandfather young, when she was about 16.

I know she has 13 children. I know Dottie is my Grandma's oldest child, I know Audrey came second, my mother is third, Ike was the first son, and he came about 4th, but after that I lose the order of the children. Til this day, I still don't know the order of all the children; it's too many children. I just know that Shanda is the absolute youngest out of all my Grandma's 13 children, and Johnnie is second to Shanda. All of her children are by the same one man, my Grandfather. And all of my mother's brothers and sisters are older than me. To them, I am a baby.

My uncles might entertain me preach to them a little bit when they was sitting there drunk or buzzing off they high. They prolly thought I was tweakin. But eventually they would roll on out on me, and I would be left alone.

But that left me alone. And when I was alone, I consoled in my congregation. At my Grandma's house, I had all different pillows. Since my uncles left me there; I used their pillows and posted me up a congregation.

Then one day my Grandfather, Isaiah, caught me. He has a towering 6 foot something and at least 180-pound physical presence. He would stare down behind me from on top of the three rungs of stairs, that separated his living room from the boys' rooms. Sometimes he would try to crack the door, so he could sneak up on me. But the wooden white painted door was old. It always squeaked. That's how I knew he was there.

I stared up at him, not knowing what else to do. His reflection would even glaze along the long mirror on the bedroom's right wall.

"Go 'on preacher!" he rustled out to me. Then he'd leave the stairs.

Later, he told my momma about me preaching, when she came to pick me up. At first, they probably all thought I was crazy to be talking to myself, but then the word got to swirling around the family, and they just chalked it.: that I was following in my father's footsteps. That one day, I would be a preacher.

During this time, I was only like 4 years old. How was I supposed to be a preacher, and here it is I can't even read??

And what's even worse, I was too young to know anything about it then, but I didn't have no life experience.

I was only 4 years old. I ain't even went through nothing to preach about. But one thing I did have: an invisible vision. My invisible vision is what gave me my courage. When I wasn't preaching, I would find other things to get into. I would plunder through my uncles' rooms for all they jewelry and money. Once they knew I was stealing from them, they knew they had to do a better job putting things up. Otherwise, I was gon have they jewelry back at my house, and rockin it wit my bell bottoms wit the patches in the knee; and even had money to go cop me some candy, some ice cream, maybe some extra milk... something.

While I was still going to Zion, one time there was this teacher. I think he was a substitute, but he was regular enough for me to develop a dislike for the brother. One day while I was on the swing, swinging high as I could go, back and forth. And he walked; he got too close to my swing. So I spit on him. At first I thought I missed him, cause I couldn't see it land on him. But he looked up at me. He said, "You spit on me."

I tried to lie like I ain't know what he was talking about.: "It must've been 'a wet leaf."

"You spit on me," he said it again.

I tried to aim fo his head. But he kept looking at the sleeve of his arm. So... that must've been where it went.

"Get out that swing," he commanded me.

I ignore him. I keep on getting it. So, he walk up and stop my swing. Take me off the yard and into a room. The room got like soccer balls, basketball balls, there was some table board games, and I think I saw soccer net.

He was still talking bout me spitting on him. I was still lying.: "It must've been 'a wet leaf."

He screamed, "You did! You did!"

Then he looked around... he saw a baseball bat. He grabbed straight for the bat. When he swung the bat, he ain't swing the bat like a batter at a baseball. That's what I thought he was going to do. My first reaction was to shield my head, to try to stop him from busting my head open. But he grabbed the bat and then hit me with each end of the bat. I held onto the bat. Every time I would swing for his face, he would dodge his head, and get back control of the bat.

He struck me mostly in my arms and in my back. A few times he did hold the bat like a hitter, but he ain't all the way forcefully extend the swing. But he did still hit me. Then he went back to hitting me with the ends.

He never actually beat me down, cause I never hit the ground. And at the time, I really couldn't feel it. I guess it was my adrenaline was going. But, later that night when I got home...

"WAAAAAAAAAAA!! WAAAAAAAAAAA!! WAAAAAAAAAAA!! WAAAAAAAAAAA!!" I was a four-year-old child, I didn't know nothing else but I was supposed to cry.

"Jamie, what's wrong wit you?" my mother cut my light on and questioned me. I had broke her outta bed with her husband.

After I told her. I didn't tell her the part where I spit on the teacher; only the part where he beat me with the bat.

"Larry. Larry, get up! Wake up! Something is wrong with Jamie. Something is wrong-- something happened to your son," she told him.

By the time my Daddy came in there, I had to explain out the story again to my father, but again I left the first part out. I ain't need him to know that.

My father was about 5 foot 9 and over 260 pounds, he was a gentle giant. "Let's get him to the hospital," he told my momma.

My momma got me up and got me dressed. I was in

so much pain!

My parents rolled straight out 27th Street, to Hampton General Hospital. It was Whittaker and the other hospital; I could've went to straight down 16th. But my Dad wanted me to go to Hampton General. The doctor took x- rays and I had to tell him the same embellished version of the facts.

My x- rays came back negative. Praise the Lord. I didn't have no broken bones. And I think he gave me Tylenol for the pain, so I could sleep.

The next day.: my momma took off work and my father took off work. They was up in Zion Baptist. They was up in Ms. Daye's office. And again I had to tell the story about what happened.

Ms. Daye sat at her desk, and she listened to me. She listened to me tell half the truth. I came to find out that the teacher had been an ex- felon. And he was working that job as part of his parole/ probation. Ms. Daye terminated his employment. I don't know what else she did; whether she reported him to his PO or whatever. But I never saw him again.

I wasn't going to see him any more anyway.: my parents weren't satisfied. Especially my father.: "We're withdrawing Jamie from the school," he said to her.

"Oh please, Mr. Miles... Mrs. Miles," she tried to plead them down to keep me enrolled.

My mother followed my father's lead. They wasn't having it. My father kept asking who the teacher was,

"What's his name?" my father wanted to know.

Ms. Daye wouldn't give him his answer.

My father was trying to get her to bring him down to the office. She wouldn't do it. And once he got out to the hall, he tried to find out the classroom, but he ain't know his way. Ms. Daye wouldn't tell him. That's when he turned to me.:

"Jamie, where is your classroom?"

I was gon tell him. But Ms. Daye cut me off. She threatened my father that if he didn't stop, then she would call the police on him. He still left in a fury.

Thinking back on it now.: both of us was wrong. I did disrespect him by spitting on him. But he was wrong to beat me with a bat. A better adult resolution should've been done to discipline me for what I done. Whatever animosity we had against each other, that led up to that day ever happening; I don't wish no further ill- will towards him. It just is what it is, and it was what it was right there. I'm just BLESSED that God protected me as a child, that was in a fight, against a grown adult man that was armed with a baseball bat. The Lord protected my head from being crushed and my body from being killed.

But, that was my last time ever at Zion Baptist. My momma still wouldn't put me up in Buckroe. Zion was a private school, and it was a Christian private school. My parents tried to match that. They sought to keep me in private school, and a private school where "Christ" was the head of the institution.

But the Gospel Spreading Church was only a church. It wasn't a school. My parents even took me up to the Catholic school, they'd thought about enrolling me. Could you imagine "me" going to school everyday in one of those exclusive Catholic school uniforms.: WHOA! But to make a long story short.: there was no school that my parents could afford to send me to that was equal to or better than Zion Baptist.

That's how I ended up in public school.

Chapter 2.

For public school I ended up going to Newsome Park Elementary. The school was big as hell for my lil 5 year old body. It was a lot walking I had to do. It was longer walks from the bus to the classrooms. It was longer walks to get to the cafeteria. And a whole lot more students. I wasn't used to being around all these many people at one time.

I don't remember none of my teachers. None of my classmates. Much of nothing. I had transferred from Zion in my First Grade year. I wasn't there a whole year. And in that same year; I was gone.

I ended up moving twice by the time I left Newsome Park.

My mother had outgrown living on 16th Street up under her mother- in- law. She pressured my father that she wanted to move. My parents found a house on 30th Street, over in between Madison and Jefferson.

My Best Momma is very spiritual; and in a lot of regards conservative into being old-fashioned. She didn't own a tv. Not that she didn't believe in it; she just didn't own one. She did own furniture.: that still had the hard- shelled plastic on it.

Won't nobody's jherri- curl juice gon get up in there and ruin her classic antique living room suite. You won't gon spill no cup of kool- aid on it neither. It was a hard summer, on that crusty- sweaty plastic. Won't no A/C.

She had one stereo. One stereo with one main record. One record that used to play:: Music.: "Lord, It's gonna rain---/ It's gonna rain--/ You betta get rea- dy/ and bear this in mind/ God showed Noah/ Showed him the rainbow sign/ He said, "It won't be wa- ter, but fire next time..."

That's the gospel song she usually plays, that's sung by the Sensational Nightingales.

See, my Best Momma she loves people. She loves genuine relationships and real conversations. She loves the Lord, and she loves all the family that the Lord BLESSED her to have. She ain't have time to get distracted watching tv.

My father had a young child in the house. He had a good job making good money in the Newport News Shipbuilding. The Shipbuilding, to this day, is our area's biggest employer. Almost everybody from our peninsula, at some point or another, go through employment in the Shipyard. If not you-- then somebody in your family. Somebody you know. Somebody you close to. I had multiple family members that were all employed at the Shipyard at the same time.: My momma's brothers; Dottie's husband, my Uncle Carter; and my father. That's at the least.

You know how parents try to do the best for

they children: so my father had went bought me a color tv. Back then, a black family owning a color tv was a big deal. I was able to see all my cartoons in actual living color. Top of the Line!!

And my father had (2) cars. He had a long shot- out 4- door green Oldsmobile Ninety- Eight. It had a tan top and tan cloth interior. Automatic, and everything was electric. All the way down to the windows. White- wall tires.

That was his town and country luxury mobile. He loved it like a Cadillac. He only drove it to church and on his days off. He had another car to drive to work.:

He had a car that was a blend of being in between a beige and a yellow. It had a body style like a Chevelle. I wanna say that's what it was. It won't an SS, but it was still hard. It had the all black vinyl interior. But it was 2- door and you had to roll down the window.

But Mottie had grew attached to my tv, cause all I really watched is Bugs Bunny, Tom & Jerry, the Flintstones... After that I ain't care for the rest of tv. And the day my father came to get the tv from his mother's house, it really hurt Mottie. And I hurt to see her run upstairs to her room.

But my mother had put us in the middle of that. She wanted the tv on 30th Street. On her days off, she could watch soaps. But my Daddy did right by his wife.

On 30th Street, it was a split-level house. We lived downstairs, and a whole nother family lived upstairs. The house had what I was used to.: roaches, rats, and mice. The rats was so huge!! I used to think they was black kitty- cats crouching all over the floor. But my momma wouldn't let me go pet em. I'on know why, but they never came out the kitchen.

It's crazy, cause we had to walk through the kitchen to get to the bathroom. We ain't have but one bathroom.

In the bathroom-- there wasn't no shower. Only a sink, toilet, and tub. The tub was made out of porcelain and had shelled porcelain feet on it. It stood up for itself, off the black and gritted white square- tiled floor. We ain't have no A/C. Just fans. Something else I was used to up in the house.

In the winter, we had to insulate the windows in plastic to try to trap heat in the house, and throw 'a old blanket down at the base of the outer doors. Ask me if that ever worked.:

I had met (2) NEW friends; my friend, Kirby, had left me behind back on 16th Street. My NEW friends names were Tank and Man, and they lived right across the street. Tank was real real red and Man was real real dark skin, but they said they was brothers. They was raised by they momma. She ain't care what the hell her kids really did. She drank. She smoke. Most of the time, she prolly be drunk. Tank and Man had a tree house. And they wanted me to come over and play in they tree house.

"Come on man," they said.
"Just hurry up and run cross the street. Yo

momma ain't gon know. We got girls..."

I wasn't really into girls yet. But, I liked em. I had attraction for em. So, I was looking...

"I don't see no girls over there," I said to them.

"Yes it is. It is girls. Come on. Just come on."

I was holding onto my lil green superhero. He was foam and had a yellow cape, so he can go in water.

"Man, ya'll ain't got no girls over there-- call em and tell em come here."

Tank started calling off some girls' names. But ain't no girls never come out. I just kept seeing they same dingy- ass kitchen curtain blowing off the breeze of the opened window.

"Jamie get in this house." My momma came out. She heard the whole conversation. She poked fun at the composition of them knowing anything about getting some oochie- coochie at they lil young age. Then she sent them home before she tell they momma.

Community was different back then. The hood looked after each other, but I still don't know why I had to get in the house.: what did I do wrong.

I had another friend on 30th Street. His name was Andre. But he was younger than me. But he was cool. We always got along, but by me being a little bit older, when I play sometimes I would hurt him, and he would get to crying out real loud, and that would get me in trouble.

He was raised by his Grandma. She wouldn't let
him play with Tank and Man either. When they
come out the house.: she would make Dre come in
the house. A lot of times, I'd get stuck outside by
myself, until my momma came out to check on me.
That's one thing about it.: God had BLESSED me to
really have a MOTHER. And not jus a woman who
so happened to have a baby. There is 'a difference.

But Tank and Man was cool, for the most part. They
just looked like trouble, but they wasn't violent or
nothing like that. I think they was just
misinterpreted.

Something else about me being on 30th
Street was my father's service of the country in the
Marine Reserves. That's when more and more, I
started noticing that one time a month, when I'd
see him grab that camouflaged costume he'd have
stashed up in his closet. And it went wit these real
tall, big ass black boot, and the laces came almost
up to his knees.

Every time he put them clothes on, I knew what it
mean.: It mean he was leaving alone me and my
momma.

My momma ain't drive, so one of his
friends, somebody, or one of the brothers from the
church would have to drop him off at the Armory
over on Warwick Blvd. I would ride with him to see
him get dropped off. It would be so early in the
morning; the sun still be laid in his bed. As soon as
he got out the car.:

"WHAAAAAA!! WHAAAAAA!! WHAAAAAA!! WHAAAAAA!!" I'd start up. I wouldn't do it til he got out the car.

I cried, kissed, and hugged for him so hard, I would knock his tight- fitted fatigued hat right up off his head. After a while my mother would have to come separate me from his shirt and his neck.

"NOOOOOOOO!!" Just like a child, I'd holla, scream, and kick.

"Come on Jamie, he got to go," she would say to me.

'Go where??' What's more important than him being with me and his wife...

"Go. Just go on Larry; he'll be alright." She would hold on me so tightly, so I couldn't run back to him.

He'd grab for his large green duffle bag up out the trunk, and I'd see him exit my life through those fake silver handled doors.

Most of the time his friend, Elder Mc Nair and his wife Sister Mc Nair, used to drop him off for service. Elder Mc Nair was a man just like me.: he loved to hear my Father preach.

Elder Micheaux was a 20th century preacher, that was truly ahead of his time. Before all these big preachers that are out doing it today... that are called "Evangelist." Elder Micheaux was also an Evangelist. He just didn't call himself that, because in reality, he was the predecessor to the

Evangelist preachers that you might see today.

He wasn't in competition with Billy Graham; nor
could he really ever be during that time, cause Billy
Graham was a white man. Elder Micheaux
was a light fair skinned man. He probably could
"pass," but you can clearly see, he ain't no
Whiteman. Just like Elder Micheaux, Billy Graham
was also a predecessor of today's evangelistic
preachers. The difference was-- Billy Graham didn't
have a church. He'd travel and air his Crusades, but
he never physically had a church where Believers
could go to attend. So, with the help of the Lord,
Elder Micheaux built (7) churches along the east
coast, from New York and Philly, all the way down
here, to Virginia.

His era was predecessor to "Evangelism"
and the architectural molds of the great designed
big mega churches that you see today. Elder
Micheaux was LIVE and IN PERSON, but during
his day, RADIO was king. TV was new technology.
And by the time he passed in 1968, color TV was
NEW space- aged technology for him. He'd died in
the same year that Dr Martin Luther King was
assassinated, so he never had the luxury of
experiencing administering a sermon at the grand
scale of what a Bishop TD Jakes, a Joel Olsteen, or
what a Creflo Dollar might experience today.

But before he had passed, Elder Mc Nair
had went to him and asked him for permission to
build a branch from off one of his (7) main stay
churches. It would still be called The Church of
God, but it would be a branch from off the tree,
whereby the Spirit of God, he was able to found.
And so Elder Micheaux ok'd him and gave him

32

permission. And Elder Mc Nair went and built a church off of Tidewater Drive out there in Norfolk, Virginia, and he called it, The Church of God.

It was a small, what you'd call "a hole in the wall" styled building. It had great big store front aluminum and clear glass paned windows. They was old. And huge squared black and muddled white checkered tiled floors. A lot of the tiles were split, broke, cracked, or missing. We sat up in some brass- plated aluminum backed chairs; with the pads for your back and yo butt to sit down. It was the same chairs you might find at a kitchen table. We had a few rows of em.

It did have a stage for a pulpit, the pulpit had red carpet, and at the altar, it had a table, and the table had a chair, for the deacon to go sit down. But we ain't have no deacon.

We did have one piano for Elder Riddick's sister, Sis Mary to go sit down and pipe us out some tunes. And the back had some extra checkered tiled floors that was split, broke, cracked, or missing. Then, it was a pile of tiles huddled up in right a corner, that ran like 2 feet along the wall, that was split, broke, cracked, or missing off the floor.

There was an open room, that was over to the left side. But it was just an open space. It looked like it was hanging around for some bright ideas. Finally, it did have (2) bathrooms, that were off to the right, before you walk into 2 feet of tiles. It was supposed to be one for men and one for women. It was supposed to be. Usually, only one bathroom worked at a time, so we all had to wait on one toilet. And, there was a back door.

Our church got broken into-- a lot.

We'd get there on Sunday mornings, and Elder Mc Nair would say, "Somebody been in here."

And we'd all go check. We'd be all scared, tip-toeing in a line to the back, praying the robber ain't still in there; and shown nuff, the back door would be kicked wide open.

"I don't know why they keep breaking in here. It ain't no money in here anyway," Elder Mc Nair would say out loud, as he scuffled to push back close the door with the faulty security lock.

Then we'd all go back and get down to service.: Elder Mc Nair, Sis Mc Nair, Sis Mary, my mother, me... and my Daddy. If he was there.

When he wasn't there, Elder Mc Nair would say, "Junior, you gon be alright."

And Sis Mc Nair would correct him, "Dear, his name is Jamie."

I liked being called "Junior."

He and my Grandfather was the only (2) that gave me my first nicknames. My Grandfather didn't call me Jamie. He called me "Peanut." He never said why, but probably cause of the shape of my peanut head. He and a few of my family on my mother's side might call me "Peanut."

I liked being "Peanut."

34

But I saw Elder Mc Nair exactly the same as I saw my Grandfather or as I might see Pee- Wee.: I saw him as my Grandfather. I love him like a Grandfather. He was always very friendly, always nice, and he was an extremely good man.

All my life I never seen him do nothing but good. After my father went off, he'd drive me and my momma back to his house. They lived out of a small town called Grafton, in Virginia. Just off the road from Route 17.

Back then his house was all rural. It was about 2 or 3 houses in front of his drive, but when you go all the way to the back.: there was his house shuttered by pitch black dark woods of grimacing trees. I was a fan of Horror movies-- what today they call "Slasher Films"--- Friday the 13th, Nightmare on Elm Street, Halloween. I could just see at any time, Jason standing up, and chasing us through the damn woods.

One of them would go and turn on the porch light. But once you get inside their coupled home was so nice, warm, cozy, and holy love. They had central heat, that blew through the vents of the floors. And Sis Mc Nair loved to cook.

She would go in her kitchen and she would cook for me, her husband, and my mother. It was always good.

Just like her husband, Sis Mc Nair was always very nice, friendly, and good. They never got out they bed to do evil. And just like her husband.: I'd wonder why Sis Mc Nair wasn't my Grandmother? I'd loved her, and she'd loved me, like a Grandmother would a Grandson. I value her like a Grandmother; I just had never called her that.

The way she cooked; it would take my mind off my father. And she almost always kept me a fresh piece of cake or other some other sweet tasty dessert, and some sugar hard candy. Umm, umm, umm, umm, umm.

I was so BLESSED in my early childhood to be surrounded by quality good people.

My family had moved from 30th Street to Paula Maria Apartments, up on 76th Street. I was rezoned. That's why I had to stop going to Newsome Park. I ended up going to Parkview Elementary School to finish out my first-grade year. Parkview is on the corner of Jefferson Avenue and Mercury Blvd. I only went there for the first grade. The only thing I didn't like about Parkview, they would cut into my play time, they kept on trying to teach me something.

One minute it was alphabets, then how to write the alphabet, then it was numbers, and colors, you know; stupid stuff like that. I didn't care for none of this stuff, all I wanted to do is play. I liked to do art, but my conceptualization of how to do art was different from my teacher's. They had disciplined structures and formats.: my style was far from conventional. As far as me learning how to write and distinguish all these different alphabets and how to count-- HA! I could care less! As long as I could read my mother's cursive notes.: I was good. Plus, the alphabets they was trying to teach me to write didn't look nothing like hers.

I took some of my first pictures at Parkview.
I took one on construction paper. I stood on my left
side and they turned me to 'a silhouette. My teacher
used a pencil and traced me from the egg shape of
my head to the collar on my shirt, onto a red sheet
of construction paper with a white construction
paper background, and it had a black construction
paper border.

The next Parkview picture I had, was more
like a real picture. They had the whole first grade
sitting Indian- style out on the lawn, in front of the
school, according to homeroom assignment.
Everybody was in the picture-- students, teachers,
probably kitchen staff. All I remember was seeing
this red car coming from across the James River
Bridge, and onto Mercury Blvd. I was looking to see
was it my Daddy's Chrysler. I turned my head on
the picture, to see if it was him coming to pick me
up. To this day, my parents have that picture of me
looking off to the side.

At Parkview was where my attraction for
females had heightened. When I got to Parkview, I
saw beautiful and female both in the same package
for the first time. The girl's name was Makeba. It
was the first time, a girl my own age, caught my
attention. I had never seen a girl like her before.
She had smooooth brown skin, big pretty bubbly
lips and brown eyes, and she had a butt. She won't
flat like the other girls. She had 'a body more like
one of my momma's friends.

It was just one problem.: Makeba lived out
Woodsong. Woodsong was the most dangerous
projects out Newport News. It was well
established.: if you ain't from out there, don't go out

there. Woodsong was so bad, the police ain't even go out there.

Woodsong was so bad, they built 'a hospital right up next to that muthafucka. If you got shot, if you got stabbed-- if you can get to Newport News General Hospital-- you might get 'a chance to make it. But you gotta get to the hospital now, cause the ambulance ain't comin to pick you up.

I'm tryin ta tell ya.

Back before it was called Woodsong, it was called Chantilly. All that shit was bad. A bad bad place. So bad, they probably had they own section out Pleasant Shade Cemetery, just fo niggas that got smoked out Woodsong or Chantilly. And they ain't care how old you is; how young you is.: if you ain't from out there, don't go out there.

As for Makeba, I saw her again in 2nd grade. That's crazy, the baddest girl on the planet, and outta all places, she lived in the most dangerous project in the city. By this time, we was going to Briarfield Elementary School. Briarfield was in a fence, just right of Woodsong Apartments, where Makeba stayed, and footsteps in front of Briarfield Apartments. On the corner of Marshall and Briarfield Road.

After only one year at Parkview; they tore the school down. They turned it to a strip mall. That whole little area; they put up a Roses, a Subway, Pic N Pay Shoes, a Pizza Hut, a Hot N Now... I guess that's what they really think of a child's education.

In 2nd grade I finally tried to holla at her.

But I was too scared to talk to her myself. I went to her friend, to express to her girl I had an interest in her. But she sent word back she already had a boyfriend, some nigga named Butch. I was fucked up.

By the time, I started 3rd grade, I got changed schools again. They closed Briarfield down, like they did Parkview. They jus ain't tear it immediately down, and make it to a strip mall. I'on think nobody woulda shopped at that mall, except people who lived out Woodsong. But eventually they did tear Briarfield down. And years later it would turn to Heritage High School.

For 3rd grade, I got sent to Sedgefield Elementary School. Only one problem.: Makeba ain't here. After 2nd grade, I would never see Makeba again. I thought we would grow up together, that maybe sometime around High School, Butch would be gone. But now, she was gone. And I had to adjust to a life of not being around her.

Since Makeba was gone, I guess it was time to get back into my ministry. One day I had brought my ministry back home to the house. Well it was an apartment, but uh.:

When I brought my ministry back home, I wasn't welcomed with the warm church hospitality and Christ spirit filled comforting arms I had hoped for. I was opposed from...

my Father.

Of all people.

Despite the fact he had heard I was doing it-
- I think when he saw me doing it, there was a
whole different reaction.: "JAMIE, WHAT ARE
YOU DOING!??"

My Father would pull off his belt, and he would
beat me.

He would whip me, and whip me, and whip
me, and whip me. I don't think that that's how this
is supposed to work. I wasn't supposed to be gettin
beat by my inspiration. But that's what happened.

His eyes would be bulging blood shot red. I
would wait to see if tears would bubble up in the
panes of his great big wide dejecting eyes. In his
passion, he saw what I was doing was "playing"
with God. And he took this as his chance to gruffle
out, "You got the devil in you!!"

I guess this was his way to physically fight the devil.

But despite how many times he would whip
me-- was I ignorant? Was I stupid? Or was I
courageous and curious? I would still keep to
preaching my ministry. Either I would preach, or he
would beat this devil out of me.

Then one day, the LORD must've looked down from
Heaven. Because HE sent me some help.

One day I was preaching when both my
father and mother was at home. At the time, I was
probably about 8. My mother and father were still
at the dinner table, finishing dinner. I went into my
room and I closed my door to start preaching a little

bit above, "Amen," "of," and "the." My Father already knows what I'm doing, so he tips up behind me with his belt in his hand to beat me.

I ducked his first swing and grabbed his belt. At some point he gotta work for this ass whoopin. Then the unthinkable happened...

My mother came in to stop him from beating me. This had never happened before in history...

It was unusual because my parents always supported the side of the other. If one of my parents ever decided to beat me, the other wouldn't stop it. Sometimes, I even got doubled teamed. I used to get whippings so much, I thought it was normal. But this time, for the first time, my momma had stopped him. WOW!!

The LORD had given me protection in my nurturer... in my mother.

And later when my Father caught me doing it again at my Best Momma's house, he pulled for his belt to beat me again. But this time he was stopped by my momma and by his momma. Pretty soon after that he was no longer pursuing me. If he would catch me doing it, he would just leave back out the room. Even if it was just me and him at home alone.

That was one of my first obstacles that the LORD had brought me through.

But I still didn't fully know how to read.

I had some very sluggish learning habits throughout the 1st, 2nd, and 3rd grade. In the

41

summer of July 1983, following my 3rd grade year, Elder Mc Nair had gotten extremely sick. He went into the hospital.

He had been doing so bad, that I couldn't even go with my parents into his hospital room to see him. I would have to wait in a small air space, that swung over top of the parking lot at Riverside Hospital and wait for my parents to come back out. Sister Mc Nair was there, but I would barely even see her, she was faithful to her husband's side.

We would go to the hospital almost every night, if not every night. Then one night, it all STOPPED.: I had heard that Elder Mc Nair... had DIED.

He had passed in July from cancer in his pancreas. But I didn't go to his funeral. I couldn't take it. I couldn't take it. In more ways than one, I couldn't take it, and by July 1983 I had developed a fear of funerals.:

My grandparents used to keep (2) dogs in they backyard named Bossy and Trixie. Trixie had had puppies, and my grandparents let each of the grandchildren, that existed then, to take a puppy. I wasn't the oldest grandchild. Debbie was. But I was the 2nd oldest, and the oldest out of all the male grandchildren. I don't know how it happened, but I ended up with the prettiest puppy of them all. He had this bushy brownish- orangish fur. Like he would change colors in the sun, sometimes he looked orange. Sometimes he looked brown. Sometimes he looked both. And he had patches of fluffy white fur, all around his neck, and tipped his chin, and on the paws of his feet.

The apartments we lived in didn't allow us to keep pets. So, my puppy had to be kept at my Grandma's house. I loved my puppy so much, that I named him Puppy. It's all I could think of. When I saw him the first time, I held out my hand, and snapped my fingers, gave him some little doggy calling whistles and said, "Come here Puppy."

Puppy came up to my hand, smiling and wagging his tail. He was so happy, he fell over on his side, by my feet, just so I could rub on him. He been Puppy ever since.

I used to love to go to my Grandma's house. I didn't care; day-- if it was night, then I would just throw the back porch light on, cause it was too dark. I would come through the front door and quickly get out the back door. I went straight to the backyard, to go pick up and hug up Puppy. I'd rub him on his golden brown and white fluffy fur. I'd hold him up, so he could look at me. He'd look at me and lick out his tongue.

It got to where I would call him, and he would walk up to me, crouching low to the ground, he would keep licking his tongue back and forth, and I would rub him til he fell over on his side. He even liked me to rub the spot of white fur God put on his chest.

He rarely barked.

If my grandma stopped me from getting to the backyard, then I would just stand at her screen, and call out for Puppy.

Then one day I came to my Grandma's

house and I went to go outside to get to Puppy. But.:

"Peanut," my Grandfather broke the stripe of my plight.

"Huh," I answered him.

"Come here," he called to me.

I thought he had just wanna see me. I was standing in his kitchen, headed fo the backdoor, when I heard him kept calling me,

"Peanut...

Peanut...

Peanut." I gotta go see what he wants.

Then I'm standing there, looking at him, at his bedroom's door. He stayed a lot in his room wit the door open, the only time his door be closed, is if him and his wife be in there together. I'on know what they be doin-- they say they be sleep.

But, usually his door be open, that way he can sit up on his bed and watch tv, and know what we doing out there in the living room. My momma the one who would go in his room, sit in the wooden brown chair propped up by his bed, and spend time chopping it up with her Daddy.

But now he wanted me to go sit down in the chair.

"Sit down..." then he would talk, and say, "Go sit down.

I went and sat up in the cushion of the hard wooden chair. He had a general conversation. He could tell my mind was on Puppy. He knew I wanted to get to the backyard. That's when he casually leaned into telling me, "Puppy broke out the fence and he got hit by a car... Puppy DIED."

DIED.

Puppy what!?? Got hit by a car!?? Puppy DIED. What is DIED??

At this time, I had been alive like 5 or 6 years, nobody in my life had never DIED before.

So, "you know-- DIED." He kept trying to explain. I wasn't catching it.

Then he went into, "You know-- went to Heaven. Puppy went to Heaven."

I guess he thought he would give it to the preacher from the church perspective. When that ain't work, he got my momma in there, and both of them trying to explain to me about DIED. What DIED was...

A few months later, in the same year, this like 1980/ 81, my Grandfather had had a brother that all of us were fond of named George. My momma used to always call him Uncle George; and so growing up, that's what I called him. I called him, Uncle George.

At times, we would go to Norfolk, to see Uncle George. Well, one time we went to Norfolk to "see Uncle George." But this time, when we go "see

Uncle George," it was in a church. The church was packed. We was near shoulder- to- shoulder. And I'm seeing people. I'm seeing my family, and everybody keep crying. I'm small. I'm short up in the pew, but when I can, I keep looking up to the front of the church. And I keep seeing this long oblong object, laying out there at the front of the church. I see something in it. I guess Uncle George was in it. And he was laying down. But I took it like he was resting, in something like a bed. Then the rows got up to start moving to go "see Uncle George." Next, our row got up, it was time for us to go "see Uncle George."

My mother held me by my hand. And when we got up, she picked me up in her arms, and I saw something-- it looked like everything was swollen, dried up, and glued together.

"WHAAAAAAAAA!!" I HOLLERED, I SCREAMED, I KICKED, WITH EVERYTHING THAT WAS IN ME!!

I don't know what happened to him. I don't know what it was that got him; but I didn't want no parts of that!! That was how I learned what "DIED" was. The fear was put in to me. The Lord say in HIS Word, "The fear of the LORD is THE BEGINNING of knowledge." Proverbs 1: 7 (emphasis added); "The fear of the LORD is THE BEGINNING of wisdom: and the knowledge of THE HOLY is understanding." Proverbs 9: 10 (emphasis added); and in Proverbs 8: 13 He say, "The fear of the LORD is to hate evil: pride, and arrogancy, and the evil way, and the froward mouth," (emphasis added).

Just to name a few. But what I feel about that day, and from that day is that The LORD was putting the fear of God in me. And from that day, through me watching what had DIED or DEATH, God was putting in me the order of respecting the purity of HIS Spirit; and what life is like without HIS eternal breath.

But in the 2 or 3 years later, when Elder Mc Nair had died, I didn't go to his funeral; I didn't want to see him look like the last time, when I went "to go see Uncle George." In a way, that woulda had me up in my momma's bed, in between mommy and daddy, cause I woulda been jumping out mine's all night. Just seeing those images over and over in my head...

When I got to 4th grade, I used to go to Music class once every week. My teacher's name was Mrs. Clark. She was a great teacher, because she made me love singing out as loud as I can to a lot songs. Every class we would all compete to sing our ways into her heart, until the end of class, then she'd write us out certificates of appreciation for our participation in her class. Her certificates told us just who was her Most Outstanding student. But I lost interest in her music class, because she had me singing stupid songs like.: "Doe, a deer, a female deer. Re, I needs a lot of sun. Me, a name, I call my- self. Fa, a long, long way to run---"

The do- re- mi song. What I had wanted to do was to sing Michael Jackson. Michael Jackson was THE KING OF POP. That's what they called it, cause Michael Jackson didn't sing do- re- mi- fa- sa- la- ti- do.

Not even normal r&b wasn't enough for
Mike. Normal r&b singers just made songs for girls,
about girls. They used to use metaphors and word
play to romanticize to woman how much they loved
them, and they loved they body, and how much
they wanted to have sex; you know; it was friendly
for the radio.

But not Michael Jackson. Mike would go and make
songs, singing to men. And in these songs he would
sing to you, just how BAD he was gon KICK YO
ASS!!

So white people couldn't just go and call
what Mike was doing r&b, funk, disco, or soul; not
even hip- hop. They went and came up with a whole
New word to explain the genre of music that
Michael had been doing.: they called it POP.

And boy was Michael an EXPLOSION!! at it.
I been alive 46 years, at time of this writing. That's
almost HALF A CENTURY. I never in my life seen
another singer/ artist/ performer dominate the
scope of the globe the way that Michael Jackson
did. He could, sing, dance, perform-- the way he
entertained was DYNAMIC and ELECTRIC on a
level like we never seen.

The only one that comes close is Beyonce.

But back in the 80s, he had everybody in
world wanting to be Michael Jackson-- white
people, black people, Indian, and Asian people-- all
over the world. Regardless of young or old.
Regardless of male or female. Everybody wanted to
sing like Michael Jackson. Everybody wanted to
dance like Michael Jackson. Everybody wanted to

dress like Michael Jackson.: from the Thriller Jackets, to the Beat It Jackets, to the one left hand glove, to the penny loafers and glittered socks, all the way back up to his jherri- curl.

Whether it was r&b, whether it was soul music, whether it was hip- hop, dancing, or break dancing, every one of us were fingerprinted by the impact and influence of Michael Jackson. He had the music, the rhythm, and the fashion.

When he dropped that Thriller video on MTV; I didn't even have cable in my house. I watched it at my homie's, Omar's house. All of us was packed up in there-- even his momma was up in there. And nobody talked-- nobody talked, until that video WAS OVER. Then we waited, to see was they gon play it again. A lot of performers and artist I see today are mediocre. Mike used to do that shit! All the way through, Mike used to do that shit!

J- Lo today, she work hard!! But Beyonce, on the female side, got it on smash today; she's the best that ever did it. Because she's absolutely the most constant and consistent. But by Mike being male, he could more easily transcend the influences; not just in his music, but also in how he dressed and how he danced, to BOTH the male and female genders of his audience.

Mike had it sewed from the Hood to Hollywood. Wanting to be like Michael Jackson and being like Michael Jackson was 2 different things. Other than Michael Jackson there were other artists, whose songs that I fell in love with.: The Fat Boys and New Edition.

When I listened to the Fat Boys and New Edition do their rendition of "making music." I related to it in a way that made me feel like, I can start doing this. And that's when I discovered my new stimulation.: That's what made me start writing my own r&b songs and I started rapping.

I had wanted to be fat like the Fat Boys, but my Dad was already up to about 280 pounds, it won't enough food in the box for both of us to be The Fat Boys. So I had go choose something else.

Michael's fashion influenced every genre of people and music, but Mike's fashion was POP! it wasn't necessarily street. And that's where hip- hop had stepped in.: next thing you know, niggas was out rockin Gazelle shades, FAT shoelaces, and raccoon hats-- like The Fat Boys. FRESH!! Kangol hats and iced gold chains-- like LL Cool J, and all black leather, leather hats, tight blue jeans, three-striped track suits, and ADIDAS--

like RUN- DMC!!!!

Niggas ran and tore Foot Locker's down to get a feel for that RUN- DMC life. My aunt Theresa took me to Sears, up in Newmarket North Mall, and she bought me my First Adidas track suit, and she bought me my First ADIDAS!! Man, you couldn't tell me nothing-- I rocked that ADIDAS sweat suit till the sleeves shriveled up to my elbows. Til my pants capri'd up to my ankles. Til my big toe was busting out the front of my right side shoe. You feel me? I couldn't wait to put my ADIDAS suit on at least one time every week!

But after that, won't no more Adidas for me.

It costs too much money for my momma to dress me like RUN- DMC. The closest I got back to it, was to put on a pair of all suede Jox. The dark blue and whites one. The black and reds ones. They had four stripes. But man, that shit ain't Rockin, understand what I'm saying? But I still used to coat it in my Fat Boy shoelaces. It's the best I can do.

I couldn't get clothes out of Thalheimers, out of Foot Locker, Sears and stores like that; for real, not even A&N.

When my momma wanted to buy clothes for me, she took me to a store that was something like a thrift store; something like on a level as a Salvation Army... man, my momma took me to The Outlet.

It was strung out on Mercury Blvd, and in the summer time, when you roll up, The Outlet would have they front doors opened up on top of this tall and high curb, and they lil DAV flag flappin loud in the wind. He felt so good, you can hear him pop out his crinkles at his joints. The DAV was stores that made poor people feel better and tried to fit dignity in a paper box or up under 'a piece of plastic, all for under $10.00.

Won't no new brand names up under there. Combing the isles was like walking round in an indoor yard sale. Plenty of old clothes, that dead people probably wrote out in a will.: "I won't be caught dead in this shit."

Some washed- up bell bottom pants, 8-track and used cassette stereos, some old Intellivision video games, tentacle webs of ten-speeds and racked up banana'd seat bikes, and a wall of $20 black and white TVs. Besides my bed, my dresser, and my blue trunk my Best Momma gave me, my whole bedroom came up out The Outlet.

I used to wear the faded bell bottoms like I was back in the 70s. They wouldn't even cuff. I used to use safety pins and clear tape, or cram em in my socks like I was Mr. T, just to tame em down.

So yeah, my school pictures was all fucked up.

But, uh, back when I was in 4th grade... that's when I got introduced to Chapter 1.

Chapter 1 was a remedial reading program designed to bring me up to at least a 4th grade reading level. And-- it worked!! My reading ended up going beyond the 4th grade level!! If I could see the word, any word in English, it didn't matter what it was, if I could see it... I could read it.

I could read so well, that every January during Martin Luther King's birthday and every February, during every Black History Month, I became the kid to always get called on by the teacher to read Dr Martin Luther King's speeches.

Because of my background of growing up in a southern black church; of having a father as a minister and hearing the other soulful oratory of the other elders preaching in the Gospel Spreading Church of God, it was easy for me to imitate the cadence that was made world- famous by Dr King. Soon as I learned to read, I just got "Dr King Speech Reader" stamped across my forehead every January and February. That's what followed me all the way up, even to my 12th grade year in high school.

The other advantage to learning how to read is, I started advancing in rounds of the Spelling Bee. I always died like the 3rd or 4th round. It's my fault. I didn't like to study. I had poor lazy study habits.

The Spelling Bee was different in the 80s than it is today. In the 80s, the Spelling Bee didn't come on ESPN and ABC. If I would've had that kind of visual, I probably would've put more time and energy into studying and taking it a lot more serious.

We used to hear there was a National Spelling Bee. But we never saw it. The incentive just wasn't there like how it is today.

But to get back on track with the story: sadly enough, after I had mastered learning how to read words, I had stopped wanting to preach. I think the passion behind me learning to be able to ready, naturally had came from me seeing my father preach. His preaching was the fuel that drove me to want to learn to read. And the two went together. So when my family saw me preaching or with a Bible, they just automatically presumed, I was trying to be a preacher.

But after I had learned to read, that's when I took up other interests.

Chapter 3.

I was into liking kung- fu and karate, because of Bruce Lee. I was into to football, because football players made a lot of money to run around wit 'a football. I had wanted to do something with myself, where I could buy my momma a house.

I liked boxing, because of fighters like "Marvelous" Marvin Hagler and "Sugar" Ray Leonard. I loved hip- hop and r&b, starting from New Edition and The Fat Boys. And I liked girls.: but after losing Makeba, it was particularly hard finding that special one.

Makeba had a shape that you ain't particularly find on girls my age, you ain't even find it on too many older girls. You might find it on one of my momma's friends-- well, only one of my momma's friends.

It's crazy, because I was surrounded by girls. I had a grandma. My grandma had eight girls. Then, I had cousins.: Debbie and Sabrina. They was girls. They had friends that was girls. That's on my momma's side.

On my daddy's side, I had my Best Momma. My Best Momma had three girls. Mottie and Esther didn't have children, but Novie had a son, and TWO GIRLS, named Stacey and Colleen.

I was closer in age to Stacey and Colleen, and right before their brother Keith. Keith was a little younger than me. Keith was alright, but I always loved Stacey and Colleen more. And this part will really get me in trouble.: but Colleen was that cousin-- you know-- that you wish wasn't really yo cousin. Especially when we got older and into high school.

My momma had friends. Her friends was girls. And all my momma's friends mostly had girls.

My momma had friends from work, friends from at church, and she had friends in general; but none of her friends look like Ms. Lois. Cause Ms. Lois had some Booty, who was that "only one of my momma's friends," I was talkin bout earlier.

Ms. Lois would wear long black hair. She had this beautiful creamy light- browned skin. Pretty brown bubbly eyes. She won't flat, like the other girls. And she was always CLEAN. They had an apartment out Newsome Park. When my momma would go to see her friend, Lois, we always went in from the back of the apartment.

The back of the apartment means, you go in through her kitchen. There was these long brown beads that hanged from the opening that separated her kitchen from her living room. The wooden beads dropped down long, almost hitting the floor. And when you stepped up in her living room; her apartment was always clean. Always CLEAN.

Surprisingly, I'on know why.: but she was single. She was the mother of (2) girls that was older than me, named Monica and Belinda. Belinda looked closer to her momma than Monica, but neither of them ain't have nothing on they momma;

not even both put together.

It was one time I got sick, and Ms. Lois watched me in her home. I messed up. I messed up so bad. I was so sick, when I pissed, I didn't clean up after myself. Ms. Lois didn't like that. After I left, she told my momma, "Oh, he can come around here; but I'll never keep him again."

So much for the future.

Then, my momma had a friend named, Phyllis. But I had to call her Ms. Phyllis. It won't Ms. Phyllis, but Ms. Phyllis has a shy and quiet daughter, named Nicki, hopefully I'm spelling that right. One thing going for Nicki is she was red. But we was just friends, cause I ain't even know what it meant for a girl to be red back then. I don't think neither of us had a sexual attraction for the other. But she was still real cool.

Nicki had a father. His name is Ralph. Her mother's husband. We was in Virginia, and Ralph was locked up somewhere all the way out in Tennessee. But Ms. Phyllis loved her husband. Ms. Phyllis loved Ralph.

My momma would kick back in her chair, and get her started, and Ms. Phyllis would go off, "Ralph... Ralph... Ralph... Ralph... Ralph... Ralph... Ralph..."

She would get to grinning, batting her eyes and blushing, and patting the curls they put in her wig. And my momma would rock back laughing and enjoying her friend.

My momma had another friend, she used to like, who used to always do her hair. Her name was Ms. Joyce. But Ms. Joyce ain't have no kids. Then, she had another friend. Please forgive me, because I can't remember her name. But she had (2) children--

A son named Junior, and a daughter named Tee. All of us was about the same age. But when we go see them, I spent more time in Junior's room, playing with his toys, than I did around Tee. But we was friends; there was no sexual attraction between me and Tee.

But her momma had this long-- shot out-- I'on know what the hell it was. But we would ride around in it. She would drive; cause my momma ain't have no license. My momma be up front, and all (3) of us would be in the back.

She would stop us for Burger King or some Mc Donald's. She smoked. But she would never smoke around my momma. And she did something else, in a way my father didn't do in his cars.: she would play her radio.

My momma didn't take offense to it, but she would be surprised to hear I knew some of the songs. She would hear me singing out loud with Junior and Tee, and she would look back at me, and I would stop that singing. These won't the songs Elder Mc Nair taught me to sing.

Junior and Tee would just laugh, and laugh, and laugh.

Then, when I finally got a little bit older, and I

would go to Buckroe for the summer. That's when I would see my NEW summer school bunny, um-um, I mean teacher hhhh, Ms. Penny.

I won't in my momma's class no more.

Ms. Penny was a white girl, but she had a BODY like 'a black girl. She won't flat, and she had breast. I used to see when she brush or comb her long brown hair. It would fall in fine healthy strings or it would bounce down past her shoulders.

I had NEVER seen a white girl like Ms. Penny in person. Girls like her, you saw as center-folds in magazines, on tv, or in black kids' porn. I didn't know they lived in real life. I didn't know they lived in my real life.

She used to like to tan. We was so young, she had the whole class laying out on top of a towel, tanning in the sun. We ain't know no better.

She would be reading a book, laying on her back, in a one- piece bathing suit one minute. Then she might look and see me watching, and then she would roll away to not see me or roll over on her stomach. She would tan in the back yard of Buckroe Baptist, or she'd tan on Buckroe Beach. But she tanned mostly on Buckroe Beach.

I would go from black to crisp, while I watch her go from white to brown, wit brown hair, and brown eyes, and 'a phat juicy bubbled butt. In summer school we always had activities.: One day every week we' d have one day for the roller rink. Then we' d have one day for bowling. Then we' d have one day for the library. But it was TWO days a week.: we had one day to go to the beach, and one day to go to the pool. And that was gon be TWO days a week that Ms. Penny was gon go from her tight ass blue jeans, to jam all that ass up in that one little one- piece. Umm, umm, umm!

And yes, she used to like to get wet. The way you see her get up out that pool-- good gracious!! She was 'a white Halle Berry but badder than Pamela Anderson BADDD!! But she did restrain herself being around her children. She still did keep herself adult and professional.

Plus, I was too young to even know what to do wit it all back then, but I did like to look at it. One thing I knew how to do was to run and keep getting me some hugs. Ms. Penny was always nice and friendly to be around. One day she asked the class if they could change their name, what would they want their name to be. When she got to me, I don't know what made me think of this name, but I said, "Pierre."

I don't know what made me think of that name. But it stuck. And every time she'd see me, she'd say, "Hi Pierre," and hit me wit that smile. Woooo! Woooo!

Man, Ms. Penny is HOT!! HOT!! HOT!!

But she did break my heart when she went and got married to Rusty. Rusty is a police officer, for the city of the Hampton Police Department. Just like her, he is cool. They do make a super couple. And I'm happy she found a husband that can love her, appreciate her, and make her happy.

My momma had another friend. And she had a daughter named Althea. Althea was a special needs child. She couldn't talk. But she would sit in her wheelchair, and she'd radiate in so many smiles. I'd do silly stuff just to make her laugh. And she would laugh. I would put toys in her hands for her to hold. She could hold it, for a little while. She wouldn't throw it or drop it. Her mother used to work, but she stopped to care and share time with her daughter full- time.

That was how my mother got to meet them, cause Althea was once enrolled at Buckroe as part of early child care. My mother has the kind of love and compassion in her heart, that's not just confined to laying around on the job.

Of course my mother was friends with Ms. Wilson. Ms. Wilson only lived, maybe like a 5-minute drive from the school. And sometimes my daddy would drive us over there to kick it with her.

Or sometimes, he'd drive us over my momma's other friend house.: Ms. Meredith.

I loved Ms. Meredith like one of my momma's sisters. I saw her like a aunt. She was kind and always sweet. Almost every time we go to see her, she wanted to feed me. "Jamie, are you hungry?"

She probably would ask.

"Naw, he don't need nothing." My momma probably answer for me.

Sometimes she would let me eat. But she used to always teach me, "Never wear out your welcome."

That's one of her all- time golden rules, I still follow even to this day. The other one is.: don't be eating after other people.

She would teach me it's not good to eat behind other people, and to be sharing cups and things to put in my mouth. That was her way to warn me against germs and harmful bacteria, that could hurt me and get me sick.

One thing about it.: momma ain't got money to keep running me to the hospital.

Then suddenly up out the blue she came.:

It happened when I was going to my momma's school, in the summer. There was this girl named Tiranease Vaughan. But everybody called her Niece. Pronounced Niecey. I don't know where it came from. Niece wasn't on Makeba's level. We was the same age. So she definitely wasn't on Ms. Penny's level, or my momma's friend.

For real Niece was the girl you didn't like. She was the girl you couldn't stand. She was the girl, that when she come around, you would tell her just how ugly she is. What?? She would do it to me.

That's how our conversation always go, a great big dialogue of both of us telling the other one just how ugly they really was.

So what happened??

I had a friend named Jonathan. Jonathan was a white boy, but we didn't see race or color. To make a long story short.: when we used to go to the library once a week, they used to show us Laurel and Hardy, The Honeymooners. The Three Stooges. Yes, stupid shit like that. But every now and then, they would show us movies.

One day they played this movie, where it was a Native American and a white guy, and the two made themselves bleed at the wrist, and they touched blood, so they could be blood brothers.

WHAT A GREAT IDEA. If my momma won't gon go get me 'a brother, then I would take matters in my own hands. And who was better to be my blood brother than my Best Friend Jonathan?

We both thought it was cool. So, we got back on Center, trying to find something perfect that would slice us open at the wrist. We started with a piece of mulch, we picked up on the ground. It just scratched my wrist and made me ashy. It did nothing to cut open our wrist.

Of course some idiot would keep glass up off the ground to keep us from cutting ourself. We had to look for the next best thing.:

Jonathan found a rock. We used it, but it didn't cut. He had to find a rock with a sharp edge. He found one. And when we used it, it only cut a little bit, so we kept searching for rocks wit sharp edges. That the idiot didn't get up. We picked them up, and kept scrubbing a series of them, until.: WE HAD BLOOD!!

Ha, Ha, Ha, Ha, Ha, Ha, Ha!

Once we had blood, we locked ourselves up by the wrists. But it wasn't good enough, we needed to make this all the way official, like the Native and the white boy did up in that movie. So we got my Fat Boy shoe laces out one of my shoes, and Jonathan tied us at the wrist. And BOOM!! just like that, I had made me a brother. I'on know what was takin my momma so long. If that's all it is, she coulda been had this out the way.

OK, back to the Niece story.: So we got took for a field trip out Yorktown, in Virginia. They kept trying to tell us something about a Civil War that went on around and up in there. Then we ate lunch. Then we went to go play. Which was what I didn't need a history lesson to learn how to go do.

I was a boy, so I do what real boys do... I went to go play in the dirt. My Best Friend Jonathan came with me; he like to play in the dirt too. When I look up, out from the shrubs and grass, I could see them.

You know, THEM.

It was Katie. Katie was Ms. Penny's freckled- faced niece. And Ms. Lewis' best beloved granddaughter. But she ain't look like no Ms. Penny. She was the typical thinned- ass white girl. You know.: typical young dirty blonde-haired stuff.

I wasn't at the least impressed.

Then, she had that other girl strolling across the grass right tagged- along with beside her.: It was that ugly ass Niece!

They didn't just find us-- they came fuckin wit us. Katie came and picked Brother Jonathan, right up out the dirt, holding him by his hand, and she gave him a BIG kiss. Huh- just like 'a woman, ain't it.

'UUUHGGGGGHHHHH!!' I wanted to think to myself. This is NASTY!!

"Look, they kissin. They kissin," Niece kept saying to me.

"I know." I gotta do something to stop it. I grabbed Jonathan by his arm. But it was too late.

I'd lost my Blood Brother to Katie.

And if that wasn't bad enough, the next thing I knew.: Niece had kissed ME.

'AAUUUUGGGGHHHH'!!!! This supposed to be the part where I hold my stomach and go spit out on the ground. But Katie had broke my train of thought. I heard her say,

"She likes you... she likes you."

This is all too fast to process. The next thing I know.: Katie and Jonathan, was standing there, holding hands, kissing; boo'd up! And me and NIECE was standing there doing the exact same thing. Suddenly, Niece didn't seem so ugly to me after all.

She still wasn't no Makeba, Ms. Penny, or a Ms. Lois. But she definitely started making me feel some type of way, and gradually, I started developing an attraction for the girl I least expected. I started falling in love with Niece.

When we got back to the Center, over days and weeks, she would send one of the other students to go running up to my momma to holler out to say,

"Mrs. Miles... Mrs. Miles, Hey! Niece likes your son."

When my momma found out about me and Niece, I expected her to do the same thing she'd do to all the other girls.: I expected her to run her away.

She did it when I had TWO GIRLS!! TWO GIRLS!! Yes, BOTH AT THE SAME TIME!! I had pulled two identical twins.: Ella and Loretta.

Well, I ain't pull em. They chose me. Heh, heh, heh, heh, heh. And my momma was impressed, cause I could tell em apart.

They would rub on each one of my arms. Then they'd sit me down in 'a chair. They would massage on each part of my shoulders, rub on my chest, all while singing me songs. I'on know where the hell they got these songs from. I never heard nobody else singing them, but the two of them. But they both knew the same song.

If I had on a jacket. They would rub me out the jacket. After I found that, I always grab my jacket whenever I see these two bitches coming around. They had this very sensual way of rubbing my legs all the way down. When they get to my feet, they would look up at me smiling and singing, then they would giggle at each other, then they would look back up at me. They might rub back down my legs. Whatever one did, the other one did, like they was synchronized swimmers.

I would see a side of their face get lost down in their long brown hair. They might fan their hair from out they eyes. If their hair kept falling down in they eye, I did my part.: I would hold their hair up out they face for them.

"Thank you," they would smile up at me.

Then they would undress both pair of my shoes, and massage both of feet and all tens of my toes. They'd put my shoes back on, and tie them if I had laces. If I had straps, they'd strap em. If I had Fat Boys laces, they'd slip em back on my feet. Then...

They'd come back up.

I'on know how much these two little twin bitches know, but I was lined up to find out. I think one of them was about to sit on top of me, or some'thin like that, when all of a sudden-- out of no where we hear,

"GET OFF MY SON!!"

Momma. No, no, no, no! Not now! Not right now! Come back in 30 minutes please!

"Y'all get off my son, before I tell yo grandmomma."

They scurried to get theyself together, especially since she threatened to tell the guardian who had raised em.

Some other day; not that same day, they would do it all over again. But it was no use- - every time we was about to get somewhere,

"GET OFF MY SON!!"

"I'm gon tell yo grandmomma." But my momma was snatching. She ain't never tell they grandmomma. Of course, we ain't no that then. We was too scared to try her.

But with Niece- - she didn't act like that. When the kids would run up to her.: "Mrs. Miles... Mrs. Miles, Hey! Niece likes your son."

She would just, "Oh," and start her little happy inverted smile.

'What the hell does that mean??'

I never seen my momma act up like this before. She was on some new shit. I wasn't expecting this. I'd had girlfriends before. But I had girlfriends for like one day. Two days. A coupla weeks. Me and Niece was going past two weeks, and I ain't know what the hell I'm supposed to do. My momma won't helping me get out this shit. She liked Niece. Not only did she like Niece, she also liked Niece's parents.

Niece came fromma good family. Both of Niece's parents was active duty military. And they both drove IROC t- top Zs. At one point of time, that was the shit.

After me and Niece went 2 weeks, then a month, and a month and a half, then we picked up where we left off last summer- - I started developing more and more of a liking for Niece.

Niece wasn't just black, at the same time, she was working this sexy lil Asian look into her. You can see it, in her eyes. All up in those sexy- chinky auburned eyes. And now she'd burned LOVE!! into my heart.

Chapter 4.

It was other things that caught me off guard about Niece.: she had a brain. She was an extremely smart girl.: at history, at geography, at math... I think she was an Honor Roll Student.

She had a brother, named Jamelle. But he was younger than us. But he was cool. He was quiet. He never got in the way.

Niece didn't sing to me like Ella and Loretta did. She ain't rub on me the way Ella and Loretta did. Goodness! I'on know what ever happened to those girls, but I can bet they went on to make a lotta men happy. Damn!

But Niece did do stuff the twins ain't do. She would kiss. She would let me kiss her. She would lay up under my arm. And she was extremely hairy. The girl had black hair everywhere. She even had hair up under her armpit.

Older women would've handled this with a razor, some trimmers, a pair of clippers, something. But Niece was still too young for that. She liked to tickle me. Then when I go to tickle her back, up under them hairy ass armed pits, she would scrunch all up, so I couldn't get to it.

But one thing, Niece did that Ella and Loretta, or no other girl ever did.: she showed me my first piece 'a pussy.

Damn, she even had hair on that. I ain't bullshittin.

That bitch had 'a little bush. But she ain't let me touch it. Every time I would go to reach for it or kiss it, she'd cover it back up in her shorts and panties. Then when I move back, she would show it to me again. What 'a tease.

But I always count Niece as my First Girlfriend. Plus, Niece was the girl that kind of dissolved the crush I'd had on my teacher, Ms. Penny. I ain't no how it was gon happen, but I saw us growing up and being together. Getting married and having matching IROC Zs.

But then 5th Grade happened...

5th Grade means the summer was over for me and Niece. It was time to get to work. In 5th Grade, I'd had a homeroom teacher named Mrs. Pollack. Mrs. Pollack wasn't as phat as Ms. Penny was, but it ain't e'en matter. Ms. Pollack still had a nice shape.

She wore her hair cropped short up in the back, and off to one side. Her hair was brown, but she'd dye it in the front, and that one long side, she'd lazily let slap her in the face; she'd painted it blonde. And boy was she good at it.

Ms. Pollack was another crush, that looked like she could've been a center- fold, on tv, or in my homeboy Arnold's Playboy book. She was BAD!!

She used to always smell her right fingers a lot. But she had these pants-- they was my favorite pants. I think they was hers too. They was all white, and they was see through. And she would get to

70

writing up on the chalk board. And she would write... down...

down...

down...

down...

down...

She would write all the way down, to the last space on the board, and her booty would spread out, in them all- white see-through pants. Umm, umm, umm, umm, umm! She ain't have on a thong, you can see the panty line.

I would stop writing, jus to see her write. But after she got back up, I would complete my assignment, before she go and erase it. 5th grade was when I developed a new attraction.: Bodybuilding.

I started to fall in love with Bodybuilding, because of Rocky, because of Conan the Barbarian, because of Hulk Hogan, because of Apollo Creed and Mr. T. I wanted TO BE RIPPED!

But just like wit football and everything else, I wasn't putting in the work. I wanted to play football, but it cost money to play football. I wanted to box, but it cost money to box. I wanted to do karate, but it cost money to do karate. Everything I wanted to do, my parents didn't have the money. I didn't even feel like setting myself up for failure, by telling them I wanted to do something. That shit hurt in my childhood development.

I had some more friends I'd met from going to Buckroe.: The Stith Boys. Anthony and Shawn Stith. They lived right over the Hampton city line from me, on 76th Street; out Freda Court.

It was walking distance from Paula Maria. But I didn't go. My momma don't like me to be too far from the house. She always want to be able to find me and get to me. It's jus how she is.

I had a mother; and not just a woman who had a baby.

I hear other people's stories, of people, especially men, talk about when they was growing up, how they was raped and molested. Those types of things never happened around me.

For #1) the Spirit of God put a shield of protection, so those types of spirits couldn't even enter in, and for to happen; and

#2) Momma won't having that Man!!

If my momma didn't watch me or my father didn't watch me, my momma would only put me with people that was like her. Seriously, certain family she wouldn't leave me around. Not that they was bad people, or she feared they might rape or molest me; but it's just they lifestyle- - if they was into smoking, drinking real heavy, and getting high... she ain't leave them to care for me.

It's like she saw those people as potentially reckless and careless. My mother would never put me in a position to get hurt, harmed, or killed.

But what I was saying.: when I saw Anthony, show me his football uniform. He was playing for the Aberdeen Raiders. I was happy for bro. But that shit kinda crushed me, cause I knew I couldn't get the same thing.

Then it was crazy cause, in my whole hood, I was like the only kid getting raised by both his real parents. All my other friends came from a single parent household.: Omar, Carlos, Junior, Tina, Yolanda, and Dirty Red, Corey Mc George and his brother, Jimmy. My nigga Dwayne Sessoms. Corey Ford. JR... all my niggas.

Even Anthony and Shawn Stith. They momma was a single parent; but she worked hard for them children, UP IN THE SHIPYARD, to get them children everything they had.

She went hard on they birthdays and on the Christmas. Then, I had my nigga Mike Jones. His momma was around, but he was raised mostly by his grandmomma.

My father had long been laid off from The Shipyard, but I still wondered why I wasn't getting it, with two parents being at home.

When I first moved out Paula Maria, I didn't even have black friends. My best friend was a white boy named Robert Henderson. This white boy was cra- zy!! This the only kid I know, that used to come outside, and play in his draws. After it would rain, and you would see this white boy, barefeeted, in nothing but undergoes, stomping and dancing out the water puddle.

But he was cool.

He was real cool.

He had a little sister named Crystal, and he eventually had two identical twin brothers named TJ and James. They was all raised by they real momma and real daddy. But Barbara, the mother, was a stay- at- home mom. And um,

"Which one is it- - Roscoe or Boscoe?"

"Which ever one you wanna call me," was always his response.

But he was the father.

And that man put it down for his family. He was the only one in the house that worked. The only one. But he provided for his wife, all four of his children, and himself. He smoked like 'a drunken Russian horse.

But especially when Christmas came, you'd see the candlelight blazing at the top of the tree, decorated down in ornaments, and lit up. Then there was presents. My friend Robert had Big Wheels, GI Joes, Hot Wheels, He- Mans, robots you put oil in em, you name it. Roscoe, or whatever you wanna call him, would buy his son everything but some damn pants.

But he was so happy, I guess he really ain't even need em.

Then, there was times, I get to playing a little too

aggressive with Robert's toys. I wouldn't break the toy, but often Robert would get hurt, and...

"WHAAAAAAAA!"

My momma kept saying, "Don't wear out your welcome." I guess that what she meant.

Because that would be Robert's defense mechanism, for starting with his father, and then later on his momma to say, "Jamie, just go home."

And I would move back to my lonely room abode, without any Big Wheels, without GI Joes, without Hot Wheels, without He- Mans, and without those little plastic robots, where you just hold him by the head, and put the oil in em. I had toys, but my toys wasn't fun toys. It's 'a difference. Nothing I can do with a 1983, signed auto- penned Orioles World Series Baseball Bat. There just isn't.

Not a cool toy.

I just had to wait it out for Robert to miss me, then his family would invite me back over. Usually, it was Spaghetti Dinner. Umm- umm! Til this day, still one of my favorites.

And the happiness would last, until the next time I accidently hurt Robert again. Then, we'd have to start all back over. But to this day I love Robert and I love his family. Even, Ms. Barbara's family.:

She has a sister named, Ms. Joanne. Ms. Joanne used crutches to get out her husband's, John's long- shot out blue Pontiac station wagon, she even had a wheelchair in the back, if she felt like grabbing it, but nothing was going to stop her from the love she had for her sister, for John, and for her family.

They was all good people. I hated to see when the Henderson family packed up and moved.

After Robert moved, I started getting Big Wheels. But on my Big Wheels, the handle bar might be loose, I gotta keep punching back down on the steering column, or slightly pinging it with a hammer, so I don't crumble the plastic. It might be missing the brake, from where you get out in the street, across a cool drag of strip, then you go real, real fast; then you pull the brake and cut the wheel, so yo Big Wheel will start burning in donuts!

It might be missing one of the plastic petals, so you can strap in yo feet, and go for a ride. I just had to put my foot down on the bare metal. And the worst part was when you purchase your Big Wheel, your front tire was already splitting from being rode on concrete. Man, all my Big Wheels came from The Outlet.

I might have me a Big Wheel, that might last me 2 weeks. A Big Wheel was an alternative to riding a ten speed, a Schwinn, or a BMX Bike. And unlike a bike that had only 2 wheels, a Big Wheel HAD 3; having a Big Wheel, was having a tricycle-- ON STEROIDS!!

Unlike a bicycle, a Big Wheel, sit cool, low-gripped to the ground. A Big Wheel was a cool kid's ride from freedom from his parents. I could roll up to 7- 11, buy me some bubble gum, buy me some

Doritos, buy me some Nerds, some ice cream, and an Iced Cold PEPSI, and roll on back round to the house, and my momma won't even know it.

And just like a bike; a Big Wheel, you can have it on- road; off- road-- a Big Wheel was a turn in its own lane. I'd ride my Big Wheel past 2 weeks. When the front tire starts caving in, or when the front tire just falls off its axle...

That's it.

It's nothing else left you can do, but go and buy another Big Wheel.

But after Robert left, that led me to meet new friends. I had friends, I could play football or basketball with- - but it was this one kid that was a dickhead or sometimes an asshole. His name was Terrence, and he lived in the apartment right over top of us, with his single mom, Ms. Cynthia.

Ms. Cynthia, shoulda been called Ms. Cinnabon, cause she was brown- skinned. She definitely was sexy. And she was BADDD!! like coated in cinnamon- brown sugar BADDD!! She was small, but she was a little taller than me, and she was mad in shape. Cause she danced. She did ballet and she danced. Damn, I wish I coulda saw all that. But all she had was muscle tone, she ain't have no body fat! It's crazy.

But her son- - yeah, he was a dickhead. An asshole. His name is Terrance. He was about 5 years older than me, and for some reason when he saw me playing, especially football, he would come over there, and start fuckin around.

Every time I get the ball, he would run into me, and just hit me wit everything he got-- BAMMMM!! Hit me with a hard tackle.

I shake it off a little bit, after I kinda got used to him; I get the ball, and here he comes again-- BAMMMM!!

I couldn't get around this guy. I couldn't outrun him. I couldn't beat this guy. All I could do, is do what I saw Robert used to do,

"WHAAAAAAAA!"

Hey, I was still young enough. My momma come out there, or my father come out there, because the field was right beside our apartment; and they would run Terrance off.

My momma usually went to go get Ms. Cynthia. And she would call Terrance in the house. One thing I'll say.: he ain't like too many other people, but he always had respect for his mom. And he never disrespected my parents. I used to wait to see him say something crazy out the mouth. I'll flip the switch to a whole new level, if it come to fighting for my father or my mother. But we never got there. He ain't like what they had to say, but he'd just walk off.

I appreciate him for that. I talked shit about him, but it was a long time ago. I'm just talking shit, because for real, he was my First Bully.

But he never broke my bones, or made me to where I was sore the next day. Just, he just kept coming back around me; around me; around me; around me. And when I got tired of him fuckin wit me, I knew what I had to do, so I can play in peace.

I said all that to say: Hey! won't I supposed to be in 5th grade, talking about Mrs. Pollack?

OK, alright. That's what I thought--

OK, so I had this crush on my 5th grade teacher, Mrs. Pollack. I just took you to the woods, to explain to you that I couldn't afford weights and gym equipment. But I wanted to be a Bodybuilder-- like the kind of guys I saw up in Muscle Magazines and competing on ESPN. You know.: BIG!! Strong and Muscled- Up!! So when I go to school, I would suck in my gut and ooze out my chest, so Mrs. Pollack could be turned on by MY huge developments in muscle.

I don't think it worked. She wouldn't say anything about it. She would just call me over to her reading table, with a few other of my classmates, and she would have me READ. Of all things.

When my parents used to shop, we often ran into her at the Food Lion, right down on Jefferson. Then she'd be in something baggy and standing up there with her goofy looking husband. It won't the first time I ever seen him. "Jeff," is what she called him. But it was spelled something stupid like, "Geoff."

He supposed to be some kind of painter. A few times I'd see him jot up to the school, in that small tiny blue 2- door Rabbit. He would have a ten- foot ladder poking out the back, like he really was about to go put in some work. But he be on her job. Prolly there askin her for her money; hmm, you do know how dem husbands do. Every time I see him, I just think.: 'I'on know how she could want him over a chiseled specimen like me.'

My mother would ask her, "How is he in school?"

And she'd just look at me and bounce back to my mom like, "Oh he's..."

'The man'o yo dreams.' You know you wanna say it. But NOOOOOO!!

"Oh he's... a good student. He don't give me any problems."

Yeah bitch, you betta does not get me in trouble in fronna my momma.

But (2) more things about Mrs. Pollack real quick.: It was one day she had asked the class if they had brothers and sisters. How many brothers and sisters did we have.:

I was gon say Jonathan, but he was only one. So, I told her I had (13) brothers and sisters.

My mother came to the school one day, I think it was a PTA; a parents and teachers meeting, when she sprung the question on my mother.:
"Mrs. Miles, I didn't know you had (13) children?"

My momma looked at her like she was crazy and said, "No. My momma got (13) children. Uh- huh," she rashed out into the humor.

"Oh, but your son, said it was you-- he said he had (13) sisters and brothers."

See, there she go.: tryin to get me in trouble wit my momma.

"No. My momma got (13) children," my momma said to her again, in the same polite voice tipped in her courtesy of humor. "Oh Lord, child please. Don't put that on me," my momma said rubbing her belly.

Then, Mrs. Pollack looked back at me, wit those soft coated hush- brown puppy eyes and sadly said, "Oh."

It's not good to tella lie. Fortunately, that was one lie I didn't get punished for. My momma chalked it up in good fun. She delighted into laughter about me trying to make HER my sister.

The other was when Mrs. Pollack got pregnant. I can't blame her little silly ass husband for that. He ain't just knock her up-- HE KNOCKED HER ALL THE WAY UP!! Man, Mrs. Pollack got pregnant.. with twins!!!! She musta showed him that ass all up in them all- white see-through pants, squatting down and spreading out. Good-gracious!! I think that'll do it to any man.

But at the same time my crush on Mrs. Pollack was closing in on a stalemate, there was a girl in my own class that came polarizing my constant attention. Her name was Shoshoni. And guess what her last name was?? JACKSON.

Shoshoni Jackson.

And now, I always trip off that line by Kanye that go.: "She gotta light- skin friend/ Look like Michael Jackson/ She gotta dark- skin friend/ Look like Michael Jackson..."

And this might sound crazy.: but that's what Shoshoni look like-- the dark- skin Michael Jackson.

But that was the swag. Michael Jackson had the whole world sewed like fig leaves. Everybody wanted to be Michael Jackson. He took a West Coast fashioned style and made it a flowing international transcending concept-- black people, white people, young people, old people, men, women... it ain't make a difference. And this shit ain't 'a costume, it was real everyday life. But Shoshoni wore it well. Too good. After Mrs. Pollack finished giving up shots in them damn see- through pants; I had Shoshoni over there in a jherri- curl and some tight ass jeans.

It was 'a helluva life.

But I was scared of Shoshoni. I didn't know how to approach and talk to her. I ain't have no rap game.

It's crazy, cause I could write rap songs, even rap songs about girls. New Edition had an R&B song and video called, Popcorn Love. My follow- up response to that was a rap/ r&b version of the song, that I called, Coca- Cola Love. I don't remember how it go. I just remember the title. But I was too scared to ever perform it. And I was too scared to approach Shoshoni.

I won't use to pulling up on girls. I had always had girls who liked me, pull up on me. That's how I got Niece.

I tried to wait her out.

She ain't come to me either.

I wanted to try my Makeba approach. I'll get one 'a Shoshoni's girlfriends to holla at her for me. But that didn't work. Shoshoni didn't have no friends. She was a loner. Which made hollering at her that more extremely difficult.

I had tried to sweep reading up under the rug, but once God gave it to me; I got it. I kept getting called to Mrs. Pollack's table to read vocabulary. She rarely had to correct my reading.

Then, in 5th grade, by me being an elementary school senior, I kept getting called to the Principal's Office.

But not for being bad.

The Principal would call me in-- it was a group of students that got called in to do The Morning Announcements. And my contribution to The Morning Announcements, was to recite The Pledge of Allegiance.

I'd see the other students speaking into the microphone instrument, that would project their voices out over an intercom system, all over the whole entire school; all over the whole student body.

When it was my turn.: I froze up.

I was nervous.

"Go ahead," Principal Kane would waive the microphone to me.

I'd step up to it, and say, "I pledge allegiance to the flag, of the United States of America..."

WOW!! I would hear my voice stand stilled and stoned, and stutter the cold stared microphone into a melted sheltered echo.: "... and to The Republic, for which it stands, One Nation, under God, indivisible; with liberty and justice for all."

I had flipped into an oratory voice, like the voice I would hear my father speak, and not just my normal speaking voice...

My voice was cadenced so solemn, when I finished, I could hear Mr. Kane eyes bow into an, "Amen."

I got called often. Sometimes, as many as three times a week. I was finally at "the Good" stage of my life with Principal, Mr. Kane. But it didn't start like that.:

Chapter 5.

I first met Principal Kane in the fall of 1983. It was September. It was just after Labor Day. It was winding into fall. I was in the 3rd grade. I had a homeroom teacher in the 3rd grade. Her name is Mrs. Stewart.

Mrs. Stewart was the hardest teacher I ever had my whole entire life. She is the epitome of The Diary of a Mad Black Woman. Believe me when I tell you.

Mrs. Stewart also had a reading table. This is before Mrs. Pollack's reading table, and before my voyage into Chapter 1. I would go to Mrs. Stewart's reading table to read, and I would mess it up. I made mistakes, and Mrs. Stewart's way of correcting me was with the point of a sharpened red pencil.

She would say, "THINK," and meanwhile she would be stabbing me, with the lead, in my head and in my scalp, of her hard reddened pencil.

That shit would hurt so bad. But I never hit her. I was raised not to hit women. And I had never told on her to my parents or reported her to the Newport News School System. This is my absolute first time ever speaking on it.

I was used to getting so many whippings as a child growing up, for real, I didn't know what to think of it. The line was blurred for me to categorize it as abuse.

She would do it so often, that I developed a tolerance for the mistreatment and suffering she was forcing me through. She would do it like every time I come to the table, then when she'd get tired of me, she'd say,

"Go to the Principal's Office."

And that's when I started getting introduced to the bad side of Mr. Kane.

In the summer of 1983, the Newport News Public School System had sent a form to my house. And in the form the school system asks the parents for permission "to discipline" their child. But the Newport News School System's version of "to discipline," means they was asking the parents for permission to whip, or to beat they child for doing wrong. Of course, my parents checked, "YES." Granting the school that permission.

So my bad introduction to Mr. Kane, was in the form of him grabbing a hard woodened paddle from out the top drawer of his desk, putting me across his knee, and WHAMMMM!!

"That's one," he'd say. "Move your hands."

Naturally I was crying and covering my Lil Junie cakes from the blows of his weapon.

"Move your hands," he'd say again.

He'd hit me again, WHAMMMM!!

"That's two."

I'd cover back up.

"Move your hands."

I would hold my hands there. He'd take the end of the paddle and beat it against my hand until I moved my hands. Then, WHAMMMM!!

"That's three."

WHAMMMM!!

"That's four."

I'm crying, hollering, and hysterical; I'on know when this gon end.

WHAMMMM!!

"That's five," he finally said. "Alright, that's it." And he pushed me up. "Now go back to class."

He was fighting and defending for a teacher he didn't know was maliciously corrupting the integrity and morals of a public education. He was Principal Kane, or Mr. Kane to me. But to my father, he was,

"Coach Kane," he excitedly call whenever my Father was called on to reinforce discipline to MY "disruptive behavior," or to come remove me from school. When I was suspended.

My father loved to shake Coach Kane's hand, the man he'd been to him, back when he was at Huntington High School. If Mr. Kane gave my parents a bad report, that stemmed from my corroded teacher- student relationship, then my parents was going to put on the strap where Coach Kane's paddle had finished me off. And that's how it was every time.

When I was a child, I had a real bad plundering problem. I was always tampering in other people's stuff that ain't mine. I had started doing it with my mother's brothers, and when my Grandfather got on my mother's brothers about putting up they stuff, I moved on to plunder in my parent's stuff.

Well like I said, my father had been an active-duty US Marine, and following his tour in Vietnam, he became active-duty reserves. One day I was plundering through my parents room. My parents had a desk in their bedroom. The desk was shellacked in black and had shellacked white doors.

When I go through the drawers, my dad got a cut off clip of bullets. That looked like real Rambo bullets. That's the part that intrigued me, so I went to go show the bullets off in school.

After all, it was time to see something more, than Arnold's daddy's Playboy magazines. So I took the bullets to school. I was showing the bullets off to some friends in the hallway. And Arnold was there.

"What are you doing?"

Mr. Kane had crept up behind me.

"Let me see that."

I gave it to him. I ended up in the Principal's Office.

"You coulda hurt somebody. Somebody coulda got killed. If you throw this down, and this thing explodes..."

I'on know. He was talkin like I had a bomb. The crazy part about it, he didn't whip me. He didn't even call my parents. I never did get my daddy's bullets back. (It was a disassembled clip of the bullets that go to an M- 16 machine gun). I was relieved not to get in trouble or suspended.

But, Hi Daddy.: yes this is the first time I'm revealing this to you. I apologize for losing your souvenir war memorabilia. Please don't whip me.

Alright, I got (2) more down notes.:

First off.:) When I was in Fifth Grade, our classroom had got an outside visitor come sit down in our class. The woman had a round circle hole through her throat, and she spoke to the tune, of something like a robot would, with the help of something she held in her hand. The woman had cancer.

After she told us her story, Mrs. Pollack asked us to write letters to her. These notes she would take with her. I don't remember specifically what I wrote, but basically it was a positive spiritual message, but the most important part is that that was the first time I really experienced that the message that I had to say about God, had a lasting effect on a woman who was dying from terminal cancer.

The design of what I said; because I had even put in there about where I attended church. This woman went to the business office of my church, and I think back to my school to find out where I lived. And I was surprised to look out the window and see this incredible woman pull up in my parking lot.

The amazing part about it I was discussing her to my mother, to my Grandmother, and I think to my Best Momma; and here it was, now she'd come back into my life. What a joy it was.

She came and rang our doorbell. Both of my parents were home, I forget which one answered the door. But she came, sat in our living room. She unfolded my letter from her purse, and she gave it to me. She wanted me to READ what I wrote her out loud. And I did.

I saw her tear up and cry as she listened to me read to her from a piece of paper. I kept pausing as I read her the letter. My soul was absorbing her pain.

I wasn't judging her. The letter wasn't judging her for being a chronic cigarette smoker, or whatever it was that led to her cancer. But the letter, if you really think about it.: was a ministry that the Lord began to put into me. A REAL ministry that wouldn't affect the lives of stuffed animals and pillows, but a ministry that would help the lives of actual real people. Even to a woman that was literally pressed down into her very own valley of the shadow of death and despair and dying from cancer.

And I was able to give her that ministry, and she received it, from a 10-year-old.

I think she did come out to my church one time, but after that I never saw her again.

Second.;) My mother did get pregnant in 1985. She had said some young girls was laughing at her for being pregnant, I guess because my momma was in her middle 30s. 35 to be exact. But I never caught them.

It was in December, the same month I was waiting on Santa Claus. My mother had entered Mary Immaculate Hospital, way up at the top of Newport News, right before Virginia start changing into Ku Klux Klan County.: Gloucester, York County, Poquoson, Tabb and all that white racist shit.

But that's where they had put my momma, all the way out on the outskirts of integrated civilization. Then, I'll never forget it as long as I live, December the 6th had happened.

Of all days, my daddy ain't have his car.

Theresa, my mother's sister came out Paula Maria to pick us up in her Chevette. That was a 4-door car. Economical. Good on gas

When we get to Mary Immaculate, I got to wait in a waiting room, while Theresa and my Daddy go back to see my momma. They did finally let me go back. When I go in the room, I see Theresa. I see my momma. I see my father. What I

don't see is my brother, my momma supposed to
have for me.

Ain't my brother supposed to be somewhere in
here, waiting to get held by me in my arms??

"Come here, son," my momma called for
me. She was in a hospital gown and reclined in her
hospital bed. Her hair won't done. It was just hand
swept-- straight to the back.

She kept holding on my hand and she kept talking
to me, "I got you. The LORD Blessed me, and I got
you..."

Yeah, ok Momma, but where is my brother at?

"I love you. I love that I got you," she kept
soothing me in this long-warmed voice.

I'on know where she was going with this.
She actin like she can't get to the good part. I was
fed up and impatient. So I just come out and say,
"Where's my brother?"

I'm looking. I'm looking around for my brother. I
want to see my brother. Then she say,

"Your brother is at the morgue. He went to
the morgue."

Now, this don't make no sense. He just got here,
how the world he get to go somewhere without me.

"He went to the morgue," I say.

"Yeah."

"He went to the morgue," I say again.

"Uh- huh."

I can't process what a MORGUE is; so I say, "He went to the mall?"

At first she paused, and listen to me.

"He went to the mall?"

"Yeah. Yep. Uh- huh," she agreeingly said.

She could tell I was having trouble processing the information. I did some reading, but I had never seen the word "morgue," and even if I did, I wouldn't know what it was. She woulda been better off just telling me he DIED.

At least now I knew what DIED was.

My father had named his 2nd son, Terry. Terry Miles. I left out the room, to go return out to the waiting room. The nurses brought my brother's stillborned body in the room, after I was gone.

My mother was given (2) Kodak pictures of her deceased child; including (1) where she had where she was able to put on his named bracelet.: "Terry," on his left arm. And his fresh baby cap on top of his head.

We would've got a tombstone for him eventually, to replace his temporary paper marker. But Pleasant Shade Cemetery, in Newport News, did some real disrespectful shit.: when we went to go find Terry's grave, because my mother wanted to lay flowers on her son's grave, we could never find his grave.

The Cemetery's Management kept swearing he was there, and that he was buried over in the baby section. The baby area was small. They couldn't even show us where his remains was. My mother always remained very troubled that her son's body was lost. She just took comfort in that her baby was resting in the Lord, and she would massage herself in her husband's arms.

After I got grown, I even went back out there so I could say I found it. But I could never bring my mother back that news. Them graveyards so greedy for money. My family didn't have any insurance for Terry.

But to get back in line wit the story.: I was hurt I didn't have no brother for the Holidays. No brother for Christmas. And I jus went 'head 'on and took it out on Santa Claus.

"It ain't no Santa Claus. Santa Claus is FAKE! Santa Claus ain't real..."

And my daddy just sat there, shaking his head agreeing with me.

"Hhhhhh! Santa Claus really ain't real..."

And jus to think all these Christmases this jolly fat white man done got away with holding me on his knee. And Tina... Whatta bout Tina the Talking Tree...

Chapter 6.

     1986 was young Funky FRESH!! Funky FRESH!! That probably was a young dope fiend's phrase, that was somewhere out there gettin BLASTED!! up off the drug. But Funky FRESH was a phrase that was relevant in music. It was relevant in hip- hop.

     But in 1986, I won't round fiends gettin funky. I just wanted to be around friends who was FRESH!! Our music was Doug E FRESH and DJ Jazzy Jeff & The FRESH Prince.

     The FRESH Prince was out before anybody ever really knew his name was going to be Will Smith. Before anybody knew he was an actor or a great big movie star. For us, he was our hip- hop star. His oratory in how he could lyrically narrate a story, is an amazing incredible talent.

Slick Rick was also a master lyrical story teller. But Will's stories were more entertaining, comical, and humorous. And his videos had so much more animated COLOR.

     He could manipulate the fragrance of reds, whites, blacks, golds, greens, whatever colors he want, into the delivery of his songs. I still listen to his music to this day; before he was the Hollywood Will Smith, and you can hear the potent seed of potential in his voice. Even at 17, you can hear where he could've been anything he wanted to be in Hollywood or in entertainment.

A lotta ancient hip- hop heads probably spit names to you like Grandmaster Flash, Kurtis Blow, Kool Hurc, duh- duh- duh- duh- duh. But hip- hop for me didn't start wit none of them. Hip- hop for me started from Blllllllllur- STICK EM!! Ha- Ha- Ha- STICK EM!! Blllllllllur- STICK EM!! Ha- Ha- Ha- STICK EM!!

That whole Human Beatbox and sound of The Fat Boys. That's what did it for me. It's what made me start payin attention to real Rap Music, in'a whole nother way.

My mother's brothers.: Ronnie, Johnnie and Pernell used to throw block parties in my Grandmomma's backyard, and they used to play songs by The Fat Boys. They used to play a whole lot of Funkadelic and Parliament, cause that's what was painted onside they treehouse, and they used to play this rap song that was rapped by a little known named artists; a group- named Newcleus.

Off- top it's the only song I can think of they ever sung. The song they used to rap was called Jamony or Jam- On- It, I seen it spelled both ways. But when you pump that song to any house party, or all up in some summertime heat-- you can best believe, it's gon be some sweaty chested black men bumping, grinding, and humping hard and fast up on some ass from the back, all over toppa the dancefloor.

I liked Run- DMC, but I was never a Run- DMC fan. All my friends was. They'd have Run- DMC posters taped, stapled, and thumb- tacked up from Word Up! Magazine. I liked leather coats. But

I ain't never been no nigga in no leather pants. And Run- DMC coasted the town in Cadillac cars. Cadillac is not just a popular American man's car. It's also a popular Black American man's car. A lot of Black men love Cadillacs. Even a lot of my friends loved Cadillacs. But not me. I never been a fan of Cadillacs.

You need Run- DMC in hip- hop, I'm not denying that. But I can blow past Run- DMC, and be alright. Cause my favorite rapper following The Fat Boys... in 1986.. was KRS- One of Boogie Down Productions.

My father owned a stamp collection. In the summer of 1986, he had obtained this stamp that he believed to be WORTH A FORTUNE. He couldn't find what he was looking for in the local Hampton and Newport News area. He believed that if he went to New York, that he could get the stamp's anticipated value.

My mother took her whole paycheck, and off we went up north, in my daddy's red and chrome 1969 Chevrolet Impala. It was like a 13-hour trip, but when I woke up, I could see the face, body, and torch of Lady Liberty, illuminating up the Hudson River.

We not only got to see the World Trade Center, but I actually got to breakdance in the lobby of one of the buildings. I emulated the hardcore breakdancing styles that I'd seen in Breakdancing and Beat Street, and even in music videos. When I saw myself drawing a crowd, that's when I stopped. Cause I got nervous. New York Citians and international tourists all took the art of

Breakdancing extremely serious. They could tell who the real break-dancers was, or they can carve you up in a fierce Breakdance Battle.

Breakdancing beat the streets with graffiti, DJs, MCs, subway trains, broken cardboard boxes, and NIKE AIR JORDANS.

Air Jordan's was the very first sneaker, that even had young kids getting killed, so somebody else can put em on. Niggas won't doing this for Dr Js or even for Run- DMCs ADIDAS. But when them Air Jordan shits came out-- the shoe was so raw and authentically exclusive, not only was it the most killed for sneaker shoe ever built!! but; where you seen generic knock- offs of valuable brand names before; Jordan's was the first sneaker I remember, where the literal shoe in and of itself was FAKED. So if you went to shop for a pair of Jordan's, you had to be sure that you was really buying NIKE Air Jordan's. It was the only FAKED fabricated sneaker on the market. If anybody had on Jordan's, never mind who he was, never mind what he looked like; never mind what else he had on; the whole time your attention be on what he got on his feet. And yo eyes followed his shoes all over the room. All over the street.

But Jordan's was more of a middle- class luxury, than a poor kid's reality. And that's where BDP-- excuse me; Boogie Down Productions crushed it in wit the hard crisp high- top Delta Force NIKES.

The NIKE and Mike combination had smashed Pumas, Adidas, the Stan Smith Adidas, Diadoras, and even Ballys, all outta- style. With

NIKE it wasn't about a particular color or style, or brand. Just by having NIKE shoes on your feet you was making a statement, and the best part of it all, you didn't need no FAT LACES, or no other accessory to go wit em or in em.

In the World's Most #1 City, everything was more high- priced, than what my momma's whole paycheck could afford. We couldn't buy a hotel room. We wound up just sleeping in the car, alongside a rough in the face New York City curb.

My father and mother took turns on watch, while I got to go to sleep in the backseat. I got to see Madison Square Garden and I wanted to go up in the Statue of Liberty. But the lines was long of other people wanting to get up inside her too.

I wasn't disappointed. I was excited to be walking the streets and plazas of some of my most favorite rap music superstars.

There was something that happened in my time in New York, that still strikes a cord in me today.: it's the sight of homelessness.

I don't think I seen homelessness any more than what I did at the big black gate of Ronald Reagan's White House. In DC there was billions of shitty- ass pigeons and homelessness for blocks and blocks, and miles and miles. They be standin out all in fronna Mc Donald's. 'A nigga can't bite 'a Big Mac without somebody not asking you for spare change.

In DC, I used to just walk past it or through it. We was poor, but even poor people looked down on homeless people as being bums. But I'll never forget it.: I was in 'a Mickey Mac's bathroom in New York's Manhattan. I was at the sink washing my hands, from pissing, and a homeless man entered into the bathroom. I tensed, cause I thought I was going to be in danger.

But, I didn't see him using the bathroom and washing his hands like me, I actually saw him grooming himself. At the sink and at the mirror. I let the water splash through my hands, as I looked at the mirror and looked in his face, it's like I could see his soapened washcloth rinsing and absorbing the skin of his pain; the dreds of his struggle. Maybe he was getting ready for work, or a job interview.

But that shit hurt.

New York ended up being a nice vacation, but we was more broker than we was going up there. It ended up, what my father thought he had, he didn't have. And on the trip back, we started having problems out the old ol' school Chevy. The radiator kept overheating. And we had to keep pulling off the interstate, or to the side of the road, to cool the engine down. But the Lord was with us, and we made it back safe and sound.

I was kinda glad to get back, cause it was summer. And that mean, I can get back to Niece. Niece was my baby.

After all, I'd justified passing Shoshoni up for her.

'You already got a girlfriend,' I kept telling myself.

But fo real, I fucked up, I fucked all the way up- I was in my freshman year at Huntington. The same school both my parents graduated high school from back in 67 and 69.

But now this shit done downgraded into a middle school. And I searched all over the whole school fo this bad lil bitch, named Shoshoni. She won't nowhere to be fount. Not only was she nowhere at the school; she was nowhere in the city. And just like Makeba, I never saw Shoshoni again.

By the time the school year wounded back down, it was into the summer again. And that meant I could kiss my future wifey again.

So I thought.

Niece was on some new shit. Not only was we not kissing-- we was not holding, touchin, or talkin. Niece won't giving me attention. I'on know where she got this shit from. She kept laughing and talkin to Anthony, like she was tryin to fuck wit him. I'on know if she was tryin to get me mad, or what. But that shit won't workin. I damn sure won't gon get in my emotions over that bullshit.

Then I heard Jamelle say she had a boyfriend. A new boyfriend, so I guess that was it. Niece come. Niece go. It was hard just looking at her, and being around her, and she was no longer mine.

Later that summer, just before the fall, the church had it's annual baptismal service in Washington, DC. This was a good time to clear my head and get my thoughts off Niece. Generally, my father always uses the annual baptism in DC, as an invite to go and see his uncle. Best Momma has a brother named Jake. And Jake has a beautiful wife named Ruth. And Jake and Ruth have (2) children.: one boy named Junior, cause he named fo his daddy, and one girl, named Michelle. And they have a loving (2) story home out Silver Springs in Maryland.

This was the only time I see them out a whole year.

I had another cousin named Junior, on my momma side. But me and him used to fight. Me and this Junior didn't fight. He used to ride me on his bike and let me play wit his robots and toy guns. But the scariest part about going to see Junior...

When I first get to his house... First of all, the whole family come to the door.: Jake, Ruth, Junior, Michelle. Everybody standing there hugging and greeting, in this lil yellowed light bulbed foyer, then all of a sudden this GREAT BIG and HUGE.. DOG!!

I was bigger than him. But he looked like he was bigger than me. Man, this dog look like he was about 6 foot tall. Then, I grew, but he was still a big ass dog. They had a Doberman Pincher. I'on know his name. All I know when I see him, it's time for me to run-- even if the door is closed.

I remember my Aunt Ruth, holding her Doberman, and saying, "He don't bite."

Well, why he got all them teeth? He look like he kept tryin to get to me. I see him keep jumpin and jumpin up, and looking like he trying to lunge at me. I won't gon be his next Scooby- Doo snack.

"Junior, take the dog. Put up the dog," whatever his name is, she might say it. And Junior would go take his precious puppy, and however long I stayed, THAT DOG STAYED LOCKED UP IN A ROOM.

It was like that EVERY YEAR!! I had developed my fear of dogs, I guess, from my momma. That's what she said. And every time I see that dog, I was always afraid of him. It was time to run.

Especially back then, cause Dobermans was the shit in style. In the 80s black houses either had Dobermans or German Shepherds. Either one scared me like an intruder. I won't tryin ta feel what that bite be like.
When I leave, I can see him run up to the screen door, looking out at me, like, "Come back here nigga! So I can BITE the shit up out'cha!"

But now that I done got a little older, my dad stopped going to Maryland. If he did, it was to buy a room, in Maryland or in Washington. Mostly in Washington, and his spot was The Econo Lodge.

Hey, after sleeping in 'a car out New York City, the Econo Lodge, might be a nice spot.

I think I been to the Washington National Zoo like (1) time. It's alright. I didn't really like it. I liked it better, running up the grass of the Washington Monument, or that long ass sidewalk by the pool, leading up to the Lincoln Memorial.

But my most absolute GREATEST TIME about

Washington DC, was The Smithsonian and The Air and Space Museum.

Man those huge GREAT BIG dinosaur bones, and hearing the history of the antique fossils like the brontosaurus, pterodactyl, and tyrannosaurus. That's the most popular, and the ones that stuck out for me the most. But my absolute most favorite dinosaur EVER!! is the Pterodactyl. I'm fascinated with how a bird can exist that huge, and with a wing span so enormous.

I would spend (1) WHOLE DAY in The Smithsonian, and the next WHOLE DAY in The Air and Space Museum, looking at old military planes and walking through fragments of NASA space rockets.

That's a part of my past, that always stuck with me to this day.

Then, to go to the service itself. Seeing all the saints from Virginia, from DC, from Maryland, from Philly, New York, and North Carolina... everybody happy, smiling, it's nothing but the love you expect to see when you get in Heaven.

And we'd see the choir, dressed in ALL-WHITE. All you see is God's holy children decorated and flowing in white, like some sheep. And they would sing and march in a military formation, that'll shut 'a Jack In The Box DOWN!!

Then we'd finally get out to the stadium, to see the new saints, that were getting dipped over backwards to wash away all they past, in a pool, for the sake of the Lord Jesus, and for the remission of their sins.

It's so colorful and comforting to watch. My eyes soothed into the warmness of the pool, to wash Niece up out my thoughts, and to wash a disturbing 1987 from out my mind. Cause as I told you my mother has a brother named Johnnie.:

Usually every Sunday after church, my mother goes to see her mother. Cause we see Best Momma up in church. But this particular Sunday, my momma said,

"Take me home," she said as my Dad piloted the wheel. "I'm tired. I wanna go home," she told him again.

Then the closer he drives her home, she said, "I'll just call momma from home."

Something else unusual, cause we usually ain't got no phone. But this day, Hey! we had a phone.

We get home, and my mother gets on the phone wit her mother, and my Grandmother was as cool as 'a ice cube on 'a hot summer arm, in San Antonio heat. What she said was, "Evelyn, you need to get round here and see yo brother. See what the police did to yo brother."

This was way before George Floyd, way before Breonna Taylor, Philando Castille, the whole entire Black Lives Matter Movement, way even before Rodney King had his tumultuous run- in in California. This was back in NINETY- EIGHTY- SEVEN. And Police on Black violence had attacked my family.

My Uncle Johnnie was walking back home from a party, over by The Atmosphere, in downtown Newport News. He was drunk. He had been drinking. But the Newport News Police stopped my Uncle from his walking. They grabbed and shoved him and slammed his face to the parking lot with his hands handcuffed behind his back. And pushed their foot down into my Uncle's neck, with his hands handcuffed behind his back, and beat my Uncle, where ever they could, with hard black woodened night sticks.

They beat my Uncle's brains out.

My Uncle Ronnie, he didn't go to the party. He just so happened to be walking up the street, when he saw a crowd standing around by the street.

"What's going on?" he asked.

"Man, they over there beatin his ass," somebody out the crowd had informed him.

My Uncle Ronnie looked.

He looked,

He looked,

"HEY!! THAT'S MY BROTHER!!" He ran towards the frenzy.

The only way he really recognized Johnnie was by the pieces of the clothes he had on. He remembered what Johnnie had wore out to the party.

"Get outta here before the same thing happen to you," the police had threatened my Uncle Ronnie.

Ronnie was so PETRIFIED, that he ran all the way home to get my Grandfather. And my Grandfather grabbed his gun. For his son; he was gon kill the police.

"Johnnie sit up so your sister can see you," Grandma said to him when we got there.

Johnnie mumbled the groans of his pain, as he peacefully sat up in his bed. I had wanted to hold my hand to my Uncle's shoulder. But I didn't know if it would hurt him. The left side of his face was smothered in bruises from being stomped on the concrete. And where the officer had kept his foot, my Uncle's neck was bent like a piece of rubber. He was SWOLLEN. My Uncle's neck looked like the curve round the rubber of a tire.

But his neck was bent all the way over, and the muscles of his neck was so SWOLE, it looked like he had (2) necks!

I didn't know whether to cry or to be angry.

My mother is The General of the family. She'll know what to do. She's the most active child out all my Grandma's (13) children, and she's the most influential. When she's around, my Grandma and Grandfather just fall back and let her go.

"We going to that police station," she said.

107

OH SHIT!! I'm thinking my momma gon finish where my Granddaddy left off.

"Daddy, you going?"

"Naw, I'm staying."

My Grandfather rocked back into comfort that, Yeah, my babygirl got this!

At the same time, he had to stay back-- my Grandfather was a war man. A US Army military veteran, who had helped to take down Adolf Hitler in Germany, all the way back in World War II. And he was a decorated Purple Heart recipient. It was too much for him.

He also kept his wife home wit him

Rolling in the car was me, my daddy, my momma, my Uncle Johnnie, and my Aunt Woodrina. My momma's little sister, but Johnnie's big sister.

I could watch Johnnie from the backseat. It was amazing that he was still alive from that much pressure being applied to his neck and back of his throat. Most black men wouldn't survive this level of abuse from the police. I never seen nobody's neck as bent and as swollen as his neck, and still be alive. But Johnnie was special.

I never told him.: but Johnnie was always my most favorite uncle. Why?

Cause Johnnie was Smooooth man. Not to judge.: not only was Johnnie handsome, but Johnnie was swagged.

I can remember the first time I saw Johnnie. My first thoughts of him is, 'Why him and Ronnie ain't twins?' Didn't somebody tell my Grandmomma when you got babies wit close- n- rhyming names, they supposed to be twins?

Hey, I guess not.

Ronnie had 'a style. He had 'a little kick to him. But he couldn't do like Johnnie.

I ain't never see 'a nigga rock 'a tux like this nigga. Johnnie had a picture shoved up in the edge of his mirror, at my Grandma's house. He gotta picture where he rockin 'a all- black tux wit the all- red bow tie and cummerbund. Then he got another picture that go wit it; where he got on the same tux, but he got on some dark pitched shades, covered in all- white frames.

Ronnie was rough. Ain't nothing really wrong it. As a man, it's a time to be rough. But Ronnie, like his older brothers, Pernell and Charles was more rough.

Ronnie rode mopeds, and his first car, was a van on wheels. But Johnnie-- was smoooooth. His whole style was smoooooth. He never owned no motorcycles or moped bikes. And his first car.: was an all- white stretched long Oldsmobile. Wit chrome dish rims, thick- trimmed white- wall tires, and a smokin!! all- red interior. It won't just Smoooooth; it was HARD!! Johnnie was that nigga!

If Johnnie could only sing; man, he can be like the 6th, 7th, or 8th member up in New Edition. That's

Word!

But that's before drugs and alcohol crept into my family and started to deteriorate Johnnie's life. He still had glimpses of it. But he never got all the way back. Perhaps drugs and alcohol was the only penicillin, still sittin him up.

When we got down to the lobby of the police station, we was trying to figure out which way to go. Two police officers passed us in the hall, one of which, being a white Sergeant.

"What happened? What's going on?" he had asked.

"My brother... the police beat my brother..." The General went off.

"Mam. Mam. Please, calm down..." the Sergeant responded to her.

I think all of us was feeling some assurance, that we could talk, and we would find out who these dirty cops was, and bring some "Justice," for Johnnie.

I say "dirty cops," now. But at the time, I didn't know what a "dirty cop" was. Police Officers are supposed to be very nice and friendly. They're the ones you can go to to chase the bad guys and restore the peace and serenity to the community.

That's what's supposed to happen.

"My brother..."

"Mam. I'm talking to him."

"But, the police BEAT my brother... look at him... look at his neck..."

"Mam, I'm gon ask you to keep quiet. If you don't shut up, I'm going to have to arrest you," you can feel that racist aggression raise in the Sergeant's voice.

"You're going to what??"

"I'm going to have to arrest YOU. I'm going to have to lock YOU up," he had said to my momma.

WHOAAA!!

Just that fast, I witnessed now us become "THE CRIMINALS," the ones "WHOSE AT FAULT," the ones "IN THE WRONG."

My mother never been arrested in her life. She never even caught a parking ticket. When I saw my mother keep quiet,

I knew this was serious.

The Sergeant asked Johnnie was he drinking or high on drugs. Then he twisted it to say that Johnnie was hallucinating that the (2) officers had jumped him. Instead he said that Johnnie was attacked by someone else; some other people, and that the police had come TO STOP IT.

The two Newport News Officers put Johnnie on an elevator, by himself, and took him somewhere upstairs "to talk to him."

We stood waiting for Johnnie to come back down. They spooked him. They'd spooked him. When Johnnie came back down, he was just ready to leave, to get up outta there, and get back in the car, and pull off. Whatever they told him, he wouldn't even tell us.

Til this day, he won't even talk about it.

For the 2nd time, DEATH, had threatened an uncle in my family. The First Time.:

My momma's other brother, Charles. Charles was my momma's second oldest brother, behind Ike. Charles was named after my Grandfather's brother.: Charles. But my Uncle Charles was 'a hood nigga. He even used 'a hood name. They called him Bird!!

Everywhere he go in tha hood, we called him Charles, but the streets called him Bird!!

I don't know why. I'll have to ask him. But Bird, is what they called him.

One day BIRD was at a party, and he got to beefin wit 'a nigga. And I think it was over 'a girl. Of all things, right? I'on know if Charles was tryin to fuck wit the girl, or if the girl was tryin to fuck wit Charles, but she musta been 'a pretty attractive lookin bitch. Cause the nigga threatened my uncle's life over her.

He had told BIRD he would kill him; or he would kill him the next time he see him. It was some stupid shit like that.

But Charles came home and said, he would take his own life.

After that.: we rushed Bird into Whittaker Hospital; right there on the corner of 28th Street and Orcutt. It's 'a BLESSING that that hospital was 2 blocks from my Grandma's house, if not Uncle Charles would be gone.

Charles had pumped his body with suicide medication. That's a whole bottle of Aspirins. And he drunk it with rubbing alcohol.

I wanna pray right now for someone going through the crisis of contemplating suicide, and wanting to take his or her own life.:

"Yahweh is HOLY!! Yahshua is HOLY!! The Ruach Hakodesh is HOLY!!

HOLY!! HOLY!! HOLY!! is the NAME OF THE LORD, WHO MADE THE HEAVENS AND THE EARTH!!

O Mighty YAHWEH, We believe in you as The ONE and ONLY, TRUE AND LIVING GOD. NOT THE GOD OF THE DEAD, BUT THE GOD OF THE LIVING. We believe in Yahshua, YOUR precious son, as the Living Light of Heaven and Earth. And our Messiah of EVERLASTING LIFE. I come in prayer, to pray for those suffering right now, and contemplating suicide, and considering to bring an end to their own life, to FREE them of the permission of the devil. To release them from the devil of frustration, agitation, repression, depression, and fear. In Yahshua's HOLY NAME I pray. Amen, amen, amen, amen."

By the Grace of God, Charles did not die. He did not leave his family. And the Lord BLESSED him all the way out. The same guy who said he was gon kill him; changed his mind. Charles recovered from getting his stomach pumped, and the next thing I know, we was at Patrick Henry Airport, waiving good- bye to Uncle Charles.

Uncle Charles had signed into The United States Marine Corps. He was stationed in Okinawa, and got busy out in Desert Storm. Then when he came back, he got stationed in San Diego.

It all ties in to the story about Johnnie, because after Johnnie was brutally stomped, beaten, and spooked by The Newport News Police, he pretty much didn't want to have anything else to do with Virginia.

As soon as Charles offered his brother the invitation to head out west, Johnnie Was Gone!!

Chapter 7.

1987 won't just hard in my break- up wit Niece, and my momma's side of the family. My father has 'a brother too. Name Bobby. My father and Bobby got different daddy's, but the same momma. Best Momma. And Bobby has a different father than Mottie and Esther. Pee- Wee.

Nobody never seen Bobby's daddy. I ain't never seen em. I'on think my daddy never seen em. I'on think Bobby never seen em. I think Best Momma the only one ever seen em. You know.: before her Glory Days. Hunh.

Bobby is 'a cool dude. 'A thin, dark-browned- skin dude. Just like me. Maybe a shade darker; and Bobby wears glasses. So he can see. One thing about Bobby, he like to eat.

When I was small, and my Best Momma used to put my lunch box in the refrigerator, you gotta watch Bobby. Bobby be done ate up all my peanut butter and jelly, and bologna sandwiches, and drank all my juice. Whenever my Dad would get in his face to defend for me, Bobby would just run off. He used to get bullied a lot by my Daddy when he was young, and I'on think it never wore off of him. But other than that, we never had no problems out of Bobby.

Bobby is real nice and friendly. He's not a mean, evil, or violent person. He's not very social. A lot of times, he just keep to himself.

He does have 'a few friends, but Best Momma don't let em in her house. So that isolated a life for Bobby that was away from the family. Whatever business he kept away from us, Bobby kept out in the streets.

My Best Momma knows that Bobby is a alcoholic. She knows he loves to drink, but because of his isolated life, I don't think she knows the extent of his drug use. She don't know Bobby get high, or how much he get high. She don't know the extent of exactly what kinds of drugs he was addicted to.

To an extent, she probably didn't want to know.

Out of respect that Bobby has for his mother, he keeps it out of her sight. If he brings it around her, it's hidden in his pocket, or disguised in his system. But as long as she couldn't see it; as long as she couldn't smell it; as long as she did not hear about it; she did not know about it. And that's how she parented Bobby.

It was easy for her to pick up on that he was an alcoholic, or that he had been drinking. Especially if he been drinking beer. She can smell the alcohol on his breath, and she would say,

"Bobby you been drinking."

Of course Bobby would lie, "Ma, I ain't been drinking." Because he wanted to experience her love and affection. He wanted the comfort of being around the only real parent he ever knew, and to be around his family.

But when it was too much, and my Best Momma couldn't tolerate it, SHE'D PUT HIM OUT. And we laughed, and laughed, and laughed, and laughed about it then. It was funny to us how she would throw Bobby out, back through that door.

But what she'd put Bobby back out to.:

Back into the cold, dark, and isolated night of the streets. And there Bobby played more with the demons of not having his father, and with addictions. That was probably puppetted to him, by his friends and hoes of the street, who engineered a form of social acceptance.

After me, my father and mother had moved from 16th Street, Bobby had moved in our old crib. Up in the house, pushed right next to his mother. And there Bobby lived. He struggled to be as sober as he can, to be around his mother.

Bobby want to be loved. Bobby want to be respected. Bobby want to be accepted.

But Bobby is Bobby.

One day, Bobby went out to the pier on 16th Street. Bobby had wanted to catch some fish. But Bobby was drunk. He had been drinking. And Bobby lost his balance, his shoes lost its grip, and Bobby fell over in the water, trying to catch some fish.

Bobby had to be smart. Bobby had been in the Air Force. But Bobby was drunk. Bobby been drinking. Bobby couldn't swim.

Bobby went down.

Bobby drowned in the demons of his own depressions. When Bobby floated back up. Bobby was lifeless. Bobby was without a soul.

Bobby was dead.

Fortunately for Bobby, God had shown him some favor. For #1.) Bobby's body, when he drowned, his body went all the way down TO THE BOTTOM to the pier of water where he had been fishing.

It woulda been easy, so easy, that Bobby's body could've stayed remained for many more minutes, at the bottom of the pier of water where he had been fishing; he could've drifted away in a current.

But the Lord brought his body back up to the surface.

For #2.) That Bobby was with some friends. Probably some friends that we never seen, cause Best Momma run them away from the house. But Bobby's friends had enough love, compassion, and affectionate care for their friend. That they didn't want to see Bobby die.

They retrieved Bobby's body and started resuscitation efforts on him. By the time the ambulance had arrived, Bobby's body was still without a pulse. And the first responders, or out of respect for Bobby's friends, should I say the second responders, began their CPR and advanced methods of resuscitation. They had to pump the water from out of Bobby's body, liver, and lungs, that Bobby had ingested from sinking down to the bottom.

But after they cleared his lungs and water from out the way...

For #3.) God had breathed into his body, again, the breath of life: and Bobby became a living soul. (Ref.: Genesis 2: 7).

Best Momma didn't know what happened to Bobby, until Bobby came back home. I think the Lord wanted Bobby to see that he really was loved, respected, and accepted; not just by his mother but by his family.

We hugged and was happy, that Uncle Bobby was back alive.

After that, Bobby was grateful to the Lord, that HE had given him another chance, and Bobby got him a suit and he got him some dress shoes stretched. And Bobby started showing up at the church, for service.

On his very first service, he didn't just show up, Bobby went all the way to the altar, to give the preacher his hand and Christ his heart. Bobby got saved.

Bobby got saved and he still striving to maintain his new unique lifestyle. But doing drugs and alcohol is not just an addiction, it's a habitual appetite.

Bobby began back drinking. Drinking and drugs was more than a coping mechanism for Bobby. It's how he function. The same way we put up with Bobby being around us... in doses.

Is probably, the same way he tolerated being up and around us... in doses.

Cause it won't all the time Best Momma would put him out. Sometimes, things be going fine, and Bobby jus choose to up and leave on his own. The poison of certain drugs and alcohol-- haaaaaah!!

You already know. I don't have to say it.

It had a hold on Bobby. And after days and days, and months and months, and years, and years and years. Drugs and alcohol HAD A HOLD on Uncle Bobby. His liver began to deteriorate with sclerosis.

The Dr told Bobby, "IF YOU TAKE ONE MORE DRINK-- YOU'RE GONNA DIE."

It's not that Bobby didn't believe what the doctor had said to him. But what was he supposed to do? He was hooked. He was already addicted. The drugs and alcohol already HAD A HOLD on Bobby. What else can he do?

Bobby took a drink.

My cousin Colleen was there. She was staying with her Best Momma then. She had went to go get her boom box radio. To her, Bobby looked sleep on his couch.

She walked back on the other side.

When my Best Momma get home, she's thinking of

her son, 'Where's Bobby? He's mighty quiet. I haven't heard his mouth all day.'

"Bobby... Bobby," she called out to her son, living on his side of the house.

He looked sleep. Bobby didn't respond.

"Bobby... Bobby," she called out to her son, again. But she went to go touch him, to wake him.

When she felt to go touch him, Bobby was as stiff as a board. Riga mortis had already set in. This time, there was no getting him back.

Bobby

was gone.

It was 1987, seven years from the time I had went to my first funeral, and no, I did not go to Bobby's funeral.

I couldn't take it.

The fear of death. The fear of funerals was still in me. I couldn't see Bobby look like that. I only got to see Bobby through the eyes of a child. I never got to see him as a grown man.

Let us pray.:

"YAHWEH IS HOLY!! YAHSHUA IS HOLY!! THE RUACH HA' KODESH IS HOLY!! HOLY, HOLY, HOLY, HOLY IS THE SPIRIT OF GOD, WHO MADE THE HEAVENS AND THE EARTH, O MIGHTY YUD- HEH- VAV- HEH, I INVOKE YOU

BY YOUR HOLY NAME!!

The same God who said, "See now that I, even I, am he, and there is no god with me: I kill, and I make alive; I wound, and I heal:" (Deuteronomy 32: 39).

O Mighty FATHER of Abraham, Isaac, and Jacob, I come before you LORD to pray for the soul of Bobby Miles.

I pray O RIGHTEOUS AND EVERLASTING FATHER, that you remember Bobby Miles-- the soul of Bobby Miles, on his day of "JUDGMENT."

I advocate O Heavenly FATHER, that Bobby was a good man. He was loving, he was peaceful, and he was non- violent. And when he came back to life he accepted YOU, as his personal LORD and SAVIOUR.

Judge him not for his drug addictions, O HEAVENLY FATHER; for you say in YOUR Word.: "wherein there is life, I have given every green herb for food: and it was so." Genesis 1: 30.

Judge him not for his alcohol abuses, for YOU, O RIGHTEOUS, JUST, AND HEAVENLY FATHER say in YOUR Word.: "And it shall come to pass, if ye shall hearken diligently unto my commandments which I command you this day, to love YAHWEH your Elohim, and to serve him with all your heart and with all your soul,

That I will give you the rain of your land in his due season, the first rain and the latter rain, that thou mayest gather in THY CORN, and THY WINE, and THY OIL." (Deuteronomy 11: 13- 14)

(The Word of Yahweh).

    I pray O Mighty YUD-HEH- VAV- HEH, that YOU see all of his alcohol uses as WINE. And in the Blood of the HOLY MESSIAH, YAHSHUA, I pray that ALL of Bobby Miles' sins be Forgiven. Both seen and unseen, heard and unheard, and known and unknown.

    I pray O HOLY YAHWEH, God of this world, and God of the world to come, to see Bobby Miles again, in the Kingdom of Heaven. This I ask and pray, in YOUR Precious, Mighty, HOLY, Gracious, and Heavenly NAME, and in the NAME OF YAHSHUA, The HOLY MESSIAH. For it is written.: "Ye have not chosen me, but I have chosen you, and ordained you, that ye should go and bring forth fruit, and that your fruit SHOULD REMAIN: that whatsoever ye shall ask of the Father in my name, he may give it you." John 15: 16 (The Word of Yahweh). "Let the words of my mouth, and the meditation of my heart, be acceptable in thy sight, O YAHWEH, my strength, and my redeemer." (Psalms 19: 14). Amen, amen, amen, amen."

    "May we see Bobby Miles in HEAVEN. Amen."

Before 1988, there was still so much that happened between 1986 and 1987. Robert's little sister, Chrissy had died from leukemia.

They had moved, but we was still in the same place out Paula Maria. Plus they knew my momma's "job."

    So Ms. Barbera had found my mother to

give her the news. I didn't go to the funeral. I went to the wake.

It hurt to see Chrissy lose her life so young. I was 12, she had to be at least 8. I can remember her running around and playing and trying to keep up with me and Robert.

And her mother would pull her back, "No, you're a little girl. Come sit here with mommy."

And Ms. Barbera would cuddle her daughter in her arms, on the couch.

It did hurt to see Chrissy look like that, but I did notice that her body was better preserved than Uncle George.

But I still wasn't touching it. I would stand at a distance from her casket. The fear of death was still in me.

My Best Momma has a youngest daughter. Her name is Mottie. Stancil is her last name, cause her parents are married.

Mottie is shy. Yellow and quiet. She is lighter than her mother; and even lighter than her father.

Mottie is sisters with Esther. Mottie and Esther. Esther is good, for the most part quiet, and Esther is very smart. She spends a lot of time in school. I think Esther is older. But it go, Mottie and Esther.

That's just how we always say it.

One day Mottie came up missing.:

The world always been bad, and of course, we feared the worse for Mottie. The Police had some efforts to find Mottie as a Missing Person. But turned up no results.

After about 'a month, Mottie came back home. And she was pregnant. She had told Best Momma that she had been kidnapped by a Whiteman, and the Whiteman took her all the way out Norfolk and raped her.

It might be true. Best Momma didn't believe it.

Mottie know she was out givin up that yella butt.

But Best Momma had compassion. She didn't make Mottie abort the baby. Mottie ended up having me a cousin, named Christopher. Stancil, like his momma and Best Momma.

And yes, Christopher is even lighter than Mottie.

The father came there; looking for Mottie. Of course, he would. Ain't it. And yes, he is 'a Whiteman.

But Best Momma wouldn't let her go with him.

Eventually he gave up, trying to take Mottie.

And he refused child support to Christopher. Which put Mottie on welfare. When that happened, Mottie was able to get an apartment for her and her baby, down the street from Best Momma, out Stuart Gardens.

It's so much in the dark with Mottie, about what happened in the one month she was gone. It is. But it's not. The bottom line is that we are grateful to God that Mottie is alive, and we got to add Christopher into our family.

Chapter 8.

In the 7th grade, I tried out for Ms. Nora Moore's Drama class, as an elective. I don't even know why I made that decision, I guess it was just trying something to do. I did good in it, but for my 8th grade year I was ready to move on and do something else. I had wanted to take Foreign Language classes. Pierre wanted to learn French. I signed up for French.

Between my 7th and 8th grade year, I didn't have a phone. My Grandmomma's phone was listed as our phone. Ms. Moore had called to figure out why I didn't sign up for her class, for my senior year of middle school. After the conversation I had with her, I changed my elective back over to Drama. And I'm glad I did.

I had the opportunity to see Marcelle Marceaux, LIVE, at the Chrysler Coliseum. That never would've happened if I wasn't in drama. It never would've happened if it wasn't for my momma.:

My momma's class goes to the library every Monday, and while her class was probably sitting down in a vast educated setting, watching The Three Stooges, my mother had found some flyers on mime artist, Marcelle Marceaux. But she didn't know who he was.

I didn't know who he was.

My mother had brought the flyers home to me, because she thought he was "an actor."

I took the flyers with me to school, and showed them to my teacher Ms. Moore. When she saw who it was on the flyer, she asked me,

"Where did you get these?" with her mouth all astonished and dropped opened.

To make a long story short.: MARCELLE MARCEAUX COMES TO TOWN!! WOOOOOOO!!

Ms. Moore made arrangements. We did have small fees to pay, but we got to roll into the Chrysler Coliseum, Custom Coach Style: Ms. Moore rented us a bus; and I got to see Le Monsieur. The Living French Legend himself.: Marcelle Marceaux. LIVE! IN THE FLESH!

The Greatest Pantomime Artist that EVER LIVED. Who can dispute that?

Then, we did one major play called, The Lion Who Couldn't. Roscoe Orman from Sesame Street was the original actor selected to do the part of the Lion. He had to cancel "due to personal matters." Which in this case, means, he had a baby by the chick on the side. Which in 1988, having babies outta wedlock, and babies by your mistress, was not good public rapport.

He had to cancel "due to personal reasons." Hunh. And the part ended up going to actress, Francesca Roberts. She drove out from California all the way to Newport News, Virginia. Before that time, I had never heard of her. She was such a beautiful actress that worked well with us. And she kept letting me get many- many hugs. She was so soft.

To this day I see her on TV, and of course now, I know who she is. She makes guest appearances on quality hit shows. Generally, she'll always play a judge. She's been on The Fresh Prince and on Martin. Reruns of those shows still come on BET at this time.

To this day I am thankful to her and I thank her for helping our play to happen.

During my 8th grade year, I developed more love for hip- hop and rapping, even though, I wasn't really allowed to play that kind of music in my house.

See, my father was a preacher, and my mother is his wife. And to them, that kinda music was "the devil's music." I wasn't permitted to play it and blast it.

Not, when they wasn't home.

But I was a latch key kid. That is a kid who got the key to the house. You feel me?

I can let myself in anytime I want. Especially, when mom and dad ain't around.

When my parents ain't around, I can BLAST!! Boogie Down Productions, Eric B and Rakim, EPMD, Big Daddy Kane, LL Cool J, Run-DMC, PUBLIC ENEMY, Eazy- E, NWA, all the music the devil was probably good to see me dancing to.

In the Hampton Roads Area, which consists of 7 CITIES of Norfolk, Portsmouth, Chesapeake, Virginia Beach, Suffolk, Eastern Shore, Hampton, and Newport News, and other surrounding areas; we had a local radio station-- that wasn't even an FM station-- called WRAP. RAP. But spelled with the call letters W- R-A- P. And it started out on AM channel 850. Later the frequency changed to AM 1350.

But you catch that channel at the right time, and it played just as crystal clear as an FM channel. The "right time" for us, was 4pm- 4:30. That's when WRAP played, THE RAP ATTACK.

THE RAP ATTACK was 30 minutes of the hippest, rawest, latest hip- hop music, with all the rappers and groups I afforested, and too many more to exhaust on this writing. But WRAP kept us in the loop with the progression of hip- hop music and culture, at a time FM radio was discriminating against it.

And when that 30 minutes came on, I'd be strapped to my tuner, like 'a bale of hay be strapped to 'a cow's tongue, with my tape recorder pushed up to the radio. My finger was to the pulse. I was recording. Every single song.

For poor kids that didn't have the freedom and luxury to go to the record store and buy the music; WRAP was THE SOURCE for me to get all the top- HIT hip- hop. And I won't turnin loose.

Sometimes, I be so turned up, in playing my

music back so LOUD!! after I had recorded it, that sometimes I wouldn't hear my parents come home. I'd be caught. Or if I see them pulling up to the house, I'd go flying through the house, to my room, to go turn the music down.

My father didn't like it. He had wanted to beat me with a belt for playing it. But my mother suffered for me to listen to it. She said,

"Just play it through your headphones."

Man, I had some dumb- ass headphones. My headphones came from the Everything's A $1.00 store. What that means is.: you gotta spend $2.00 on 'a pair of headphones. Cause when you buy a pair of headphones from Everything's A $1.00, only (1) side of the headphones is going to work. So, I gotta buy another pair...

Then bring them home, cut and splice a pair, and make it into (1) headset. That's how I got headphones. But them $1.00 headphones used to THUMP!! I get em right.

When I listen to rap; you got people who can listen to songs word- for- word. I didn't hear the music like that, cause I was a rapper myself. I got favorite rappers, even favorite rappers in groups, but I didn't spit their lyrics word- for- word. As an artist, I wanted my own raps. My own lyrics. To me it was BITING, to rap another rapper's lyrics. That's just how I carried it.

It was about this time I met another friend. I was out shooting the basketball in the monkey bars. In Paula Maria, that's how we played basketball. We had a full basketball ball court, but Management would take down the rim.

It was a lot of welfare moms, or single moms who stayed out there, but our hood was a good, wholesome, quiet area. Other areas in the city was outbreaked with crime and crack, or dope, and gun violence. Kids getting killed over a basketball game. But looking back, Paula Maria did an excellent job to protect us and to push the harmful and negative effects of those types of things from invading our community, and from desecrating our lives and killing us.

Basketball courts drew a lot of attention.

For some young niggas, shootin hoop through a rainbow rim of the monkey bars, as a goal, it was probably boring to crime, crack, dope and guns.

So one day I was out shooting, when--

Up comes this kid. I never seen him before. I throw up the ball, to see what he gon do, and when I miss, he'd catch it and start driving the lane for me to check him. His name was Damon Chandler. He was from New York. From that day we first met, the impact and influence of my friendship with Damon, would be the first dynamic that would take my childhood to the whole NEXT LEVEL.

Chapter 9.

Damon was raised by his mother, Karen, and his stepfather, named David. Just like me, Damon was from a good family. But my family was a good CHURCH family. All the things in my house I wasn't allowed to do.

I can do it in Damon's house.

I was just glad my momma let me keep going over there. Ms. Karen and David smoked. My momma really didn't let me over nowhere, around people who smoke. My Granddaddy smoke and my Aunt Paulette, but when they see my momma, they always put they cigarettes out. They might be in good mid- smoke. But they see my momma; they put it out.

Another thing that brought me and Damon together, both of us were single children. We didn't have brothers or sisters. And we were both boys.

When I go over to Damon's house; Mrs. Karen loved him. The boy had everything.: Nintendo; Super Mario Bros, Duck Hunt, Track and Field, Double Dribble, Double Dragon, Donkey Kong, Mike Tyson's Punch- Out, Legend of Zelda...

You name it... he prolly got it.

Not only did I get a chance to play NINTENDO-- something that's definitely not at my house-- but both of us had love for rap. Hip- hop music and culture. Of all things a momma could buy a son.: Mrs. Karen bought her son twin Technic turntables, wit the mixer, and woof box speakers for a Christmas gift.

Damon turned into a DJ, right there in fronna my sight. He would cut, scratch, and spin, and work on his mixing. I would listen to him do that, while I grabbed the Nintendo controller.

Then at some part, Mrs. Karen had bought Damon (2) dolls. A Chucky and 'a My Buddy. By this time, I had outgrown preaching to dolls. I had 'a new place for em. The world of professional wrestling.

I'd pick them damn dolls up, and clothesline, hit 'a brain buster, wrap a figure- four leg lock, or an earth dropping DDT on My Buddy or Chucky. Ain't make no difference. Then I'd tag Damon in, as my tag- team partner so he can getta piece of the action and shoot for the pin.

My last time loving to play wit a doll, was a bad experience.: It had been 1985.

Cabbage Patch Kids was the dolls that was poppin! In 85, 'a kid won't 'a kid if you ain't have 'a Cabbage Patch Kid. But Cabbage Patch Kids got expensive. My momma won't payin $50 fo some lil scrappy ass doll. That money gone go somewhere else; like payin her BILLS.

And Cabbage Patch Kids can range into the low HUNDREDS OF DOLLARS. Cabbage Patch Kids was expensive and too much for me. But I still wanted one.

My momma had a cousin.

Gwen told me and my momma, "I can make you a Cabbage Patch Doll."

I shoulda known something bout this ain't sound right. Now remind you, that Cabbage Patch Kids start at $50! Gwen said she would make me a Cabbage Patch Kid for 25!

I shoulda walked away from this shit right there.

I gave her a chance. I gave her a chance. I gave her a chance.

Man, when that doll came back-- she done stuffed some cotton inside some damn PANTYHOSE. The Cabbage Patch Kid whole body made outta pantyhose. Gwen done sewed some eyes, a nose, and a mouth. Stitched him some hands. Put him some black slip- on shoes, pink overalls, and sewed him on a wig.

My momma had paid the money up- front.

I was so mad...

But that's what I get. The only way you might getta Cabbage Patch Kid for $25, is if it's stolen.

So after my Cabbage Patch experience, I was done wit dolls, except for when I got my Charlie Mc Carthy. I was fascinated with ventriloquist dolls and how they work. But other than that, I had outgrown playing with dolls.

Playing at Damon's house was better than

playing at Chuck E Cheese. He had Nintendo. He had the rhythm and the beats. We just couldn't play it too loud. He had old neighbors that lived up under his apartment. His momma didn't mind buying him stuff. But she wasn't trying to buy them replacement stuff.

Damon had bunk beds that was built like a jungle gym. And I saw him do something more wit a piece of bread than just dip it in syrup. He would take a slice of bread, put pasta sauce on it, and add some mozzarella or parmesan cheese. He'd Turn it into 'a PIZZA.

Damon was a cool dude. He was just chubby. And when he walk, he almost look like he was rockin over his Patrick Ewing's. He looked clumsy. But he had speed. He could play football, basketball. And when you think you got him, he had a jet engine on him. And we both was into girls.

We both liked girls.

Damon had a clear phone in his room. When it ring, it light up. "Hello," he would answer it. He'd be pickin his tall high- top fade, grinnin, and talkin to girls. But in our hood, it won't that many girls to talk to. Most of the girls was younger than me. I ain't like girls that was younga than me. I had to have a girl that was my age or older.

The only girls my age was Monica. Yolanda, but we all call her Baldy. That musta been her baby name, cause the girl had a hair full of hair. And Tina. Baldy and Tina was sisters.

Won't none of these bitches Bad Bitches. That's why

they ain't absolutely captivate my attention. Plus, I had already had Baldy.

We ain't never have sex, but she was one of them on and off again. One. Two- day girlfriends. She was before Niece. And now we was 13, and she was still suckin her thumb.

Tina had a phat ass butt. She'll let 'a nigga rub on it, smack on it, and squeeze it. But she won't givin 'a nigga no pussy. She was rockin 'a nigga up fo nothing.

They momma, Ms. Antoinette, had one mo daughter, named Dirty Red. But she was too damn young. She won't nothing but like 6. Fuck I'm supposed to do wit that?

It's one more honorable mention.: Andrea. Andrea had been the baddest bitch out there. But Andrea was older than me.

She had already growed up and moved out. Some years later, she had lost one of her children. One of her sons got killed playing on the playground. Not out Paula Maria, but out Aqua Duct. It was some reckless nigga, tryin to shoot at a nother nigga, and ended up erroneously having a bullet hit her son.

After Andrea moved, I never saw her again, except for in The Daily Press and on the news, after the tragic death of her son. Then she moved to Richmond.

Oh, and we had Chrystal. Just like Andrea, Crystal was Red. But Crystal was REDDER than Andrea.

My first celebrity crush was Whitney Houston. But after they put Lisa Bonet on The Cosby Show; I saw flashes of Salt, from Salt- n- Pepa; and Tisha Campbell; all the way back on School Daze-- it was o'va wit! I was hooked on Red Bitches ever since. I wanted me 'a Red Bitch.

And Crystal was everything. She was RED. She was PHAAAT. But she was 'a virgin. She won't givin 'a nigga that pussy. Me and Damon had tried her, at different times. And I know that was crazy, cause Damon used to dance, and do a lotta shit, a lotta girls liked Damon. Plus he was the most advanced nigga in our whole hood. Corey Mc George won't even fuckin wit this nigga; and Corey was in high school.

Damon had cable tv in his room, and when Ms. Karen ain't home, we had a VCR in her room. We had a spot to bring the girlies over. So when I saw Chrystal ain't even give that nigga no pussy-- Damn! She won't even lettin 'a nigga see that pussy.

So other than that, everybody else was somebody's momma. Cory Ford; my nigga JRs momma; Ms. Charlene; Candace, she was too young, but she had a thick Red ass momma; or Chyrstal's momma. Unless them bitches was 'a pedophile, they won't givin no lil young nigga no pussy.

I was out back.

The only thing, I ain't like about Damon, is he'll act different when other niggas get around; sometimes Omar, sometimes Carlos, sometimes Eric Bell, sometimes Eric's cousin Maurice, but always Barry. Especially Barry. If it's me and him, he alright. But soon as he see Barry, he'll change up, and act a whole different way. Barry was that ol pretty smoooth ass nigga-- he could dress. And all of a sudden, when he get around Damon, these two niggas thought they was Kid N Play.

Barry had both of his parents in his home. But he kept trying to tell me, his Daddy is his Step-Daddy. I ain't believe it. I'on believe it to this day. A lotta bitches liked Barry. Even out the younger bitches, that was like 3 years up under us. He ended up pulling the baddest one. Her named was Trice, Tisha, something like that. But Barry ended up taking her virginity.

And Damon ended up taking Kim's virginity. Then he ended up taking Candace's virginity, and Erica's.

Then it was supposed to be a girl for me. She was a chubby lil red girl. She had told me she liked Barry, and I won't mad. Cause I really didn't like younger girls anyway.

Even kissing her, I won't feeling nothing. Younger girls just won't fo me. She won't feeling me and I won't feeling her; so it worked out fo both of us.

Oh, and I forgot.: it was another girl named Deborah that was our age, but she ended up fuckin a nigga named Mike, who was older than us. She lost her virginity to him. It was a lotta mommas mad that summer.

Other than Crystal, believe me, I won't missin nothing.

While I was young and in the Newport News Public Schools System, once a year, the Physical Education (P.E.) Health Instructors would have me to lean forward and to touch my toes. I was about in 6th grade when they started to notice a hump in my back. They noticed the hump again, a year later, when I was in 7th grade. And a year later, when I was in the 8th grade. But this time, my PE Teacher, Mrs. Danley reported it to my parents, to get me checked out.

I went to see a doctor out Executive Drive out in Hampton, in Virginia. He told me my spinal curve had gone too severe. He recommended me to go see an Orthopedic and Surgeon Specialist out Virginia Beach, on Virginia Beach Blvd.

At first glance, Dr Porter talked to me about wearing a brace. The brace was like a beige- pinkish color. And he said, "You'll put the brace on up underneath your clothes, and the brace will cover up your neck and support you up underneath your chin." And I would have to wear this brace everyday until my spine is straightened.

I agreed to wear the brace.

But the brace wasn't ready. Dr Porter said I had to come back and get the brace, because it would have to be specially made.

It was about 2 weeks later, I returned to get my brace. But when I thought I would get the brace, Dr Porter came with more shocking news... he said, "The curve is more severe than I thought."

140

Before it was just "a hump," or "a curve" in my back; I had suspected that. But Dr Porter was now confirming, "You got scoliosis." He'd examined through my X- rays. He advised me that I should get surgery to correct the curve in my spine, rather than wear the brace.

This was back in 1989 and I was 14 years old. This part may sound bad, but there was a janitor at Huntington Middle School named Mr. Crawley, and Mr. Crawley had a very crooked curve in his back and spine. It had curved him over like he was a question mark. That's not to speak bad about Mr. Crawley. He was always very friendly, nice, and kind. But it was because of me seeing him, that propelled me to go on ahead and go through and get the surgery.

To have surgery on your spine; being that everything rolls off your spinal column. You know you got a brain. And your brain, it sends messages down your spinal column, and your spinal column sends messages out to the whole rest of your body, then it sends messages back up to your brain.

When your body is in pain... Ouuuuch!!

Elder Edwards had just died in 1988, and this was 1989. I was going under the knife!! Everything was 50/ 50. A 50/ 50 chance I wouldn't stand. A 50/ 50 chance I wouldn't walk. A 50/ 50 chance I wouldn't run. A 50/ 50 chance I would live permanently with another physical abnormality. A 50/ 50 chance I might die!

I was scheduled in June of 1989 to have surgery on my back, in Norfolk, at the Children's

Hospital of the King's Daughters, about 2 weeks after the school year had ended.

On the day of my surgery, I had a small number of family there.

"Are you alright?" Asked the Queen. That's my Best Momma, if you didn't know.

She sat diagonally across from me.

"Yeah. I'm alright," I said.

"You sure, you ok?"

"Yeah, I'm good." I responded to let her know. I thank her for checking up on me.

Her mother is brown skin. But she is dark. Just like her Daddy. And her black wig is pulled down and barbie- pinned into her real hair. It nips at her ear.

She kept talking to me. I guess to see if I would change my mind. But I didn't. And my mother just keeps walking back and forth to tell me about Jesus and that, "Jamie, you got the prayers going up from the Saints. Going up to God from the Saints."

And she would share information back and forth between the separated groups of our family. Then she went back to talking about Jesus.

When the nurses finally came with the bed to push me off to surgery, I let my momma hold my hand. She was the only one allowed to walk me back to surgery. And so, she went to talking about

Jesus. All the way, she held my hand, and talked about Jesus. She talked about what HE would do for me, and how HE would bring me through.

I let her do it. But my mind won't on Jesus. Jesus was the furthest thing from my mind. What I thought about was Ric Flair. "The Nature Boy"'who had survived a plane crash in 1975. He had broken his back in three places, and he went on to be an NWA World Heavyweight Champion. WOOOOOOOO!!

Ric Flair is my most favorite wrestler of all time.

Then, there was my second most favorite wrestler of all time-- "The Immortal" Hulk Hogan. See, I had been eatin my vitamins and sayin my prayers since 1985. I used to workout and train off one of Hulk Hogan's Hulka Mania workout kits, since I was 10.

My body was cut different than most ordinary 14-year-old boys, my age. I had friends who played football who didn't have as much chisel as me. A lot of that came from my attraction for wanting to be a Body Builder.

Oh yeah, and I used to train off Rocky. Can't fo'get that. It was an all-cardio workout set that my momma got me from the Everything's A $1.00 store. It's amazin how well my abs and my breathing began to sculpt, fo jus 'a $1.

Three days a week I used to combine both the Hulk Hogan and Rocky Balboa workouts together as one workout. And, I had thought about the World Champion, Iron Mike Tyson and Sugar

Ray Leonard. And probably somewhere down the line, even Mr. T was taggin, "I pity the fool."

Why not??

I wanted TO BE TOUGH. Like all those guys. Not like Jesus.

I was rolled into a room for surgery. My momma had walked me all the way down to the room. Then I didn't see her no more. I saw nurses. I saw Dr Porter. I saw Anesthesia. I counted, "10, 9, 8, 7, 6..."

I saw unconsciousness.

When I woke up-- I saw PAIN!! So much PAIN!! What did you do to my body!!??

I got up to move. Cause you know; it's the normal thing to do. I felt like 90- 100 lbs. of weighted metal was stitched up inside my back onto my spine.

'WHAT DID YOU DO TO ME!!??' Is what was in my head. But it would've been in a lot of curse words had it actually come out.

I just kept trying to move in my new altered body. I tried to jerk up. I tried to walk. I tried to run from these people who had just finished Frankenstein my young 14-year-old body.

When a nurse got close-- I punched her right in her face. I tried to knock the bitch out! I just couldn't catch the full flush cross her jaw. Other nurses and Dr Porter wrapped me up and held me down. Then they hit me with more anesthesia.

I went out.

When I woke up, I was in an air-conditioned dark room. There was a window that goes from my room out to the hall. But the blinds was closed. There was a door. But it was closed. I was stiff. Solid. I was on my back, like a board. And I was alone.

I tried to move.

I tried to jerk.

I tried to roll.

I tried to walk.

I tried to run.

I was stiff.

I was solid. Like a board.

And I was all alone.

I wasn't in pain. But I was tired. I went back to sleep. When I woke back up, nothing changed. It was pitch black. It was quiet. I had woke black up. I won't dead, yet. I moved my hands to crack and spread my fingers. Then I went back to sleep.

When I woke back up, my Father was at my bed's side. The lights were on but the blinds to the hall were still closed. And my momma. I was angry that I didn't know where they was. But you know, it's against the law to cuss yo parents out, so I just politely asked, "Where y'all was at?"

I thought my parents had left me... forsaken me... abandon me.

My momma stared down at me, and I was still waking up, in her soft warmed- ovened hashed brown eyes, when she said, "Son, we haven't went nowhere. They wouldn't let us up. We had to wait for them to let us up to see you. We been here the whole time."

All I could do was shut up and soak in that kind of joy. But physically after pumping all the iron in the world, I was down.

I was in ICU, but when Dr Porter examined me, he said I should be moved to a regular hospital room. I moved to the new hospital room.

When I got to my new room, I had a visit from my Grandma Carrie. My father has (2) parents. After his father and his mother divorced, Best Momma wasn't the only one who remarried. My Grandfather had remarried too. My Grandfather had married Mrs. Carrie.

Best Momma is my Grandma, but Carrie always loved me and cared for me too, just like my biological Best Momma. I always called her Grandma Carrie. I never called her step- Grandma. I would never disrespect her like that. I saw it that I had 3 Grandmommas. The same way that I had 3 Grandfathers. I didn't know it wasn't normal. I just knew it was my normal. And it felt good. Everything got along.

My father's sister, Novie was there. And of course, The Matriarch. My Best Momma.

"We chipped in and bought you a new mattress." They happily told me they bought me a new twin- sized mattress.

"Ohh, Jamie you here that? I can't wait for you to get home and see it," my mother smiled and encouraged.

I had a roommate but he left the hospital, maybe like the next day. Then I had another roommate. He had stayed maybe like 2 nights. But when Dr Porter came to see me, he saw a lot of red tape and Biohazard signs stringing up everywhere.

Me and my momma didn't think nothing of it. My roommate was cool, laid back, and chillin.

"Dr Porter," my momma amicably welcomed him into the room. She's always very friendly.

But Dr Porter had left out as fast as he came in.

When my momma had cracked the door Dr Porter had broke loose to cursing out the nurses, at their nursing station.

Then he left and broke around a corner.

Those nurses scurried up in there!

"Hurry up! You gotta go! You gotta go! You gotta go!" They were hollering at me.

'Go? Go where?'

They forced me and my momma to leave out the room. I had to be helped to a nearby waiting lobby. By the time we came back, my room was scrubbed clean and my roommate was gone. I never saw him again.

What had happened was my roommate had an infection in his leg, and I had an open incision in my back. Me and him had the same nurses, or if my mother, or his family could've touched him and came back and touched me, his infection could've gotten in my back. I could've gotten sick. I could've died.

"Are you ok?" Dr Porter asked me.

"Yeah, I'm alright," cause that's all I could think to say.

"I'm sorry about that," he apologized.

I just shook my head. It prolly was a good idea I ain't knock his nurse out. That mighta made him my enemy. After that I didn't have no more roommates. My dad would go back and forth between the hospital and home. Only my momma had stayed with me in the room, the whole time.

She was a nurse and a 24- hour caregiver to me.

Then one night, it was on the fifth night, but start of the sixth day, that I was in King's Daughters. I was a CRACKED BACK in PAIN!! I was in so MUCH PAIN that it broke me up out my sleep. And I strained to roll over on my left side.

I couldn't do it. At all. I couldn't make it. I struggled for a minute, then I stopped, I didn't want to rip my back open. My incision was still healing.

I rested for a minute.

Then, I went to roll over on my right side. I didn't even know if I could do it. I ended up having to press the heels of my feet down into the mattress, and that's how I made it over on my right side.

There's a screen- curtain that's usually up at night between me and my roommate, when I had a roommate, so he could have his privacy when he went to sleep. But now that he was gone, there wasn't a screen- curtain that was up. And the curtains from the main window were still wide-opened from the daytime. I could see straight to the main window, and the blinds and curtains were fully drawn back.

I could see straight through the window, and I could see straight and clear out to the bulb of the parking lot's light, and I could see up to the sky.

My small hurtful eyes were drawn to look up into the sky.

Then... there it was. It was an orb. It was blue, and it was radiated.

A blue radiated orb bulb of light came down from out of the sky. I saw it drawl down from out of the heavens. The orb had bent over near the parking lot's light, without bumping or touching it, and it curved at a perfect 90-degree angle. It came. It came straight. Directly through into my window.

I was TERRIFIED!! I was as scared as 'a fluffy white rabbit in 'a red fox's ambush!!

I wanted to holler!

I couldn't holler.

I wanted to scream!

I couldn't scream.

I wanted to run!

I couldn't even move.

It was like I was drawn into and being mesmerized by this tantalizing blue light, both at the same time. But what if it was a UFO? What if it was an alien? What if I would be abducted? What if it was a ghost? What if it was something else? What if it was going to kill me and make me DIED? My brain was eating it's hairs out. But then

the orb...

It stopped.

It looked at me.

It glided through air
and space.

It stood at my bedside.

Then

the orb...

It grew,

It grew,

It grew,

It grew,

and...

There was light.

Light.

Light.

Light.

Light.

Light.

Very Bright Light.

So Much Light...

It grew bigger, bigger, bigger, and bigger.

The Light.

It grew brighter, brighter, brighter, and brighter.

It was like I was in the room with the sun. But, I

couldn't be burned.

And I was still so frightened. The only thing I could think was to call, "Jesus."

I did that because I was scared. I did that out of the greatest fear! And because there was a teacher who worked with my mother at Buckroe, named Ms. Charlotte. Ms. Charlotte had had a second job working as a convenience store clerk. One night a man had robbed her in her store.

She told me that he had started to hit her with his cane. He was beating her across her head, knocking her to the ground. And she said, "I put up my hands to stop him from hitting me, and I just called out, "JESUS, JESUS, JESUS, JESUS," and he stopped beating me. He just looked at me and ran off."

So I always remembered that. It always stuck in my mind from that time that I was like 10, 11, or 12, that whenever I get stuck out in some trouble... that I should call on the name of, "JESUS."

So that's why that happened.

My eyes stayed open; I was trying to see, and I just kept saying, "Jesus, Jesus, Jesus, Jesus, Jesus..." over, and over, and over again. I could see a glimpse of HIS hair, and HIS face moving towards me. THEN,

HE spoke to me.

I PHYSICALLY HEARD HIS VOICE. HE was

talking to Me.

At first it was in English. Like HE was calming me down. Then, HIS hand came forward out at me; out of the blue light. When I saw HIS hand. It was in the shape of a human hand. It had light wound all around it. But I could see it.

And when HIS hand got closer to me, HIS light got brighter. I no longer could see any of the blue aura at all. All I could only see was very, very bright light. HIS light is BRIGHTER than the sun. Because when the sun shines, you can still look and see everything around you. But when Jesus lights up, you can't see Nothing but HIM.

You can't even see anything around you or right next to you. I couldn't even look down and see my own body, or the bed I was laying in. All I could see was HIM. All I could see is HIS Light. It's like I was in the bosom of The Messiah.

And when HE lit up, HE turned the whole "night" time atmosphere, very very bright, it turned into "daylight."

Then, HE began to shine so bright that I could no more see out of my physical eyes, unless I saw HIS light. I strained my eyes to stay open. Then, I heard HIS voice again. But this time HE didn't speak any English. HE only spoke in a very fluid and in a very rapid tongue. I interpret today that it probably was Hebrew or Aramaic. And HE was very very LOUD!! But the whole time I felt calm and peace. I didn't feel disturbed.

Then HIS hand...

HE touched me.

When HE touched me-- I was on my left side. It was on my left arm. Between my wrist and elbow. HIS hand felt as real as a human hand. HIS touch felt as real as a human touch. It literally felt like flesh touching flesh. I felt calm and I felt peace. Then...

After HE finished, what I interpret now as HIM praying over me. I saw HIS hand, it redacted back into the light. As HIS hand climbed back towards HIM, I could see the blue aura light again reappear. All the light began to gradually dissipate back into HIM, back into the orb. Then the strength of my full sight began to come back.

HIS Glory had shrunk back up into the orb. And once again the orb was beside my bed.

HE stood there for a few seconds, then the orb glided straight back up out of the room. HE traveled back the same exact path that HE had traveled in. HE had went back out through the window and went right back by the parking lot's light, bent up at a 90 degree angle, and went right back up into the sky. The exact same path that HE had came down. HE went right back up into the sky and HE was gone.

After HE left, I felt a kind of sadness. Coming into that kind of contact. I experienced a certain kind of happiness and joy, that you can only feel when HE'S around--- when HE'S in your presence. After HE left I was too tired to think about it anymore. I went to sleep.

I woke up later that morning, and I looked all the way around the room, and everything was back to normal. My mother had woke up and came to me. She was in the room all night. So I asked her, "You ain't see all that light that was in here last night?"

And when she said, "Light!? What light!?"

That's when I just shut up. I ain't wanna go from the hospital to the coo- coo house. Before the Messiah came in, I looked over at her, she was knocked out fast to sleep in the chair. And after HE came in, HIS light was so bright, I couldn't even see my own momma. But, maybe I was crazy.

But then she asked me a crazy question. She gon ask me, "You wanna get up and go to the bathroom?"

It's crazy cause she know I can't walk. But it's crazy on top of that cause I actually answered her, "Yeah. I'll try it."

My father was a preacher. My mother was a teacher. She missed work because of me. She is a living nurturer. She nurtured me. She ain't a nurse. But she nursed me. She ain't a caretaker. But she took care of me. She ain't just a woman who had 'a baby.:

She walked me to the bathroom.

She washed me.

She cleaned me up.

And then she asked me the next crazy question-- she asked, "You wanna walk to the Cafeteria?"

'The Cafeteria?!'

Momma, the Cafeteria ain't even on this floor.

The question was crazy, and the answer was just as insane! I said, "Yeah, I'll try."

And so out we set. I had one hand on the rail and one arm around my momma. And off we went.

Then, when I was walking back up...

I was coming back up to my room. I was walking, in the middle of the hospital's aisle, like something in between a cowboy and a tin robot. My mother was walking behind me to make sure I wouldn't fall.

Then, we saw Dr Porter...

Dr Porter was standing beside the nurse, behind the nursing station. His mouth just dropped and hanged open. My room was just right there, diagonally across from the nurse's station. I was just trying to get back to my room.

Dr Porter glared at me like he was staring down a ghost. When my mother called out to him, "Dr Porter. Dr Porter. Look. See. He's walking. He's walking."

With his mouth still hanging open. Dr Porter dropped the clipboard from out of his hands!! And he hauled off away from the nurse's station.

I went to my room.

"What was wrong with him?" my mother asked me.

"Momma. I don't know what's wrong with him." I was just trying to get back to bed.

A few minutes later, we could hear Dr Porter's voice back at the nurse's station. My momma opened the door and went back and went back out there with him; where he was.

"Dr Porter.. "'she said. My mother has a very cordially tender voice, unless you get her mad.

"I never seen nothing like it." Dr Porter stood out in the hall, between my room and the nurse's station. My door was open. I could see and hear him and my momma from my bed.

"I never seen nothing like it," Dr Porter repeated, while staring over at me. Bubbles of water almost curled up in his eyes.

"I did that surgery myself..." He demanded.

"It's no way; it's no way!"- - "You was supposed to be down for no less than two weeks!" He hollered at me. I thought he was about to cuss me out. Then he said something to me that was implausibly incredible, he said, "Just give me a bowel movement and I'm gonna send you home."

My precious Jewish and Church friends, I

tell you the truth.: Dr Porter touched my body, and in one day, I went down. Six days later.: YAHSHUA, the Holy Messiah, touched my body. In one day. And in that same day; I got up, I walked, I defecated, and I went home-- all in the same day!

The crazy part about it, about a week after I came home from the hospital, the normal time I should've been doing a normal surgery recovery, I was out with my friends playing tackle football. I had (2) fresh new metal rods, and I still had my dressing healing on my back.

When Dr Porter had did my surgery, he stitched me up from the inside. He pulled all his tools and equipment from out near the bottom, near the small of my back. So the bottom of my back had to naturally just heal up on it's own.

We had a living room mirror when I got home. My mother would change my dressing, and she would always try to get me to look at my back, and to see my back and how I was healing. But I never did look at it. I didn't want to see it.

I only wanted to heal.

I wanted to play football, because I had always wanted to play football. I wanted to be a Body Builder. But football players made more money than Body Builders. I wanted to buy my momma a house. I'm only five- eight. Too short for basketball. I wanted Muscles & Money. I wanted to be a football player. But Dr Porter had checked off a list for me of everything I couldn't do for the rest of my life.

For the rest of my life I could never play football. I could never play basketball. I could never play soccer. I could never take karate, or do Body Building. I could never lift more than 40 lbs. I could never do tennis. I could never run track. I could never do bowling, or swimming. I couldn't even fish. So it's obvious, I wanted to prove Dr Stanley Porter wrong, like I did with my surgery.

But when my momma had saw me out playing football. She busted out that house, "Jamie, what you think you doing!? Boy don't you know you on my insurance!??"

She can say all that without cursing. Sister Miles don't curse. My surgery came to $81,000. Bout the cost of a small house. Blue Cross and Blue Shield paid 80 percent. Sticking my momma wit the balance. What Mrs. Miles wouldn't pay, to see her son have 'a normal life.

But that was it, my football career was over, because I knew my momma won't going to financially support it. In my upcoming freshman year my momma took a copy of Dr Porter's report up to Warwick High School, so they would be aware of all of my medical restrictions. She didn't trust me to take it to them. She was right. If it was up to me they never would've got it.

And although I tried out for different sports, I couldn't make any of the teams. Either way, I still would've had to get a physical. It's no way I ever would've passed a physical with a protruding scar vertically down my back, and two rods on my spine, that would've popped up on any X- ray. I had to relinquish my dream of wanting to be an athlete.

My father used to tell me something smart, he'd say, "Use your brain and not back." But I used to always feel like he was teasing me. It wasn't easy for me to transition, because I'd always been a physical guy.

AND I WAS TOO YOUNG!

After the Messiah had touched me, I was still trying to adjust to a life of being back regular and being normal.

I WAS TOO YOUNG!

I was too young to understand how to receive Yahshua's (Jesus') kind of POWER and BLESSING at age 14 into my life. I had received it, but I was too young-- too immature. I still had to develop into it.

After all, what did I do to deserve it?

There wasn't any absolute reason for The Messiah to show up and heal me. My absolute life and safety wasn't being threatened. I didn't run into any infections or complications after surgery. I would've healed up naturally anyway within the timeframe predicted by Dr Porter.

But apparently God had a Higher Plan.

A part of me wanted to finally join the Church to align myself with what God wanted to do in my life. I had grown up in the Church, but I had never officially joined. My father used to pressure me to join. But my mother gave me the lead way to choose on my own; when I was ready. And even though, I thought about actually joining the Gospel Spreading Church and singing in the choir; I had took to my mother's side. But all it did was give me that street to still keep running from God.

Still a part of me wanted to be that 14-year-old kid who was into rap, r&b music, Nintendo and playing games, and being into girls. By the ways I was raised; I was still wanting to sin.

So that's what made me repel from following the Lord. I was young. I wanted to be young. I wanted to follow the Lord when I was old. Sometime before I die. I thought I might follow HIM. Spiritually I was torn. Consciously, I was running from God.

And I paid for that decision.

Weeks after my surgery, of the same summer, I didn't have nothing to do. I was 14. Two years too old to go fo the summer at Buckroe. We had tried that last summer, when I was 13; shit didn't work out. I guess they thought I was supposed to be some kinda unpaid employee, who supposed to go up in here and help these lil young ass teachers hand raise they lil young ass students... HAAAAH!!

Young kids like to play. They don't see wrong and harm in what they do. None of it is with a malicious intent. Right!? Like when they throw that eraser past Ms. Theresa's head.

"Ha, ha, ha, ha," and like kids, we all laugh.

But when I laugh; guess who get in trouble?

A lotta child's play kept happening, and because I laugh and not tell on who was doing it, I was the one who kept getting in trouble for every damn thang.

But finally these lil bad ass kids had went too far.

I was on the see- saw with one of the other children, when this lil white boy run up with a hand full of dirt, and throw the dirt at me, at my back and in my hair. He must ain't know I was a master at jumping up off the top of that see- saw. When he saw me coming down, his eyes swole up real big like he was lookin up at Spider Man.

He started running, but I was walking him down. And I reached out to grab him-- the other teacher was Ms. Ann.

I'on know what she thought she was. I guess she thought she was white intervention. She put her hand up; "NO! Don't you..."

I didn't even wind back. I just-- WHAAAAAPPPP!!

The way that bitch jaw dropped-- I coulda start bein her pimp.

I heard her say, "Huuhhhh!!!!"

I ain't punch her. I just threw 'a fast back-hand chop cross that bitch face, like how Ric Flair throw 'a chop cross 'a nigga chest. That bitch was lookin at a mirror reflection of her face- - inside her hand.

"Huuhhhh!!!!" that bitch went hollering and went running off to the building.

She left the white boy standing there. I could'a pulverized him. But when I saw Ms. Ann running, I already knew where she was going- - this bitch was gonna tell my momma.

And that's jus what she had did. She told my momma and she told Ms. Bailey. Well, she wasn't Ms. Bailey by that time. She'd gotten married to a Wolfpack Alumni, named Carter, and her name was now Mrs. Smith. I like Carter. He is cool because he always talk real smart. He never loose sleep talkin bout stupid shit.

But that won't gon help me now. Mrs. Smith didn't suspend me. She let my momma handle it. And my mother's idea of handling it, was with a leather belt.

When I got home, and she told my father what I did, they both beat my ass. I got double- teamed. Wit TWO leather belts.

This shit was almost as bad as what had happened just a few years back.:

This was out Paula Maria. Paula Maria had a lotta grass. A whole lotta fields fo us to hop and play around. They had fields that intersect fields. The best way I can explain it is-- I was up in one of the fields behind my apartment.

There was a stray cat.

There was a stray kitten.

The stray kitten was more adorable than the stray cat. So I played wit the kitten.

"Meooow." You know; that little soft noise they make.

"Meooow." He keep doin it. He look like he hungry. I was gon feed him.

All of a sudden...

Here come these three little girls. They see the cat and like me they come to play wit the cute little kitten. I pick up the kitten, and this one girl, the kitten is facing her, and she step in to tickle and rub the kitten. Next thing I know,

"WHAAAAAA!"

I'm holding up the kitten. I move the kitten. To see. The kitten done clawed and ripped open the girl bottom lip. She was leaking.

Man, I had some bad luck wit lil kids, when I was a kid.

I threw the kitten down, to grab her and calm her down. She kept trying to fight me off. What the fuck can I do?

I let her go.

And she went straight home and told her momma,

and I'on know what she told her momma, but I know what her momma told my momma

that I HAD THREW the cat on top of her daughter.

And it was nothing I could do. No matter what I said. How much I explained.

"Jamie. GET IN THIS HOUSE!!"

She meant it and her face bald up in serious- meant. Momma backed me all the way up into my room. And just how convenient-- there's a Return of the Jedi Sword standing right there by the door.

There was a Return of the Jedi Sword out, that took (2) Double D sized batteries up in the handle, and when you flick the switch on the handle,

"WHOOOZZZHH!!" Your Return of the Jedi Sword would turn on and light up the night right there right there in fronna yo eyes.

Ah yeah, but that Return of the Jedi Sword, cost about $39.99. I ain't have that one.

I had the other one.

I had the one that ain't take no batteries. The one I had, you had to wait for it to get dark, or yo ass go find some dark, and this shit would jus start glowin; up in the dark.

But anyway, I heard my momma say, "You threw that cat on that little girl-- huh?? You did huh??"

And when she turned, the Return of the Jedi Sword was stickin up right there. She picked it up, like she was Luke Skywalker. And she popped me and beat me so much wit that sword. That by the time she got finished, that sword won't shit butta good piece 'a trash.

That shit was all bent up, and it had so many dents and dings, I couldn't do nothing, but throw it in the trash. And she was at the kitchen table laughing at me take it out to the dumpster.

But after I was double teamed. I took that ass- whoopin like 'a strong young man. And I showed back up to Buckroe the next day, but after that the atmosphere had changed.

I heard Ms. Ann tell Ms. Theresa, "I'll never put my hands on him again."

So that was it. That was my last Casa Ra Sa Ra at Buckroe. Mrs. Smith wasn't having me back no more, or next summer. But I won't mad.

There was no Niece. Even Ms. Penny had quit and went and got a better job. And Hey! I won't gettin paid to keep showin up at this place. I might as well move on to something better myself.

So that next summer, after my back surgery, I had to do something different. My daddy has another sister. One that ain't by Best Momma. They got the same father, except Mrs. Carrie is her mother. Her name is Berthel.

Berthel is married to a husband named Robert.

They invited to take me with them to King's
Dominion, a very popular local theme park, up in
Northern Virginia. So I go. A few weeks after
surgery. I'm feelin myself.

Walkin round. Shorts. NIKES. Tank top. My
muscles harder than Sid Vicious.

I had a real good time. At least at King's Dominion
you might actually ride the roller coasters...

        The previous year, after my summertime-
slaughter of Ms. Ann, I guess she didn't feel like she
was in a safe environment being around me. After
talking to my mother, my Uncle Lucky and Aunt
Audrey had agreed to come down from Richmond,
and to take me with them the rest of the summer.
They came to pick me up and they ended up taking
me to DISNEY WORLD.

Hold tight... this gon be a long story. But I gotta
give it to you long, cause it's the only way you'll get
caught up.

Chapter 10.

Alright, so my mother has an older sister named Audrey. They like 2 years apart. And Audrey is married to a man named Delmas. But nobody call him that. Nobody never call him that. We always call him Lucky.

And he is lucky to pull my Aunt Audrey, away from Butch, or any other man. Not judging.: but Audrey is the most attractive out all my Grandma's (8) daughters. Theresa is the second. In my opinion. But Audrey is light but browned, jus like her momma. That's all I'm gon tell you.

But I had grown to see Audrey like a 2nd mother. I never told my momma she had a replacement. I was the ring bearer at Audrey and Lucky's wedding back in 1979. Somewhere around that time, is where my substantive memory starts of Audrey and Lucky.

I remember 1983:

They supposed to went on a date to the Marvin Gaye concert. Shanda had posters all on her wall. Audrey and Lucky supposed to came down from Richmond to the Hampton Coliseum, to go to the Marvin Gaye concert. But he died. Actually, he got killed. So they had to cancel the concert.

They really missed out on something amazing. A chance to see Marvin Gaye LIVE!! That performance woulda been HUGE!!

I call Audrey my 2nd mother. But that's not
really by her own doing. It was who she is married
to. Lucky didn't have any children. He didn't have
any sons of his own. So what he really did was, take
a liking to two of his nephews; me and Hugh. And
put us up under his wing-- like we was his sons.

Yeah, Hugh. The other Junior. The Junior
that was on my momma side. Junior, just like the
other Junior, is named after his father. My momma
and Audrey have a younger sister named Paulette.
And Paulette gave birth to the Junior, that is on my
momma side.

He is from Richmond. I'm from Newport News. Bad
News. Both in Virginia. 'A hour and 'a half apart.
But our cultures are worlds apart. It's jus how it is.

Even though Lucky was from Richmond, he ol
school, so he can master pulling these (2) distant
cousins together; and makin us; somethin like
Brothers. And it was cool.

I didn't have no brothers or sisters, and Hugh,
when he first started out.: he didn't have no
brothers or sisters either. So it kinda clicked.

Audrey and Lucky would always bring me and
Hugh together. Whenever, they was going to do
something for Hugh, they might come all the way to
Bad News, to go get me. And we did all fun shit.
Like, go crabbing and drink ICED- COLD PEPSIS
from out the cooler. That's the only soda Lucky buy
is PEPSI.

Lucky taught us how to crab. We'd be standin,

where it look like somebody else ought to be swimming. But we'd be standing out there in some swimming trunks, not swimming, but holding tight onto a long white string, strangled tight around the breast of 'a raw piece of chicken, and wait til I feel a pull on my string.

That's how you know the crabs is biting.

And Lucky would inch the string, tugging it back to him, until he can swoop up under the crabs and the chicken, with a wooden handled net, capture the crabs, and pour them in a bucket.

That shit was so cool. Then, we'd take em back to Grandma's house, boil em in Bay Seasoning, and eat em. The crazy part, Lucky didn't even eat crabs. He was just showing us a good time. I felt like one day, Lucky was gon take us out to hunt. But we never got there. What we did get to was TWO TRIPS TO WALT DISNEY WORLD!! WHOOOOO!!

The furthest north I've ever been was when my Daddy took me to New York. That was in 1986. But the furthest south I ever been, was when Audrey and Lucky took me to Florida. My first time.: that was 1986. I had went to New York and to Florida; both in the same summer.

On the way down, I got to see South of The Border, in South Carolina, for the first and second time. The first time, we went to go down to go see the Sunshine-- it was me and Hugh, Audrey and Lucky, and Pauline. That's my Grandmomma, and my momma's and Audrey's momma.

We rolling in a custom cab van. So everybody

stretched out. It's plenty of space. Lucky gotta radio and Lucky got 3 tapes. Man, one tape is Al Green. But it ain't freaky- freaky Al Green. It ain't the soul-r&b, splashed wit funky elements of Al Green.

It was the saved. Gospel Singing. Born again reform, after you get some hot ass grits throwed up in yo face Al Green. But Hey! What do I know? Al Green was killing this gospel tape. And after he sing on one side, Lucky's radio was so advanced, the radio would flip the tape over, and ol' Al would start gettin it on the other side.

Don't even got to touch the radio. Ain't that something?

The second tape he had was of, um, arguably my second inspiration, Dr Martin Luther King. It was a tape on his history and excerpts from his speeches. So that's two tapes that we listened to over and over and over; and yes, they'd flip over and over and over. If you leave em in there long enough.

Then Lucky, had this third tape. He'd waited to put it in. He was quiet. No heads up; and all of a sudden it was this.:
"WHAT'S THE TIME?

IT'S TIME TO GET ILL!!!!

WHAT'S THE TIME?

IT'S TIME TO GET ILL!!!!

WHAT'S THE TIME?

IT'S TIME TO GET ILL!!!!

WHAT'S THE TIME?

... IT'S TIME TO GET ILL!!!!"

Unc had threw in a tape of License To Ill. The Beastie Boys classic first album. This was on my first trip down to Disney World. This was 1986. And I was flying down 95 South, in a custom cruise cab van, BLASTING!! "BRASS MONKEY!! THAT FUNKY HONKEY!!"

Hhhhh, I was Living The Dream.

I got to see South of the Border, and Georgia, is just before you get to Florida, so we stopped in Georgia. That's when I got to see-- that my Grandmomma had a momma!!

Named Mary. And she was still alive. But...

"What about Leroy?"

"He dead."

"What about Mr. Stanley."

"He dead."

"What about Mr. Robinson?"

Yep, yep, "He dead too."

Ain't nobody left alive, but my Grandmomma's momma, and my Grandmomma's brother; Uncle Robert.

They lived in the house where my Grandmomma once lived. It was a rinky- dink farm in Millen, Georgia. It used to be a hog farm, at some part where my Grandmomma's daddy was still alive. But now it was just LAND. And it was out in the middle of nowhere.

At night, the main road be pitch black, if you don't got on headlights, it's absolutely no light on the road, and she had no neighbors. Across the street was a farm. Beside her farm was a farm. The left side was some trees. When you look out on the other three sides, all you see is grass, farm, and dirt. And her house was halfa mile from her mailbox. Her mailbox was all the way out at the main road.

And she only had one tree hanging on the right side of her house. Being out here was even more scary than being at Sister Mc Nair house. It look like the Ku Klux Klan was gon come rollin down the street at any minute.

After we picked up my Great- Grandmother, Mary, we went rolling 'on down the I- 85, and we went to Atlanta, Georgia. We stopped by my Grandmomma's sister's house, and we ate some neck bones. She got to see her sister and her momma, then we headed on back to Millen.

Being down that part of Georgia was the first time I got introduced to a grocery store chain called Piggly Wiggly. To this day every time I think about that cartoonish pigged face, or I see the commercials, cause Piggly Wiggly is out in South Western Virginia too, I think about those first two trips to Georgia.

Piggly Wiggly was my Great- Grandmas favorite store. That's where she shop to get her groceries. And I know my Great- Grandma also believes in Jesus. Not only is she a church going woman; she took us down the country street, and up the rural route to see her in church. Then we came on back to her crib. Then the next day, at last- - it was time to go to Disney World!

Orlando, Florida.

I remember my first time in Florida. I never saw so many palm trees and fluorescent lights in all my life. So much shit was in pink, light blue, and turquoise. I read every sign going to Miami. Seem like the deeper we got in Florida, Miami moved further and further away. I was thinkin this state bigger than it is on the map.

We got to Orlando, and Miami was still over 3 HOURS AWAY!! By 312 miles. That's a lotta riding when you comin from Virginia.

I got to go to Disney World. Seeing all the lights, the magic, music everything was in full electricity.

"... if you wanna ride Space Mountain. WOOOOOO!!" That's a piece of one of the famous quotes from Ric Flair.

The line to Space Mountain was so backed; I don't even think he ever rode Space Mountain.

I did ride 20,000 Leagues Under The Sea. Me and Hugh went on The Dumbo Ride. Then we would start walking. We had to keep stopping, cause we did have my Grandma AND my Great-Grandma. I would see the sweat pour down my Great- Grandma's wrinkles. She was so hot, her pantyhose be rolled down to her ankles. I'on blame you Great- Grandma. And my Grandma keep fanning and fanning, until Audrey had to get them rested in the A/C and hydrated.

Eventually... we finally walked all the way down to see Cinderella's Castle. By the time we got there, it probably was night. But Hey! That's the best time to see it anyway. If The Lord let me live it over 'a trillion times, I wouldn't change it.

The next day we went to The Epcot Center. And that's where I got to see,

Musical Beat and Rhythm.: "Duh- duh- duh- duh - duh- duh- duh. Duh- duh- duh- duh - duh- duh- duh. Duh- duh- duh- duh - duh- duh- duh. Duh- duh- duh- duh - duh- duh- duh. Duh- duh- duh- duh - duh- duh- duh. Duh- duh- duh- duh - duh- duh- duh.

Dume- dume. Dume- dume. Dume- dume. Dume- dume."

Come on man, it was Mr. Billie Jean aka Mr. Michael Jackson himself. But he won't calling himself that. He played a character in a 3- D movie he did exclusively for Walt Disney, that was called Captain EO. So if you had never been to Epcot around that time, you probably would never know that.

It was a huge screen and a huge theatre, that probably sit 100- 150 seats. And they give you these

pink plastic shades you put on. The shades are the
3- D glasses. And you sit back and kick up in the
A/C, and you chill and watch you Michael Jackson
aka The King of Pop, aka The King of Perfection,
aka Captain EO. Act, rock, sing, and THROW IT
DOWN!

Mike is 'a bad boy. He'll sing to you an R&B
song how BAD!! he gon kick yo ass. Then, he'll spin
on you. After he kick you in yo ass, then he'll laugh
at you, "HEE- HEE."

or he might deeply humiliate you wit the, "HEE-
HEE- HEE."

That's when you know, you really fucked up!

I'm doing this writing, I just asked my girl on the
phone last night.: "What's the best Michael Jackson
song of all time?"

And she said, "Thriller."

And I can understand that. That's a real smart
answer, and statistically of course, it is the correct
answer. But for me-- it's that.:

"Duh- duh- duh- duh - duh- duh- duh. Duh-
duh- duh- duh - duh- duh- duh. Duh- duh- duh-
duh - duh- duh- duh. Duh- duh- duh- duh - duh-
duh- duh. Duh- duh- duh- duh - duh- duh- duh.
Duh- duh- duh- duh - duh- duh- duh.

Dume- dume. Dume- dume. Dume- dume. Dume-
dume."

It's that Billie Jean, man. The rhythm. The beat.

The lyrics. And that's the song, if you thought you was fuckin wit him; he get the foot all the way good in yo ass. Spin out on you, and, "HEE- HEE- HEE."

That Billie Jean take me to a whole nother planet.

Then on my second time ever in Da A; it was on the FIRST trip back from Disney World, we went to this museum. I was wondering why they took me to a museum. That's usually some shit you go to on a school field trip. But Hey! I was on vacation with (2) Richmond City school teachers.

When we get all the way back, it's doors you go out of, and it's a pool. I'm looking at the pool. Then my Uncle, he just stopped there looking. I'm thinking, why we walk past the gift shop, to get here at this pool.

Then, I see my uncle looking to his left, out at the pool. So I see a concrete slab stretched out over the pool, and when I go to read the slab-- it hit me!

I knew we was at the King Museum. But what I ain't know, they had my school- hood idol buried up out there. And Audrey and Lucky had physically took me out there to see him. I shoulda let him hear me say somma his speeches.

And it all tied in to Lucky kept playing that Dr King tape over and over and over. Even on the ride back from Disney World. It was amazing!

But yeah, Audrey and Lucky gave me TWO vacations to Disney World. Those trips had to cost a fortune from 'a poor man's pocket. Audrey and Lucky had paid for EVERYTHING. The food, the travel, the gas, the Disney World tickets, the Epcot tickets, the hotel rooms IN ORLANDO. And it won't just hotels, but hotels with swimming pools. All the way FOR SIX PEOPLE. Everything was so awesome. They gave us an amazing time and experience.

After coming back to Newport News. And coming back home to poverty; I'm gon have to be honest- - it made me look at my father and mother different.

It fucked me up, cause psychologically I was split between (2) different hemispheres. I mean, my home was my home, but it was times I didn't want to come back home. I was wishin for the day, Audrey and Lucky move me up with them to Richmond.

They probably would, if I ain't take so long up in they shower. By the time they get in it, the water be cold. They ain't never say nothing to me. Audrey said something to my mother, and my mother relayed it to me. It won't anything special about they shower. I just always take long showers. If you wanna call it that. Like 20... 30 minutes.

I'm the same way now; I'm gon get clean.

And that was one of the benefits to being in poverty; the water bill, gas, electric, all the utilities is included in the rent. Audrey and Lucky had to pay a water bill. If my momma woulda had to pay a water bill, I probably would've been more conscious about it.

Alright, that was The Long Story. Hopefully, you enjoyed all of it. Now, to get you back on track, following my surgery, and my trip to King's Dominion.:

Lucky and Audrey picked me back up that summer. But, this time, we ain't go back to Disney World. Lucky and Audrey had paid and signed me and Hugh up to the YMCA in Chesterfield for the summer. Chesterfield is a county just to the southern and western outskirts of the city of Richmond.

In the morning, I think Audrey cook us breakfast. But I know, Lucky usually the one to take us to The Y and drop us off.

When we get there, I'on know nobody but Hugh. So I'm sticking close to cuz- o. We shoot basketball. But mostly, I'm watching out for him; fam shooting the basketball. I'on know what to make out of these other kids, but I ain't gon let nobody fuck wit him. He'on know I'm gon fight for him. I'on tell him. But I'm on point.

I know he can't fight. I beat him up all the time. So somebody gotta fight for both of us.

He 13. And I'm 14. We ain't have grandma and granddaddy, my momma, his momma, or Audrey and Lucky. This was the first time we was together completely alone. So if I gotta fight, I gotta fight for me and him. Even if I gotta fuck one'a these teachers up. I'on trust these people. I had a poverty mentality, and it just made me aggressive, even in situations I probably wasn't even in.

But we was alright. I thought this center was going to be it-- it wasn't it.

179

They board us on a bus and ride us out to the woods. It's a campground. All the buildings made outta log cabins.

They had different activities. They had instructors putting us in groups. Fortunately, they had put me and Hugh in the same group. Cause it woulda been problems out in them woods.

They gave me a bow and arrow. They was trying to teach me archery. Something I never done. I was struggling to spread the bow on an intermediate set. I would see the target. Load up the bow. But when I pull the string.:

Szzzzz- BOOM!!

The arrow only go like 3- 4 feet.

So much fo my Native American side. I guess that's one time, my name won't be Long Arrow.

The chow hall was even in a log cabin, where they feed us lunch. So, me and Hugh, be standing out there waitin to meal. Jus standing out there kickin it. Chillin. I keep noticing this girl.

She got that Red Gold. And she got these BIG ASS titties. She look at me. She keep kissin this guy. Named Guy. How ironic. Even to Teddy Riley.

Then she look back at me.

She keep smiling at me.

But I don't say shit to her. The next day: well it

seem like the next day. But this time when she see me, she come walking up to me and Hugh in the chow hall.

"Hi. My name is Tashia."

See. See how this work. I ain't even'a pimp, and these hoes be choosin me.

She was doing it right. That's how this shit supposed to go. Shoshoni and Makeba need notes off this girl.

To make'a long story short.: got the name, got the number, and by swimming pool time-- Tashia was in a one- piece grinding all that ass into MY dick. Hunh.

But on some real talk-- Tashia was 'a BAD BITCH!! Straight up and down! In every meaning of the words. Tashia was TTP- - "THE TOTAL PACKAGE."

This girl had legs, thighs, ass, titties, lips, eyes, her own long hair, and she was RED GOLD!! TOP OF THE LINE!!

And the crazy part on toppa all that- - she won't but 14. It's grown ass women that won't fuckin wit her body. I was in the pool squeezin on the Baddest Bitch in The World.
From Poverty, To Prison, To Prosperity

I was looking for Guy. He looked like Steve Urkel before Steve Urkel even came out. But I ain't never see him again.
It's 'a good thing. Cause I woulda fought him for

181

this girl. I woulda broke my own rule. Because I ain't never have no girl make me feel like this girl. She was 'a present.

Hugh had a girlfriend too.

Her name was Anitra. But Hugh won't doin what I was doing.:

Me and Tashia used to do a lot of kissin. My favorite time was swimming pool time. That's when I hug her from the back, and she start grinding that all that juiccccy ass all up on my dick. She'll let me feel all on her. But she wouldn't let me touch that pussy. She'd always stop my hand goin up her leg.

So, I would grab them big ass titties. Her nipples would go through my fingers. One day I told her, "Damn, you got some big ass Milk Duds."

She burst out laughing. That bitch was THICCCKK, PHAAAT, and she was SOFT. She was rockin me up.

ALL THE WAY UP!

Audrey would let me call her. Even when I came back home, I would call her long- distance. We talked, maybe like a little past a year. I'm just gon fast forward this story.: Tashia would send me pictures through the mail. And I was TOO proud to have a girl like Tashia, that I was showing all my friends MY GIRL. Cause NONE of they bitches won't fuckin wit this bitch. Hands Down!

Tashia was the paradigm of perfection.

And, I slipped up. I was showing her pictures of to the wrong person. I was too immature to know the power of what I had. And I listened to Kenny say,

"Oh, that's dead. You know that don't you?"

He was referring to the physical distance between me and Tashia. Trying to imply to me, that that was somebody else's girl now, or somebody else was hittin it now.

And I bought into it. See, you can't let somebody else beat down yo Blessings. People talkin negative on what you got and what The Lord BLESS you wit. Cause they definitively will do it.

And Tashia definitely was a BLESSING!! Believe me what I tell you.

But at the time, I fucked up! I never called her or talked to her again.

I was looking for Guy. He looked like Steve Urkel before Steve Urkel even came out. But I ain't never see him again.
It's 'a good thing. Cause I woulda fought him for this girl. I woulda broke my own rule. Because I ain't never have no girl make me feel like this girl. She was 'a present.

Hugh had a girlfriend too.

Her name was Anitra. But Hugh won't doin what I was doing.:

Me and Tashia used to do a lot of kissin. My favorite time was swimming pool time. That's when

I hug her from the back, and she start grinding that all that juiccccy ass all up on my dick. She'll let me feel all on her. But she wouldn't let me touch that pussy. She'd always stop my hand goin up her leg.

So, I would grab them big ass titties. Her nipples would go through my fingers. One day I told her, "Damn, you got some big ass Milk Duds."

She bust out laughing. That bitch was THICCCKK, PHAAAT, and she was SOFT. She was rockin me up.

ALL THE WAY UP!

Audrey would let me call her. Even when I came back home, I would call her long- distance. We talked, maybe like a little past a year. I'm just gon fast forward this story.: Tashia would send me pictures through the mail. And I was TOO proud to have a girl like Tashia, that I was showing all my friends MY GIRL. Cause NONE of they bitches won't fuckin wit this bitch. Hands Down!

Tashia was the paradigm of perfection.

And, I slipped up. I was showing her pictures of to the wrong person. I was too immature to know the power of what I had. And I listened to Kenny say,

"Oh, that's dead. You know that don't you?"

He was referring to the physical distance between me and Tashia. Trying to imply to me, that that was somebody else's girl now, or somebody else was hittin it now.

And I bought into it. See, you can't let somebody else beat down yo Blessings. People talkin negative on what you got and what The Lord BLESS you wit. Cause they definitively will do it.

And Tashia definitely was a BLESSING!! Believe me what I tell you.

But at the time, I fucked up! I never called her or talked to her again.

Tashia Jeffries from Midlothian, Virginia. That girl was just so beautiful. I wonder what ever happened to her; cause if she fall into the wrong hands.: the wrong man will string her out on dope, crack, coke, pill poppin, alcohol, verbally tongue lashing her, and physically keep beating her. To control and dominate her.

Because that's what insecure weak-minded men will do to restrain a woman that powerful. Tashia was pretty, beautiful, sexy, all in the same package. She was smart and came from a good middle-class home. You got scum bag men out there, that's gon try to break all that apart.

And with the way the world is today, women will do it too. You got women that will do the exact same thing to another woman, as what a man will do. So, you gotta be extremely careful and mindful. These women are just as aggressive, especially over other women they psychologically see as more superior. You got females that will drug yo drink; and lead you off somewhere, you might never come back from. You'll never be the same woman again.

So, I pray that Tashia is still alive and

healthy. And I pray for all the young ladies out there that the Spirit of YAHWEH will BLESS You, and keep You safe from kidnap, verbal and physical abuse, and rape. This I ask and pray in YAHSHUA's precious and HOLY NAME. Amen, amen, amen, amen.

Alright, I gotta get my mind offa Tashia. Cause that shit hurt every time I think about it.

Before I go further into the story, I got to redress my mother's sister, Theresa. Her name is Vivian. But we all call her Theresa, cause Grandma call her Theresa. So, her name'll be Theresa.

I already told you the part how she bought me my First and only Adidas suit. But it's one more imperative part how she impactfully helped my childhood and upbringing. I gotta put this part in real quick.:

It was one time; I was sick and couldn't go to school. So, my momma had to find somebody to watch me. Theresa volunteered that she would watch me. She was married by this time, to Michael Daniels. He was a chef that graduated from Johnson and Wales University, in Norfolk, Virginia.

They had an apartment out Newsome Park.

I get to Theresa's house. My Uncle Mike ain't there. And Theresa leave me in the house on my own. She "go to work." She work for the city. I'm in the house by myself. Nothing is on TV. I wanna hear some music, cause I look over, and Unc gotta rack of cassette tapes. You'll think he 'a DJ. The man got 'a 1,000 Memorex tapes.

It's all in boxes.

But Unc, he mo ol' school than me. Goin
through his collection, you prolly gon find some
Marvin Gaye, some Frankie Beverly and Maze,
Parliament/ Funkadelic, some George Clinton, you
probably get some Spinners, and a whole buncha
people I ain't never even heard of. I ain't lookin fo
all that, I'm lookin to hear some NWA. Some Eazy-
E. Something like that

I'm thumbing through the crates. Unc ain't
got no NWA or no Eazy- E, I can knock through his
system. What I do see.: Unc got this tape. It's magic
marker inked in BIG Bold capital letters.: EDDIE
MURPHY RAW.

EDDIE MURPHY RAW!? What the hell is that!?

I pop this tape in, and I listened to Eddie Murphy
performing a comedic strip of himself and acting
out in other different characters in dialogue,

"Ed- die, why you treat me like an- i- mal?"

Oh my goodness!

So the next day, I come back over there, cause I'm
still "sick" and,

"Alright Peanut."

BOOM!! My aunt leave me at home again.
My uncle got boxes of VCR tapes, all in the same
living room. So, I'm thumbing through crates of
video tapes. And he got MOVIES. But, I didn't want

to watch a movie, I wanted to see some porn. All adult men supposed to have 'a porn collection. I'm thumbing through it. Couldn't find porn. All of a sudden.:

BOOM!!

There it is... EDDIE MURPHY RAW.

Are you serious? He really got this shit on video? Sure enough, he did.

I rushed to pop that tape in! And now I had the visual to go wit what I had heard on the tape. I'll say this.: for Eddie Murphy, and all the comedians of his generation, they looked up to Richard Pryor and maybe Redd Foxx.

For me, I didn't know Redd Foxx for doing standup. I only knew Redd Foxx for doing Sanford and Son. I only knew Richard Pryor for making movies. For me, hearing Eddie Murphy and watching him perform stand up was my breakthrough discovery of "comedians." That whole art and craft of "comedians" telling jokes and being funny. I got that from Eddie Murphy.

Eddie was RAW! Cause couldn't nobody bring it like Eddie.

My house didn't have cable, didn't have a VCR, a lot of times, didn't have a phone. By me finding those RAW tapes at my Aunt Theresa house, Eddie Murphy became for me the same staple that The Fat Boys and New Edition were to me in hip- hop and R and B. He made me want to be funny, like he was funny. And bring a sense of humor and joy, and make people laugh. It would be hard to work my craft. Especially when it come to making light of life's hard life conditions. But watching Eddie, inspired me on my way.

My family already had one comedian.

My momma.

Sister Miles can have you cutting yo side, all the way to the flo, the way she talk about people, how they be acting, and what they be saying. And she do it all, without even cursing. I would actively have a tough family act to follow. But Thank You Eddie Murphy for giving me that RAW comedic light of inspiration.

Chapter 11.

Following my surgery, when I was ready to start my 9th grade year, I didn't know how the hood and my high school peers would receive me.

Maybe like 2 years after Terence had moved, we faced an all-new kind of being bullied. This shit was at an all- time high. We was Paula Maria. We was 76th Street. But just right across the street, we had rival apartments called Glen Gardens.

Glen Gardens was across the street on 76th Street, but the heart of their entrance was on 79th Street. So, they was 79th Street.

The guys out Glen Garden, and they mimicked and imitated to be like Woodsong. Which was the hardest section of our city. Glen Gardens competed to be the new and next city terror, by following after the Woodsong model.

If Woodsong had dope. Then Glen Gardens was gon have dope. If Woodsong sold crack and coke. Then Glen Gardens was gon sell crack and coke. If Woodsong was gon fight, shoot, and kill. Then Glen Gardens was gon fight, shoot, and kill. If Woodsong was gon have a gang. WSP. Woodsong Posse.

Then Glen Gardens was gon have a gang. GGP. Glen Garden Posse.

Glen Gardens was more advanced than us. Our neighborhood was clear, clean- cut, and wholesome, in comparison. Even down to the numbers, they greatly outnumbered us.

We had nothing to match it.

You couldn't fight em. They roll together. If you fight one, you gotta fight them all. They gon surround you, and they gon jump you. The only weapon we had was to RUN.

They ran us from the bus, all the way home every day after school, when we went to Huntington. In our apartments, all the old people stayed up in the front. Me, Damon, Dwayne Sessoms, Eric Bell, Carlos Marrow, Barry... all of us lived in the back. They get tired of chasing us about halfway, then they start going back.

It was one day, they'd call for a fight in Glen Gardens. If they had called it on 79th Street, they probably would've got us. But they set the ambush up on 77th. We some young dumb kids, thinking we gon go see a fight; the fight turned on us. They chased us so they could catch us and beat us.

They started chasing me. I slip past em. But it's this one kid that won't give up. His name is Five- Four. Pronounced like Five- Fo. I guess it was cause how tall he was. Five- Fo 'a fat pudgy brown skin kid. But he got speed.

I turned the jets on him. I thought about my favorite football player. Walter Payton. I had always wanted to be fast and a running back, like Walter

Payton.

I'm running.: and there's this great big water and mud puddle feet up ahead. The ground was too muddy. Not enough traction. If I run around the puddle, I'm probably gon get caught. I gotta get airborne. It's a BIG puddle. I'on know how long it is. I jus know I gotta clear it. Five- Fo was gaining on me.

The puddle was inches. Footsteps ahead.

I jump. I get up. I think he jumped and tried to grab for me, both at the same time. My speed flashed his hold. I cleared the puddle, hit the ground, and was gone. In my ears, I hear Glen Garden side laughing. I turned around to see. Five-Fo had bust his ass in the mud. I was gone.

I was just BLESSED won't no cars coming. I coulda got killed by a car, running from these niggas.

And after all that, we all still had to go to school the next day.

But nothing came out of it. They'll fuck wit me on the bus, cause they know, if I get on the ground, won't no catching me. All of us had an embedded fear of GGP. Cause, we ain't know when one of them was gon pull a gun on us. I won't in the mood to go out Pleasant Shade. Y'all already know my momma ain't got no insurance.

My 7th grade teacher, Mr. Ross, had lost his only son, Derek Ross to a gunshot wound out Glen Gardens.

192

And around that time, my homeboy Gary Peartree had died from a self- inflicted gunshot wound, from playing Russian Roulette out Woodsong.

So kids was definitely taking eternal rest spots out in cemeteries. This DIED thing, won't no joke.

That's what we had to worry about. These niggas might fight. But the fact they was gon jump you, means they won't gon LOSE. If you get yo shit off; it's 'a good chance they gon come back, they gon smoke you. I know I won't ready to take that chance. I'm not gon stand there and let these niggas hit me and jump me. And being good kids, it won't even in our imagination to get guns and pull guns too.

But it's a BLESSING from Yahweh, that at the core, GGP was good kids too. Cause they never crossed that line on us. But we ain't know that's how it was gon play out like that, back then.

When I get on the school bus, to ride for my freshman year at Warwick High, I'm expecting from them the same thing we was getting in Huntington, but they had calmed down. They had matured a little bit. It was times it did flare up. But it won't never quite as bad as it was at Huntington.

Some of them niggas was cool ass niggas, individually. That nigga Karl. That nigga Tony Pope. Casine. That nigga Eric Harris. He had a brother named Martellus. Spelled something like that. Them two niggas looked nothing alike. They looked bout as much as brothers, as Mottie and Esther looked like sisters.

193

They had another brother, but I forgot his name. He was way too young. He was a baby compared to us. Five- Fo had moved by this time. He won't going to Warwick wit us.

One day they came to Paula Maria to play us in football. I was checking Eric. Not Eric Harris, another one. I forget his last name. He won't fuckin wit me. I Al Bundy'd on him. 4 Touchdowns in one game. But all in the first half.

And, I picked (2) of Eric's passes in the end zone.

But that might not all the way count. Barry was the all- time quarter back for both sides. Me and Barry play football every day, so he know my playing style. He know where to put up the ball, and I can get it. And he know, I got power. I got strength. I boost up the speed. WHHHAAMM!! Throw that stiff- arm to yo chest, I'm gon drop and blow past you. Damn near every time.

Most guys will just try to grab my stiff arm, bring it in, to wrap my body, and tackle me to the ground.

Not Barry.

"I got something fo yo stiff- arm."

"I got something fo that stiff- arm."

"Watch, I'm gon show you."

He talk shit to me every game. We against each other more than we on the same team.

And I get the ball. I'm running. I start cutting the

field to coast against the sideline into the end zone. But Barry. He know my style. He know my game. He know right where to meet me. I see him.

Hhhuhh!! I shoot out a rough stiff- arm, like it's 'a right- cross cross 'a nigga chest. But when Barry see that arm shoot out-- I see him do some stupid shit...

This nigga stiffen his body up and dive out to the ground. You should see this nigga face, doin this stupid ass shit. But it work. I run right into him. He get me EVERY time.

He throw his body and use the momentum of his weight to roll his body into my knees. Almost like the same thing a dog will do to trip you up and stop you from running. This nigga'll do that dumb ass shit.

But it worked.

Not only do he tackle me-- my ass go tumbling down the field. When I get up, bitches is laughing on the sideline. One thing bout it.: I ain't fumble the ball.

Glen Garden tightened up they defense on me. I got yards, but I ain't score no more in the second half.

After the game everybody is starting to walk away. Then what happen?

The nigga that was checkin me, Eric. He was mad they lost the game; he approach to swing on Damon. Then two other ones run up to steal on Damon. They run him in the house. But the boy get away. They chased Barry a little bit. But Barry ain't run home, he just ran around in the street. After that they ain't fuck wit nobody else. They went 'on head and went back home.

After that me, Eric Bell, and Barry went to go get Damon, so he'll come back outside. It was glad to see they ain't jump him. And I was just glad, that was onetime my momma didn't show up outside to check on me. I'on know what would've happened. The situation coulda got real crazy. That's why I had never talked to my parents about me being bullied by Glen Gardens. These was times crying bout it won't gon get me out of it. I had got too old for that anyway. I never wanted to draw my parents in to a violent and potentially life-threatening situation.

Then when Woodsong and Glen Gardens get together, they don't fight each other, they go out and look for somebody else's life they can fuck up. When you see Woodsong and Glen Gardens walking down the street TOGETHER, it's time to get ghost, before you be 'a ghost.

But outside of all that I competed to live a regular life. My 9th grade year at Warwick, I had signed up for Drama. I tried to pick up from where I left off at Huntington. I had a good teacher, that was perhaps teaching rather too thoroughly. She was teaching about Thespians. She even had a Thespian Club for drama students to sign up for and participate.

But I got 'a short attention span. At Huntington, Ms. Moore had us writing and performing skits. We did plays, and one big major play, that brought the city out, and even the local

ABC News. I was a Star bout that ACTION.

In High School, the school schedule is shorter than middle school. At Huntington, I didn't get outta class until around 3 o' clock. At Warwick, shiiiit, I was gettin outta school by 1: 45.

That's 'a hour and fifteen minutes early. Which means that if I didn't want Drama, then I'd have to make a choice, to change my elective.

It wasn't easy. But I did it easy. After the first semester, I dropped Drama as my elective. I signed up for JROTC.

Military Science.

I thought about following in my father's footsteps in a whole nother way. To be 'a US Marine. I hated to run, unless it was for football or for my life. But, I loved to work out. I thought about being a combat soldier, from watching Bruce Lee and Chuck Norris as my favorite martial artists. I was a fan of all the American Ninja movies. And every time I go to the school library, I always run to check out Black Belt magazine FIRST, before I even go to check out any of the other books.

The martial arts culture had fascinated me ever since, like I said, watching Bruce Lee and Chuck Norris, and even Kung- Fu Theater every Saturday morning, before wrestling. And of course, the Karate Kid franchise contributed to the popularity of the culture.

I was locked in.

I wanted to do what they do. I used to sit in the car, and we ride past Frank Hargrove's Karate Studios, on Mercury Blvd. Sometimes my momma used to go wash her clothes at a laundromat, all the way on Warwick Blvd. They had a karate studio over in the same section of the strip mall, I'd leave her in the laundromat and walk down the short sidewalk to the karate studio.

I would go look up to the door. And look through the huge clear- pane store front windows. My momma washed her clothes at night. The karate studio was always closed. The lights was always out.

But I could see the parade of karate medals and trophies plastered for display, all up against the back brown panellined wall. Side- kicking and karate chopping, all up against the store's front glass.

I wanted to tell my momma to sign me up. To tell her I wanted to go to karate class. But I lacked the confidence to go and ask her, when I knew she was struggling to pay her bills.

I wanted to tell Lucky. But I ain't have the confidence to consort him concerning it either. I left it alone.

But in high school, I felt the confidence. To do it for myself. I can run away from home wit this military gig, and pay for my own karate, kung- fu, or jeet kune do classes myself. To me, the Marines and Karate went hand- in- hand.

So, I signed up for Military Science.

The other factor, was in ROTC, they give you 'a uniform to wear every Tuesday. In poverty, that means one day 'a week, you'n gotta think about what you gon wear to school. In high school, I had had (3) pairs of pants. The same pair I wore on Monday, I wear em on Thursday. And the same pair I wear Tuesday, I wear em again on Friday. Just put it wit a different shirt.

Now wit an ROTC uniform, that means I only had to go out and find one pair of extra jeans; not two.

Warwick had Navy JROTC, which was cool cause Marines work side- by- side wit the Navy. When you think about HARD!! and being TOUGH!! in the US Navy, you think Navy Seals. But what if I could be that MARINE that train and work side-by- side wit Navy Seals?

Hunh.

After Commander Wheeler and Master Chief Bateman, issued me my uniform, it was just a matter of days when I was in lead of the company;

"LEFT FACE!

RIGHT FACE!

FORWARD... MARCH!!!!"

Anywhere, I moved them, they would go! We was out in the grass. In the middle of the track and field track, out in the front of the school. That won't good enough for me.

"TO THE REAR MARCH

... TO THE REAR MARCH

LEFT FLANK... MARCH!!"

They go down the curb. Walk down one parking lot. Lift up on another curb. They still keep marching.

Now we rolling...

"LEFT FLANK MARCH

... RIGHT FLANK MARCH!!"

We end up in a whole nother parking lot.

And I'd still be, "Go left, left, yo left right, left..."

I'd be so gone. Marching to the beat of my own cadence. Meanwhile, they done stopped!! They just standing in place, looking straight forward, stomping the ground real hard in full- step.

What went wrong?

Why the hell you stop GOING!?

Probably cause it was that car coming.

Bad, Company Commander.

A good Company Commander don't lead his cadets to go get killed by a car.

I'll have to work on that.

They looked so invisible though. Right.

Sometimes Commander Wheeler or Bateman would bring in upper classmen, to march, train, or advance our freshmen class. I used to like when he bring in these two niggas who looked like they coulda kilt 'a scene on A Different World or any Spike Lee movie. They was named Ezra Mc Millian and Antoine Mc Clain.

These niggas might dress like twins. They best outfits, was when they throw on these matching NIKE tennis tracksuits, wit the black and white Cortez Classics. You couldn't tell these niggas nothing. These got to be like da two illest niggas in ROTC.

When we get to class, these two nice and smooth ass niggas already up in there. His name was Ezra. But nobody call him that, except maybe his Daddy. To everybody else, for where we was from, this was EZ. Pronounced Eazy. Just like Eazy-E. But I'on even think Eazy-E was smooth as this nigga.

Toine be talking to us. EZ be kicked back wit his feet up on the desk. "Um-hmm," shakin his flat top fade.

But Toine was a thorough teacher. He did help me out a lot on my marching steps. My formations, and when I'm leading the company.

But when it get down to the BOOGIE DRILL team. It won't no nigga fuckin wit that nigga EZ. This nigga had more rhythm and beat, in his arms, hands, and knees, than a fraternity nigga on 'a drill

, or 'a HBCU nigga leading out 'a marchin band. He could do it all. Holding on to a dummy rifle.

When Commander Wheeler do class, he'd give us the lesson, but it was easy to drift him off into talking about the military. I loved to hear him talk about Aircraft Carriers, and the planes flying up and off an Aircraft flight deck. Listening to him, sold me on an attraction for Aircraft Carriers, and all of sudden, maybe I didn't want to be a Marine next to the Navy Seals no more. BUT AN F- 16 FIGHTER PILOT.

I didn't even have a driver's license, and here I was fantasizing about flying a fighter jet! Only in America.

I did good in ROTC. Probably not as good as Escondido. This Mexican kid had every damn ribbon decorated on his uniform. Like he was'a Five- Star G up in this bitch!

I used to watch him. A lot niggas don't like him. But I understand why.: Escondido is cool. Quiet. Laid back. He'on fuck wit nobody. He don't do NOTHING no different than anybody else would do, for real.

But for some reason Commander Wheeler kept decorating him. This nigga ain't even have no more space left on his damn chest to get all this shit they kept giving him. That shit was crazy.

The best thing I'll say about Escondido to his credit.: every uniform day, his uniform stayed cleaned, creased, and in pristine condition. That nigga could Brasso 'a brass buckle, til it turn to

GOLD. And his black shoes be BEAMING B!! That's word.

But like I was sayin; I did good in ROTC. I might've only had two or three ribbons. But Aye! I worked damn hard to get em.

Master Chief Bateman had taken a notice in me and offered me an Administration Officer job working in his office. I accepted. It was other cadets that also had other various positions. I was surprised out the whole class, he chose me.

I had had what my Assistant Principal, Mrs. Broadnax consider a behavior problem. I guess adjusting to high school. I'on know. I remember being down in her office like once 'a week. I used to see her so much, I was sick of seeing her.

One day I had to go to the nurse. I was throwing up.

The nurse didn't see me throw up. So she asked, "What color is your throw up?"

"Pink."

She smirked at me and gon say, "What you eat that was pink?"

'Prolly yo pussy BITCH!!'

But I just left it alone. I'll just go back and see Mrs. Broadnax, so she can jus gon 'on head and suspend me. Fo something.

But after she started seeing me in my uniform, all of a sudden; "Miles."

Hunh. I ain't Jamie no mo, huh?

She was admired to see me sharp, and impressively straightening out my life. I didn't know the importance of wearing the uniform. When I put on them navy blue pants and top, I became more than just a student. I represent so much more. I didn't know that. Nobody expressly told me that. I had to find out, THE HARD WAY.:

In my next semester, I was adding a class called Business Law. To make 'a long story fast.: I wasn't feeling the class. It wasn't what I thought it was going to be, then me and the teacher started bumping heads.

Pretty soon, everything that's wrong wit her class, end up being MY fault. I'm getting blamed for everything, even when I'm sitting there good.

Next thing I know, she done strutted herself down to Master Chief Bateman, and told him some kind of lie she said I said. Which wasn't true. But of course he gon take her side. Huhhh, can you believed that?

It ain't demote me in rank, or knock me out of ROTC class, but Master Chief Bateman stripped me of my Administrative position, and never would he give it back to me.

It made me feel some type of way. I can still remember that stupid ass laugh on her face, when I no longer had my job in Administration. He gave my job to of all people-- who else could it be?

Escondido.

That made me lose any interest whatsoever for Contract Law, and my interest in ROTC started to dwindle.

In the summer after my freshman year, I didn't get to go to Disney World, but Lucky picked me up to work helping him. Lucky did side hustle jobs, which mostly consist of him cutting grass. And he would pick me up, and take me with him to go cut and manicure people's lawns.

He used to tell me, "This shit don't pay a lotta money."

But in between his summer school schedule, I worked with him over the course of about 2 weeks. When he would pay me, he always paid me more than what I was expecting. He would pay me almost double, what I was expecting. And I think that was just his way of encouraging me and supporting me.

Lucky is like this.: If you go to him and ask him for money, he probably not gon give it to you. He'll tell you,

"Man, I ain't got no money."

And that's probably to get you out his face. Lucky was about work. If you work. You work hard. You work for it, then he'll pay it to you. In my house, I never made no allowance, nothing like that. Every time I wanted money or needed anything, I had to wait for my father or my mother to buy it for me.

What Lucky did-- Lucky gave me pay that gave me PURCHASING POWER. So when I go back home, now I can go to the record store, and I can BUY my own rap and hip- hop music. Whatever I want to listen to.

The First rap album I ever bought was ICE CUBE- - AMERIKKKA'S MOST WANTED. I had bought it from K- Mart. When I bring it home, it was all clean and censored. That's before I knew that K- Mart was whitewashing black culture music, identity, and free expression. I still had money left- - so I went to the mall and purchased The Real ICE CUBE- - AMERIKKKA'S MOST WANTED. Either way, that became the First rap album I ever bought.

But Lucky had instilled a hard work ethic in me, at a young age, that is still in me to this day.

Audrey and Lucky even took me to my First wrestling match. They knew how much I loved professional wrestling, and they picked me and Hugh up, to take us to the Richmond Coliseum to see NWAs hottest wrestling stars.: The Rock n Roll Express, The Midnight Express, "The American Dream" Dusty Rhodes, Lex Luger, Tully Blanchard, Arn Anderson, The Road Warriors, and of course, "The Wheelin and Dealin," "Jet Flyin," "Limousine Ridin;" Mr. "Stylin and Profiling," himself.: "The Nature Boy" Ric Flair. WOOOOOOOO!!!! aka My Most Favorite Wrestler of All- Time.

This was during the time the National Wrestling Alliance (NWA) was merging with the UWF (Universal Wrestling Federation), that brought in stars like "Dr Death" Steve Williams, The Fabulous

Freebirds, and Sting. When the Fabulous Freebirds bounced out to the theme.: Music.: "Bad Street Atlanta G- A/ Bad Street in the whole USA,"

I was, "WHHHHHAAAA!!" I was excited hollering and jumping up and down.

Unc kept slapping down my hands.

"Sorry," I said. I thought I was doing something wrong. I ain't wanna be on his bad side. Not right now.

"Oh, you ok," he whispered to me. "I just ain't want you cheering fo that Confederate Flag."

And that's HUGE, because racism and racist symbols were subtle, yet prevalent, even in our American entertainment.

One of the biggest hit shows of the 80s was what? The Dukes of Hazard.

Loved the show. Would never miss 'a episode. But Bo and Luke Duke drove around, and bunny hopped hills and haystacks, in an iconic car called, The General Lee.

The car even had the Confederate Flag pin painted right there ON TOP of the car. But young Black kids didn't pay attention. We wasn't properly taught what these things were and that they represented racial discrimination, and massive deprivations of social, civil, economic, and political equality against Blacks.

And here we was, "Yerrrrrr'n," racing that bullshit

all cross the flo.

Man, what we was thinking! And letting
Daisy Duke mentally seduce us, wit them tiny- n-
tight lil blue shorts 'on. Even Hardee's had a
version of Happy Meals, where you can go and
collect pieces of The Dukes of Hazard franchise.
Not just the General Lee, but even Uncle Jesse's
truck.

By 1989, Blacks had dominated in real life.
We had multi- weight class, Sugar Ray Leonard, as
a World Champion. Even the Va homie, "Sweet
Pea" Pernell Whitaker was on the wake, for The
Best Pound- For- Pound Best Fighter In The World.
And "Iron" Mike Tyson was The King of
KNOCKOUTS!!

Blacks dominated in all the major sports of
football, basketball, baseball-- on every level. From
the amateur leagues, all the way up to the NFL, the
NBA, and Major League Baseball. Even in Boxing.

And in other areas of entertainment. You
don't like to hear this now, and I understand; but
Bill Cosby was The King of tv and comedy. He
played a fictitious character on tv, but he
dominated in Real Life. Whether you believe it or
not, Bill Cosby was the model that more than 90
percent of any black tv and movies you see from the
early 1990s- moving forward are inspired by his
model. And that's a fact.

But back to what I was saying.: Black people
dominated in Real Life. And whites dominated... In
Fiction. Back in the 70s, the Champion was "The
Greatest" Muhammad Ali. And he was the greatest

foot fighter in the world, but In Fiction, it was "The Great White Hope," Rocky Balboa.

Rocky had so much impact and influence over social pertinence of our hearts and of our minds, they even erected a statue up in the streets of Philly, for this FAKE muthafucka.

Muhammad Ali ain't even got that kinda respect. Not "Sugar" Ray Leonard, not "Sweet Pea" Whitaker, not "Hitman" Tommy Hearns, "Marvelous" Marvin Hagler, not even "Iron" Mike Tyson. The ones that was running that shit, FOR REAL. But no larger-than-life city statue.

And even as much as I love pro wrestling, you still can't negate the facts.: In the NWA, the World Champion was a white blond haired man, named Ric Flair. He would come out in $10,000 suits. Genuine leather Gator shoes. He'd flaunt to the ring in decorated sequined and colored feathered robes, with the symphonic opera harmony of Also sprach Zarathustra screeching in the speakers, open up his robe, and flash you with his 40-pound gold Championship Belt.

The HARDEST!! championship belt I ever seen, in all of World History. To this day, it's no belt alive fuckin wit that Ric Flair Championship Belt. The only belt that comes the closest, is the AWA (American Wrestling Association) Championship Belt. Held by pro wrestling champions like Rick Martinez, Sergeant Slaughter, and Nick Bob Winkle.

But in the NWA, the best Black star was a man, named "Pistol Pez" Whatley. And "Pistol Pez"

Whatley when he come down to the ring-- he hunch at his neck, back, and knees. He look like a Jim Crow caricature when he walk out to the ring.

In the WWF (then World Wrestling Federation. Now World Wrestling Entertainment), we had what? "The Immortal" Hulk Hogan.: "Six-foot- Sheven. 3 inches from Heaven; and I weigh 3-0-5, and can whip any man alive."

Yeah, but probably NOT FOR REAL.

But the closest thing we had to Hulk Hogan, was what? The Junkyard Dog.

The Junkyard Dog was a Black man that came out to the ring, "with a manacle" strapped around his neck.

They never let Pistol Pez Whatley be The World Champion. And despite his popularity and success, they never let The Junkyard Dog be the WWF World Heavyweight Champion. Not even for three months.

Back then, the NWA had never had a Black World Heavyweight Champion. After Ted Turner purchased the NWA from Jim Crockett Promotions, and changed the name to World Championship Wrestling (WCW), that's when we got our First Black World Heavyweight Champion, former Florida State Football Great, Ron Simmons.

And him and Butch Reed was The First Black World Tag- Team Champions. They had a team managed by Teddy Long, that was called DOOM.

When Ron Simmons got to the WWF, Vince Mc Mahon had sterilized him into a Black Militant, replica of a member of The Nation of Islam character, named Farooq. But in WCW, he was dominant and ON TOP.

This is not racism. Racism is what whites did to us.

In WWF, the First Black World Heavyweight Champion they had was The Rock. And for people who say The Rock is not Black but Somoan- - you need to read yo lessons by The Honorable Elijah Muhammad and shipped to you in mass production by Clarence 13x.

We had Booker T as a World Champion in WCW and WWE. We had Mark Henry. Now we got Roman Reigns. On the ladies side, Nia Jax, Sasha Banks, and Bianca Belaire. And on RAW, we got "THE ALMIGHTY" Bobby Lashley. Hopefully he has a long reign. And in this writing, I also gotta send love and respect to "The Octopus" Mr. Jonathan Gresham.

Alright, back to the story.:

In my 10th grade year, I still wasn't doing talent shows, or showcasing with The Buddha Brothers, on our local radio station 103 Jamz. What I was doing was rapping and rap battling in the hallways at Warwick. I was rappin about stupid shit, like "aqua colored Benzes." My opponents liked to gangsta rap. That credit goes to Dr Dre.

Whereas New York rap was more like'a boom- bap. Boom- boom- bap. Dr Dre made rap music sound more like, "Whuuuuur, whuuuuur, whuuuuur."

In other words.: He dumped the game on toppa it's head!!

In other words.: He putta lotta New York rappers outta business.

But anyway, West Coast Gangsta Rap had transformed the whole entire texture of rap and hip- hop music, and before long, even rappers from Bad Newz was rapping like they came up off the west coast. There was one homie that took notice of my style. And my friendship wit him, would grow my life to the next level.

Chapter 12.

One day, I had stayed after school. Warwick had certain activities, like on Monday, Wednesday, and Friday they would open up the gym, where I could go lift weights. And they had days, where they would open up the other end of the gym, where guys could go and shoot basketball.

That's where I was.

But, I wasn't running a game or shooting the ball. I was chillin up in the bleachers, when this guy came bopping up to approach me.

"Hey. You the one that be rapping?" he said and asked me.
"Huh?" I was looking, cause I never seen him before. A part of me is entertained that he was paying attention. The other part is tryin to figure out where the hell he goin wit this.

"Yeah. You. Yeah, it's you," he keep pointing to me.

'Man, who the hell is this nigga?'

But to speed it up, his name was Leonard Trower. But he introduced himself to me as,

"Lynn."

And let me know he was a DJ. I already had a friend who was a DJ, a dancer, ladies man, and everything else but a rapper. But for real, I had squandered myself with Damon. Cause at his house it was too easy to get distracted. I didn't focus on my craft.

So I don't know what it was, but I tried my hand. Next thing I knew I was back on Wickham, from where I had grew up. But the city also growed up, cause we ain't call it Wickham or Wickham Ave no more. To our new young, raw, and wild teen age generation- - this was Wick Zoo!

And I had found a new home away from home, 3 blocks from my Best Momma's house; I was wit Lynn down on 13th Street.

847 13th Street. That was the address. I ain't never see so many Black people live in one house. His Grandma live there. With Aunt Rea live there. His Aunt Wanda live there. His cousin Mike, Rea's son live there. His cousin Poodie, Wanda's son, and Ja' mont, Wanda's other son live there. He live there. And sometimes, Rea's other son, Ray live there. Man, this house was packed!

He told me he was supposed to be a DJ. This nigga ain't even have 'a turntable. What he did have was a slender black briefcase, and when he popped it open, he had a Tougher Than Leather album by Run- DMC. I coulda laughed. I probably did laugh. Shit was funny.

But I ain't give it up on the bruh. He was good company. And he was good peoples. He took me out and showed me his hood. Which is wild, cause most of the hood is in his house. But he lived like 2 doors down from one of dem illest niggas in ROTC I was telling you about. EZ.

I got to hang and chill wit that nigga outside of Warwick. A nigga name JJ. JJs brother, Dwayne. And a crazy ass light- skin nigga uppa block, on 12th Street, named Kane. Not only was 13th Street the shit. It was a swing through and hang out spot. Niggas came through like DC, Keith Still, BJ, 'a nigga named Sweets, other niggas from time to time, and EZ had an older brother name Bae Mc, and an older sister name Lea.

I got to meet them and meet his parents. I found me and EZ had more in common than I thought. Both of us was PKs. Preacher Kids. Both his father and my father were preachers. And I saw something else about EZ, he wassa happy kid. He loved to laugh a lot.

Lynn lived next to a girl named Meaty, but we rarely even saw her. Later it was Jessica and her sister down on the corner, but JJ ended up getting at that.

I was just chillin.

I liked my newfound friend, but I still had my original homie, Damon. At first Damon was into fuckin this red girl name Tamera. I think she went to Warwick wit us, but the only time we really ever see her was when we jumped the 20 foot fence, in back of Damon's house. And quickly walked a dirt trail beside a lake of ditch that ran out to Marshall Avenue. And I would go wit him to her house, off Marshall. When we get there, her lil fast ass sneak him inside.

I gotta wait for him outside, or at the homie Tori

Stith's house. Wit him and his lil brother. Like
every time he would come from fuckin this girl, he
always talkin bout his nuts was hurtin.

That bitch musta been draining that nigga.

One night we was round Tori's house;
Damon was trying to get to Tamera. But her
momma was home, or something like that. Tori had
ordered the fight. I see my mans, The Heavyweight
Champion of the World, "Iron" Mike Tyson. You
know Mike. All Black. Wit the black flat top fade. Lil
hook part at the top. Black trunks. Black shoes. No
socks. Right.

His opponent- - this nigga looked scared on
the tape. Fuck they get this guy from? Man, Mike
gon KNOCK!! this nigga out in ONE ROUND. He
ain't fuckin wit Mike. Right.

Shhhhhh...

That night, look like the whole world shook upside
down--

Iron Mike got KNOCKED OUT!! by James
"Buster" Douglas. This shit was unbelievable. This
shit had to be FAKE. No matter what I thought, it
won't gon change the facts.: Mike Tyson was no
longer invisible. Mike Tyson was no longer the
Heavyweight Champion of the World.

We was so mad, we left Tori's house and walked
back home.

The next thing I know, Damon and Tamera had
broke up. It was a nigga named Derrick that went to

Warwick wit us too. I think Damon found out she
be sneaking him over there. That's prolly why his
nuts was hurtin.

But anyway it ain't take Damon long to
finda new girl. She wasn't really attractive. But what
she was was good people. Real Real good people.
Such good people, that we rarely had to walk to her
house. Damon's momma would drop us off o'va
there. And we met her momma and her uncle. And
they was such Real Good people that next thing I
knew, my momma was round over there, and her
sister Theresa.

Simone. That was Damon's new girlfriend
name. She didn't have no sisters. She had a cousin
name Mandisha. But we called her Dee. This bitch
was something else. She stayed round down the
corner from me, off Aberdeen. Out Sweetbriar.
Brittany. One of them damn apartments. They right
next to each other and look identically alike. I get
em confused.

Anyway, I walked to her house on a HOT!!
HOT!! summer day. It was so damn HOT!! the
Virginia Cavalier iron- on on my basketball shirt,
was smelling like crayons. And I had on a pair of
loose silver pants, so I could look like MC Hammer.
I just was missing the patented leather shoes. But I
showed up to her house.: sweating, fresh sheets of
heat bumps, and black- n- crispy. In 'a incomplete
ensemble.

Dee was kinda small. Cause she was skinny. She
wore glasses. But she was Red. Simone cousin
looked Real sexy!

But when she saw me, she ain't give me no kick- it. That bitch went and started talkin on the phone. I couldn't get no kiss. And she told me she liked BARRY.

'How the hell this bitch know Barry?'

Oh well. That's o'va wit. I went back home.

I see Dee a few days later round Simone house. I'on know what happened but everything changed. Maybe it was Simone's radio. Maybe it was BBD singin, "Tell me when will I see you smile--again..."

Maybe. But it worked. I had Dee in my arms. My hands slidin back and forth, between holdin her back and squeezin on her ass. And getting kisses!

We couldn't keep our tongues outta each other mouth.

I remember feeling her round her waist. Dee ain't have NO body fat. No stomach. No muffin top. And wit her glasses, she had that sexy lil bookworm look.

When BBD went off, we was still on. It felt like we finally had a connection. But Simone had neighbors and her momma in the house.: won't no way to get pussy in the backyard. The only way was...

Simone and Dee had family up in Baltimore. To make'a long story short.: It's supposed to be a date for Damon and Simone and me and Dee. We had to go outta town.

Damon's momma, Ms. Karen was down fo it. Jus one catch.: gotta run it past Sister Miles.

My momma listened to Ms. Karen, "Yeah, it's gon be 'a good time. Damon gon be there... duh- duh-duh." Then she fucked up when she said, "SIMONE." That "SIMONE" was gon be there.

And something bout SOME GIRLS was gon be there. Fo my momma that was it. She clapped it. She shut it down. After she found out I might possibly get some pussy there; she won't ready for the possibility she may be made to 'a grandmother. I still ain't got my high school diploma yet.

After that, I saw Dee a coupla times. But ain't nothing more materialize. We won't never boyfriend/ girlfriend; no shit like that. So I started hollering at Simone's friend, Celeste. Celeste was a brown skin girl, wit bumps on her face. The teenage acne years. But I ain't hold it against her. I go to her house. She on the same block as my Grandma house. But she don't know that. We ain't make it that far.

"I think I wanna go wit Barry."
'WHAT!?' I wish she'd told me that before I got here. We shook hands and I was gone. I really didn't have time to think about it.

My mother had a student, whose father was trying to give away a puppy. We live in Paula Maria. We can't have puppies. But for some reason, my momma really wanted me to have it. My Dad took me in his truck to go pick it up. The puppy was half Black Lab. Half Doberman. So when I get there. His daddy won't there. Just his momma was there. And she kept snapping at me inside her fenced cage. I still had a fear of Dobermans.

But unlike Junior's friendly faced Doberman, I was advised, "Watch out. Don't get too close. She'll bite." Probably so, since my Aunt Ruth won't there to hold her back, and especially since she recently gave birth.

They all look like. I'on know what made me pick the one I did. I think her student's father picked it out. It's the one he gave me, and it's the one I accepted. He tryin to give me the dog, and I'm trying to run from the dog. I still had a fear of dogs.

He won't even 'a dog, I was running from 'a puppy. My Dad calmed me down, and we put the dog in a plastic milk crate. I was looking at him, in the crate. I started thinking of a name for him.

"That dog stinking. You gotta get him outta here. Put him on the back," my father broke my concentration. Somehow my father got a real funny nose.

I used to say he got it broke, when he played for The Washington Redskins. But my daddy ain't never play fo no Redskins.

I put the dog in the back. We had to keep stopping, because he kept trying to jump out the back.

"You gon have to get back there and hold him," my father told me; IN THE BEGINNING OF FEBRUARY!!

So I had to sit in the back. Holding the dog in the

crate. Shivering.

"Whaaa," he was crying.

Probably for his momma. Cause I was taking him to a lonely and a foreign place. I just kept looking at him. Still kinda afraid to touch him. We drove him to my Grandma's house. My Grandma agreed to keep him. Cause we ain't have a place for him.

"What's yo puppy's name, Jamaica?" That was my Grandfather's new nickname to give me. Jamie Jamaica.

I say it almost wit no hesitation; "T- Bone."

"T- Bone," they all say.

"Yeah. T- Bone," I locked it in.

They don't know where I got that name from. But I know. Ice Cube was my favorite rapper. And he had a group out called, Da Lench Mob. In his new rap group, he put out, he had a right hand man named T- Bone. So, I named my puppy T- Bone, cause he was my new right- hand man.

Ah, soon as I could overcome my fear to touch him.

I walked him in the crate, across the street from my Grandma's house. We was in the backyard of The Doris Miller Rec Center. I put the crate on the ground and tilted it until he fell out. But he landed on his feet. I watched to see him sniff at the ground. He walked around a little bit. He ran up the hill and stood at the fence. He probably could smell the chlorine from the pool.

He ain't know I used to swim in that pool when I was small. I didn't tell him that. And he probably really didn't care. But what he did next, I think was him telling me that he now trust me.

When I go to walk away from the pool, I went back down the little hill. He was sniffing around. Then he look up and over and see I'm gone; I see his lil short stubby puppy legs running toward me wit all his might. At first I was scared. But something said, "Don't run."

And he ran- - not to me, but right beside me, and he stood there. Like he wanted me to trust him. And he was just laughing and licking his tongue out, when I rubbed him on his side. I took him back to my Grandmomma's house to feed him and get him some water. Then, I had to get in the truck to leave him, and to go home. I really didn't have time to think about it.

Best Momma was sick.

When we went to the hospital, my Grandmother was down to skin and bones. Her father had just died a year ago. The February before. My Great- Granddaddy Lloyd. Lloyd was his last name. All I know is we called him Lloyd so much, I can't even tell you what his first name is.

My Great- Grandfather was a very dark- skinned man, with white wooly hair, and he wears glasses, so he can see. Less than two- years ago he was just telling me about heart attacks.

"You can have hundreds of heart attacks in yo life." He spread his fingers out to show me.

"Your heart got veins." He talked about these white spots. "One of those spots hit that vein--that's it."

That's it.

It's enough I can say about my Great-Granddaddy Lloyd. My Great- Grandmother and Great- father didn't share the same bed. They didn't even share the same room. Yet, they was married. In the same house. I wonda how they figure out where they was gon make the kids?

But, I was his great- grandchild. Probably now, in more ways than one. When I used to stay at his house, I was small when I slept in his bed. Aye! That was in my glory days. When I could pee a mattress like I was pissin out a house!

I would pee him out his own bed.

By the time I grew up, he probably finally changed his mattress.

And my Great- Grandparents house is very tidy and neat. Just like Sister Mc Nair's. Very clean. My Great- Grandma won't even let 'a speck of dust, up on her china cabinet. And she keeps plastic over her couch, just like Best Momma. This is the same house, my father lived in from time to time, after his parents divorced.

My Great- Grandfather Lloyd is a good man. I never seen him hurt or harm anybody. I never seen him wrong any person, and up to his dying day, he still

223

drove and operated a car. Even into his old age, the Lord BLESSED him to be fully functional.

By now.: That's it.

He DIED from a heart attack. His funeral was in February. His church was a block down from Simone's house, on 43rd Street. It was colllllld. Good gracious. The wind was whipping. And when you step inside the smallest church, that was like 2 feet bigga than 'a chapel. This was where my Great-Grandfather had made into a living sanctuary. This was where he worshipped, prayed, and praised; and where he called on the name of The Lord. (Ref.: Genesis 12: 8 and Genesis 26: 24- 25). He laid on post, at the door of the church, with the greatest biggest grin on his face. He only had on his suit and his glasses. But he had no regard for the weather outside, or the hawk that was whooping at his face.

For my Great- Grandfather Lloyd, I had to show up. I had to show him his respect. But believe me, I paid for it. Those images haunted me ALL NIGHT. I was 14 going on 15. Too grown to jump up in my momma's bed. But I left that light on ALL NIGHT!!

Not just that night, but EVERY NIGHT!! fo like 2 WEEKS STRAIGHT. That subconscious fear of God was still in me.

Whooo!

Now a year later, I was looking at stages of it again. Stage 4 cancer was eating my Best Momma alive.
She usually wear glasses. But her glasses were off. Her eyes were opened WIIIDE. She barely

even blinked. And she could tell, she was in her
final stages. She ain't put nobody out... and she kept
talking.

I listened to everything she said. I had to. It
was the last days of her life. It was the last time I
would hear her talk, in this life... on this earth. That
was it. My father turned 43 on February 18th. I
turned 16 on February 19th. On February 20th,

Best Momma was gone.

We buried her out Pleasant Shade
Cemetery, in a gray casket. She had wanted a gray
casket- - just like her Daddy. She was faithful to The
Lord, and faithful to HIS service- - just like her
Daddy. She had erected her life as an altar before
the Lord- - just like her Daddy.
I went, to lay my Best Momma down to rest. With
that word. What they call it? Interment. But yes,
again, I paid for it. I kept seeing my Best Momma
over and over and over again. The light stayed on,
at least 2 weeks.

But this year was a little bit different. About
the same time we got T- Bone, my father had got a
fortune. No not really. It just seemed like a fortune
from where we had been. He had got a huge lump
sum settlement, due to a back injury he received,
while working on the job. About the same time, our
lease was running out at Paula Maria. My momma
didn't wanna renew it. She wanted to move.

We moved from Paula Maria in January,
about the first of the year. Then we moved
temporarily into the Golden Sands, out Buckroe, in
Hampton. Generally not a safe place. The Golden

Sands is a high drug area. Fortunately, we was
BLESSED, it wasn't a high violent area.
From Poverty, To Prison, To Prosperity

My momma had all the connects. She had
been a teacher to one of the manager's children,
who operated the motel and efficiencies named The
Golden Sands; and so, we was able to live out The
Golden Sands for a discount price.

In our efficiency, one side was the living
room with included cable, and a kitchen. The
bathroom was in the middle. 2 beds was on the
other side, in the bedroom, with a phone.

We stayed there maybe like a month. After I
left Paula Maria, I didn't go back to see Damon or
BARRY. I still did keep contact wit Lynn. I had
brought T- Bone with us out to The Golden Sands.
After the manager found out, I was keeping a
puppy, she told my momma the dog got to go. Hey!
I had to take him to the bathroom; and I think he
like sniffin round swimming pool water. So Hey!
What I'm supposed to do?

T- Bone had to go back to my Grandma's house.
Until my Daddy find us some permanent place to
stay. Naturally, my mother would want a house.

My father had the down payment for a
house, but he actually did something kind of smart.
He went and bought a used car. A chestnut brown
Oldsmobile Royale from Oyster Point Dodge. He
didn't want payments. He paid it in cash. Then
instead of buying my momma "a house." He bought
her a trailer, from a cool Vietnamese dude, named
Wynn. That's not how it's spelled. That's how it

sound. It's actually Nguyen.

And my father didn't want payments, so he bought my momma a mobile home. He paid it in CASH.

He started to say, "Praise The LORD, I gotta house and a car paid for." It became his new mantra.

We lived out Warwick Mobile Homes. 101 Troy Drive to be exact. In the Oyster Point area of Newport News. Offa Jefferson behind the Crown. Just down from Oyster Point Road and Patrick Henry Mall.

Once we got out there.: we had a yard. T-Bone now could come live wit us and be at home. At the end of all this going on, Best Momma was in her last days of life and had DIED, we buried her. And I was haunted out my mind.

T- Bone was still a puppy. My Uncle Ronnie had house broke him in, so I could bring him in the house. I keep him wit me in my room. Wit the light on.

Then my daddy would get to crying, "Get that dog- - put that dog outside man." Wit his funny nose having... I gotta get up, sometimes after I just fell asleep, and put T- Bone outside in the metal tinned shed. In February. In the colllllld. And close him in.

He was good long as he was sleep.

When he get up, "Whaaa, whaaa, whaaa." He would cry, jus like 'a baby. I gotta get up, go wit him in the shed, hold him in a dusty chair, and rock him back to sleep.

After seeing my Grandmother DIED. He gave me life. I could rub the warm of his pitch black fur. But I could still think about my Grandmother's funeral. My Grandfather was there. My REAL Grandfather. I may have seen him like 5 times in my life.

I'm just counting.

My father used to take me out Yorktown to see him. I guess so he can see who his grandson was, when I was small. After that, my dad stopped going to see him. Wouldn't call. Nothing. My father started resenting his father for divorcing his mother and leaving him and Novie. But he would just close his eyes. He never did admit it.

But, now here he was.: at my Best Momma's funeral. I watched him and my father to see what their interaction would be.

They spoke. Kept it moving. My Grandfather spoke to me. Kept it moving. We didn't touch. I didn't hug him. We didn't even shake hands. I saw who he was. I knew where he live. But we ain't have no Grandfather and Grandson relationship. I was closer with Pee- Wee, than I was with him.

That's what happens when it's a breakdown in communication and a disconnect in families. I know my father still loved his father. He took him in and cared for him, after the divorce, leading up to my father joining the Marines, and even gave him A HOME until he got on his feet. Now, he was going against all that.

And somewhere down the line, somebody probably saying, "It ain't nothing but the devil."

No it's not.

The devil don't got no power. He gotta get permission. (Ref.: Job 1: 6- 12). And in Proverbs 19: 23 it says.: "The fear of Adonai leads to life; one who has it is satisfied and rests UNTOUCHED BY EVIL." Complete Jewish Bible version.

Stop giving the devil permission over your life, over your love, over your family, over your relationships. The devil didn't destroy my family. DECISIONS made by people, such as my father, such as my grandfather is what deprived me of the opportunity of having my Grandfather active in my life.

I'm just grateful to Best Momma and Ms. Carrie; the ladies had better since than the men. They had love and respect for one another, despite the fact at some part, they both shared the same man, and afterwards at different times, the same husband.

Ms. Carrie was never selfish to keep Junius out of his children's lives, or to keep him from his first wife's funeral.

When we lived out Hampton, out the Golden Sands, my father used to drive me to Warwick every morning. Then after school, I would catch the bus to Lynn's house. And my peoples pick me up from round there, or they get me from my

Grandma house. But when we moved out Warwick Mobile Homes; we was back in Bad News city limits. I could now catch the school bus. I was rezoned to attend Menchville High School; and I welcomed it with opened arms.

I was glad to be outta Warwick. Warwick was alright. I'on know what it was, but I didn't adjust good at Warwick. When I got to Menchville, it was a different campus. A different atmosphere. It was bigger. A whole lot bigger. And where Warwick had a predominantly black student population, with white students being a minority; Menchville had a predominantly white student population with blacks being the minority.

Then Newport News had (4) city high schools. Two of the schools were DOWN closer to the black neighborhood communities. At Warwick and Ferguson, there was a predominantly black student population, with white students being the minority. But in the UPPER part of Newport News, in the schools of Denbigh and Menchville, white students were predominant while blacks were the minority. At Menchville, the whole attitude was different. They had a motto that was decried to excellence in athletics and in academics.

The campus was made like a community college. It was clean. The wax concrete floors stayed spit shined. I was in a better place, and I could feel it.

I was round all brand-new people. A few I knew, but most- - I never met before. I was in a all-new world, that was free from my past at Sedgefield, Huntington, and Warwick. I was free from Paula Maria and the bullies of the GGP. I just felt a breath of a brand-new start. And I was down fo it.

When I first settled in at Menchville, my first priority was to enroll in JROTC. I did. Menchville had Air Force JROTC, but it didn't matter. The only thing that mattered was me getting this 3 years of JROTC up under my belt in high school. Take the Armed Services Vocational Aptitude Battery Test, which is the ASVAB, so I can get military placement based upon my level of education, skill and trade. Then I can run off to FREEDOM for a life in the military. Right.

Long as I got that 3 years- - following basic training, I automatically go to an E- 3. That's a Sergeant in the Army, Marines, or Navy; and an E-2 if I go join on with the Air Force. My attraction was to be a Marine; or I could go to college after high school. Take me some ROTC at a higher level, or if I could get enrolled to the Naval Academy in Annapolis, then after 4 years I would be a Commissioned Officer. Where I could climb on board of my very own fighter jet!

I still couldn't drive. I still didn't have a license. Wishful thinking.

While I was in ROTC, it was this girl that liked me. I can tell she like me cause she keep looking and smiling at me. Her face ain't all that. She gotta phat butt. But she gotta real sweet personality. Her name is Tara. We get cool. I like Tara. But as a friend.

My heart was on a different girl. Upstairs. In English class. I would say she was the Baddest Bitch in The World, but I already said that bout Tashia. I would say she was The Baddest Bitch In School, but she probably wasn't. She was ONE of The Baddest Bitches in School. The other (2) was Contessa and Quanette Moore. The Q make 'a W sound. It pronounce like Wuanette or Juanette. Don't ask me how that works. It just do on her. Quanette look exotic. She look like she Black and Puerto Rican. Like banana troppa- ca-nana all pushed together.

Tessa is pretty too. Thin. But RED. A Real beautiful face. Natural beauty. No lip stick. No make- up. She already had the chemistry of a world- class model. And she was Smooooth. Tessa is Too Smooooth. When she had broke up with her boyfriend, he tragically shot and took his own life. I was just getting there, so I didn't know him personally. But Ace's sudden death definitely upset a lotta people and a lot of students at Menchville who loved him and cared about him.

Tessa definitely is an ace of 'a girl. But no girl is ever worth you taking your life for.

That's why fo me, my bells banged for Joy Jackson. Umm, umm, umm, umm, umm, umm, umm! Joy Jackson was The Baddest Bitch In School, for me. Every time I see Joy--

She looked like Tisha Campbell. When she was on House Party. Maybe a shade browner. Eyes like Tisha. Lips like Tisha. But I think her booty was phatta than Tisha. And Joy wasn't loud.

And we both got the same- - I guess it's wisdom tooth, poking through our gum on the right side. Like in the exact same spot. She is perfect.

What's wrong is, I perceive Joy as too smart and beautiful. I think she's outta my league. And therefore, I don't got the confidence to approach her. She has a friend, name Anitra. How ironic is that?

I send Anitra to let Joy know I gotta interest in her. The next day, when we get back to English class...

"Did you tell her what I said."

"Yeah. I told her."

"And..."

"And what!?"

"What did she say?"

"She say, why you ain't man enough to come ask her yourself."

What!? I held my desk and scooted down in the seat looking at Joy. She look like 'a sweet juicy bowl of cherry- iced ice cream. But I couldn't do it. Damn I couldn't do it.

She was sitting 2 rows over from me, and at the front. She is quiet. She is lookin so smart.

I still jus felt like Joy was out of my league. Like she was too much! I was intimidated.

Then it got crazy. I was chasing Joy. But I had other girls chasing me. It won't just Tara. At Menchville, I got a lot of female attention. It was enough for me to notice.

My Hulk Hogan and Rocky Balboa contraption had put me in there. It was still holding up. Plus my dad had an old sand weight laying round in the yard. I used to bench, curl, and military press on that. Though I wasn't an athlete, I had the shape and build of one, and these Menchville girls was taking notice.

I had started my 10th grade year at Warwick.: "We are Warwick Raiders... and we like to par- ty. Par- ty Har- dy. Par- ty Har- dy, all- night long." That actually was a drill song, I picked up from Toine.

I transferred from Warwick and finished my 10th grade year at Menchville. I was now a Menchville Monarch. Whatever their drill song is. Prolly got something to do wit, "Razzle- Dazzle... MARCH!!"

"The Razzle- Dazzle," that was the best military marching breakdown EVER!! When I led the ROTC Company at Menchville... I had to get at least TWO Razzle- Dazzles in before we broke rank. I can't even explain it to you. I just know it was awesome!

The summer after my sophomore year, I went back up to Richmond, to work with Lucky. Lucky never paid me fair. To say that he paid me fair, would be to say that he paid me what I deserved. No more- - No less. Lucky always paid me MORE. MORE than what I expected to receive. Which is even greater than fair.

I always looked up to Lucky, not just as a father, or 2nd father figure. But for as a mold of a man and as a husband. Lucky was very loving and expressively romantic towards my Aunt Audrey.

He would kiss his wife. Something my father and mother did not do. My parents were never openly loving and romantic. So, I picked up on this contrast.

Lucky would always kiss Audrey before he leave out the house. No matter where he go.

And when he come back, despite he had the key to his own house, he would always announce himself to his wife,

"It's me Babe."

And he would holler it out loud, despite the fact she might be in the kitchen, or a whole nother room.

"That's you Lucky?" we would hear her say.

"Yeah, it's me," he confirmed back to her.

She would come to him, and Oh Lord! here they go... kissing again. Audrey be tripping off me, cause I turn my head. I be thinkin they bout to get it in.

But when he really did wanna get it in, he didn't take her to just a local hotel. He would take her to a hotel in Hawaii, or take her to a hotel in The Bahamas. Lucky got class.

And it's something else about Lucky.: he and my Aunt Audrey was the second ones in our family to get their house built from the ground. A house. Not just a house, but a rancher. That means the whole house is spread out all over one story of the ground. But it is very luxurious. And he moved my aunt from out the City of Richmond and into Chesterfield County. A Richmond City suburb.

After I left "the ranch," I was back to my reality. Back to my poverty. When I come home, I feel some type of way. But I've grown to accept, it is what it is. It's been like this all my life. I go to my room, change my clothes, and go out in the yard to play wit my growing dog. He done come along ways from small cans of puppy food. It's getting more expensive to feed him now. Because of the budget, I gotta feed him generic.

Generic brands of quality, generic brands of value, and generic brands of nutrition. I'm buying bigger bags of dog food, but his large bags still economically cost me about $8.99. Under $10 bucks.

My father doesn't work for an employer. He's now self- employed. Which, in this case means, that my father got a whole lot of transmissions, engines, and junk piled up in our yard. You walk up and you think you on the set of Sanford and Son. And my middle name being Lamont, ain't help me out.:

"You Big Dummy!"

He scraps the engines, transmissions, and junk for copper, aluminum, and brass. Then he drives it on his Ford F150 out to a salvage yard, mostly in Chesapeake, and turn his small profit.

My mother "worked" at Buckroe Baptist

Child Care most of my life, before that she worked at Shalom Kindergarten. But I was too young to remember that. But basically, her twice a month income is what staples our family together.

I seen my mother's whole two-week paycheck be as low as $450 dollars. That means she was financially supporting a family of three and a dog, off of $900-- less than $1000 a month. And only $10, 800.: for an entire year.

And I still was in school, I wasn't working no regular pay wage job.

We gotta do the best we can do.

God Bless the man that made Ramen Noodle Soups. That took 'a nigga up off 'a syrup sandwich. Didn't it!? We used to go to Food Lion, you get 10 for a $1.00. Then 15 for a $1.00. Then it went UP to like 20 for a $1.00. Shiiiit fo $5.00 'a nigga got like 'a hu'ned soups in da crib!!

And back then, I was eating swine. You get one of them BIG red juicy pork sausages. When you boil it in the pot; that bitch BUST!! open!! Put that shit wit them noodles... Aye! 'A nigga ain't have to eat 'a syrup sandwich again!!

'A sausage and 'a hu'ned soups.

I'm not condoning it. To all my kosher and halal eating people. I'm just saying back then, that's what the reality was.

It was summer, and I was chillin wit my homeboy Lynn. He want me to walk wit him up Seven Oaks

From Poverty, To Prison, To Prosperity.

to see another friend, name Dwight. So that's
walking from like 13th Street up to 39th Street. But
in downtown Newport News, all the streets close
together, so it's not a bad walk.

On our way up the Wick, it's this girl in the yard. I
hear Lynn say, "Hey, Ericka."

He smiling. Waiving to her and shit.

"Hey," she answer back.

At first I ain't know who she was, until I
looked real close. Then, I kinda knew who she was.
Ericka was a girl who I used to see in the hall,
before I left Warwick. When I left, I was a
sophomore. She was a freshman.

But in high school, I didn't see girls in
classes. Like she's a sophomore. She's a junior.
She's a senior. She's a freshman. I just saw them in
high school. As long as they at least was in high
school, then they was good enough for me. Ericka
and another girl was like the only two big girls, out
they whole little team.

But this was my first time seeing her out of school.
Lynn asked her about the yard where she was
standing.

"This my Grandma house," she said to us.
So that perfectly explained to us who's roses she
was out there watering, in the middle of August.

The sun was BEAMING!! her ass. But Ericka is a
RED girl. The sun had tanned her into a golden
brown. I saw her sweating. Then, I saw them big

238

bubbled eyes. I shot my shot...

She told me, "Nawww." Turning me down. But then she said, "Y'all wanna come in," she warmly invited. "Come on."

We walked up in her Grandma's yard. She told us to go straight to the back. The back yard. Lynn walking first. I'm in the middle. And she behind me. She swiped at my hand. So I think I'm tripping. So when we walking back from the back yard, back to the front yard- - she swipe my hand again. But this time, I turn around.

And when I turn around, she walk straight into my arms. She let me taste them THICCCKK JUICCCY ASSS Lips!! And she gave me the tongue. Ohhh!! Audrey and Lucky ain't know how to do it like this. I was LOCKED holding my hands round her thicccckkk juiccccy ass and hips. Gosh o' mighty!!

"Hi, my name Ericka. My number is 244..."

I think it was gon be the start of me loving all Ericka's. However it might be spelled.

Chapter 13.

This was my first real girlfriend since Tashia. Ericka was a big girl. Some say fat girl. If we had The Fat BOYS. Then I guess, somewhere down the line, you gotta have The Fat Girls. It's not always nice to call them fat girls, unless they KNOW you're not saying it to be offensive. You not being malicious. So, I'll just say big girl, so you'll have 'a thought to plug into your imagery imagination.

But, I didn't see her like that. It's more to her than that. I didn't know I had a sexual attraction for big women. I didn't really think about it. Ericka might be big. If you wanna call it that.

But man this girl was BEYOND Beauty. She was pretty. Naturally. That means without lipstick and make- up. And when she walk, how them legs rub together- - ummm, ummm, ummm!! This girl was sexy, sexy, sexy! I couldn't naturally resist her. And above all, she was RED!! She was TTL- - TOP of THE LINE!!

That same summer, Sister Mc Nair would get me to cut her grass. Out Grafton.

"I got the lawn mower," she would say to my mother on the phone. And my mother relay the message to me.

I would load up on my father's pickup truck. That means.: I would just take me, my dog and his (2) dog bowls.

My dad would drive us out to Sister Mc Nair's house. We'd drive out Route 17, and cut over to her long drive way; her house was the last one to the back. On the left. My dad'll pull his F- 150 up behind her little small blue hatchback, and let me and T- Bone get out, and his (2) dog bowls.

"God Bless You," my father would politely speak.

"God Bless You, Elder Miles. How are you today?" Sister Mc Nair is not just friendly and good, she's also very respectful.

"I'm BLESSED. The Lord been keeping me," you can hear the somber baritone in his plaid buttoned- up chest.

Then my father would leave, and Sister Mc Nair would walk with me to get the lawn mower, unless the lawn mower was already out on the side of the house.

By now, that grimacing- menacing nightmare scene of a slasher film waiting to happen... had long gone. Real estate developers had laid stake to building up a shopping center, two sets of apartments, and one set of condos, with an indoor gym and an outdoor swimming pool, just right there past a smear of trees, in fronna the specs of Sister Mc Nair's past intimidating property's eyes.

But Sister Mc Nair herself, still had a huge piece of yard. I fed T- Bone some water, so his throat won't go dry, and strapped him to a tree. I took to thinking all about Ericka as I cut- cross Sister Mc Nair's grass. To pass the time. I thought Ericka was gonna be the one. I wanted Ericka to be the one. We talk. But shit was going slowwwww.

Slower than me chopping this quarter of a football field.

When I finally do finish, Sister Mc Nair have a hot plate of something delicious to eat. And maybe a dish of a piece of cake. She just about always kept hard candy out in a glass jar.

It was a fashion for a lot of old ladies to usually sit a glass jar of peppermints out on her coffee table. Best Momma was like that. My Great-Grandma Lloyd was like that. And Sister Mc Nair was like that. I guess these lil old ladies didn't want nobody sittin up there talkin to them, wit some stankin- ass breath. They was conscious bout this kind of stuff.

Sister Mc Nair did not just feed me. She fed T- Bone too. T- Bone got spoiled going to Sister Mc Nair's house, cause she fed him more than dog food, and better than table scraps, in his bowl. T- Bone would be lickin his lips and patting his paws to the ground. He'd be making noises, like he just wanna run and hug and give her a kiss.

Me and T- Bone would be out there for like 5 hours.

Then she'll give me my check. And I read what Lucky was telling me, when he tell me.: "People don't wanna pay you nothing."

My check be for $20.

My dad get me to the bank to go cash it. My name wouldn't even be spelled right on the check. It be spelled J- a- m- m- i- e. Jammie. But the bank'll still cash it. And I wasn't mad, cause I remembered what Lucky had told me when he taught me the skill. And I never lost any respect for Sister Mc Nair. I still saw her like a Grandmother.

When I get back to the house, my momma let me know Ericka done called, and that Sister Mc Nair was pleased with my work. Since Elder Mc Nair had died, she was living alone, and she had proposed for me to come out there and live with her.

I thought about it. Her yard definitely wasn't as scary as it once had been, when I was small. But my life wasn't in the county. My life was in the city. My friends was in the city. My girl was in the city. I wanted to be in the city.

Plus, Sister Mc Nair is a very spiritually conservative person. She don't even keepa tv in her living room. My lifestyle was more fast- paced and loud listening to my Gangsta music. My parents tolerated it. But Sister Mc Nair might not go for all that. It was best for me to stay at home, where I better fit in.

The school year started, and I was back at Menchville. I was back in classes wit Joy. I would tell myself, "You gotta girl. You gotta girl. You gotta girl."

Boy who was I foolin?? I still wanted me some JOY!

Plus, my girl, won't doing nothing. Just talk, kiss, and look at each other. But I still ain't have the confidence to go at Joy. What was I to say? "I wanna eat yo pussy in the rain, in 'a trunk of 'a cherry coated Range..."

HA! Yeah right.

And it's crazy, cause I had girls chasing me. Tara was still chasing me. I went to check to see was she doing this with me, or was she like this with everybody. I couldn't find proof she was naturally after every man. So she be chasing, chasing, chasing. And I just stay nice to her. Keep her close.

"Just wait." That's all I could think to say to stall her.

"Hhhh. Ok," I'd hear her respond.

She had more balls to go at me than what I had to go at Joy. She did have a phat butt. I wanted to see something more in her. But Tara really likes me, and I knew she wanted to be more than just having sex. There's more to life than that. It just don't always work like that. Tara wanted to be boyfriend/ girlfriend. I wasn't ready to give her that. So I just had to keep being nice to her. My attention was quietly at Joy.

But Tara ain't know. Plus, Tara ain't know, but as that school year progressed, I had a girl that was showing me her pussy. Niece had did it when we was young, but she was my girl. These girls really ain't even know me. It's generally a man's behavior-- for a man to pull out his penis on a girl, and show her how big the muscle is. But in

Menchville, I was seeing that women can be just as aggressive as men, when it come to getting what they know they want.

But the crazy part about it, I thought less about Ericka, I was more mindful that something I do might get back to Joy. I ain't say nothing. I'll just sit there and watch the show. Some of these girls really was Bad. But to me they won't fuckin wit Joy. I didn't wanna fuck that road up. That's why I walked away.

Just like Sister Mc Nair, my Great-Grandmother Lloyd used to call for me to cut her grass. But unlike Sister Mc Nair, my daddy wouldn't drive me out there. I had to catch the bus. I had to catch like 2- 3 buses from Oyster Point all the way down to Greenbriar, down from Shell Road, just before you get to Victoria and Kecoughtan Road, out in Hampton. So, T- Bone just gotta see me leave alone.

My Great- Grandma's yard is small. Her whole yard can fit on Sister Mc Nair's front porch. But I cut her grass anyway, and it take like 2 hours to rake up all the leaves and bag up all the sticks, and sit it out in front of the ditch, in her front yard.

Then I gotta go in her house, and wash my dirty hands, in her clean and tidy space. When I go sit at the table, she feed me peanut butter and jelly. But I ain't set trippin. I love peanut butter and jelly.

That's part of my pay.

The other part of my pay, a check to "Jamie," for $5.00.

That was damn near my bus fare. I can't even buy dogfood wit this. But I won't tripping. It just made me know I wanted more out of life.

When I get back home, I grab my dog, and take T- Bone for a walk. He was happy to see me. I was happy to see him too. It was time to relieve some stress. I walked him by his chain, up Troy Drive, or through the trailer park. Clayton Mobile Homes be closed by this time. So we would cut through his property. I never vandalized nothing. I never even let T- Bone piss on the tires.

Then just right past the new mobile homes he had for sale, be some used, broken down, torn apart mobile homes. T- Bone liked to play and run around in those. I was afraid for him. I don't know how he did it, God must've been with him; he never got yoked up by his leash, and he would walk over top of broken glass, and not get cut; or get the shards of glass up in his feet.

When he would scare me too much. I would have to go pick him up and bring him out all the way to the sidewalk, and sit him down, so he wouldn't try to run back. Once, I get him through that, he loved to trot past that tiny lil furniture shop on the left, the golf club place, and Carlos' Mexican Restaurant. I'll cut him through Oyster Point Apartments, and he'll ramble in the back of 7- 11. I'd cross wit him, over Oyster Point, and take him all the way to Bally's. By the time he get back, his tongue be lappin up in his water bowl.

T- Bone is adorable.

He was getting bigger. But I would feed him. Get on the phone wit Ericka and hold him in my arms. Rubbing him and rocking him, on the back porch. He would fall asleep in my arms. I could hear him snore. Just like 'a human. It was fascinating, he was making me and my momma get over our fear of dogs. Our fear was subdued by our love for da T-Bone.

In my junior year, I wasn't in ROTC no more. I did enough fuckin up when I was at Warwick. My Menchville Counselor Mrs. Long used to call me to her office, at least once a month, just to keep up wit me. All the counselors at Da Ville did it. I can't say they had a golden blueprint to get 'a nigga a billion dollars. But they did their best to care, and to be there, and be supportive of students, to help them achieve their goals, and get to the next level.

Mrs. Long told me, "Mr. Miles, you are behind on your credits."

Informing me that I had to catch my credits up, in order to graduate on time with my class. Her brilliant solution, to drop my regular after noon classes and electives, and to start a vocational class program, called New Horizons.

New Horizons had (2) campuses. One on Butler Farm Road, in Hampton. And one on Woodside Lane, in Newport News. New Horizons had trade and skill courses like Carpentry, Brick Masonry, Auto Mechanics, Cosmetology, Horticulture, and I think it was 'a Electrician class. I went to the one on Woodside Lane, in Newport News. I took carpentry. Because I wanted to learn to build my momma a house.

Completion of my votech class, would give me 3 credits, as opposed to 1 and a half. Not that I couldn't get about that anyway. But I was trying to avoid going to summer school and night school. They wasn't free. I'd have to pay. And I was looking at it, hmm.: If I couldn't get my momma a house through the NFL. Then I'd learn to build it myself, in carpentry. So I went into William (Bill) Padgett's class.

Ericka still wasn't fuckin. I thought she might be a virgin. So, I pulled up on niggas in her hood, to see what's up wit shorty.

"A VIRGIN?! Hell naw she ain't no virgin."

They damn near laughed at me when I said that. I was waiting for at least one to say,

"Shit nigga, I just finished fuckin her, right fo you rolled up."

But nobody never said that. Or that somebody just fucked her, yesterday, or last week, or last month. But it was bout December. It was almost Christmas. I forgot if it was in person, or over the phone, but she wanted to break up.

I was glad. Cause I thought it might give me the strength to go at Joy. What was I gon say? "Girl, let me hit you wit this horn, till I wring the whole elephant nose out, up in that pussy, BITCH!"

I still didn't know that yet.

Joy was too intelligent. I didn't know how to approach her. I didn't have no other mutual friend to try to bring the (2) of us together. I probably would've kept pursuing, but by the end of January,

"Hey." Ericka was calling me back.

And I went 'on round there.

When, I first get there, it's the same frustrating shit as before. It drip into February. A few weeks go by, then, we get the call.:

"Evelyn, come Quick! Your father is in Hampton General Hospital," my Grandmother said to my momma.

"Huh!? What!? What happened!?"

My Grandfather had suffered a chronic stroke while he was home, in the yard. The ambulance had to rush him to Hampton General Hospital. Now here it was February, again. It was collllld. And my Grandfather was now fighting for his life.

Chapter 14.

I don't know how much of this I was supposed to take. In February 1991, my Great-Grandma, Grace Miles had died. Her funeral was the same day and time as my Great- Grandfather Lloyd. I couldn't be at two places at the same time. Plus, I was closer to him. Then another family member had died. Three of em, at the same time. In February 92, Best Momma had died. Now I was looking at my mother's father.

He laid in his bed. With his eyes closed. Everybody was talking around him. But for some reason, he only respond when my momma talk.

"Daddy; this Evelyn. Can you hear me?"

He would start smiling and laughing.

"Daddy if you can hear me, blink your eyes."

His eyes wouldn't open. But he'd blink his eyelids for The General.

"Touch your nose."

He tried to move his hand to his nose. I think one time he did it.

"Isaac," my Grandmother called out to him. She was the only one that can call him that. Even, to his only sister Ruth, he was also called, "JUNIOR."

He might laugh or smile. But his eyes stayed closed. Like he could hear, but he couldn't see and he wouldn't speak.

Periodically, everyone would step out of his room. I went back in by myself. I can remember the first time we met,

"Jamie, this is your Grandfather," My little smalled hand was introduced to my Grandfather by my mother.

At that time I thought I only had Pee- Wee. But here it is... it was another one.

My Grandfather was a landlord. He owned a house on the ONE WAY 27th Street, in between Marshall and Wickham, where he provides low-income housing to community residents.

Before my Grandfather would only stick to one lane on the highway, driving his browned Ford Econoline van on I- 64 to Richmond; he had the cool light yellow Ford cab truck, wit the green top.

"Come on Peanut. Come on and go with me."

He gave me my FIRST nickname.

He'd drive me around, and show me off to his friend, Mr. Washington on 27th Street; or to his brother, Uncle Charles; or to (I thought it was his brother. But Debbye said, it's his nephew).: Uncle Jimmy.

He'd proudly say, "This my Grandson, Jamie. This Evelyn's son."

But by now, even Charles and Jimmy had DIED. He named his son Charles after his brother Charles. That's why it's (2) Uncle Charles.

I remembered one day he was keeping me and my cousin Sabrina. We was chewing gum. And for some reason, we thought the gum would go better in our hair, than chewing it in our mouth. And he caught us, downstairs in the shop.:

"What y'all doing!?" He saw that gum!

"WHAAUGHHH!!" His mouth and eyes got big both at the same time.

"Look Granddaddy..." we thought we was playing. Like the bubblegum supposed to go in there.

He pulled off that old white leather strap, quicker than The Lone Ranger can click out "Silver." That man beat the shit out us. Well I got it worse, prolly cause Sabrina was 'a girl!

After he beat us, he took us in the bathroom, to get the gum out our hair. He was washing it, in soap and water. I don't think these was NON-STICK BUBBLES. The more he scrubbed, the more the gum reacted as an adhesive to my scalp.

My Grandfather is a war veteran, and man of all trades. He ain't no barber. He done went and got the scissors,

"Hold still." He cold clipped the gum from out our hair, as best he could.

"Ha, ha," I can laugh about it now. It wasn't funny back then. I was losing my Grandfather. The same Grandfather that would later call me Jamaica, as I grew; and Jamie Jamaica. My 2nd and 3rd nicknames.

Every birthday, including every celebration we gave him, out Gosnold Hope Park, after we would sing Happy Birthday, and he'd blow out all his candles; he'd wish, "I wanna live to be 99 years old."

February 18th my father turned 44. February 19th I turned 17. February 20th Best Momma had DIED. February 21st, my Grandfather was gone.

My Grandfather died at 72.

"Wgyhdftbft. Sfddcvrgge," that was Ronnie high and drunk.

That's what he might as well been saying, cause he was fucked up. He lost his father. He took it hard! His father was his father... and his best friend.

Yes, I went to my Grandfather's funeral.

He was a World War II fighter soldier, who bravely and courageously fought against the hysterically tyrannical Adolf Hitler, and to end the unconscionable extermination of Jews. He was not only a Father, a Grandfather, and a future Great Grandfather and a Great- Great Grandfather to future generations, but he was also a valiant combatant, and Purple Heart recipient, of the United States Army. To this day, my Grandfather, Isaiah A Jones Jr, is buried on hallowed ground, out Hampton Memorial Gardens, in Hampton, Virginia.

Believe me.: my light stayed on. I couldn't bring T- Bone in the house no more. My Dad had already kicked him out a year ago. I couldn't go no where. I go to the bathroom, I see my Grandfather. I walk past the living room, I see my Grandfather sitting in the chair. I couldn't even go to my own room.

His eyes were closed. He was semi-responsive. There was no clear speech and no clear indicators. The time came when the doctor pulls the family aside into a waiting room and asks the burning question concerning disconnecting his life support system. The sisters of the family made the decision to pull their father's life support system. They did not want their father to be a vegetable, nor would he want that for himself.

My Grandfather entered the arena to do his battle versus death. He soared during his first hours following his disconnect from the machines.

I said to myself, 'My Grandfather is a fighter. He will pull through this;" but death rallied in the fourth quarter and prevailed.

His casket was an after sunset sky colored bluish- gray. He had praying hands creviced on the outside chromed corners of his casket. The inside top half of the lid had a stitched- in praying hands design. He wore a dark gray suit, white shirt;

there's a tie.

Cooke Brothers Funeral Home gave him a nice haircut and freshly cut shave. He looked in fit. He looked in shape. His hands wasn't folded or crossed. Not like a mason. His hands was straight down to his side. Just like a soldier. As if he was standing at attention. Prepared to march off into his afterlife.

I gotta get out this house!! I was haunted out my mind!!

It's not that I was afraid of my Grandfather, I know my Grandfather loved me and would never hurt me. It was the respect for The Lord, that God was burning into me. I had to fear DIED, so God could use it as a rod, for me to straighten out and comply to HIS order.

I still won't there yet. I was at Ericka's house.

While my Grandfather was in Hampton General, it had gave my family time to meet Ericka. To meet her precious Grandmother, Mrs. Washington; and to meet her Uncle Sonny, and Aunt Beatrice.

And her family met my mother, and various ones of my mother's seven sisters. They would come pick me up from Ericka's house. She lived just two blocks down, and a block over. Perfect walking distance. But now those days was changed.

It was just me and her sitting up late in her living room. We watched every damn show on BET, every Comic View. We watched Martin. In Living Color. I got tired of hearing the bubbles in the damn fish tank.

I was fed up.

I was tired.

By body was changing.

My hormones were developed.

I was 17, but my body was a full-grown man. We got into a argument about nothing. I knew what my reasons was.

"Look, I'm out," I headed to the door, and put my hand on the knob. I wasn't coming back.

She must've felt that junk. Cause she said,

"Jamie, come here," she seductively called out to me.

I needed HER. I needed to feel LIFE. I needed to feel ALIVE. I needed her.

I needed to feel HER. I needed Ericka more than ever.

She had on this red Chicago Bulls t- shirt. These like purple acid wash denim shorts, and these all- white Reebok Classics. A girls favorite. Hair slicked straight to the back. Won't even done. But she ain't need to.

She went and grabbed that blanket, and we went on her Grandma's back porch. UMM!

We finished in the grass, up under the clothesline!
We ain't just make love. Ericka had took my
virginity.

After that we had sex maybe like (1) day a
month, like the first (5) months. But for real, it
helped our bond. We spent time together. Her
Grandma or her Uncle Sonny would invite me for
dinner. Grandma Washington was one of the best
southern cooks your lips could ever taste. She
cooked with the same form of passion that I had
been accustomed to from my own Grandmothers
and Mother. I started calling her Grandma, just like
her Granddaughter that I was dating. She had the
same genuine natural qualities and characteristics
that must have been embedded inside of most
Southern Black Americans, back during the era that
she was born and raised.

In Ericka's family, I saw a continuation of my
family. And in some regard I guess the family l had
that was dwindling. I started to really fall in love
with Ericka.

After the five months, she wanted to come to my
house. Not just to see where I live, but she wanted
to make love. Well- - somethin like that.

"Shit. Alright." What else I'm supposed to
say?

The only catches.: we had to skip school. And my
father. And T- Bone was at home.

Alright.

So she catch the bus up to Patrick Henry Mall. It's early after 6 in the morning. I think she was the only one on the bus.

"Hey," she speak to me.

Ericka is fat and phaat! BOTH AT THE SAME TIME! UMMM! UMMM! UMMM! This shit is TTL- - TOP of THE LINE!!

'Baby, come be my cherry on top!' I shoulda told her.

Them juiccccy lil legs and thighs rubbing all together-- 'a BLACK MAN'S Dream!!

She walk up to me.

"Hi. You," she like to smile and say to me. Ericka like five- seven. Five- six. One/ two inches shorter than me. She step up on her tippy- toes.

"Mmmmm, mmmmm, mmmmm, mmmmm," that's me meltin on her lips! Lickin her tongue, like I'm eattin that pussy. Grippin on that big asss butt!! YES!!

"You gotta feed me. I want some breakfast," she say to me.

"Alright." It's 'a Mickey Mc's cross the street. I walk her across Jefferson to Mc Donald's.

I'm broke as a joke. I got like $2 in my pocket. But I spend it all on her, so she can eat, and I can make her happy.

After she finish eating, we stroll locked hand- n-hand, in love, back to my trailer.

My dad's car and truck parked in the front. I know he home. What I don't know is if he at the kitchen table. It's windows in the kitchen. Our trailer is on the corner of Troy Drive. It's only a fence on 3 sides of the lot.

I gotta sneak her round back.

Then when I get to the back, I gotta hold her up. T- Bone be at the back. I gotta see where he at, what he doing. He can smell me. If he know I'm in the yard, he gon be trying to play. If he see her, he gon lunge at her, and bark. Either way, that's gon make my father come outside, if he make too much noise.

And remind you.: I'm supposed to be at school.

Alright, so I tip- toe through the back. T-Bone is SLEEP inside his doghouse. His doghouse don't got a door. It's a rimmed tire laying on the ground, that I use for a door, when I need to shut him in. I use that.

I'm quiet. I don't need the tire to jerk his chain. I stay there for a few seconds. He don't move or come look out the front of his dog house. That's how I knew he was sleep.

I had already left the hook off the backdoor, before I went to pick Ericka up at the bus stop.

The backdoor was still unlocked. I went in. My dad was sitting in his chair, facing me, but his eyes was closed. He was in his spiritual meditation.

I went back and told Ericka to come on.

"Shhh," I said to her. She kept looking over at T- Bone's house. "My dad in the living room. You gotta be quiet."

I held her by the hand. Took her straight to room and closed the door... man this bitch pussy so damn good! I'm thinkin, 'Deg, that English Mc Muffin musta really paid off.'

She keep making noise.

I'm like, "Ericka, you gotta stop! My father in the next room."

Shit, the damn wall made outta soft ass paneling.

"I can't help it," she told me, and she still keep making noise.

She turning me on for real, but at the same time.: I ain't tryin to get in trouble. This girl got me skippin school and gettin pussy in 'a preacha house.

I put my hand on her mouth.

This bitch TOOO DAMN JUICCCCY!! She still keep making that noise.

Next thing I know.:

"Jamie!? What is you doing in there?"

Alright, to speed this up.: we get caught! My dad

left back out my room. My door don't got no lock. After he leave out, we start back. SHE STILL MAKING NOISE.

I move my hand now. Shit, we done already got caught now. Fuck it! I might as well go head and finish POPPING this bitch head off!!

"Rrrrrriiiiing, rrrrrriiiiing, rrrrrriiiiing, rrrrrriiiiing, rrrrrriiiiing," that's the phone ringing.

He ain't answering the phone. We ain't got no answering machines. That shit ring like 35 times. That shit breakin my concentration. I go get the phone-- it's my momma! Calling from at work.

"Jamie, what is you doing wit Ericka in that house."

'Up in here dustin her BIG ASSSS off.'

But, I couldn't say that. Not to my momma. I said somethin that sound more like, "Huh!?"

She got tired of talking to me. I wasn't giving her her answers. She wanted to talk to her husband. My dad was standing outside. I passed him the phone. He took it, and I went back in the room, and back up in Ericka. She broke me all the way in to Big Girls. These bitches take dick! She had me about to flip this whole trailer to 'a popsicle stand!!

Good gracious. This bitch was loose, soft!! Wet!! Deep!!

Despite all that, I don't rub 'a round off. I really hurt and upset my physical father. He called the police. It was nothing they could do. We was both minors, and I lived there.

So the officer told me, "Just leave. Let him cool off... be sure to take her wit you."

We finished getting dressed. I got pocket change out my room, and now I was on the bus, wit Ericka. Catching the bus back down her way.

"I hate you." WHAAAAP!! She said and she slapped me.

She caught me SO HARD!! I heard 'a nigga in the back say, "OHHHHH!"

At the same time, 'a nother nigga said, "DAAAAAMN!!"

She hit me so hard, I saw stars. But I ain't hit her back.

"I wanna break up," she said to me. "It's over."

I knew she was scared. She thought my momma was gon tell her Grandmomma on her. But she didn't. We was broke up, and I didn't come back home. I went to Lynn's house. I was down there like (4) days. Lucky drove all the way from Richmond to come pick me up. My momma was wit him.

In the van, I just shut up. I didn't bring it up. I just listened to them talk and speculate about what they think really happened. I wasn't gon address that bullshit; gettin pussy is 'a young niggas rite of passage. When I went back home, I didn't bring it back up either. I blew right past my father. I tried to play it off like,

　　"T- Bone," I went to go grab and hold my dog. T- Bone has 'a heart bigga than a teddy bear.

I don't plan on bringing it up to my father. I didn't plan to. Then, like the 5th day, it brought it up itself.:

It was in June. The weather was warmed and muggy. I'm stickin to my own sheets. The trailer ain't got no A/ C. I put the fan on in my room.

It felt like I'm sweatin on the inside.

I roll my window out. It's not working. I'm horny. But that don't even feel good. Then...

I go piss.

　　'WHAAAUUGGHHH!! What was that?' I feel my shit burning.

I can't sleep.

I keep getting up going to the bathroom. I got frequent urination.

　　'WHHHAAAAUUUGGGHHHHH!!' every time I piss. I feel like I'm pissin out RAZORBLADES!!

My momma had a Home Remedies book out on her

living room shelf. I went and I go get the book. It was just a year ago that Magic Johnson announced that he had HIV. That he was HIV Positive. The first thing I did was go to HIV. Read it.

Shewww! I don't got that.

I go to AIDS. Read it.

Shewww! I don't got that.

I go to gonorrhea. Read it.

That's what it was.

I check syphilis. I check chlamydia. I had gonorrhea.

I ain't say nothing that morning. My dad took my momma to Buckroe and he left. I ain't drink kool- aid, soda, nothing all day. I'm running from 'a glass of water. My momma get back home. She about to start dinner.

My dad kicked back, in his favorite chair. The kitchen table. Looking at the news.

I gotta let them know. I say, "Momma."

"What!? What is it?" I know she tired for real, she just got in from work. But this is important.

I say, "Momma, I'M BURNIN!!"

Both of them stop and look at each other, then look over at me. I'm in the living room. I say it again;

"I'm burning. I think I got gonorrhea." But I knew what it was from reading the book.

My momma tell me the impossible.:

"Just wait til tomorrow. I'll get yo Daddy to take you tomorrow."

I had to go A WHOLE NOTHER NIGHT wit that shit up in me. I was disgusted.

The next day my Daddy took me to Mary Immaculate Hospital Emergency Room, I beat him to the car. 'Come on! Let's Go!'

That shit won't NO JOKE!!

When I get to the hospital, the nurse taking my information. She ask me what I'm there for. I tell her, the same thing I tell my momma,

"I'm burning. I got gonorrhea."

I ain't even make it to the chair. I think I got back there faster than a gunshot victim.

I had to strip down to a gown. The doctor came in there wit that metal cotton swab. Put it in my tip and spin't my dick.

"YEOWW!!"

He came back.

"You got gonorrhea."

'No shit Sherlock.'

Then he got something else wit him. This BIG
PHAAAT JUICCCCY LONG ASSSS NEEDLE!!

"Where you going wit that?" I asked him.

"You know," and he smacked himself on the
ass.

I said, "NAW! Hell Naw!"

He said, "Well, you can leave outta here, and go
back home with it."

I said, "Go head."

No way in the hell, I'm gon take this shit back to the
crib. I roll on my stomach. He hit that big long ass
needle in my left buttcheek.

"AAAUUURRRGGHHH!!" I holler out

"Hold, Hold, Hold... you bout to break the
needle!!!!" he shouted out to me.

This shit was about to get real horrible. After that
shit was finished, the doctor asked me, "How old
are you?"

"Seventeen," I answered him.

"You got lucky this time. This coulda been a
whole lot worse."

Then my father talked to me in the ride back to the
house.

"See, Jamie, that girl seeing other men."

"That girl seeing other men," he kept telling me over again.

I didn't want to hear it. Cause I didn't want to believe it. 'Man my baby didn't burn me. Not my Baby.'

'Not my Red Rabbit.' Hunh. 'Man my girl LOVE ME. MY GIRL faithful to me.' And the whole time I'm tryin to think of where else I got this shit from-- my Pops wit more life experience and wisdom than me, was giving me the truth.

No wonder that pussy was so damn good!

I thought he was gon bring up what happened the other day, but he didn't. This the first time, I'm formally revisiting it.

When I get home, I take a shower. The penicillin put me to sleep. When I get up, I check-- no discharge. I go piss. No burning. No razorblades.

IMM'A NEW MAN!! The doctor said, I was lucky. No, I wasn't lucky. I was BLESSED The Lord brought me back. I coulda been finished. At 17.

All the clothes I wore those (5) days, I threw all that shit away. I never wore it again. I called Ericka and told her what happened.

"Nah- uh." She ain't believe me. Then she was acting like I gave it to her. Then she started talkin like she had got raped by a nigga out her way.

She was upsetting me.

When she was talking about she got raped, I gave the phone to my momma to talk to her. Cause you know.: I ain't the pussy police. But I'm tryin to get this girl some help.

After she finished talking to my momma. My momma said, "That girl wasn't raped. She lying to you."

And that makes it hard for a woman who actually does suffer being raped. The struggle of being believed.

All this shit was going on. I went round to her house, and she still didn't believe me. If that won't bad enough, not only did this bitch give me my first STD... but when women make STUPID ASS decisions- - sometimes they just keep it going.

She went from burning me, to giving MY FRIEND Kane some pussy. She ended up burning him too! After he came round there, and showed him his pills, that's when she finally believed it, and carried her lil dirty pussy ass 'on to the doctor. Running round here clapping niggas.

After that, her and Kane BROKE UP. But Kane just went 'on head and fucked her, cause she was attracted to wanting to give him the pussy anyway. He ain't never have no love for her.

I was fucked up. It took us like (2) more months, before we started back talking. I was doing something to get back to life, and stop feeling fucked up. I went and got me my first Real job.

They hired me as a Groundskeeper at Water Country USA, in Williamsburg. That mean, I was sweeping up trash. They paid me minimum wage $4.25/ hour. I worked full- time, and got paid every (2) weeks.

I could use my badge and get admitted for FREE to any Anheuser Busch theme park. And I got (2) free tickets, every paycheck, to invite any family or friends I wanted to the park for a day. I always gave my tickets to my father and mother.

It's the least I could do, fo bringin that heathen into they house. And thank my momma for using her Blue Cross and Blue Shield to get that demon up outta me.

I liked my job. It was fun. For 17 years old. They had a professional diving team, that was a clownish- comedic diving board version of the Harlem Globe Trotters. That's the best way I can explain it. They would flip, trip, flop off the board, from tens of feet HIIIIGH into the air, and splash down in a relatively small tub of water.

And get up every time.

Then the finale to the show, would be like a triple or quadruple backflip high dive from like 50 foot up into the sky. Their entertainment was awesome. They'd repeatedly perform these feats and diving board circus acts at least (3) shows a day. Everyday.

From time to time, I'd catch them sitting, eating, chopping it up, in the break area. And I'd respect them for the superstar athletes that they was. They had one Black guy on the team. He was keeping up, and even a few times, he himself would nail the 50 foot drop finale.

I ain't pressure him for an autograph. Though I probably should've. Instead, I was happy he just let me shake his hand.

It was a water park, it wasn't a roller coaster park. So, I got off work at 8. When the park close, all the people had to leave. Me and a few other niggas that was groundskeepers, would go to the small stretch of food court. They had beer on tap. But they would lock the machines. I don't care. I was a social drinker anyway. I'on drink on the job.

Honeybuns locked up. Moist chocolate chip cookies locked up. Cinnamon rolls. I wanted some PIZZA!! That's all we could really get to. They never kept the pizza til the next day. Whatever, they ain't sell, they'd throw it away. Whole boxes and pies of PIZZA!!

America too spoiled.

Once they learned what we was doing, they tried to stop us from getting it. Even by rushing it into clear plastic trash bags and throwing it in the dumpster.

I almost DIED at Water Country.:

From time to time, they would be short on staff. They needed Ride Attendants. I get called to go up on like this BIG, TALL, HIGH ass slide. Besides The Wave Pool, and that big dumb ass 25 foot hardboard sliding board, this probably the second or third biggest attraction. Water never stops gushing out these rides.

The instructions are simple.:)

It's three buttons up at the top. It's three sliding boards. Two of each end slides, spiral you up at the top, and splash you out at the bottom. The middle, is just a regular tube slide. You sit in it, and it just squirts you down, straight into the water. Each slide lands you to a different direction of the pool. When you push the button, the light goes GREEN. The slider knows they can GO. Right.

Easy.

I can't push the button until the previous swimmer is clear up out the way. Now, of course it's a water park. For kids, a place for FUN! Kids love to do stuff that's FUN! The light is still RED. I didn't push it.

I see 'a kid look at me wit that lil seagull look in his eye, then "VROOOM!!" Kids start throwing themselves down all three slides left and right, all at the same time. One behind the other. I see all these lil white kids, and one lil black boy, skipping hands and feet all cross the water. They crashing all up into the previous swimmer's backs, and shit.

The lifeguard stand up out his chair, and he lookin up at me like, "WHAT THE FUCK!!??"

Shit, what I'm supposed to do? I ain't push the damn button.

I get back control of it. Now, they leave me

up there the whole rest of the day. Instead of me climbing down like a regular land lubber; it look like fun to me too. I wanna try my hand down a slide. I jump on the spiral slide. Once you let go, it's no coming back. I slide up, down, and shoot out the side.

My ass is FLYING through the air like, "Aaaaagghhh!!!!"

Then, zruurh!! Boonga!! Boonga!! Boonga!! BOOM!! I end up in the middle of the water.

'A LONG ASS WAY FROM GETTING THE FUCK UP OUT THE POOL.

It was something I forgot. I can't swim. I tried to put my feet to the bottom of the pool, and hop along the bottom, til I get to the wall. I start going down.

Down.

Down.

Down.

I keep going

Down.

My eyes open under water. I breathe in some water.

"Wrrrrugggghh!! Wrrrrugggghh!! Wrrrrugggghh!! Wrrrrugggghh!!" I'm struggling to get back up to the top.

It was something I didn't know.:

That this pool was 10 FEET DEEP. Not the 5 feet I was used to.

I'm punching. Kicking. I had a flash thought of my Uncle Bobby drowning on 16th Street. I'm fighting fo my life at the top of the water. Then, all of a sudden...

"Shrrrruggghh!" That's my best rendition of verbalizing the lifeguard blowing his whistle. The same lifeguard that got in to it wit me earlier, about the kids on the slide. He jumped in and swam me out to safety.

I made Water Country News; "Yeah, you the kid that almost drowned."

They put me back up to work the slide again, but I never shot back down. I had new respect for 10 feet water.

August 13th was Ericka's Birthday. She turned 16. And I missed it. On purpose.

I got ME 'a check!! Ha, ha, ha!!

I made $4.50 an hour. I got paid every two weeks. That's 80 hours in 2 weeks. My checks was $360.00. Even after taxes and social security, I still had about $300. I think it was like $298. But that's still more money than what I ever had at one time.

And the annual baptismal service was coming up. My momma had wanted to use my check, to go to Washington, DC.

Wit 'a paycheck, I had control. I had economic freedom. I had what they call... uhh... uhh... oh yeah! PURCHASING POWER!!

And I know, Ericka wanted me to buy her something sweet fo her 16th Birthday. And my momma wanna spend all my money in DC, but eh-heh... flip da script!

I'm gon BLOW this money on me. So I can go SHOPPING. I was in Mother's Record Store, buying rap tapes every two weeks. My senior year of high school is coming up too. Jeans fo school! Shirts fo school! Bookbag! Yes! Paper, pencils, pens, erasers. And...

SHOES...

I gotta get me some SHOES!!

When I was 4, I wore a size 4. When I was 5, I wore a size 5. When I was 6, I wore a size 6. When I was 7, I wore a size 7. When I was 8, I wore a size 8. When I was 9, I wore a size 9. When I was 10, I wore a size 10. When I was 11, I wore a size 11. When I was 12, I wore a size 12. And that's it. My feet stopped growing since I was 12.

The only real shoes I had in my WHOLE LIFE; well it was two.: a pair of penny loafers, and the pair of Adidas my Aunt Theresa bought for me back in 4th grade. Other than that, my momma bought me shoes out The Outlet. I had $13 all-white sneakers from Pic N Pay, or $9.99 all-black sneakers from Payless. In two weeks my big toe point straight up out them muthafuckas.

I was gon get me some SHOES!!

At the time Filas was in style, fo da niggas and da bitches. Bitches, bitches, bitches, bitches, bitches, bitches, BITCHES! They came in all flavors- - black, white, orange, red, blue, purple, yellow, pink, green. Gosh o' mighty. They came in high- tops. Low tops. And almost everybody had em in suede.

I didn't want mines in suede. And erry' body was rockin low- cuts. I didn't want to be exactly like them. I rather had my first pair of Jordans. But Jordans woulda broke the bank. Buying $70 Filas was way more affordable. $71 wit da tax.

"I'll take a size 12 black leather, please high-tops."

I was 'a lil too late to be FRESH!! "Hmm," that's my momma ain't like it. But that's what I was.

I bucked on her Birthday. I was fucked up over girls right now. And even though Ericka had broken up, she knew I was the best love for her. She was good peoples and her family was good peoples. We gradually started back talking.

She was still friends wit Kim. The girl I'd set Lynn up wit to date, while I was wit Ericka. And one day, he and Kane went around there. Kane was more advanced than me and Lynn. I didn't have a car or drive. Lynn drive but ain't gotta car. Kane drive and got his own 5.0 Mustang, wit the 5 star HUBCAPS. Aye! Erry' body can't buy da damn rims. Plus they look like rims from far away.

Anyway, after all that, me and Ericka was back talkin. At first, I ain't want Ericka back. I'm real frustrated. I still got some pin't up anger. And I ain't rock off last time. I'm thinkin bout just Grudge FUCKING!! this big assed bitch. But Ericka know me. I think she can see right through me. She won't jus gon let me hit it like that.

I meet up wit her at Kim's house. Ericka is a very very pretty girl. And damn! this bitch be looking real real good! Like most big girls, wit big butts! she's extremely sexually explosive. She made me get back wit her first.

"Yeah. Yeah. Alright. Alright..."

I walk her down, like 3- 4 blocks, to my Grandma's house,

"Hey, Grandma, this Ericka. Ericka this my Grandma..."

I take Ericka down in the shop. In Johnnie's old room. Johnnie long gone to California by now. Pernell and his family is too. Charles got parts of the family out on the West Coast with him by now. I'll get into all that later.

Right now... I'm getting into Ericka. I'm hitting this bitch in Johnnie's room. She makin noise. I can't even get to flippin it and hittin all this BIIIG RED ass up from the back. Cause I gotta keep covering her mouth.

"I can't help it." Here she go again.

276

But my Grandma don't come down there. This time Ericka ain't the only one that get to cum. After we finish, we straighten up our clothes, and leave out my Grandma house. But I hear it, when I get home.

Grandma told my momma what I did.

She prolly was mad I brought the same girl, who burnt me wit gonorrhea at my own house, up in her house. My Grandma never saw me the same again. She didn't say nothing. But she didn't have to. I could tell she'd lost a lot of respect for me. I'd defiled my momma's house and her house, both in the same spring and summer.

I monitored myself over the next 5 days to one week, after, I didn't see signs I was reinfected with gonorrhea-- it was o'va wit. I was cool wit being back wit Ericka.

I broke my fresh Filas in on the sidewalk at The Washington Monument. Why wait fo the first day of school?

"Hmm." That's my momma again. Looking me up and down. She not impressed.

She was mad I didn't have the whole check to go to DC. I already gave her 20. I pay her $20 every time I get paid. I was giving her allowance. But I was cool wit it, all my momma did for me since Seven Oaks. $20 the least I could do for the woman who kept me out 'a mouse mouth.

In DC all I had left was like $70. My Dad just said, "That's ok." And he paid most of the trip, as usual.

We still got the Econo Lodge. We still got the Washington Monument, Lincoln Memorial, all the live DEAD exhibits at The Smithsonian, and the rocket and plane fragments at the Air and Space Museum; and of course, the Baptizing Service itself.

This might be a BLESSED year after all.

Chapter 15.

When I get to 12th grade, I was set. The first time, I took myself school shopping, and I even got the cash to pay for my own senior pictures. When I get to class, there is the love of my life. Um... Joy... I mean to say, Joy is there.

I try to act normal.

I'm wit Ericka. Maybe.

Tara still chasing. At Da Ville, I got at least (2) lockers. I got a locker over on one side, for like morning classes, and I got another locker over by the auditorium, before I get to Vo- Tech. When I go to spin around, it's this mysterious dark skin girl. She keeps standing there. Staring at me. She never say nothing. She just standing there. Staring at me.

This shit happens like every week. At least once every week. We never speak to each other, even when I walk right past her in the halls.

One day, I had just finished leaving her; I'm walking down the hall, down by the gym. When this whole nother- other girl pop up out the blue. I'm walking, and she just walk straight up to me, she wouldn't let me pass around her;

"Hey. How you doin? My name is Kie- Kie..." (Pronounced Key- Key).

I already knew who she is. Who didn't.

Kie- Kie is this very popular girl around Menchville. In that she has a lot of friends, both males and females. Everybody in the school naturally loves Kie-Kie. I had no idea I was on her radar.

The one thing about Kie- Kie having a lot of friends, is she is always extremely happy in her HIGHEST social state; and that means she is LOUD!! Almost every time I see her, she is LOUD!! I'm not generally attracted to verbally LOUD!! women. It ain't like they gotta political, social, or radical reform message, or like they artist making music, naw, these just bitches hollering out making a whole buncha dumb ass noise.

But Ericka is like that. Typically, she is a quiet girl. Especially if you isolate her. But when she get all up round her homegirls and she gets EXCITED, that's when them bitches gon start gettin LOUD!! and making a whole buncha dumb ass stupid ass high- pitched noise!

But what trapped me about Kie- Kie, first, cause she is like one of the most popular girls in school. She won't on the level of a Tessa or a Quanette. I can't give her that. But based upon her popularity, she was like a local status symbol. That's one part about it.

The other part is.: is Kie- Kie got that fried caramel butta- pecan troppa- canana. In other words; that's what color she is.

She a big girl. But her upper body was kinda small. She ain't really have a big stomach. All her weight was from the waist down. She was built like how Ghetto Barbie is now. Kie- Kie just got more thicker legs, hips, thighs, and assss! DAMN! I done fucked around, and pulled the PHAAAATEST girl up in the school!!

Like, I say, she ain't really have a big stomach. She was BIG BONED from the waist down. But, I don't get into all that wit men. To me, I don't care if a woman got a small stomach, or a big stomach. The bottom line is.: a BIG BOOTY BITCH is a BIG BOOTY BITCH!! And Kie- Kie was 'a BIIIIG BOOOTY BITCH!! The PHAAAATEST bitch up in Da Ville.

So, I'm jus gon speed this story up, cause it's plenty of overlapping parts. I go to her house. We do a senior skip day, at her house. One of her friends; Trice is there. Trice is the ideal red bitch. If you wanna red bitch, you want Trice. She had thick ass lips, and 'a ass phat like Salt. I wanted to fuck Trice.

Couldn't get to her.

Her boyfriend, Rodney, is here. He ain't never letting up off that bitch. I'on blame him. Trice was tough. Rodney has 'a car, so the two of them always rolled together. He looked like he could be 'a dope boy. He had real cool, very smooth D- boy swag. But if he was or not, I'on know. I ain't never ask em.

Then, it was Kie- Kie. I wasn't there for Trice. I was there for Kie- Kie.

It was some other people in the living room. But

soon as I get there, Kie- Kie take me in the room. I'on know what's up wit bitches watching tv. But that's what we was doing. We watched tv, then we watched the whole damn Jerry Springer. That shit went off.

We get to kissing. Playing around. I end up getting her pants and panties off. I hadda rubba. Me and Ericka ain't use rubbers.

I don't make the choice when not to use rubbers, or to stop using rubbers, and start having unprotected sex. I always let the female make that decision. We get to that level when she ready.

So, I had a fo Kie- Kie.

We do a little 4- play stuff, but this girl is RACING!! my mind crazy. Kie- Kie didn't know I hadda sexual addiction to fuckin big girls wit real big butts!!!!

Music.: "I needa BIG BOOTY BITCH/ 'a BIG BOOTY HOE/ 'a bitch witta booty dat's BIGGER dan 'a do'."

Damn, right. 'A bitch witta booty so BIIIIG!! she gotta turn sideways jus to get thru the do'.

Damn Right!

      'A bitch witta booty so BIIIIG, she can break'a toilet seat!! She make 'a nigga gotta go out, and spend $200- $300, just on 'a toilet seat, to hold her BIG ASS up! That's when you know, you fuckin 'a Real BIIIIG BOOOOTY BITCH!!!!

Damn right! You need'a bitch that can hold you

From Poverty, To Prison, To Prosperity.

down, when you doin 'a hu'ned miles in 'a hurricane.

Kie- Kie was PHAAAATER than Ericka. I'm tryin to get this dick up in 'er.

When, I get up in her, a coupla times. She start makin that noise, I like. Then she said, "Stop."

I'm like, 'What!??'

I ain't even get to eating this pussy real good, or nothing. I ain't get to the whip cream and syrup. I ain't even get to sopping all this Great BIIIIG JUICCCCCY ASSSS up, like'a piece 'a candy. Nothing.

I ain't even finished stretching out yet. I guess she was used to fuckin 6 inch niggas or something. I'on know. But she said, Stop.

What can I do?

She say, Stop. I gotta Stop. I gotta get up offa her. I'm not gon lay here and rape the bitch.

It's over.

I didn't have the patience. Maybe it's my fault. I ain't have the mouthpiece to talk to pussy back then. I wasn't verbal. I was just physical. A woman just had to find out the hard way; on her own, that 'a nigga Black, but muscled up like 'a bright red Ferrari. And that 'a BIG DICK NIGGA needa BIG BOOTY BITCH!! That's how this shit supposed to roll. I was ready to BUST!! all that BIIIIG shit up!! Break all that ASSSSSS up in half!!

Damn right! Crumble dat cookie.

You can't say you wanna fuck. Then bring me some weak ass pussy game. You wanna give me some pussy, you gotta be on toppa yo game. You tryin to tap me out; shit, this shit, 'a competition. I'm gon tap yo ass out first.

Kie- Kie brought me 'a weak ass pussy game. I balled that shit up. She drove me to Dwight's house, I got out the car. That's it.

IT WAS OVER! It ain't no going back.

Me and Kie- Kie never had no public relationship. A lot of people would probably be surprised that we was ever even together, to began with. I was never with her, up round her great big circle of friends. But until then, I did consider her My girl. And she did use to ask me, "How was it?" So this my first time, detail explaining it.

Al- right, moving along...

Um... let's talk about this Tara.:) Tara chased me from 10th grade, all the way to senior year. I finally got tired of stalling her; I wanted to fuck her. But I won't ready to fuck her. If that makes any sense.

Tara was phat. She looked real soft. But it was too much that come wit that... I couldn't be her boyfriend.

I couldn't let that get back to Joy.

So, I figure in my mind, I'll keep Tara close. I'll

basically bring her in my circle. Keep her close.

I introduce her to Lynn. She meet Lynn. Lynn don't gotta car, but Lynn borrows his Aunt Wanda's Sonata, or her boyfriend Larry's Chysler Lebaron. Next thing I know, Lynn driving up to Da Ville, pickin Tara up at school.

He was just supposed to be fuckin her. Keeping her close. I was bringin round 'a sexy booty bitch, that both of us could fuck. That way I can keep Tara from falling in love and keep her from wanting to make me her boyfriend. That way I could keep the sexual relationship between me and Tara a secret from Joy. That's how this shit supposed to go.

That's not what happen.

This nigga done fucked around and fell in love wit the girl. Made her his girl. But I ain't really surprised. For real, I was doing my friend a favor by hooking him up with Tara. Lynn is my dawg, but Lynn has very bad taste in women. Not that the girls he likes are not nice. But that's it. I knew Tara was his speed. She cool, but she won't all that in that in the face. That won't good enough for me. But for real.: Tara was an Upgrade for Lynn. She was better than any of the girls I seen Lynn fucking.

I was conscious of.: I couldn't bring just any girl around my homies, and be like, "This is my girl."

Naw. I don't care how phat a girl is, nothing. It's more to it than that. I had to have THE BADDEST BITCH outta all my friends. PERIOD. If my girl ain't better than yo girl, then you'll never see her. I won't bring her around my homies.

I wanna have the bitch that ALL my homies wish they can fuck. That's my secret competition.

If you in my circle, and you just pullin any girl out, just cause she let you fuck- - I'm gon pull out a girl that's TTL- - TOP of THE LINE. She gon shut down every bitch in yo line- up. And, even if you catch on, and start spitting out Top of The Line Bitches. I'm still CRUSH you; and I'm gon start showing you what TTP- - what "The Total Package" look like. And she gon shut down everything, you THOUGHT, was Top of The Line.

A lotta niggas wanted to fuck Ericka. A lotta my homies wanted to fuck Ericka. She just didn't have no discipline being up around them. She broke at Kane.

Once, other niggas know yo bitch can be fucked; that's it. Competition over. You ain't winning when yo girl caving in. So Ericka couldn't count. I had to start over.

Another reason I couldn't go at Joy, is cause I was too distracted. I don't even know how this one started. But I know it ended wit me on her living room couch.

Her name was Lynette. Lil short. Like five-five. Five- six. Lynette was RED, THICCCKK, and PHAAAT to death. Lynette is extremely pretty. She has absolutely no physical flaws. Lynette is a masterpiece. She is very very sweet. For real she is wifey material. She is the girl you should marry, have all yo babies by, and be good. Real good. Fo all eternity.

I spent time wit her after school, at her house. But we never had sex. It's my fault. It's one- hundred percent my fault. Her mother and her younger brothers and sisters was always home, when we was home.

Lynette is not the girl for you just to have sex with. I was supposed to invite Lynette out with me, to go to church. On a church date. She is bad enough. Lynette is TTP.

Is she more juiccccy than Tashia? If that's what you're asking. Lynette is worth her weight in diamonds and gold.

If I woulda took Lynette to church- -

I'll just say, it was grown women that wasn't touching that girl's body. Not only could I have took her to Newport News; I coulda took her out to Hampton.

Mostly the older saints went to the Newport News church. The cool kids, girls my age, and younger people went to hear Bishop Elder Jehu Riddick preach out Hampton.

It was only two girls I paid attention to in Hampton, or in the whole church, period. There was a girl named Marsha. Marsha was a beautiful girl. She is light brown skin and thin. She doesn't have any body fat, but she is very attractive. And yes, she is "saved," and sings background in the choir.

I never went at Marsha, because I never dated no girl at church. It's a very strict dating culture inside the Church of God. If I had asked Marsha out "on a date." We would've been out on the date with adult chaperones. Probably her mother. My mother. Or both.

It wouldn't be no sex involved. We'll just be sittin up there looking at each other, sippin soda, til we get grown and PRAYERFULLY get married. I'een have to worry bout none of that wit these secular girls. My momma won't down on me around none of them.

Marsha looked good, but if I would of showed them Lynette... which I do regret, because if I did, she very easily woulda BLEW OUT every girl up in Hampton. She woulda blew out grown men wives sitting up in the pew and the pulpit. That bitch was BAD!

The crazy thing is, out Paula Maria, I had wanted Chrystal. And God sent me a Chrystal, when HE sent me Lynette. HE sent me "a Crystal" that was in to me. I was just to young, blind, and dumb to see it for what it was. But for real, I never committed to a relationship wit Lynette, cause if I did, I knew I would've married her. HANDS DOWN. I would've proposed to her right after high school. It was just that ONE girl standing in her way.

Now, I gotta get through this other part.: Once Upon A Time it was this girl named Chocolate. No, seriously, that was her name. Cause like I told you, it's overlapping parts.

I had this "Dr Martin Luther King Speech Reader" thing tattooed, plastered; something, all over my forehead, ever since I like learned how to read. All the way back since the 5th grade. And it didn't leave me. Not even in high school. Not even 6 grades later. All the way in the 11th grade.

My English Teacher said to me one day after class, "You should sign up for the Debate Team."

To make a long story go quick- - I did.

Now, let's get to the long story.:

They take us on the bus for our first debate at some high school, all the way out in the wilderness of Chesapeake. Another neighboring city in the Hampton Roads area of Virginia. It's like a 30- 40 minute drive out from Newport News. I say "wilderness," cause I'on know where the hell I was. And it wassa whole lotta trees. The school was big as Menchville. The debate teacher said he didn't want me to debate, he just wanted me to sit and listen.

So that's what I did.

The debate wasn't Menchville versus this Chesapeake school. It was debate students from over the whole area.

When I get out to the hall, I see this black girl keep pacing, and looking at me. We the only two black kids here. It's maybe a few Asians. Everybody else WHITE. So I think that's why we gravitated towards each other.

I'on say nothing at first.

The game changed when we went on break. They gave us a lunch break, out to Pizza Hut. When I get off the bus to Pizza Hut, I'm just standing beside the juke box. Cause I'm broke. Not 'a penny in my pocket. There she is. Glancing me over again.

She walk over.

She walking like she gon walk right past me. Then she just cut right up to my face, "Hi. I'm Tatanashe. But you can call me "CHOCOLATE."

Hah, this'a Chocolate, that ain't even 'a stripper. Our first day became Our First Date. She shared with me her piping hot pie of pepperoni pizza, and her soda. And yes, from that day, me and Chocolate was friends.

Kissin and friends.

My coach told me to observe the debates. So that's what I did. I observed The Chocolate Debates. When she talk, she speaks very clear and articulate. But she still got that lil hood hook to her, when she need it.

Chocolate is a very smart girl. That's not just complimenting her. She actually is very intelligent. And that's what I grew to be sexually attracted to; a Black woman who could be powerful, prolific, and potentially poetically romantic.

That's why I like talking to her; on the phone, and especially in- person, cause she a girl that can hold a conversation. I found all that to be real sexy about

Ms. Chocolate. I would listen to her talk.

We was the same age.

She was originally from Denver in Colorado. This was the absolute first time, I had ever met and talked to anybody that was from Colorado. She was a Die- Hard football fan of the Denver Broncos. That was definitely her team; when they never won one Super Bowl.

She told me she was from a military family. Well, she was being raised by her mother. Her mother was in the active duty Air Force, that's how she ended up going to Hampton High School, here in Virginia.

Yes, them damn Crabbers.

Something else, I had to put up wit talkin to Chocolate.

"YOU CAN'T CRUSH'A CRAB!!" I had to put up with keep hearing her scream out that dumb ass shit, all LOUD!! at the toppa her lungs. Chocolate was enormously team spirited.

Hampton had won SO MANY championships, everybody from out our area, who didn't go to Hampton-- hated Hampton. During this time though, Hampton won't winning rings in football and basketball, because Bubba Chuck, who you call AI or Allen Iverson, was killing them at Bethel. Another local area high school, that was in Hampton. He was disrupting they domination.

But, I never consider Chocolate my girl. We was

just Real good friends. Kissin friends. We did ALOT of kissing. Our relationship with each other started in our Junior years in high school, and crossed over into our Senior year. I tried her. But she never gave me no booty. She might'a been a virgin, but I'on know. She never said for sure.

I was getting all this past Ericka. She ain't need to know all this stuff. But at the same time, we had a thriving boyfriend/ girlfriend...

Yeah, right.

After we got back together, we went from fuckin once a month. To twice a month. To...

I would go to Ericka's house, and she would be cooking dinner for her family. She would call her Grandma, and Grandma would straddle 'on downstairs and go to the table. Before they say grace, Ms. Florence would look back at me and say, "Boy, you want something to eat?"

"Boy" was her nickname for me. She ain't mean no harm by it. If she ain't like me, she wouldn't even let me in her house, and date her granddaughter.

"Naw, I'm good," I'd holla back from the living room. I'd be trying to have etiquette, cause my momma taught me not to wear out my welcome.

And Ericka would walk over to me and say, "Go on, get you somethin ta eat... Cause you gon need it."

I'll get up, go to the table. Ericka done cooked fresh

fried fish, greens, mash potatoes and gravy, corn-on- the- cob. After Ms. Florence and Ericka's family finish eating, they all go back upstairs. They usually don't come back down. I'll go watch tv, until Ericka finish washing dishes. After she finish washing them dishes...

I was slidin her ass cross the living room floor; like I was paying the rent!

We had went to having sex Every time we see each other. We developed a certain chemistry. It clicked! We didn't even have to talk. Erry time we see each other; you already know what it is. Compared to Ericka, these other girls was slowwww. As far as having sex goes. I didn't have to... bring Ericka up to speed. She already there.

That's why I won't absolutely hungry about having sex with Chocolate, with Tara, with Lynette, any other girl, or even talking to Joy. Chocolate was named like 'a strippa, but that bitch won't strippin!

Ericka was 16. She was a year younger than all us. Younger than Chocolate, than Lynette, Tara, Joy... But Ericka was the girl who can MATCH or EXCEED all my sexual needs.

This girl was 16 telling me, "I want 'a room."

So Hey! She say she wanna room?? Shiiittt, Daddy gon go get my Baby 'a room. I'll go do some work wit Lucky, come back home wit 'a lil doe. I meet Ericka up at the bus stop, at Patrick Henry Mall, and we go shopping. At Spencer's. It's supposed to be an adult toy store. But who knows. They let high school kids up in there. Almost everything is high as hell. They want top dollar on everything. Except for

these cute lil white bottles of motion lotion. They generic fo real. But that's cool. That mean I can buy it!

They come in all these cute lil colors.: apple, grape, strawberry, I think it was black cherry... shit like that. I let Ericka pick out the one she want, and I pay for it. We either walk or catch the bus down to Hey! The Econo Lodge.

But this one was in Newport News; not Washington DC.

When I get to the front desk; they don't ID me or nothing. I just put the money down. I used to tell them,

"One bed. Two people."

They was charging me like $39.99. Like $40/ $41 something wit tax. Then I caught on. I start sayin,

"One bed. One person."

Then I noticed they started charging me like $5 less. And I would bring her in.

So, I was fuckin Ericka for Free.

-Or-

She was fuckin me fo Free.

However you wanna look at it.

I would order us pizza. We can get a grape, strawberry, or cola 3 liter soda at Food Lion, across the street. The hotel had cups and ice. And when we get back in the room, she'll go take her shower, and when she come out, she got on a smalled tight teddy- lingerie. She'll be glowing there in this dim light. Everything all phaat, juiccccy, mushing, and squishing together; all before I ever even get there.

But Aye! Daddy gon do the rest!

Hah, who need tha otha girls!? Ericka was skinning the hair on da ram!! ALL NIGHT!!!! And in the morning when we wake up before 11. Ericka was poppin pussy like 'a cheese factory!

And a lotta niggas ain't like that. Shawn Talley tried to fight me for her. Shit, what the hell I'm gon fight fo? I was already gettin the pussy. But like I said, a lotta niggas wanted to fuck Ericka. She was 'a fat girl. But that won't no flaw. That bitch was fat and PHAAAT!!!!! That shit just mean, all that shit was thicccckkkk, juiccccy, and EXXXTRA creamy. Ericka is beautiful. She is pretty. Sexy. And she RED!!

The bitch is 'a WINNER!! In her own rite.

Alright y'all, I'll get to more Ericka shit later on. I'll just say, she definitely was better than any thing any of my homies was fuckin. JJ, won't really my homie; he was friends wit Mike D, one of Lynn's cousins. But JJ did have 'a girl named Jessica, who lived on the same block. She's not just beautiful, she is sexually attractive. But she has the raw potential to be THE BADDEST BITCH IN THE WORLD.

She got the bold ideal color of Black. Not too light. Not too dark. Her body is tall and postured, and gorgeously in shape. No body fat in her waist, but she curves in her booty and hips. Just the right place. In the right hands, Jessica can be an icon fashion model. She can be on the covers of all your magazines, hearts, dreams, and imagination.

Fortunately enough for me; JJ don't know that. Aye! She was in there, just sittin on the couch.

Then BJ; he lived up on like 18th Street. But he used to be around 13th Street, like me. He is another friend of Mike D. You not gon believe this-- he started fucking Crystal. Yes, the Real Crystal.

And I'on know how this shit supposed to work-- two light skin people together. She light skin, and he 'a lighter light skin than she is. I didn't see this coming, when we all went to Warwick. But the two of them got together. She ain't give Paula Maria niggas no pussy, but here she is; she gave BJ some pussy.

She gave BJ her virginity.

And even though, Crystal is very nice, sweet-- this was a girl that was HANDS DOWN TTL, or arguably coulda even been "The Total Package." But once she started fuckin wit BJ, her body started losing weight. Her skin started to break out in blemishes. In other words.: she fell off.

I was shocked to see, she didn't even look healthy no more.
Warwick Mobile Homes was a good neighborhood

to grow up in and to be nurtured. It's where my bond, my love and respect started to rekindle between me and my father. My father had got into the scrap metal hustle, as his means to support our family and put food on the table.

I'll see him in the sideyard hacksawin up a used up light, just to pinch out a piece of copper. He would bust down parts and transmissions mostly for aluminum, copper, and iron; sometimes steel.

"Watch yo back. Alright, you ready? One, two, three..." he'd say to me, as I helped him load up the ol Ford.

And we ride the Merrimack Bridge Tunnel, all the way over to a salvage yard that was in Suffolk. The Suffolk city of Virginia. My father loved to come here cause he say,

"They pay the best prices."

It is boasted that they are The Largest Scrap Yard ON THE EAST COAST. I wouldn't know. I ain't never been to EVERY Scrap Yard ON THE EAST COAST. But I been to this one. To me, it's not that large.

When you first roll through the security gate, they got piles and piles of used to be cars, banged down and stacked up to the heavens. Well, not that high, but it's taller than the 25 foot fence they got strapping the property. The cars are just off to the left.

And you'll notice a lot of yellow cranes over the yard. Real tall yellow cranes, as high as a light pole. Some of the cranes are yellow mobile trucks.

But all these cranes have very huge, and very strong- powerful magnets attached to them. And it's warning signs posted, and they'll tell you, not to never get up under those magnets. When you look cross the field, you might see a magnet laying face down in the ground, on broken cables.

After you get through the gate, and when you drive their path straight, it's a scale. It's a huge square or rectangle square, and you drive over top of it. You can feel it tremble and vibrate, because it's manufactured ground.

And there's generally always a black man that works in the tinted glass booth. But you can see his silhouette. And you see his hand signaling, telling you to go on head.

And my father tap on the clutch, hit his little 3- speed gear shifter out of first, into neutral, back into first, and rev his vintage American engine, just up cross the line. The front and cab of the truck, has to be off the scale. The only part they weigh is the bed of the truck.

Oh, this is after my father pull off his buckets of copper and aluminum. They weigh those on a smaller scale, inside. Add everything up, and that's how they know how much to pay.

We always swing around to the right side of the yard. The right side of the yard, is basically, lot yards of dirt, littered with scattered parts and piles of junk. It's muddy when it rains.

When I first jump out the truck, you're not

298

supposed go up under these magnets. I know. I know. If that magnet drops anything, or if it itself falls and breaks, it can easily kill a man. Or if you got on any metal, it might suck you up in the magnet. So I just got to stand at a safe distance, AS CLOSE AS I CAN.

BOOM!! And there it is. This magnet can tug up BUNDLES of TONS of heavy pounds of engines, transmissions, cars, any kind of metal you can throw at it, the neck of this crane would swoop down, and it's mouth will just gobble it all up like a dinosaur going out to lunch, man. It's awesome!

The side we was on, had less stationary cranes. A mobile crane had to come meet us at the truck.

"Get back! Get back!" my father liked to warn.

It was a black guy behind the wheel, he'd come whippin the crane round the curve, like he was pushin 'a long- stretched Cadillac. The hard hat crunched into his fro and he chillin.

He'd shoot the magnet down to the bed of the truck. I'on know how much PSI this thing could handle, but I seen this thing throw cases of engines and transmission blocks from off the back of my fathers truck. And I think,

'Man, we need one 'a these things back at house.'

All them minutes we wasted on pulling and lifting, and here it was; how easy this machine could just reach down, and pry out all these deceased carcasses, all at one time. Herald like 'a bodybuilder's bicep.

My father was a make believe do- it-yourself guy. When wanted to save money on 'a Earl Scheib paint job, he'll just hand paint his cars himself, wit a paint brush and some latex paint. Just like the red his Ford was painted, wit a streak of gold across the vent of the hood. All the way down to the wooden rails, he'd hand drilled, screwed, and hammered down into the six holes in the top part of the bed of the truck.

Sometimes, the magnet couldn't get all the way down, cause my father's homemade rails be in the way, between the magnet and the metal. He didn't want the magnet to do the same thing to my daddy's truck, that I was doin to his trailer, when I was hittin HARD!! up inside Ericka. Break all this shit to popsicle sticks!

The man on the truck would adjust the gravitational pull on the magnet. My dad'd truck came to life, like it had a soul, you could still see the truck rocking and rattling; wiggling and shaking. Pinning down it's rubber, on all fours, with all his might, to grip hold of the dust on the ground. This old pick-up was truly worth it's weight of being Ford TOUGH!! It was scrapping like a dog up against this magnet.

But the magnet was mightier. Sometimes this magnet would literally rip my father's truck from it's feet, up off the ground.

WOW!!!!

And I'd see my father's Ford suspended in the air, still wit all the pounds of junk lugged to his back.

DAMNNNN!!!!

The driver would carefully sit my father's truck back down. Cause fo 'a second, I thought me and pops was gon be footin it back to the crib. He would have to readjust the gravitational pull on his magnet. He would lower it; not drop it all the way down, and the magnet could pull up the engines and heaviest pieces of iron and steel, like sippin from a straw.

It's a good thing, this was a 70s Ford pick-up, and not one of the new model trucks. You know these new trucks all computerized. They operate on computer systems. That circuit board hit that magnet; that shit be done knocked all the fuel injection and tune- up oil up out that muthafucka.

Before I go, I gotta go see one'a these cars get crunched up..:

They have a machine that is on the left side of the yard. It hunkers like 'a bully, to the side of the gate. To trap all the cars inside the fence. It lays flat and keeps quiet.

But when he gets to running his mouth, "Yyrrrrrrrrrrrrrr." YOU BETTER WATCH OUT!

The top of his tummy is a black wide conveyer belt. Everything else is YELLOW. That's the last thing these poor unfortunate automobiles, that the insurance company deemed "a total rec" gon see. This the euthanizer to all you bitch ass cars!

The car would roll along the tummy of the conveyer belt. The machine stop him half way. Then...

"WRROOOMM!!" The Executioner throws down his metal mallet.

And it's o'va wit!

Particles of glass go EVERYWHERE! The windshield, windows, rear view/ side view mirrors- - all that shit.: GONE!! The top of the hood be smashed down below the dashboard.

And when you see the top of the tires curl and tuck up under the fenders, and the bottom of the tires snap all the way out- -

YOOOOOOOOO!! THIS IS THE COOLEST SHIT EVERRRRRRR!!!!!!!

They say, "One man's trash is another man's treasure."

It's like I had stepped foot inside a Live TONKA yard. It was incredible! To all the men and women who work this Suffolk- Chesapeake scrap yard, when you get off work tonight- - knock you back an Iced Cold Beer. Cause you got the greatest job EVER!!

When we get ready to leave the scrap yard, my father would park the truck and race in to get 'a fortune! No! But it felt good to say that. The experience was priceless.

After we leave the scrap yard, my father 'a fat boy; so of course, the first thing he do wit his cold hard cash, is go buy some food to eat. He always go to Hardee's. A hot Hardee's Roast Beef. Why not? My father didn't pay me in money. But I didn't care about that. It's amazing how God used a salvage yard to repair a splintering relationship between a father and a son.

He paid me by feeding me, keeping a roof over my head, paying the water, gas, and light bill. Things like that.

The love of having a father and having him in my life, was worth more than all the metal in the scrap yard.

When my father wasn't doing engines, transmissions, washed up lamps, and other worn-out pieces, he expanded his hustle. He would scrap mobile homes. He would do it on his own. But the landlord who owned the park, his lot was right behind our trailer.

Sometimes he would employ my father to clear off a lot. He would take me with him. The electrical and gas lines would be disconnected. I put on a hat and a mask. And my father would hand me a fiber glass handled axe. And we would go as a father- son team, and dismantle this trailer from the ceiling, all the way down to the iron axle.

We throw away all fiber glass insulation, windows, wood, and paneling. We'd scrap the aluminum or tin. My father would cut out and burn all the electric wires and cords in a barrel, to get it to the copper. My father is a cook and a welder by trade. So he'll get or rent a torch, and chop the frame down to pieces that can go on the truck. Then we'd take it over Suffolk and salvage it.

We'd pile up all the trash, transport it to the city's landfill. Rake and sweep up the lot; and that's it. The job's complete.

My father has bad shopping habits. Bad as in- - it's not good. His idea of grocery shopping is to buy Cookies. He like regular cookies. He like duplex, chocolate chip, and knock- off Oreos. But his best cookies, is Fig Newton's. I think he like it for more than they sweet chewy fruit they stuff inside. He buy regular cookies for me and Fig Newton's for himself.

One thing about it.: he know he better hide them Fig Newton's somewhere up in his bedroom. Cause if they hit that kitchen-- it's fair game!

And my father love to buy eggs. He won't jus scramble his eggs like regular black people. He want his egg in 'a omelet or fold over easy.. Then he do the nastiest shit ever! He pour ketchup on top of his eggs and eat it.

"UUUGGGHH!!"

No way I can stand here and take this shit. I gotta leave the room or leave the house.

It's crazy we had to buy eggs, since we had chickens out in the yard. My dad had bought chicks from a chick and feed store over off Big Bethel Road. Out Hampton. He was always doing something.

When I was small, it was Rabbits. My father used to raise rabbits in the backyard on 16th Street. The rabbits will break out the cage. And my momma and best momma be chasing my daddy's rabbits all round the yard.

He had one mean rabbit. This rabbit ain't like nobody. He was black and furry, wit crucible red eyes. If you think you gon eat him; he look more like he gon eat you!

I would be terrified of him. Cause he always tried to bite me. He won't nice, like the rest of the rabbits. I used could rub and pet the other bunnies, like 'a puppy. My father used to keep the mean rabbit in his own cage. It was good he never broke out; prolly woulda jus had to let him go get-a- way. One day my father finally went on head and killed him. Umm. He made'a good piece'a meat on my plate.

It was hard to believe he was gone, and we was sittin there eatin him.

Now, my father was doing the same thing wit chickens. Except these chickens su'pose to lay eggs. They can't even get to it.

Cause they all start out as chicks when he first get em. Then they start growing up. Then one morning, you hear.:

That's the rooster cock- a- doo- doo-doodeling.

They not supposed to be doing this shit, until the sun come up. But I think they timing is off. Cause they be,

"UR- URR- UR- URR- UR- URR- URRRRRR!!" at like 4 in the morning.

Maybe, the sun came up in his own lil bird head, or he gotta bright idea. I'on know.

All I know, it ain't bother me. But Mickey's wife don't like it. That's the next door neighbor's wife. She would complain, that the rooster was waking her up.

So my father gotta get up, go out there, snatch him out the cage, wring him by his neck, and chop off his head with a small sharp hand axe. Over a chopped off piece of tree.

Soon as he think that's over...

"UR- URR- UR- URR- UR- URR- URRRRRR!!" 2- 3 more of them fine feathered bastards done sprung up. Now, he gotta do the same thing to them, he did to the first one, cause Mickey's wife still be cryin.

My father would bring the birds into my mother. And she'd clean and pluck them under water in the kitchen sink.

My momma from Newport News, but I think she wassa country girl, on the low. She knew how to gut the chicken, and to get out the- - what!? I guess you call it gizzards. My father used to eat that. She would take off his feet. And other than buying my momma 'a house, the best thing my daddy ever did for my momma, was when he bought her a Crock Pot.

The Crock Pot is a slow cooker. My momma plop them birds into the Crock Pot, and we come back hours later- - UMMM! UMMM!

The meat fall right up off the bone! Juicy pieces of chicken just melt right in yo mouth. That's how we do it in da souf!

Don't feed into that. I'm jus trippin.

And my father love to eat hogmongs, chitlins, and pig's feet. My momma wouldn't let me eat it. She'd clean it and cook it for him.

It was only like (4) black families out this whole big trailer park. I probably knew all of them. My friend Shawn. He was an only child like me. Then it was another guy who went to Menchville wit us. I'on remember his name, but the basketball court was over near his house, and he would see me out his window, and he'll come out and shoot the ball. He was cool. And it was another Miles. But he moved. And when we was standing out there, dislodging his trailer. He kept on,

"Do you know Lil Kenny, he um, he Big Nikki son?"

"Naw," my father said to him.

"Do you know Jeannie and her brother Thomas, that's momma's cousin."

"Naw."

"Bobby... Bobby Miles... Oh yeah, I know him. He um..."

"Naw. That's not him."

So that was that. This all drew to a futile stalemate. Ain't nobody know nobody. We was all Miles, but we won't related.

But we did learn one thing.: "all Miles work hard." Amen to that.

There was a lot of mobile homes that touted the Confederate flag. One home, had the whole damn flagpole looming in his yard. But I only encountered racism one time being out there.:

I think Eazy- E is one 'a the coolest niggas ever. And I'm a fan of NWA and West Coast rap music. So, I like to wear a lot of black. Don't really know why. I just do. T- Bone, that's my dawg. I take my dog for a walk.

Black kid. Dressed in all black. Walking a Black Dog. Holding a Black Baseball Bat. In a white trailer park.

The baseball bat was a souvenir Orioles autopen signature bat, commemorating their 1983 World Series Championship. I got it from my Uncle Ike, back when he use to live in B- more, before he moved to Richmond. It used to be in plastic. Now... it was in my hand. Across my shoulder.

Warwick Mobile Homes has a lot of dogs. Almost

every trailer has at least one dog. And it's a lot of loose dogs, that break the chain, jump the fence, etc. Even T- Bone done broke his chain and got loose before, and my Daddy got to bail him out from the dog catcher.

So I got the bat. Not just to protect me, but also to save him, if a more dangerous dog, jump out to get after him. And it was on our way COMING BACK to the house. And on our same street. We on the corner of Troy Drive, beside the phone, they towards the opposite end, but near the middle.

I'm walking T- Bone. And here they go running,

"ROO- ROO- ROO- ROO- ROO- ROO- ROO!!" towards the front of the fence. It's not one. But two pit bulls. They 'a pretty golden brown and white, and off the chain. Neither of them got chains on. And the gate is low. These two pit bulls are running through the yard and from off the front porch, hauling at high speed.

It looked to me that these two pit bulls was bout TO JUMP this little ass gate, and come after me and T-Bone.

I reacted by swinging the bat, but I'm in the street, the dogs are in the yard. All of a sudden, I hear this weak feminine voice saying,

"Don't you (yuh- yuh- yuh- yuh- yuh- yuh- yuh)." One of the dog's owners was barking.

So, I don't say shit. I ignore the bitch, and keep walking home. I put T- Bone up. Feed him. Go in the house. Next thing I know,

"Boom, boom, boom, Boom!!"

It's 'a white man at the door.

He come in, "Your son got a baseball bat, and he's swinging it, and he's threatening my two dogs and my old lady..."

I'm explaining to him what happened. He ain't trying to hear it. He look at my parents and keep flashing back at me. You can see Mississippi burning in his eyes.

After he finish his spill of threat, intimidation, and fear, I'on know what he think supposed to happen. My parents ain't beatin me with the belt no more. My parents ain't the police or Ku Klux Klan members.

What's supposed to happen?

After he left, my father just looked at me and said, "Jamie, be careful."

I know what he meant. But this ain't the 1960s no mo. Dr King had died in 1968. And Public Enemy, Ice Cube, and Eazy- E was the head of the Post- Civil Rights Movement, not Al Sharpton and Jesse Jackson.

I ain't afraid of these ghosts.

But after that, I would check over T- Bone and the yard when I come home, but nothing more came out of it.

Chapter 16.

I saw racism, two times at Vo- Tech. I took Carpentry 1 my first year at New Horizons. Which was my 11th grade year. New Horizons doesn't just foster school and training to Newport News students, but to various students over surrounding cities and counties. Which means Black city kids gotta go to school wit white kids from Ku Klux Klan County.

Me and Julian was the only (2) Black students in the class. Ju- Jish was always into something. I'll jus say that. Anyway, he gets into it one day with one of the white guys, from Tabb County, that was in the class. The white guy gets mad at Ju- Jish keep fuckin wit him and out it comes,

"You fuckin NIGGER!"

I don't remember his first name. I just remember his last name was Burton. Cause that's what Mr. Padgett keeps callin him. But now, Mr. Padgett ain't in there. Man, Ju- Jish grabbed the pneumatic nail gun. Cut the gas on the compressor. He held that bitch back like it was 'a firing pin. Nails come poppin out that bitch,

"Thu, thu, thu, thu, thu, thu, thu, thu, thu,"

Ju- Jish don turned the nail gun to 'a fuckin Uzi!!

I heard Burton holler out, "Ahh! Ahh! Ahh! Ahh!!"

SHOTS FIRED!! That's when I knew them nails was poppin his ass!

Every time I see that scene from 12 Years A Slave, when the white slave master was talkin all that shit, but when the Black man got the whip, and start beatin his back. And the white man be,

"Ahh! Ahh! Ahh! Ahh!!" screamin and scramblin to get away. He remind me of Burton that day.

The only thing that stopped Julian, was one of the nails flew through his finger. He had to go pull it out and bandage his hand. After that Burton started apologizing,

"Man I'm sorry. I'm sorry. Ok. I won't say it again."

Pay attention to what he just said, he say, "I won't "SAY" it again." But that don't mean, it's still not in his heart. His mouth just reveal what his mind suppress.

Just because we don't HEAR him "SAY" it, he still got ways to show that he hasn't negated how he really feels. Where you think all these political lobbyist come from? They the ones wit the most money since slavery. The world's richest man is a white man. The richest white man in the world, and

312

the richest man in America, is the same person. He don't gotta run for President. All he got to do is pump $50 million dollars at the man he want to be President.

And all that racist legislation gets passed right cross the desk. And you'll never HEAR him call you a NIGGER! not one time.

You better pay attention.

It ain't just the world's richest man; but the 2nd, 3rd, 4th, 5th, 6th, 7th, 8th, 9th, 10th... and 9 times out of 10, they all right here in America. The nectar of Capitalism.

You got white people that's rich, but don't got no fame. You'll walk right past them, and not realize what you looking at. Whites who have inherited generational wealth; all the way since slavery.

Racism is not always blatant as you HEARING a white person calling you a, "NIGGER!" Most racism will be passive.

I experienced that at New Horizons. Although, Mr. Padgett was a nice man, he catered more to the white students, than what he did to me and Ju- Jish. It's like he saw these white boys more like... they was his sons.

Especially with Scott.

These white students caught on and could do the work faster. But a lot of that was embedded from how they was raised. They started out as kids,

313

doing building projects and stripping down cars and engines, and all that shit, in the yard with their father and uncles.

That's not the background me and Ju- Jish came from. I came from 16th Street, 30th Street, Paula Maria. Ju- Jish came from... Stuart Gardens. Some Apartments down on Garden Drive.

Even though we didn't have these developmental advantages that the white students had, we could still do the work. It just might take us a little longer.

Shit, I wanted to build a house. I ain't never built no house before. But I knew it could be done. And I knew that a Black person could do it. My Grandfather had built his house. He had turned a used- to- be store into a home for his wife and 13 children. But my Grandfather won't here no more; when I had took an interest to doing Carpentry. Mr. Padgett didn't take the time with me and Ju- Jish, as far as harnessing the skill and technique.

That's all I needed was the repetition. I learned good by repetition. Once I get the concept of the technique down; that's a wrap. I could master doing the trade.

Once I did something one time, Mr. Padgett was fast to want to jump onto doing something else. This was the only place I could get this practice. Tools alone are expensive. Just the tools alone can run you into THOUSANDS of dollars.

I ain't have that kinda shit at home.

And we was getting good quality hammers,

nails, saws, table saws, circular saws, drills... all way down to the sheetrock and wood. We was gettin it FREE off tax payer's income. Oh, we was gettin it. But we wasn't effectively being taught how to use it.

That's just like.: somebody can give you a garage full of Snap- On Tools, Craftsman, all the quality saws, blades, hammers, drills and bits, screw drivers, compressors and guns, da, da, da, da, da, da, da. But you don't know what to do wit what you got.

And somebody comes along and say, "I'll give you $50,000 for all this right here."

And you sell it to him, not knowing you coulda flipped projects and coulda made $500,000, or a series of projects and coulda made $5 million dollars. You understand what I'm saying?

So that's where me and Ju- Jish was at wit it. We coulda learned a trade that permanently would of been able to supply us with a lifestyle to where we can care for ourselves and feed our family; for the rest of our life. It would've kept us out the street. It would've kept us out of prison.

So from that standpoint, yes, we were given the opportunity, but the schooling still failed us.

We built wood sheds in one of the parking lots, up closest to the classroom. I used to scale up the shed like I was a Road Warrior, and walk the top like I was in a 25 foot ladder wrestling match. I wanted to drop kick Scott off toppa that muthafucka!

But Scott wassa cool- ass white guy. He was from Ku Klux Klan County, but he ain't never treat us fucked up. It won't no beef. It's just in Padgett's eyes, he could do no wrong.

My momma got something good out of it.: I made my momma this luxurious medicine cabinet. It was "luxurious" cause I made it by hand; BITCH!

It was a medicine cabinet on the top and a paper towel rack on the bottom. And I SHELLACKED it in a dark reddish- brown wood stain. It came out nice. Don't worry bout it.: My Momma liked it.

You supposed to screw it into the studs, to hold it up. But she just put it up in her kitchen. And the only thing missing; she just had to go to a glass shop. To get the glass cut and fit in there. But she didn't focus the money on doin that.

In my senior year; Carpentry was a two-year program. I didn't go back for Carpentry II, cause I didn't feel like goin through all that bullshit a 2nd year. I liked cars. I couldn't drive em. But I liked them. I wanted to work on cars, so I changed over to Auto Mechanics.

Auto Mechanics is a two year program, just like Carpentry. I was taking Auto Mechanics 1, just to get a feel for the course, to see if this was something I'd like to do for a living.

Alright, I'm gon come back to that. First, let me tell you the best part about these New Horizon courses.: once a year we took a field trip to Virginia's State Fair. Back then, it was up in

Richmond, just avenues down from our Richmond church, where my Daddy go to to preach from time to time.

The State Fair definitely was nothing like going to Disney World, or King's Dominion, or even Busch Gardens. Going to the State Fair is more like going to the carnival. Just minus The Freak Shows. The Freak Shows gotta be the coolest part about going to the carnival. Right. Especially since they don't got roller coasters.

What they do got.: Ferris Wheels.

Yo, I'll ride any roller coaster in the world, I'll even go backwards on the Rebel Yell, before I go and ride a Ferris wheel. I'll fly in a plane, before I ride a Ferris wheel.

I ain't never see nobody get hurt on one. They look real nice at night, all lit up and illuminated up. But I just think, when I get up there, that's when something bad gon happen. If God ain't make it, I ain't ridin nobody's Ferris wheel.

It's something else they got at the State Fair, a whole lotta BIIIIG ass vegetables. I saw pumpkins that's bigger than people. That's some shit... go see a 6 foot, 7 foot tall, 8 foot wide pumpkin.

They had a lotta booths that sold NFL, NBA, and college team hats, clothes, posters, NASCAR; all sports merchandise.

I bought a Raiders hat for $10. Hey! It was a Fair price.

They had a lotta popcorn, cotton candy, snow cones, pretzels, chips, sodas...

And something else they hadda lot of...

BITCHES!! Bitches! Bitches! Bitches! Bitches! Bitches! Bitches! BITCHES!!

Bitches from Halifax. Bitches from Manassas. Bitches from Fairfax. Bitches from Winchester. BITCHES!! from all over Virginia. I always leave wit long distance phone numbers. And I always get kisses from at least one bitch.

Fairfax is the richest county in Virginia. I think they say it's even the largest county. But, I never been there.

Alright, back to the story.: So I'm in my second year at New Horizons. 12th grade year, and I'm in this auto mechanics class. Mr. Roller was the other auto mechanics instructor. I used to always hear him say,

"Never let me hear you call this thing a motor. This is an engine. This is not a motor."

That was Mr. Roller's pet peeve. I don't remember what my instructor's name was. I began learning some stuff. How to do tune- ups and tire changes. Then we cherry- picked out an engine, and started stripping it down to the block.

We was filing the pistons, then one day... he was gone. He wasn't DIED.

He had switched jobs. We all think he went to Siemens. I'on even know what they do at Siemens. But hearing him explain it, it had to be a high paying job. More than 'a teacher salary.

So he left, and we got a replacement teacher, named Mr. Andes. Mr. Andes was a young skinny-thin white boy, who loved to wear blue jeans and long brown hair. You couldn't tell him, he won't the coolest thing, since the Beatles beat it back to England.

The crazy part about it- - we didn't always get along. He'll say some slick shit out the mouth. And I'll say some slick shit back.

And you know how people listening are.: "OHHHHHHHH!!!!"

Wendell, Traun, and Earl. Mostly Earl. Like he was provoking us to fight.

But Mr. Andes was cool, and he was more professional than he was a fighter. So he stopped coming at me like that. And when he did that; that's when I was really starting to learn from him.

I was side- by- side being trained by an ASE Master Technician. For FREE. We pulled in a black Camaro, and ripped that bitch, from start to finish. The engine. The transmission. The tune- up. Tires. Brakes. Muffler and exhaust.

Then we did the same thing with a Mercury Cougar. I could do the work. And I liked it, but I couldn't get a certificate in it. Cause I didn't take it for 2 years. It's a 2 year course.

If I would've taken Carpentry or Auto Mechanics for 2 years, at the end, I woulda got a certificate and my high school diploma. But it was my first time ever doing either one my whole life. So by 11th/ 12th grade, I'm already in the fourth quarter to try to figure out which one I'm really good at. And which one I wanna do for a living. Cause these aren't just courses; these are lifetime career making training.

But I did graduate the first year of both classes.

When the senior year Year Books came out, I only let girls sign my yearbook. Girls was signing my book, and signing their names and phone numbers. Lynette signed my book. But I already had her number. Hunh.

Then guess who else came to sign my book? You already know.:

Ms. Joy Jackson herself.

I didn't even call her over there. Man, I was nervous, and scared like 'a bitch! The goosebumps was chomping the sweat on my neck. Joy walked over. Oh my God, this red bitch is So BAD!!

She asked could she sign my book. Why?? Why?? Why?? could I not talk to this girl??

Cause I already had a red girl telling me, "Put it where you want to put it."

And that bitch won't doing no snatching! She meant every word!

We was on again and off again, in a year and four months, once me and Ericka really got together. In Feb 1992. We never usually stayed broke up for more than two weeks. Maybe it was cause she wanted to fuck other guys; sometimes it was probably just to recoup from each other. One time, she fucked up. She revealed to me that she was fuckin a nigga who went to the same school as me. A nigga named Jay.

When she did that, I thought we was done. Cause she ain't make this no secret. She usually keep who else she fuckin away from me. She don't let me know it.

When I saw who Jay was- - I ain't get mad. I can see why she might like him. He was cool. Quiet. Laid back. He ain't make'a lotta noise. He reminded me of myself.

He was a little bit taller than me. He looked like he coulda been on the basketball team. But he won't on the basketball team. He wore a Michigan jacket, with a hood. It could be a rain coat, if it rain.

And he was dark skin. He was darker than me.

But even after she told me, they was together; she still came back to Me. But this one went past 2 weeks; which is another reason I thought it was over. It was like 4 weeks later. I got the call,

"Hello?" Like I ain't know who the fuck it was. I gotta caller ID.

"Hey."

"What's up?"

"I miss you...

I love you...

come see me." All that's what she said.

What I'm supposed to do?

"Naw. I'm good. I ain't fuckin wit you no more. Shawty we through..."

That's what I'm supposed to say, hunh?

Yeah, right. Nigga I was goin round there.

Make- up mean, she come up out the house in some loose orange gym shorts. No panties! She sit back in the chair, pull the shorts to the side, and she show me that PHAAAAT ass pussy. And that be 'a bout it, right there on her front porch.

She let me fuck her right there. In fronna everybody. Cars rolling down the street. People standing cross the street. People walking down the sidewalk. I hadda bitch that was eatin the dick HARD!! I'm hoopin this pussy, like I'm LeBron James!

Rubbin off rounds like RAMBO!

That's how we make- up and get back together. I'm supposed to fuck all that up, hunh? Hunh.

Then it was times when I get to talking shit to her,

over the phone. I have a nickname for her--- I call her Snu. So, I be talkin to my Snu, like,

"Yeah, I'm gon fuck the shit outta you...

I'm gon fuck you so damn hard..." cause we supposed to been having phone sex. But she don't respond back.

She gets very quiet.

She let me finish. Then all I hear is, "UH- HUH. WE GON SEE. GET YO ASS ROUND HERE...

BRING THAT ASS OVER HERE!" Or, this'll be her most favorite line,

"Uh- um. Yo house or mine?"

Sometimes, I might stall her,

"Man, I ain't coming round there..."

"I said, "Yo house or mine?"

"Listen.: I'll be round there tomorrow. I'm not fuckin wit you tonight."

But it don't make no difference. She don't forget nothing I said. Man, that bitch start pumpin that pussy so hard, phaaat, and wet; feel like I'm cummin in the cotton of cantaloupe and soft honey dew melons. 'A nigga hit that lil shake. 'A nigga shake off in that stuff, man.

And she just be layin there talkin bout, "Um- hmm... um- hmm."

I can't even last 5 minutes.

Dat pussy da BOMB!! BOMB!! BOMB!! Plus Ericka was spontaneous. We was already at that level.

Lynette was definitely wifey material. She definitely won't afraid to pull up on 'a nigga. I still didn't know how to talk to pussy, Ericka had just kinda fell in my hands. Ericka was hands on. Lynette wasn't like that. She was quieter and shyer. And that's what made me feel afraid of starting over.

I needed a girl to work like Ericka, who wasn't Ericka. These girls won't doing that.

Now, my fantasy and dream girl, fo real the only girl that was standing in Lynette's way, Joy Jackson herself, had walked and sat in the seat, just right in front of me.

"Do you mind if I sign your book?"

I politely handed her my Yearbook. My tongue was swallowing my throat. This how this girl made me feel. I had never had a girl made me feel the way Joy made me feel. This shit was impeccable.

If nobody else, Joy- - Joy could make me start over. She could make me drop Ericka and be with her. She could- - if only I knew what to say.

"Here you go," and she smiled.

Like 'a breeze on a cloud, I watched her walk

324

away. After she walked away and sat back at her desk. I cracked open my Yearbook to read what she had wrote. She wrote a note. And signed it. And...

she gave me her NUMBER.

'WHAT!?' I was pulling my socks by the jock strap.

I was looking at her, and she was turned to the side, but looking forward at the board, like she was waiting for me to come over there.

But I couldn't. I couldn't move. This girl had scribbled my legs down to cottage cheese. At least I got the number. Maybe, I'll call.

I still ended up having to go to night school at Warwick for a semester, when I was in 12th grade. To make up 0.50 credits. So I can graduate on time with my class. My mother paid for me to take the English class. And I passed.

It was GRADUATION time.

I can talk like this now, cause it's legal in most states. My cousin had a boyfriend who was a US Navy veteran. He was cool. He had moved to Bad News and was with Sabrina. He originally was from Roanoke. His name is Tony.

For a graduation gift Tony gave me a dime sack of reefa.

"Hey, man it's all I got. Congratulations," he said and dapped me up.

325

I poked it in my pocket to save it for later. Bout the same time I was doing that,

"Jamie..."

It was my momma calling me. She was telling me my Grandma Carrie was here. It was the first time I saw her since Best Momma's funeral. In over 3 years.

I don't really know what to think. I didn't know if this was supposed to bring our lives closer together, since Best Momma had passed away. Did she want to replace what Best Momma was in my life? I don't know. I never asked her.

"You wanna ride wit me?" She asked me.

I had wanted to ride wit my cousins Debbie and Sabrina, and their boyfriends.
But then I thought, 'Why not?'

She showed up for me on my Graduation. I got with her in her burgundy Chevy Caprice. And we all leave from my Aunt Dottie's house, over on Roanoke Avenue, right across from F and S. The 34th Street corner store. I didn't want a Best Momma replacement. Best Momma can never be replaced. But I already know she knew that. And I just sit still and look out the window, as we go over the Interstate 64 fly over, to go to the world famous, Hampton Coliseum.

I could read, write, spell, and count, and I made it all the way without failing a grade! I went into the Hampton Coliseum. They had an order how they seated us. Joy was there. It was so many people, I barely saw her. Then after we graduated everybody went their own separate ways. We was now 18 and GRADUATED. We wasn't obligated to our parents and to going to school no more.

I do have some regrets about not attending my Senior Prom.

Who was I supposed to take?

I couldn't take Ericka. For the same reason I couldn't take Lynette. I couldn't let that get back to Joy; that I went to the prom with another girl.

I couldn't go to the prom with Joy, cause I couldn't even talk to her. Joy was even my preference if I went to the Military Ball. It was Joy or nothing at all.

So I missed out.

I honestly feel Joy would've brought the best out of me. If I had Joy, I think I woulda went to college after high school. I would've took my PSATs in 11th grade. And my SATs in 12th grade. And I should've went to Lucky's alma mater, Virginia Union University. In Richmond.

I did call Joy on the phone a few times. But I still didn't know how to talk to her. I really didn't know what to say. She told me she was leaving for Howard University.

I feel pain again, like how I do with Tashia. It hurt to even write that.

Other girls was chasing me; but Joy was the

girl I really wanted. I didn't see Joy like how I might see other attractive girls. Subconsciously, I wanted a wife. And when I saw Joy, I saw a wife. And I let her slip like a dry football pass, right through my butter fingers.

All I had to do was.: Joy could've went to Howard. Got her degree. I coulda went to Union. Got my degree in Business Management and Administration. Then after we graduated, we coulda came together.

The Perfect Love Story.

We coulda got married in Newport News, where we both from. But go move to a major city. Live together. Work. She woulda gave me all her babies.

Hhhh. Happily Ever After.

But, that's not how it went down. After graduation, Water Country had wrote to offer me my job back. But I didn't accept it. Not that I wasn't grateful. It's because Water Country is a seasonal job, and I wanted a job I could work all year long.

I had wanted a job in a restaurant. In the restaurant industry. Even if I had to start off entry level, as a waiter, or washing dishes. Nobody would hire me. Not Mc Donald's. Not Wendy's. Not Chick-Fil- A. Not Cheddar's. Not Gyro's. Not Sabarro's. The movie theatre wouldn't even let me pop popcorn.

Not the Chinese restaurants, on Oyster Point Road. Carlos wouldn't even hire me to wash his Mexican dishes.

328

I put in at Bally's. Couldn't get Bally's.

I finally landed a job at Simplicity Cleaning Services, just up like (1) block from my house, before you get to Jefferson. Simplicity was owned by black man, named Mr. Ivy. Simplicity was a part- time night time cleaning job. Mr. Ivy hired me part- time.

He had contracts to clean the local area Old Country Buffets restaurants, after they closed down, after hours. Old Country used to be the most popular buffet restaurant for poor people.

I can remember when Po Folks used to be my Daddy's most favorite restaurant. When my Daddy used to get a good check, and he used to take his family out to eat- - he used to take me and my momma out to Po Folks. Po Folks was a restaurant that was owned by some country music legends and stars. They used to have some real good fried pieces of chicken and mashed potatoes and gravy, for a pretty fair price. But once Old Country Buffet came out with the ALL U CAN EAT for $5.99, that's when Daddy stopped eating at Po Folks.

It was so many people, you had to fight for a parking space. And after you did all that, you still had to stand in line. In line just to get to the cashier. And in another line just to get to your table.

But once you get in, especially after church, it be nothing but 'a whole buncha po black people chowin down in they Sunday's best.

But by now, those days had long gone. Old

Country Buffet was still a value quality restaurant.
But no matter how cheap you put it. People had
moved on. Other buffet chains began popping up in
the peninsula and tidewater area. My mother's
whole family would come out for Ryan's. My
Granddaddy and Grandmother. Audrey and Lucky,
and most of my whole family in Richmond would
come down, so we could all eat at Ryan's, on
uptown Jefferson. And even after my Grandfather
passed away, my mother's family still swarmed to
Ryan's, when everybody comes home, to Newport
News.

Ryan's was an all you can eat buffet too. And
at a higher price. But people will pay a slightly
higher price, to not go through the headaches of
parking and waiting in line. And Ryan's was more
spreaded and spaced out, where you had less
people on top of your back. But Ryan's claim to
fame, it isn't so much the food. I mean like, how
many different ways can you fry 'a bone of chicken?

The best part of Ryan's is THE DESSERTS.
The All U Can Eat ICE CREAM and CHOCOLATE
and CARAMEL COVERED SUNDAES. Wit the
sprinkles. And COOKIES! I get through my (1) plate
of food, just so I can get to my multiple shots of ICE
CREAM, SUNDAES, and COOKIES for dessert.
Why waste time eatin real food?

So by the time I was workin in Old Country
Buffet; Old Country Buffet was outta style. But it
felt crazy cleaning the decor of my once upon time
favorite childhood restaurant. Not much had
changed, based upon the features of my memory. It
was still the same. All the way down to the carpets.

330

You never know how much mashed potatoes fall to the floor, til you down on yo hands and knees, lickin it wit 'a butter knife and a bucket of soap and water.

The best part about working at Old Country Buffet, was the part that can never go out of style- - the food! Most of the time they would leave food out in the salad bar for us. But after hand scrubbing the shit out this filthy ass carpet, who the hell wanna eat some damn lettuce?

All the best food was in the back.

We'll go into the kitchen. Cause Hey! We had to clean there anyway. And boy did we clean. They had ovens turned on back there. Perhaps the food they was preppin for the next day. But who knows? We was eatin this up tonight! Yes, pork. I was eating swine back then.

But the most popular pieces was the chicken, turkey, hens, and chops of roast beef. When you cut into this roast beef, the meat would be so tender, the beef would melt against the blade of the knife. UMMMM! Ummm, ummm, ummm!

Mostly, I went to work for 4 hours a night. 7 nights a week. A graveyard shift.: from 12 midnight til 4 in the morning. Sometimes I worked til 6; if we finished the Newport News store, then we'd jet over to help the guys finish out in Hampton.

When I first get home, I still got energy. I don't know if T- Bone ever got any sleep. He wassa 24 hour watch dog. Even when I get home at 4 or 6 in the morning; there he be,

"AROO! ROO! ROO! ROO! ROO! ROO!
ROO-- ROOF!"

He make all that noise, just so I can remember to
walk back there and pat him.

We hadda little farm jumpin in our yard. My Daddy
wit the chickens. Me wit the dog. And my momma
wit the birds.

When you get in the trailer, if they wasn't sleep,

"Chir, chir, chir, chir, chir, chir, chir, chir,
chur," be the sound of my momma's parakeets. I
think the last "chur" part was when the bird just
finished cussin me out, for coming through the
door waking him up from standing still on 'a stick.

But, I only worked for Simplicity for 2
weeks. It only took one paycheck; or the lack
thereof to kill this whole damn Parmesan Paradise.
The day came to GET PAID. And when I saw Mr.
Ivy didn't have a paycheck for me, this Big Buffet in
Bermuda was over!

Danny Ray kept trying to get me to come back to
work; even if he had to pay me out his own pocket.
Aww, you just go back to fuckin Mickey's wife.

Oops! Did I say that out loud...

I used to see her with her lil smalled- tight
two- piece bikini. Cuppin up on them tiny titties up
on top. Diggin all up in that lil butt from the back.
She'll lay out in the sun, up in her front yard. You
know.: whenever Mickey ain't at home. Cause he

wassa hard working man fo his family.

After she finish browning her abs, and burnin them buttcheeks, then it was, "Danny Ray. Dan- ny Ray..."

She'd tip it over right there to him, so he can bruise it the rest of the way. Of course, Danny Ray stayed barefoot, and his door was always open. I don't think she was into black men. But it's cool. I was too young to be into adultery.

But anyway, I declined Danny Ray's offer. It was a common culture out the trailer park for whites to walk around in the street, and in the grass, and on the sidewalks barefooted. Without any shoes on. They reminded me of Robert. I'on even think Danny Ray even owned a pair of shoes. That's probably why he ain't have none or many furniture; cause the store wouldn't let him in to buy it.

Mr. Ivy is married to a white woman. That's besides any point. I'm just narrating that fact into the story; but I confronted him in his office. I asked him,

"Where's my money?"

And he tried to carve me some lil stupid reposited story about, "It'll get straightened out. Everything'll get straightened out."

And I probably would've brought into that, if I hadn't discovered after I was complaining, that he wasn't paying NONE of his employees. Danny Ray was just working, basically so he could keep driving the company station wagon.

Even at 18, I knew I won't going for this bullshit, "Man you gon pay ME, my muthafuckin check!" I demanded from him.

"What you say!?" he started balling his face up.

"You heard what the fuck I said.: You gon pay ME my muthafuckin check!"

"What!? What!?" he started scooting back and forth in his emotions. "You'n talk to me like that. Who do you think you are? You get out my office."

I just stood there with my hands crossed. One hand holding the other, cause I already knew what I was going to do. All he had to do is stand up. Man, just stand up. I was gon rock him! I was gon stretch him! I woulda beat that nigga to death wit one of them vacuum cleaners, I was lookin at.

"Get out!" he shouted.

He didn't get up.

"Get out!" he shouted one more time.

Then, I just turned around and left. I had thoughts about doing something to him, or coming back in wit my lil black slugger, and smash him and all this shit to pieces.
But despite how angry I was. I didn't do any of it. I don't remember who the advice came from. Maybe Danny Ray. But it was 'a peaceful resolution.

I sued him.

It cost me $17 to file my small claim in Newport News Circuit Court. I was suing for what I was owed- - $238.00.

It's 'a shame, all that work. That man didn't even want to pay me $238 dollars. He and his wife came to court, and he told the judge I came in his office ranting and raving, and that I cursed him. That,

"He came in and he was cussing at me. And all this and that." He was moving his arms all animated trying to explain his point. We never did make eye contact.

Of course the judge told me I was wrong, but nevertheless, he had to pay me because that is the law, and I was his employee. So it was that simple.: I won my lawsuit for $238.00.

If I was thinking; I also could've been reimbursed my $17 for filing the case. But I was good wit just getting my paycheck. If I can get my paycheck.

I rode the bus there and back home. On the way back home I was happy that I won. I was grateful to God. But even more important.: I was glad I didn't lash out in violence. Cause I was one-hundred percent in the right, but if I did that, I woulda been going to prison, and I would be owing him money. I was worried about when and how I was going to get paid.

I got back to the trailer. Soon as I closed the door.:

"Whuudddddddddddddd.

Whuudddddddddddd. Whuudddddddddddd."
Ok. Ok. That was the phone ringing.

"Hello?"

"Come get your money," he said.

"Ok." I hung up the phone.

To me this sound like a set up. I'on know if I
should take T- Bone or my baseball bat. But I went
by myself. I went in. He gave me a check- - $238
dollars.

I said, "Thank you." I walked out; and I never
stepped foot in his business again.

Bout the same time I was getting back to the
house, my father rolled up. I showed him the check.
I was hoping it would cash. It did. And that really
meant, I would never have to step foot in his
business again.

I got paid, but only one problem.: now I'm back to
having no job.

When I was in my 12th grade year, in high school, I
was writing down on a piece of paper what I wanted
to be after I graduate. What I wanted to do. I wrote
down (5) things. I said I wanted to be.:

1) an Auto Mechanic,

2) a Rapper,

3) a Drug Dealer,

4) a Robber, and

5) a Murderer

I had wrote (5) things. 2 positive and 3 negative. I had put up the note. Somewhere. I had forgot I had it. But the kind of mother I have; she would always go through my room, when I wasn't home. To plunder; and see what I was in to. And one day, the Spirit of God led her to that note, and she questioned me,

"Son, what is this? Why did you write this?"

"Oh, it ain't nothing." And I got the note outside of her hand and balled it up, and threw it in the trash. But to this day, I still remember everything I put down on that piece of paper.

After I graduated high school, I wanted to be the first positive thing.: I wanted to be an auto mechanic. I just didn't have the tools. And I didn't have the government grant or money to get into UTI. They had one in Tennessee. But I wanted to go to the one in Houston. Because I had a liking for the NFLs, the Houston Oilers. And Warren Moon was one of my favorite Quarterbacks.

Virginia didn't have any pro sports NFL, NBA, Major League Baseball teams- - nothing. So if I went to school, I was more attracted to go someplace outta state, that was a magnet for all that attraction. Plus Texas would be an attractive state. I always wanted to go to Texas, ever since I used to watch Dallas on tv.

The only problem.: I didn't have no capital. I had

nothing monetary to manifest these dreams into fruition. So, it was still just a dream.

Moving down the list.:

When I was in my 11th grade year, in high school, I took a liking to a friend named Joe Beldo. Joe said he was from New York, but I had met Joe at Menchville. Joe used to perform talent shows up in the school.

The way he rapped and chanted reminded me of one of my most favorite rappers of all time. KRS- ONE. Joe even wore dreds, something like KRS- ONE. So we got cool, cause we had at least one of the same classes. I liked Joe genuinely, cause he was a cool friend. But I also liked him, cause I felt like being around him would help advance me to doing something I never did.

I used to rap in front of small groups, or battle in the hallways. But I never performed on stage in front of a larger audience, or at a talent show, or even recorded in a studio. This was big feats for me; I liked to rap. And I wanted to be accomplished.

The problem with my rap style, is that I didn't put enough practice into it. Two of the hardest parts about being an artist is.: finding your own voice and being original.

I didn't put enough time into finding my voice, all the way back to when I was friends with Damon. To my credit, we didn't exactly know about none of this back then. But it's not an excuse, because I was still tryin to work on establishing a voice and a style. I worked on tryin to find my voice, not by sounding like the man in the front, but sounding like the man in the back. I was a fan of gangsta rap music. Because Gangsta Rap was King.

The science to Gangsta Rap wasn't just how HARD!! you can curse when you tellin a story, but how many times and ways you can call the other man 'a bitch and a muthafucka. Eazy- E and Ice Cube was the two, in front, Gangsta Rappers in the world. But only one of them wrote their own lyrics. The man, in the back... was Dr Dre.

Even when Dr Dre did The Chronic, he wasn't known for being the in the front man. He was known for being "a Producer," who just so happened- - he was rapping. Snoop Dogg was the man in front of the show. But Dre was killin it at the same time. He was the first one who took that, "Just'a little ghetto boy--/ playin in the ghetto streets--/ whatcha gonna do when you grow up--/ and have ta face-- re- a- lity..." After that, years later, Biggie Smalls and Wu- Tang Clan did a rendition of the same song. But Dr Dre was the first one to murder that shit.

Dr Dre didn't write his own rhymes neither. But it ain't matter. The cadence of his rhyme pattern was laid back, clean, clear, and articulate. If I could just take a Dr Dre rap pattern, but make it more lyrical; that could give me the voice I need, and my place in the rap game.

There's only one problem.: the subject matter.

Dr Dre is from Compton on the West Coast. His

environment is gangbanging and gang violence. So in the process of me developing a Dr Dre into an east coast, Virginia pattern, in the meantime my lyrics are gangsta/ gangbanging lyrics, like Dr Dre. So when I make a rap about "calling for a truce."

Joe is six- two when he stands up. But for this, he had to sit the fuck down and shake his brain.

"What the hell is a truce?" he asked me.

"Ah, yeah, well you know--"

I didn't know shit about no truce. Bloods and crips won't even known of yet, or heard about in Virginia culture. He ain't never say it, but Joe won't tryin to put this bullshit on stage wit him. However, me and Joe stayed cool and remained friends until we graduated high school.

But now that we was graduated, it won't no more school talent shows left to go to. If I was gon improve, I had to do it another way. That's when I started spending more time down town. Not around Lynn. But around Dwight.

Dwight doesn't have fully developed feet. Both of his feet are cropped off about half way of what a normal size foot should grow. He wears prosthetics that comes up to his knees on both legs. And he has shoes built in as feet, at the bottom of the prosthetics. And Dwight is a large over 300 pounds. He can slide and scoot around on the floor at home, but when he goes out, he hobbles on two metal crutches.

But all that's besides the point. Dwight is

one of the best pure lyricists your ears can ever hear. I first saw Dwight on stage at talent shows, all the way back to Huntington Middle School. So just being around him and being at his home; I had the honor of being friends with a true Bad News Hip-Hop Legend.

Not only could he spit, but also, just like Damon, he could DJ. He could DJ so good, that people was paying him to come and do parties for them.

With me now being outta school and not having a job, it made since for me to spend more time around Dwight and going with him to these various parties. And that's what we did.

At the parties, he didn't rap much if at any, he would just DJ. But wherever he went, he took me wit him. And he'd get paid. He didn't pay me in money. Just like my pops, he paid me in food. And I got along wit that.

Dwight had moved from his two- story apartment out Seven Oaks to a studio apartment on 41st Street, still in Newport News. On Jefferson Avenue, right beside the cab stand. The apartment was a living room/ slash- bedroom/ slash- music studio. Then it had one bathroom and a kitchen. That was the whole apartment.

The living room/ slash- bedroom/ slash- music studio, also had a VCR for watching movies and a tv. I literally sat in that house and watched Boyz- N- The- Hood and Menace II Society EVERY DAY!! EVERY DAY almost non- stop.

Then Dwight had another way to pay me;

341

the hottest rapper in Bad News wassa ladies man.
He knew A LOTTA bitches. A whole lotta bitches.
He knew bitches from in person, from over the
phone, and over the chat lines.

So he'll pass the phone on to me to talk to
bitches, and a lotta times, some of these bitches
would show up in person. A few of these bitches, I
had sex with. I don't even know they name. I can't
even tell you the first initial. It was one night he was
on the phone, and he give me the phone to talk to
this one girl, to see what I can do with her.

The girl's name ended up being Shiakema.
I'm just gon call her Kema (pronounced Key- ma),
so I don't gotta try to break all that shit down. I'm
writing this shit, 2 in the morning, I'on got time fo
all that bullshit. Just do the best you can.

Anyway, Kema hadda very beautiful telephone
voice. And we would talk all the way until we fell
asleep. Then we got to the point where I would tell
her, "I love you."

And she would say, "I love you too."

After about 2 weeks, I said to her, "Where you at?
I'm tryin to see you."

She told me that she was out Wendwood
Square, out Nettles Drive. This bitch literally stayed
right where my momma stayed, just across the train
tracks. She lived in the backyard of Warwick Mobile
Homes. She gave me the address. I said,

"I'll be right there."

I told Dwight I'm gone, I'll holla back. I catch the bus up Wendwood Square. I get to the door. And guess who comes the fuck to the door?

No, not Joy. But I wish.

Kema was the same dark skinned girl who used to keep watching me at my locker at Menchville. And when I saw her come to the door- - I was about to say,

"Sorry. I got the wrong address."

But Hey! Maybe this might not be her; after all Kema did have friends. So I say,

"Is Kema home?"

"That's me," she smiled.

I was about to revert back to Option A. But it was kinda too late. What really got me is- - it was summer. And Kema had on these white- tight poom- poom shorts. She had these phaat chocolate ass legs, standing there lookin like a Hershey Bunny, wit them poom- poom shorts all up in her pussy.

What I'm supposed to do?

Shit, I had already told her I loved her. So shit, we was making love in the room. I started out wit 'a rubba, and ended up wit out 'a rubba- - on the same night.

And this same girl that started out as a shy, quiet, secret; mystery girl, on the halls of

343

Menchville, and who I would see at my locker, would be the same girl who would alter the future of my life, Forever.

Chapter 17.

After me and Kema had sex, I really didn't hear from her, for like two weeks. I tried to see her, and she was like,

"No- - No."

Then after about that two weeks, she was telling me, "I'm pregnant."

The word was coming from Kema that she was pregnant, and not just pregnant. BUT PREGNANT WITH TWINS.

She was telling me they was mine. And I was cool wit that. I wasn't resentful. The first thing I did; my momma's sister, Shanda, helped me get my driver's license. I had already taken Driver's Ed in high school. Shanda let me use her blue Toyota Tercel, and I went and got my driver's license.

After that, when I was searching the classifieds for a job, I came across this huge article, that was advertising to train you for trades, and they would pay you while you train. One of the trades they listed- -

No. It wasn't for rapping.

It was for Auto Mechanics. Still on the first (2) positive things on my list. Right. To apply, I was scheduled to come to the Rouse Towers, in Newport News, near the corner of Jefferson Avenue and Mercury Blvd. And Shanda took me over there. So I signed up. What I signed up for was Job Corps, and the man gave me a date that I would be leaving, December 7th.

I felt a sense of urgency about everything. I had TWO babies on the way.

December 7th arrived, and Job Corps sent a bus to pick us up in Newport News, then we stopped to pick some more would be students up, in Norfolk. Then I believe our last stop was Richmond, then we came to Woodstock Job Corps Center, in Randallstown, Maryland. That's in Baltimore County.

While I was in Job Corps, that was my first total separation from my parents, from my family, from friends, from Newport News and Hampton, and from the Saints in the Gospel Spreading Church: from everywhere I was born and raised.

Job Corps was co- ed and a kind of a scary place, because it was very violent. This was where a lot of young society rejects had come to, for one last pulse, before the judge put them away in prison.

Almost every body up there was in a gang, based upon their geographic location. Where they was from.

At Woodstock, the majority of the students was from Virginia. The second largest group of students was from DC. The fashion was wrapped up in navy blue or black flight jackets.

To them, everybody's name was "Joe."

"Hey, Joe..." or

"Young; Youngin."

"Young. Aye Young. What up Young?"

To them everybody was "Young," or "Joe."

And if you was fat, then yo name was, "Fats."

Some people took offense to it. But they ain't mean no harm; that's jus how they talk. When people first saw me, they automatically presumed I was from DC, they was shocked to hear I was from Virginia, cause I wear a lot of black. And DC did wear a lot of solid colors and a lot of black. But one of the first things I picked up on is how these DC niggas was more fashion conscious, more so than VA niggas.

Virginia niggas might rock Mikes and Nikes;

Timbo's; shit like that. But they'll put anything on wit it. For DC niggas- - DC niggas rocked a lotta POLO. A HARD!! ass colorful POLO shirt over top of some blue jeans, black jeans, or gray pair of sweatpants. But not just any blue jeans, black jeans, or sweatpants; that shit'll be POLO or brand named too- - mostly Carhartt, HUGO, and HUGO Boss.

The 3rd largest faction, was niggas from Philly. But they was still a small number. It used to be like 8, now it was like 4 of them niggas. But you can't tell these Philly niggas they ain't "The Shit!"

These niggas smoother than 'a pelican sittin on 'a green blade of grass. These niggas dress like DC niggas, except they don't wear no dark colors. All their clothes is colorful, BRIGHT, and full of life.

Everybody else there just basically fall in place. Delaware niggas run wit Philly. New York and Jersey niggas roll wit VA. And you have niggas from Baltimore. My nigga Herman live off campus, cause he lives in Baltimore, so he commutes to campus everyday.

The ideal of Job Corps is a good place. But the reality of Job Corps is very violent. Everybody from DC think they can box. Everybody from Philly, think he 'a boxer. And then Baltimore got into it with DC.:

At Job Corps as students, they pay you for being

there. You still need a supplementary income coming in from your peoples, but I was able to start my First savings account while on campus. Every (3) months Job Corps gives you vouchers so you can go shopping, primarily at Value City. The longer you stay in, the more money you receive.

And they give us FREE field trips, EVERY weekend. Trips to the movies, skating rink; about anywhere you want to go. And you don't gotta pay. Just sign your name to a piece of paper.

Well... this one was the skating rink. The skating rink is in Baltimore. Baltimore niggas orchestrated an assault on students from Job Corps, by having they neighborhood street homies meet the students up at the skating rink.

A fight and violence breaks out when Baltimore niggas start pouncing on Job Corps students, just out for the weekend to have a good time. The attack was supposed to be a Baltimore slaughter on DC niggas. When they get back on center, and DC niggas find out about that, cause most DC niggas didn't even go. But when they find out, B- more niggas was trying something at them, these DC niggas broke up in the carpentry shop. They took 16 penny nails, and hammered it to the end of boards, and came back out and start smackin these niggas off in the head, wit the nail ends of the board!

One guy they got a hold of, I'on even think he was even from Baltimore. But these DC niggas had broken this nigga arm. When I see him up in the RAs (Residential Advisor's) office, that nigga arm was bent up and curled over like 'a chicken wing. He was sitting still, and his arm was still shakin scared from what them niggas had done to him.

It won't nobody goin on snooze cruise, but it wassa lotta niggas gettin fucked up! It's a BLESSING nobody DIED that night. Some arrests were made, but that ain't kill off the violence.

Quanette was there. I told you it was co- ed. I never went at her, and she didn't go at me. But she's always very nice. When she sees me;

"Hey," she waves, as she keeps on her way.

On some weekends a combination of House, Rap, and Go- Go music culminates the bass from the area speakers, as they would turn the basement of the rec room, to an on- live club floor. I would watch Quanette dance. Quanette is phaat and 'a sexy booty ass bitch! Her booty jus look so sweet and as crunchy like some cotton candy! Like if'a nigga was to get to eatin that pussy, like yo tongue'll jus melt away right off up in that stuff. Ummm- Ummm- Ummm.

Quanette is super FLY!! and always 'a Bad Bitch, in

any category! Goodness 'a Gracious!

After the DC- Baltimore shit died down,
then DC niggas started fuckin wit Philly niggas. And
they started getting into it. After that the numbers
started dying down. A lot of students were
graduating, transferring to other centers, getting
arrested, or dropping the program.

I already had a high school diploma, so I
didn't have to wait on a GED. And Job Corps will
even help you get a driver's license. But I already
had one of those too. So I advanced into my trade. I
was supposed to be taking Auto Mechanics, but
somehow that got messed up; and I ended up
taking a class in Accounting.

During this same time, I was searching for
myself spiritually, to see where did I fit in with God.
At this same time it was a maturing time to see
where did I fit in in the world. I took notice of
people being from different geographics, and
backgrounds, and religious diversity. I began to feel
that my calling might not be in the Church but in
Islam. I was feeling compelled to want to join the
Nation of Islam.

The problem was I didn't have anybody to
personally help me to achieve the Nation of Islam
connection. I had an RA (Residential Advisor) who
used to be Nation, but he had converted to being a
Sunni Muslim. I didn't even know what a Sunni

was. I had been attracted to the incredible history and the clean- clipped and manicured mystique of The Nation of Islam. So I declined the offer.

The Islam idea couldn't materialize.

I was in touch with Kema while I was at Woodstock. My whole purpose for being there was to care for and support the two babies I had on the way. My family had made a connection to Kema; and often my mother and her sisters would pick Kema up, and they would do "girl stuff," and hang out.

But one day, I got the dreaded conversation. Kema had went into labor to give birth to the babies. When I call expecting to hear the sound of my little son and baby girl; all I hear is Kema telling me the twins.: Zavion and Zariah, did not make it.

"WHAT!? What do you mean they didn't make it!? What!? What happened..."

When I told my counselor the story, that the twins had DIED, he just kept droppin his head down and saying, "Umm, umm, umm, umm, umm...

Umm, umm, umm, umm, umm..."

He helped me though. He really did everything in his power to help me. He granted me a pass for Emergency Leave of Absence, for 7 DAYS.

That's the first thing he did. Then he reached in his desk and gave me FREE round trip Greyhound bus tickets, so I can get there, and get back on Center. That's the second thing he did.

And I was gone.

When I came to Job Corps that was my First time traveling- - distance; outside of being in a car. This was the first time I had rode a Greyhound home. I usually take Amtrak. But after this when I come home (cause we got weekend passes EVERY weekend, if we wanna come home), I started using Greyhound, because Greyhound was cheaper. It cost me about $61 for a round trip Amtrak ticket from Baltimore to Newport News, back to Baltimore. It only cost me about $33 for a round trip ticket on Greyhound.

About half the price.

And with Amtrak, the train ride you through the woods. On Greyhound, you get all the scenery. Cause you actually go on roads and on the interstate. So the counselor had put me on to something.

When I get back to Virginia, I'on touch down in Bad News. I get off in Richmond. My second father and mother was there to meet me and pick me up. Lucky and Audrey drove me to Bad News the next day.

When I get there, I don't hear from Kema. I hear from,

"Hello? Hey You!"

Um- hmm.

My mother told me she had called. I haven't spoken to Ericka in months! I didn't call her not one time I was at Center. But I was calling her now. I was returning her call.

"I'm pregnant," she told me.

I'm counting the months up in my head. After I graduated, me and Ericka wasn't together. We was seeing and having sex with other people, but we still made time for each other on BOOTY calls. Whenever she called me, and whenever I called her, we never resisted each other. Plus we still had that chemistry- - whenever we saw each other- - it was goin in! It was goin all the way in!

But anyway, when Ericka told me she was pregnant, I didn't believe her. It's not the first time I had heard this over the course of our relationship. So I think the bitch lying! I got to go see this for myself.

I get round there; and shown nuff, Ericka really is pregnant. Before I get there, she told me it won't mine. She told me it was some nigga name Leon.

'Where the hell she gettin these niggas from?'

Leon ain't even from Bad News. Leon from Hampton- - a Shell Road nigga.

Even when she telling me this, I ain't even believing this shit. I'm tryin to wrap my head around all this...

The potential I had Kema and Ericka pregnant at the same time...

Kema loses our twins, but Ericka is still pregnant with a baby by me...

I'm confident that me and Ericka had sex on her date of conception...

Is this a sign that me and Ericka was meant to be married and be together...

If this wasn't MY baby, then how else would she know THE PERFECT time to call...

All this shit racing through my head.

On toppa all that- - how is she keeping her pregnancy concealed from her grandmother? Ms. Florence is a woman, a mother, a grandmother, and everything else in between. Like she can't see her granddaughter IS PREGNANT!?

"She asked me.: "Ericka, are you pregnant?" I listened to her tell me. "But I tell her, "No grandma." She thinks I'm just pickin up weight."

This shit don't make no sense. Ericka had on an oversized tennis skirt. It's no way... It's no way... It's not no way, your grandma just think you pickin up weight.

But in the end, I didn't worry no more about it. Grandma had went 'on upstairs. And it came down to me and Ericka being too happy to see each other. She liked my shoulders; and I liked her legs being on my shoulders. Bendin all that good stuff o'va and hittin it from the back. We had unprotected sex.

I didn't feel bad, cause I felt like he was my son anyway. And she put me on to that this pregnant pussy, is where it's at!!

This bitch done took the sex game to a whole new level.

I had 7 DAYS on Emergency Leave. I ended up seeing Ericka. Never did see Kema. I ended up having sex with Ericka, like everyday I was home. And me and Ericka ended up back together. I get back on Center, back with Ericka.

"How is your baby mom?"

I don't even know how to answer that question. On many different levels.

When Kema was pregnant, and even after everything that happened, and I switched the focus over to Ericka, and my might be baby; I stayed laser focused. In only 6 short months I had completed my Job Corps education in Accounting. Now I found out, that there was still at least one more thing I can do, other than Carpentry and Auto Mechanics. I returned back home on July 1, 1994.

When I completed and came home, Job Corps paid me for finishing my course. I was only there 6 months. If I woulda been there longer, I woulda had even more money. I had $700 in cash, in my pocket. Plus my money I withdrew from my savings. And Job Corps gave me a FREE one way bus ticket Home.

I didn't stop off in Bad Newz. I landed back in Richmond. Lucky and Audrey was excited to see I could learn a course like Accounting. Me and my whole family was. Lucky wanted me to continue my education at the next level; in college. And at his alma mata, Virginia Union University.

Lucky was a die-hard Panther fan. And often when I was in high school, Lucky would come pick me up and take me and Hugh to Virginia Union's basketball and football games. He would follow them when they would come to Hampton, to play against Hampton University, and we went as far as Elizabeth City, in North Carolina. So I know how much him having me enrolled in Union means to him.

I do it.

But I'm still not sure if I want a degree in Accounting, because Accounting is boring. I don't feel like I wanna be doing debits, credits, and taxes as a Certified Public Accountant FOR A LIVING. I feel I want my major to be in Business Management and Administration. I know I wanted to be in business for myself. But what type of business am I trying to run?

I help Lucky around Richmond a coupla days, while I figure some things out.

Coming back home-- was the worst thing to happen to me. Just to fast forward this story.:

I ended up having sex with Ericka, EVERYDAY!! Then I'd catch THE LAST BUS from her house. Which is like 12 in the morning. Go to Kema's house, and end up fuckin Kema all night, and staying the night at Kema's house. Go home. Take a shower. Change clothes. And do it all over again. I was like T- Bone, I won't gettin no sleep.

This was EVERYDAY- EVERYNIGHT for a month.

July comes in. And I still didn't get my mind together.

"Audrey is on the phone," my mother said to me, "You ready?"

"Ready? Ready for what?"

"Audrey say, Lucky bout to come and get you, so you can go to college...

You going?"

'WHAT!?' I won't expectin this until August. I was off- balance. So, I give 'a off balance answer, "Naw. I'm good."

'WHAT!? What do you mean you not going!? Boy, you betta get yo'self up out here and...'

I expected somebody to say.

At least somebody to ask me, 'What's wrong?' To find out why I would wanna say I didn't want to go to college.

But nobody said nothing. Nobody challenged me on making a DUMB ass decision. They just let it go, and my momma and my 2nd momma moved their conversation on to something else.

Chapter 18.

The crazy part about it, after I declined to go to Union, Shiakema had moved with her mother. We lost contact.

July 20th came, and Ericka wasn't pregnant no more. I fell back to see if Leon was gon step in and be with her and his son, Tori.

My bubble had desiccated. I had lost my Chocolate Bunny and 'a Red Rabbit.

But after Ericka had Tori, miraculously we was still together. She wasn't giving me any signs like she wanted Leon. Even after I told her about Shiakema-- she cried. She still wanted to be together. A part of me was crazy for telling her that.

She knew about Kema. But Kema never knew about Ericka. I never not once brought Ericka up to Kema. So Kema never knew I had that underlying relationship.

After Kema had fizzed out, Snu was still standing there. I went to her house to see her and Tori. She brung him downstairs and let me hold him. Next thing I know, her Grandma was watching me feed him and change his diapers. So Ms. Florence asked me,

"Is that your baby?"

I told her, "Yes." I felt bold about it.

Her Grandmother looked at me very stern and said, "You be here EVERY week to bring that baby milk and diapers EVERY WEEK, now. Don't let me have to come and find you."

'Yes Ma'am,' I dotted my head down into her eyes.

I was thinking about what Shiakema had said to me when I had went away to Job Corps when she was pregnant,

"You left me. You just up and left me."

I didn't LEAVE her. I had went to Center to get an education and skill training, so I can get a good paying job to take care of her and our (2) babies. But now, I didn't have a job. I didn't have no income. I had nothing going for myself. I had blew Job Corps and Union both in the same summer.

I didn't know how this was supposed to work.

But I really did love Ericka. Ericka is very sexy, very pretty, and very beautiful; and we had that chemistry. After what Kema had told me how she felt when I had LEFT her; 4 years is a long time as opposed to 6 months. I wasn't prepared to move Ericka and Tori with me to Richmond. Which is one reason why I blew Union.

I was willing to make this work, because I was afraid of losing Ericka. Another part of me was thinking about marrying Ericka. But I had to give that part time to work itself out. By this time, I had gotten over the gonorrhea. What I didn't get over was the fact that Ericka had fucked not (1) but (2) of my homies.

Kane had been the first one. The second one; was cool wit Dwight. He wasn't really my homie, but I used to be around him, from being around Dwight. He had his own Jeep.

Tee was alright. Light skinned guy. He kept himself up. He felt he was some kind of pretty boy. He was kind of funny acting. Because he had slight financial advantages over me and Dwight. And that Jeep.

It's ok. I understood. It is common for Blacks in better financial conditions, or middle class Blacks to look down on poor Black people. I accepted it for what it is. I didn't hold it against him. We was poor. We wasn't broke. Broken.

Sometimes you need other people to-- you know.: it

was a day when I was at home, in the trailer park-- I get a call.:

"Hello?" It's Dwight.

"Man, Tee fuckin Ericka."

"What?" I said calm.

"Tee fuckin Ericka," he said again.

How did this shit ever even happen? How the world she even find out bout this nigga? But it all worm itself right 'on out.

"Did you fuck her?" I asked him.

"I wish!" he couldn't stop that stupid ass giggling. "She won't give me no pussy. I'on know why."

Not only do he reveal to me that He also has an interest in fuckin Ericka, but he started tryin to pick my brain on what I did to get her, so he can try to use it; and of course- - so he can fuck Ericka too. I'm supposed to give him this information, right. He's reading more about it now. I was silent back then. Back then, he was,

"You hear her makin all that noise! Tee tearin her ass up!"

I couldn't hear nothing. That's why I didn't believe it. All I could hear was him kept doing that silly ass gigglin.

"Well, where you at?" I asked him.

"I'm in the bathroom."

I didn't know if it was true. A part of me didn't care. Me and Ericka wasn't really together at that time anyway. So I knew she was fuckin other niggas. I just was disappointed she brought it back to my team.

Dwight's circle of friends was separate from Lynn's circle of friends, so I kept the humiliation away from niggas on 13th Street, so I won't keep hearing that shit every time I be around them. Later when I saw Ericka and confronted her about it;

"And!?" that was her sarcastic response to the level of disrespect that she had caused.

That confirmed for me it was true. I didn't get into all that childish ass shit about who got the bigger dick? Who was better? and all that dumb ass shit. I got into that one time. The first time.: after she fucked Kane. I asked her,

"Which one of us was better?"

She jollied around giving me the answer.

I asked her, "Which one of us got the biggest dick?"

And she said, "He was thicka, yours is longer."

One thing about it, you poke at the bear long enough, you gon find out what it is you really wanna know. After that day, I never asked her no shit like that ever again. The bottom line is, she kept coming back, and back, and back, and back. So I had to be doing something right. I let it be what it was.

But I did go to Tee. I went to Tee and I went to Kane, after they had fucked her. I asked Kane,

"She got some GOOD ass pussy- - don't she?"

"Haaaah, haaaah!" he laughed. I think he was shocked I had asked him like that. Then he said, "She alright."

I asked Tee the same question. Pretty much the same way. And he hesitated. Then said,

"She alright. Yeah, she alright."

The same thing Kane had told me. It's undeniable that Ericka got some good ass pussy, but I think the level that we had sex, and she was giving it to somebody else- - it wasn't equivalent.

We had so much more attaching to it, that poured out more passion between us.

It was times when I treated Ericka like, another man might, like she was just sex. Like she was just 'a piece of pussy.

It was recent, right before Ericka had had Tori. Her Grandma was up, so she gave me the pussy outside the house. That's how wet she get, when I just come around. Ain't it? I worked her. I'on know how many times she came. I know I did five. I was drained. This day she drained me.

I thought I was.

I was walking, leaving Ericka's house, to go to the bus stop to go home.: when this dark brown woman walk up on me. She talkin. She keep lickin her lips, and rubbin her titties; while she talkin to me. At first, I thought I was trippin. She keep doin it. It come to find out, she wassa hoe, tryin to sell me some pussy.

"I'on got but $5."

"Damn, that's it," she licked her chocolate chip eyes into mine.

"Yep. That's it." Shit that was change I had left out my $700 Job Corps money.

"Alright. Come on."

She took me to an abandoned house on 25th Street. Just 3 blocks down from Ericka's house, and 4 blocks from my Grandma's house.

I give her the five dollars. When she pull her panties down, I get back hard. We having sex in an abandoned house, on top of an old forsaken mattress. I'm on top of her, so busy locked in, I'm not even paying attention. Another guy had crept in through the back door. I didn't even know it. I didn't even see him coming. I heard her scream and she was waving her hands and shouting at him,

"NO! NO! HE GOOD! HE GOOD!" She say it again, "He good."

I don't know if the guy had a gun, a weapon on him, or what. I don't know if he was her pimp; or just checkin in on her; or if this was a trap spot for them to rob or murder niggas that was trickin. But right then and there, that could've been my time, the end of my life, just 4 blocks from my Grandma's house, and 3 blocks down from where I had just left from Ericka's house. I could've DIED.

He stood up there behind me. He looked me cold in my eyes. It did look like he might be holdin onto a gun, up under his jeans. I watched him turn and go away, out the same backdoor he came. The LORD had saved my life, even through what morally might be seen as a forbidden woman.

Even after this incident happened, it still didn't trigger me to run out to the LORD. I was still doing the opposite. I was living my young life.

I was running from him.

I have told guys in prison that story, of course more explicit, but I never reported it to Ericka, to my friends, or family. I just kept it moving. In retrospect, prayerfully, that was able to happen.

It felt good to be with Ericka. She made her mistakes. But she kept me out of trouble. When she had Tori, she qualified for welfare. She started getting assistance. It was like $230 a month.

She moved out of Grandmother's house so she could start her struggle as a single mother.

Chapter 19.

Ericka had moved out Randolph Apartments, with her cousin Kenya. They had something in common, they were both single mothers. Kenya lived in a comfortable two bedroom apartment with her (2) children.: Salone and Jonathan.

When Ericka had moved out there, that's what actually started to bring our relationship tighter together. I was takin Ericka wit me to church every Sunday, and everything. But Newport News though.

Not sayin she won't good enough for Hampton, but it won't my call. That's on The General. If I had said something, then she woulda changed it. But I ain't over ride my momma. First off.: out of respect. And for 2nd, if I had made that move, I woulda felt like, like that was me sayin I'm ready to marry this girl. If I woulda started showin her off to ALL the Saints, then I woulda been makin a statement, that yeah, I'm bout to marry this girl.

That probably woulda happened; but it's a lotta shit goin on behind the scenes. Oh boy, where do we get started wit this.:

Ericka's cousin, Kenya had a sexual attraction for me. I had already knew that. Because she went at me one time before. But I didn't take her serious. I thought her and Ericka was just tryin to trick me to see what I do. So I was like,

"Yeah. Whateva," I laughed it off.

Kenya is a caramel brown skin, and she actually hadda bad ass body in high school. She went to a Hampton school. I think she graduated from Kecoughtan. Her body changed a little bit through her effects of having babies. But she still was attractive. It's crazy I was even on her radar, cause I rarely if barely ever even used to see Kenya, before Ericka moved in with her. I saw her more in pictures at her Grandma house, than what I saw her in person.

But in person, she is really real good peoples, and a mother in every since of the word. She loves her babies. She'll work extremely hard, long hours, and over time, to care for her children, and provide them what they need.

I just had to put that in there. For me that part is even more important about Kenya, than what else I'm about to tell you. But, it all came back around. Me and Ericka was laying out on the living room floor. That's where we had made a bed. I was on my back, and Ericka was layin on my chest, and she told me,

"Kenya wanna fuck you."

What's the natural reaction to this. I laugh, tryin to read.: is these bitches playin or what!? At the same time, I'm tryin to see is they talkin bout doin a threesome.

But when she hear me laugh, Ericka jus say, "Yeah, alright. You laugh. I'm serious."

I'm pondering. My mind sweeping round all this. At the time, Kenya has a man. A nigga name Don. That's when this whole threesome thing jus blew the fuck apart. The plan go that I get to fuck Kenya, but only if Don get to fuck Ericka. These two freaked out ass muthafuckas- - Kenya wanna fuck me and Don wanna fuck Ericka.

I'm thinking bout it... until.:

Ericka strongly says, "I betchu one thing.: she might suck yo dick better than me, but I bet you, her pussy ain't good as mine. I betchu that!"

OH, HELL NAW!! That shit just shut everything down!!!! Ain't no way I'm gon let this nigga fuck my Snu.

But it still came up at least two more times, after that. When I learned this nigga was down on

Ericka, I ain't see him the same. He'll grin at me then go in the room wit his girl Kenya.

But one day Kenya tried me again. My bus get there, and Ericka's not at home. Kenya sittin up on the chair, and she fuckin wit me.

She show me the titties. She pull em out, and she suck her own nipples. Yeah, she got some big ass titties. Uhh- - but that shit ain't...

I'm tryin to see the pussy. She shakin her head, No. She keep suckin on her titties, showin me the titties. She want me to make a decision. I grab my trunk, I'm bout to pull da horn out, she put her titties up so she can see, as soon as she do that,

BOOM!! Here come Ericka right through the door. So that kilt all that right there. I did wanna have sex with Kenya, I'm not gon lie about that; but I hadda phaat booty RED freak bitch. I was tryin to weigh out... was I getting a fair trade?

Then what really kilt it was late night walks to Food Lion. Me and Ericka would walk, hold hands, and talk. I would walk wit her to 7- 11, but we had longer walks to Food Lion. The one on Jefferson. Up from Main Street. Up from Randolph and Bellwood. And that's when I heard Ericka make me a promise. When she said that,

"No matter, even if we don't get married, or

we got somebody else- - whenever one of us call, we got to always be there for each other."

So- - let me get this straight.: you sayin no matter what- - if we fuckin somebody else, or even if we marry other people- - whenever I wanna hit, all I gotta do is call You?

"Yep," she said, "We always gon have lines of communication to each other."

WHOA!! What the fuck!? This shit is unbelievable. She was giving me a license to fuck and be with other women, and she was still gon be there. Now, hol, hol, hold on Ms. Ericka; we might put this to the test. But as of right now, it's still probable me and Ericka might get married. I like it right there.

December came, and my father and mother observed me walking the stage and receiving my certificate in Accounting. That's when I realized how important me getting an education was important to my parents. When I came back home, I was still unemployed. I went unemployed into the early 1995. I was considering re- enrolling in Job Corps.

That's when the Spirit of God came back to see me.:

It was in January of 1995. I was 19 years old. I was one month from turning 20. After Job Corps,

I was living back with my parents, out Warwick Mobile Homes, off Jefferson Avenue, out Newport News, in Virginia. Then it was one night in January of 95, I went to sleep...

When the dream opens up, there are very violent random mass shootings. I can explain and articulate that now, but I couldn't back then, because I believe this dream was even before the Columbine High School incident had ever even happened. At that time, these incidents were completely unknown and unheard of anywhere in the United States.

In the dream, people were running. People were fleeing for their lives. There was rapid and frequent barrages of gun fire, from different varieties of guns. I saw people dropping dead in the street. Left and right.

Then I saw people all running to one church. The one church in the city was filled. There were so many people trying to squeeze into one church, they couldn't all fit. So next, they started running to all the churches, until every kind of church, was filled. Then, when every kind of church was filled, they all started running to the mosques. Then all of the mosques became filled, then they began running to these oval shaped, Coliseum-styled buildings, which today I would interpret as being synagogues. Back then, I didn't even know what a synagogue was.

But the people thought in the human concept.: That they might as well get close to God, and make peace with God before they die. Which is how I commonly thought. That at sometime, I would get close to God before I die.

But while all this shooting and killing was going on, I thought of the most sensible logical question.: 'Lord, where was I?'

All of a sudden, a fresh scene rips open in the dream. I see myself sitting at a bar. I ordered a glass of liquor to drink from the bartender. It looked like it might be Hennessey. The crazy part is that at that time, I didn't even drink. I wasn't getting high or nothing.

I was a clean cut kid, who had never been in trouble with the law, and I was waiting on employment.

"Nakio! Nakio Johnson!" I had hollered out loud from the bar, when I saw a reflection of one of my old Job Corps friends splatter off the shine from the bar's mirror's burnished reflection.

"Hey Mon..." Nakio had just hit me with a fake Jamaican accent. He even had long dreadlocks; a HARD!! funky Afro- Centric green, yellow, and red t- shirt; fading blue denim jeans with rips and holes; and the whole hard sole leather sandals to buff- out his entire gimmick.

As I enjoyed in conversation with my friend, two plain clothes men walked up and asked, "You Nakio? Nakio Johnson?"

It was THE POLICE!! They flashed off their badges. There was one black detective and one white detective. The black detective did all the talking. I followed them outside to a black and white cop car as they had arrested Nakio.

I asked the Police, "What are you arresting him for?"

They said, "Murder."

And in the dream, I screamed out loud, "Nakio! Did you do it? Did you do it Nakio?"

Nakio didn't talk back. Of course now it sounds crazy, but in the dream, I wanted to hear him say he didn't do it, because I wanted to help my friend.

When I saw the image of Nakio being dragged off in that cop car. I cried, and cried, and cried, and cried. In Job Corps, at one time, I had saw Nakio close like a brother. We had rode the same bus, on the same day, up to Woodstock, Maryland. So this was really crushing me. It was just then that I felt these huge massive metaphysical hands reach down from out of the sky, and scooped me, and lifted me up. It's hands kept pulling me up, and up, and up.

When I looked up, I saw these huge long spiritual arms. By the touch, I knew that it was God; and that's when I realized that the "Nakio" in the dream was really me.

God kept pulling me up, and up, and up, and up, and up into the sky. I realized that I was going up higher: past the clouds. I became conscious of life and death. I became conscious that if I kept on going up that I was going to die. I squirmed in HIS palm from God drawing me in.

At first HE kept holding me pulling me up, but at the same time cupping me, protecting me, so I wouldn't fall. Then HIS hands just started spinning me, and spinning me, and spinning me, and spinning me, and spinning me. Then HE placed me back down. Back down on earth. When HE placed me down, I was standing and preaching in a pulpit, at the Gospel Spreading Church. And I WAS HOLY! GOD HAD MADE ME WHOLE!

The crazy part is that I was standing in the Gospel Spreading Church, but I was wearing a Yarmulke and a Tzitzit. Back then I didn't know what a yarmulke and tzitzit was; and that's not something worn in the Gospel Spreading Church. So these were "signs" of things unheard of. (Ref.: see Hebrews 11: 1).

At the end of the dream, when I went out in the street, mobs and swarms of people ran, they were running up to me, to see me, and touch me, and to shake my hand. I was walking with other people, that I guess to best way to explain it, that they were witnesses to my truth. I was walking down a street, and then the last thing I saw was a Big Ball of Fire come from up out of the sky, and it came straight directly at me. I couldn't run, to the right or to the left. It came straight directly at me, and IT HIT ME! I felt both death and the end of the dream, both at the same time! God put the fear of God in me HIMSELF, during that dream.

I woke up, and I busted through the door of that lil one and 'a half- a- bedroom room trailer. I almost flipped my momma house over! It was the realest and the scariest dream I had ever had my whole entire life. And I dream often. I dream almost every time I go to sleep. So I've had billions of dreams. But this one dream I never forget. And to this day, I can still tell you every part of that dream, word for word.

"JAMIE, what's wrong!?" That is my mother. I broke her up out of her sleep with my father.

She walked up on me, from out of her bedroom, and into the living room. And she stood there, and she listened to me cry, and cry, and cry, and cry, and I told her the whole dream. In one dream Yud- Heh- Vav- Heh (God) had showed me the whole rest of my life. HE showed me how I would turn out. It was January 1995, and I was 19 years old.

Ironically, I did everything "in my power" to STOP that dream from coming true. EVERYTHING! EVERYTHING! EVERYTHING! EVERYTHING!

Cause I couldn't do it. I couldn't do what God wanted me to do. I didn't want to go to jail, to fulfill HIS promise.

At 19, I had never been arrested a day in my life. I never committed any hard crimes. I never had a charge. Man, I didn't even have a speeding ticket. I had always taken pride in not having a criminal record. Especially when I used to fill out my job applications, and the fact I could mark N/A on the section requesting information about having a Criminal History.

I never expected to go to jail or prison. It wasn't how I was raised. I was taught to be honest. To tell the truth. To be a law-abiding citizen. To have respect for the police. All good things.

About a month after God gave me the dream, I was at the altar giving Elder Johnson my hand and Christ my heart. I had waited about a month, because I waited to turn 20. I did it like a

Birthday gift. But contrary to what you might think, it didn't make my life no easier.

I rarely used drugs. I barely smoked cigarettes or drank alcohol. But by 6 years later, I WAS DOING IT ALL!! I had thought that by me joining the church, it would off- set what God had showed me in my dream. But HIS PROMISE was already set into motion.:

Chapter 20.

Ericka didn't like it, cause she think that mean we can't have sex no more. I seen the rain run down her round brown hashbrown eyes. For real, since I was already taking her to church, I thought she would follow my lead. She wasn't there the Sunday I joined; but I was drawin the stage to marry Ericka. I didn't tell her that, because I wanted her to do it naturally on her own. I didn't want her footsteps to be fostered jus to get 'a ring.

In the midst of waitin for her to make up her mind, I prayed to God for a job. My father was a welder by trade, so he used to get on wit work through a temporary work service, called Abacus. I followed in those footsteps, but instead of getting on with a temp service named Abacus, I got on wit Reliance.

Reliance hired me to go to work for a subcontractor for the Newport News Shipyard. So this was how I got broke in to my experience of working in the Shipyard. The subcontractor's name I worked for was called Nance Construction, a company out Hampton, off Aberdeen Road.

Meanwhile, Ericka had STOPPED going to church. And other than Ericka, problems are mounting at home. I thought it would be easier at home now that I was "saved," a preacher's son, and going to the same church my parents raised me up in. The dream showed me preaching in the pulpit in Newport News; so when I hear preachers say, "The Lord called me to preach." I questioned within myself, was this dream God calling me to preach? Could this be the start of me following in my father's footsteps?

My mother would look at me with a flat face, and say, "You need to get you a wife."

And my father would say, "Jamie, you need to get saved."

I don't know what the 2nd one meant. I thought that's what I already did. I thought I was just waiting to get baptized. Something like that.

I would read my Bible on my own. Something I never really done, since I learned how to READ. I'll always take my King James Version to church with me, when I go. But I read my Bible verses the same time I'm following the narrative of the Elder. And at home, I had Elder Micheaux's tapes and records. I listened to Elder Micheaux's style and cadence. I listened to him preach so much, I could perform his whole sermon back, word- for- word.

Elder Johnson himself would later do the same thing, Live, at a Tent Revival Meeting we had in Newport News.

I had never heard of a preacher preach, what Evangelical pastors on network tv today talk down on as, "fire and brimstone ministries." But that's what Elder Micheaux preached. And that's the same ministry I grew up under all my life. But in my opinion, nobody could do it better than Elder Micheaux. Even after his 1968 death, his preaching's had withstood the test of time.

Especially from a man God had produced from a 6th grade education.

Elder Micheaux had paved a foundation that we accepted as being The Truth. That's why we disregarded the dwindling attendance numbers from Saints and children in the audience. It was like that at the Newport News church, because Newport News is a larger church, and some of the other churches across the field. But not all the churches.

One of my brothers from church, Brother Nate began to pick me up, and took me with him all the way up to one of the sister branches of the Gospel Spreading Church of God in Lothian, Maryland. But it was an underlying tone to it.: maybe I would be able to go up there and find me a wife.

It was a younger audience. Something like Hampton. Except the Saints in Lothian was more fertile. Couples might have four, five, six, seven children. It was a bigger church than Hampton and listening to the choir sing; was like being at a music concert.

Nate had found a girl he was interested in, who sang in the choir. And when she lead sing, she can melt the mic down. But for me, most of these girls was too young. Any girl riding the school bus.: even 17 was TOO YOUNG for me at this age. I didn't see anything worth focusing my attention on, but I kept going back with Nate, once a month to Lothian, just for the service.

I said it was 4 black families out Warwick Mobile Homes-- my bad. It was 5. Mr. Roger Coger drove Pentran city buses for a living. He has a wife, named Mrs. Floretta. Her and my mother became friends. Then their family made friends with our family. They even came out to church with us a few times. Just like my parents, Mr. and Mrs. Coger are very spiritual people. Real serious about serving God. Roger was a Vietnam Veteran, just like my father, and through some kind of military benefit, Mr. Coger had moved him and his wife into a house off of Wickham Avenue, in between Briarfield Road and Mercury Boulevard.

And because my father was also a Vietnam Vet, the conversation Ms. Floretta gave my mother was, "Why don't y'all do it too?"

And yeah, so, we did. We got approved. And the Lord BLESSED my father to finally get my momma her lifelong passion, as a wife and as a mother. We moved into a house, in the same neighborhood, about 2 blocks down from the Coger's. At 5912 Wickham.

The backyard was HUGE!! T- Bone could now rip and run. But I had to put him on a chain temporarily, because the fence had a weak side, and T- Bone exploited this weakness by running out the yard, and into the street. Fortunately, he always come back. He never got too far where he got lost or hurt. After me and my father reinforced the lame side, then I was able to take my lil right hand man back off his chain and let him run around in the

385

yard.

He didn't stay still to watch it, but T- Bone like to play football, ever since I introduced the sport to him from a puppy. He like to play Hot Ball, out in the trailer park. Since I didn't have friends to play football with no more, once I left Paula Maria, I'd play it- - with my dog.

He understands the sport real well. He knows when he get the ball in his mouth, the object is to run, and not let me tackle him. Funny part about it, T- Bone would run from fence to fence, just like a person, running goal post to goal post.

If I run at him, he'll kneel into his front 2 paws and wait for me to get close, then he would jook, and put on the jets on all 4 feet, so I couldn't tackle him. I would have to trick him. I gotta just walk, and wait for him to lay down and start chewing the football like a dog bone. Then I would walk up on him, like I'm gon pat him, then...

SNATCH!! the football out his mouth!! And he would jump to chase me and tackle me. He reminded me of Barry, cause he would put that lil seagull look right up in his eye, and pitch his whole body at my legs.

That's when this football game is OVER! That's some embarrassing shit, to get tackled by your own dog, and go tumbling into the damn fence. And why you all stretched out, he be standing over you laughing at you, grab the football back, and get it goin the other way. When we got a bigger yard on Wickham, he'd always grab his football, and look for me to play Hot Ball wit him. I'd do it for a little while till I got tired, or he'll pace his lil seagull eyes at me, waiting for me to run wit the ball, so he can get to keep trying to rip my feet right from under me. Wit his sneaky lil dog self. He was tryin to trick Me.

I see you T- Bone.

Winters on Wickham would get so cold, my momma let T- Bone in the house to keep warm. I would come in the house, and my momma would smile,

"T- Bone in your room."

This was different than what I was used to on Troy Drive. Normally, I just heat him up some milk, on the stove. And rub his fur down in a blanket, to warm him up. But now, I go in there, and he chillin... on my carpet. Layin up in the heat. After all that time, after Uncle Ronnie had housebroke him, he stayed housebroken. He'll sit there and watch 'a lil tv. He didn't chew up nothing. He didn't try to jump in my bed. He didn't piss on nothing. He waited for me to take him outside before he used the bathroom.

I thought this might become a new permanent thing, but once the cold was over,

"Take that dog 'on back outside," my father hollered me.

Well T- Bone- - I tried.

The summer months was the same on Wickham, as on Troy. The ticks would fuck T- Bone up. And I'll have to go out there with flea and tick shampoo, to loosen them up, pull them out his fur with a hard pair of pliers, and I had a little tin can, where I would burn them bastards in hell for biting my dog.

T- Bone sure was glad to be getting this fiery furlong nuisance from up off of him. He would look up at me, hang his tongue out, and be lickin his lips. That's how I knew he was happy. And he probably was hungry, both at the same time.

Being on Wickham even put me closer to being at work. I was like a 5-minute ride. When I worked at Nance, I hadda good crew of guys I worked around.: Mike, Chad, Kenny, Ricky, Tristan, John was the Boss. Jim Nance was the Boss, but John was the Boss that drove his white pick- up truck out in the field, to supervise us, to make sure we was doin what we supposed to be doin.

I had a job setting up a pattern of bank screens, so Shipyard administrative workers can sit cubbyhole in they desk. I got, first hand, to meet some exciting sharp black men and women Naval engineers and architects. They'd make designs for ships and aircraft carriers for the US Navy, and of course... submarines. A lot of these blueprints are military secrets, so of course, they're not just gon sit there, and let you sweep over blueprints, but they'll stop for a minute and entertain a good conversation with me.

It's incredible seeing a submarine get built from the ground up, before it gets commissioned by the President to sail out in the ocean, and protect

American borders. I see a whole lotta sweat poppin from welding pipes that go in to putting together this underwater tanker, that's big as 'a whale's body.

These soon to be submerged machines are cool to watch up close, but my favorite is my high school favorite... the Aircraft Carrier. Walking the top, even in dry dock, some of these decks have to be as tall as a 30 or 40 feet buildings! Some of everything's inside man, including movie theaters, indoor basketball courts, work out gyms, sleeping quarters, showers, and chow halls, all up under my feet, it's like I'm on an on- the- water sea castle.

I was reminiscent of my military dreams in JROTC. I practiced my moves, to see if I can still get it,

"Autennn- HUUUU!"

My will to wanna be a Marine. Even after I dropped JROTC in high school, my desire to be in the military had resurrected at Job Corps. They had recruiters show up to Center, and I had took the test- - the ASVAB test just to see how well I could do,

"Right FACE!"

It's not really a pass or fail test. It's a placement test, for them to see what skills you good at, then they'll assign you to the military branch based upon need and necessity,

"Left FACE!"

I felt like a prince of armor even when I walked

around the campus of the US Naval Academy, in Annapolis. But I didn't stay in Maryland for all that. I chose to come back home, so HEY! it's where I ended up,

"Back FACE!"

So when I get back home, I go down to the recruiter, I took the test AGAIN,

"Back FACE!"

I take the test, over by the Daily Press, over on Warwick Boulevard. But I wasn't searching for full-time employment, only part-time Reserve duty,

"Forward MARCH!"

Now, I can feel the grip of the concrete surface beneath my feet. My toes sweep at the pebbles where soon refurbished white lines will be sprayed down on the deck to provide a street path for US Naval and Marine fighter jets,

"To the Left, MARCH!"

I wanted Reserve duty, that way I could have a military career and a civilian career, BOTH at the same time,

"To the rear, MARCH!"

That way I could retire from Reserve duty in 20- 30 years, and still have my civilian career and income. That was the plan,

"Half- step, MARCH!"

One problem.: I got (2) metal rods on my spine. I didn't tell the recruiter. He showed up to Troy Drive;

"What are you waitin for? Come on let's go!" he drill sergeant to me. He came to pick me up to drag me to getting enlisted.

"Wait a minute," my father said to him, "Did he tell you he got (2) rods on his back?"

"HALT!"

The recruiter shook his head NO at me.

"Parade Rest."

Then he hauled ass to his car, jumped in, sped off, and I never saw him again.

"At ease."

My father briefly explained to me that he didn't want that life for me. And I never tried to enlist into the military service ever again.

Working at Nance wasn't my first time knowing of Tristan. We both went to Warwick. And we both was in JROTC at the same time. I remembered him. He said he didn't remember me. He was an upper classman. He took me under his wing and looked to me like I was his little bro.

When I used to go to work, I didn't really get dirty. We used to dress a little bit, cause it's women all over the shipyard.: you got engineers, architects,

supervisors, administration, AND, you got
BITCHES!! Bitches! Bitches! Bitches! Bitches!
Bitches! Bitches! BITCHES!! Navy bitches and
Marine bitches, unloading from ships and carriers,
strolling all around. You know how bitches do.
These Navy bitches look REAL good in uniform
though. Especially when they in them tight navy
jeans. What!? Shit is crazy!?

But Tristan's mind is on somewhere else. He like,

"Yeah bro, you gotta go wit me to the club.
All the bitches at the club..."

He keep talkin all this shit bout goin out to
The Club. The whole time, I'm thinking he talkin
about a dance club. Shit, I'on dance; much less go
to a club. For some stupid ass reason, I said,

"I'll go."

It was on a Friday. And I got on like some
blue jeans, lil fly Izod shirt. Some shit like that. I'd
wear Izod, Chap shirts, sometimes Polo. Shit, I was
workin in the Shipyard. So it's cool for what I was
doin. Like I say, I ain't really get dirty.

Usually after work, we ride back to the shop, and
leave and go home from there. But... not today.

We leave straight from the shipyard, and go down,
and walk cross the street. We go inside this bar. It's
a Korean woman behind the counter. So Tristan is
telling her,

"This my lil brother right here. When you
see him, you see me."

And she's like, "Yeah. Yeah. Ok baby."

I don't know what the hell goin on. Then she glances at me, and she says,

"You hungry baby?"

"Yeah. Yeah. He hungry. Ma, give him that good shit," Tristan answers for me over to her.

"Ok. Ok. I got you. Coming right up."

He callin her, Ma. This woman I just met, he got me callin her Ma. It's like she's coken and grillin green peppers on a skillet. She whips it in like 10 minutes. When I bite into it, it's extremely SPICY!! I got steam and snot running out my nose at the same time.

I see some ladies come in. They all know Tristan. Tristan knows all them, and he's sayin,

"This my lil brother right here. When you see him, you see me." The same thing he said before. I'on know where he goin wit this.

And these ladies are the same way, "Yeah...Yeah... Ok. Ok."

They all come in together. They all walk together. They all go through a door I perceive as being a bathroom, together. I'm used to it, cause I'm raised by women. Women dominate as the majority of my family. So I'm used to seeing women stick together, and travel to the bathroom together. It's nothing to me.

Then,

"Hey,"

I see some more Shipyard gentlemen come through the door, they gettin off work. They come to the bar and start purchasing beer. Then next thing I know...

"Ju- ju- ju- ka- ju- ka- ju- ka- ju- ka- ju- ka- ju- ka- ju- ka," this music starts playing. And I turn around, and I see this mirrored disco ball is twirling.

Man, what the fuck these people got going on up in here!?

Next thing I know, those same ladies that went to the back, that I thought was going to the bathroom!? Now, they on the stage...

in swimsuits, bikinis, thongs, bras and panties. Grabbin hold 'a pole.

"Whooo- whooo! What the fuck!?" I'm bout to run right up to the stage.

"Whoa. Whoa. Hold on lil bro... let me explain something to you..."

Tristan explained to me The Rules of Etiquette. But that's how I got broke in to Strip Clubs. And we got paid EVERY week! So I was going to the strip club EVERY week! Every two weeks. Then it might be three- four times a week. Between Moon Light and Solid Gold.

It was a few dancers that really caught my attention. It was a young lady that went by the stage name, Polo. That caught my attention.

My home girl, Pepsi. That really was her name. I knew Pepsi from school. Pepsi was a white girl, who has 'a BOOTY like a black girl. And Pepsi is a hood girl. She was from Glen Gardens. She was cultured around Black people. And Pepsi has got since Warwick.

Mr. Plenty's granddaughter was up in there. Mr. Plenty was the first barber I ever had. He was the one who used to cut my hair close and round. My whole hairline wassa circle. Cause that's how my momma told him to cut it. When I got a teenager, and I had money to get my own haircuts, I'd go to Esquire on 25th. I didn't go to Mr. Plenty on 22nd.

It won't nothing personal against Mr. Plenty. I had just outgrown some childhood things. And being a teenager, I wanted to explore, and be where it's poppin! Mr. Plenty's ain't where it was poppin. His daughter worked with him. She was the best part of his shop. But she was older than me. I ain't never try to go at her, or no shit like that.

His granddaughter, was by another one of his daughters. Not by that one. Me and his granddaughter, were about the same age. We never went to the same schools. We knew of each other, but we ain't really know each other. But we know each other when we see each other.

Now, Mr. Plenty's granddaughter was

dancing on her back, and my head was between her knees. It's crazy. Cause I never saw her like that. I always thought she wassa lil skinny girl. When this girl strip down- - this girl gotta body. Surprised me.

Then there was my favorite... My Baby. Besides Polo, my most favorite dancer was this girl named Rio. Umm, umm, umm, umm. Mary J Blige be jumpin in the juke box. And the same time Mary J be singing, Rio was singing to me and strippin. I was in love wit Rio. Until...

There she was...

No... not Joy.

It was The Baddest Girl that I grew up with from church. No... not Marsha. Marsha was the second baddest one. Remember. This girl was asss and shoulders above Marsha. Crazy part about it.: how much she favor Kenya. She look like she and Kenya can be sisters. Like twins. Except this girl's name is Charity. And her body is still in shape. ALLLLL THE WAY IN SHAPE.

Am I gon let her dance for me? You DAMN RIGHT!!!! After she danced for me, I took her down off stage. She gave me a date In THE CLUB!?? I took her to a table. Maybe it's the puff of cigarette smoke that's in the air. Maybe it's the foam of the beer on my breath. I'on know... but I go at her.

I tried to buy her a drink. But,

"I don't drink." She said to me.

"Alright then- - I'll buy you something to

smoke."

"I don't smoke." Damn, she don't do that either. She is so precious, the girl sound like cotton candy when she talk. Everything is calm and tenda as a whisper.

So fuck it! Man, fuck it! I just go in. I keep tellin her how pretty she is. I tell her how much I noticed her at Hampton. She went to Newport News too, but mostly Hampton; or I'll see her on the Church Farm. Yes, the church has a farm, up in Williamsburg. Never mind that right now. I'm sitting across from THE BADDEST girl in church, and one of THE BADDEST women IN THE WORLD!!

The crazy part about it.: I ain't know we was gon have this much conversation. Because we never talked before. She was shocked to hear everything I was telling her. She was a little bit older than me. Now it was makin sense why I ain't seen her in a few years.

But I ain't gon lie.: Charity is BAAAAD! BAAAAD! BAAAAD! BAAAAD! BAAAAD! BAAAAD! BAAAAD! BAAAAD!!!!!! I woulda proposed to her right there in Solid Gold. Fresh off da pole my nigga. What!? Damn right! Charity is worth all that! But she said,

"I'm married."

"WHA!? WHA!? WHA!? WHA!? WHAT!?" I feel like Lil Weezy up in this bitch.

"I'm already married," she say it again.

"To who?" Man, who the fuck is this lucky ass nigga? So I can BEAT his ass!?

"You don't know him," she smiles to me, "He ain't go to church wit us."

I'm fucked up. She fucked me all the way up wit all this. I didn't know she was strippin; and I didn't know it wassa weddin.

"Well look, I'm tryin ta fuck," I go to the next thing.

I was in the wrong, especially since she just told me she was married. But I was tryin my hand, cause Charity is 'a Fantasy girl; if you ever did wanna see one. She has my brain racing too fast. This girl is soooo damn pretty, man. This shit is crazy. The smoothest butta pecan swirl caramel complexion, you could ever wanna see. Like'a jar when you first pop da top! And Charity is soooo phaat! Her body is Amazing!

"Um- umm. No," she said to me.

My head coulda dropped through the damn table.

"I'll dance for you though."

I saw her a few more times at The Club!?? But her mother and my mother are friends. She told her mother she saw me there. Her momma told my momma. And you know how that go.: that blew my cover cause I'm supposed to be SAVED! But my momma ain't really trip on it the way I thought she would. She only brought it up that one or two times.

After that, she said no more about it.

When I go to church, of course, she ain't there; but her momma and her daddy be there. They don't say nothing about it, but they be looking at me.

But I understand. I won't dare say anything bad. It's nothing bad to ever even say. Her father is passed away now. May YAHWEH BLESS his soul into Everlasting Life. And they have a very beautiful family. I have nothing but the utmost love and respect for her and her family. We never saw too much of each other after that, and then I didn't see her at all.

So, that's that.

At this time, I was on and off again with Ericka. Mostly on. Even when we was supposed to be broke up, we was still having sex. Then we was back together...

I thought.

A marriage to Ericka was possible...

I thought.

Ericka never did go back with me to church. I didn't pressure her. The same way my momma didn't pressure me. One day I go to work, I get off at 3:30. Not 3:35. Not 3:33. Not 3:32. Not 3:31. I call Ericka at 12:00.

It's lunch time. By now, she has her own apartment out Marshall Courts, for her and Tori, out Newport News. And, I'm calling from a Shipyard phone.

Don't mean shit. Aye! I jus threw it in there.

12:00 call her- - talk to her. I get off at 3:30. Not...
yeah, all that. I call her after 3:00,

"I'm on my way to yo house."

"I'll be waitin," she tell me.

Chad drops me off in the truck at Be- Lo, up
on 39th Street. Ericka's house like 3 blocks down. I
get to her backdoor. This out the projects, where
the backdoor is the front door, and the front door is
really the backdoor. Yo, whoever designed this shit
had to suck in architecture school. But that's how it
is.

"Boom, boom, boom, boom, boom, boom,
boom," that's me knockin on the door.

She don't come to the door.

"Boom, boom, boom, boom, boom, boom,
boom."

She don't come to the door.

Maybe she don't hear me. Maybe she in the
bathroom. Fell asleep or something.

"BOOM! BOOM! BOOM! BOOM! BOOM!
BOOM! BOOM!"

She still don't come to the BACK door like regular
normal people up out these projects. So, I go round
to the FRONT.

400

"BOOM! BOOM! BOOM! BOOM! BOOM! BOOM! BOOM!"

"BOOM! BOOM! BOOM! BOOM! BOOM! BOOM! BOOM!"

"BOOM! BOOM! BOOM! BOOM! BOOM! BOOM! BOOM!"

Then, she comes to the door.

She is lookin PHAAAT and lookin soft. Her juicccy RED asss in this smalled chocolate négligé. No bra. No panties. When I see this, all the guts of my anger jus fall off 'a fuckin cliff somewhere. I'on know.

So I'm hugging on her. Grippin. Squeezin. Next thing I know, 'a nigga walk down the stairs, zippin up his pants. Ericka- - WHYYYY??? What the fuck is you doin?

Man, I got the kinda girl that fit like 'a dove in 'a pimp hand.

She let me walk her over to her couch. She sittin down wit me. The nigga walk past us, and go sit at her kitchen table. He get on her phone and start dialing for his homies. I start kissin on her in front of him, and running my hand up her naked thighs. She only stoppin me before I get to the pussy. He still just watching me make my statement. He sittin over there wit her cheap checked red and white plastic table cover, and cold Chanello's Pizza.

"Mwwwah," I'm turning her juiccccy ass lips round to me and rubbin between her legs.

"STOP," she said.

This my pussy. I know it is. She know it is.

Finally she say to me, "Leave please."

"What!?"

"Can you please leave," she said.

"Alright," I get up. I leave. I go back out the FRONT door.

Before I walk away, somethin say, look up. I look at her face. She's crying. I see her lips mouth the words, "I love you."

I see her close the door. I was gone. I walked from her house, all the way to my momma's house, off Briarfield Road. That's how mad I was. The best way to get over it... just move on.

That's what I did.

When I went back to work, Chad, Kenny, and Tommy was asking me if I had a driver's license. I told them I did. And they were telling me that Mr. Nance was hiring for another driver. He needed another driver. All I had to do was go to DMV and get a copy of my driving record.

That's what I did.

And I came back to work and presented it to

Mr. Nance, inside his office. I had an A- 1 driving record, cause shit, I ain't drive shit. I just had a license. He ain't know that. I know that. Mr. Nance hired me. He took me off the Reliance payroll of $4.50 an hour, and he put me on his payroll, of $6.50 an hour. Still gettin paid the same- - EVERY week. I went from a being temporary employee to a permanent employee.

What do that mean? That mean, it's time to celebrate my new job and new $2.00 pay raise. How? That mean, IT'S TIME TO GO SHOP-PING!! I'm bout to go buy Me a brand new car.

Why not? If I'm gon drive-- Hey! I might as well drive full- time. It's no sense in jus drivin when I get to work.

Jus one problem.: I wanna stick. I don't wanna automatic transmission.

But I don't know how to drive a manual transmission.

Only one way to find out. I coulda went through Hunt's Driving School for like $150 to learn how to drive a stick or, I could say,

"Hey Rick, I'll pay you $75 to teach me how to drive a stick."

See how that work?

Ricky lives all the way somewhere out there in Smithfield County. That's at least 30 minutes from now, going fast. He doesn't even drive. Cause Ricky is 'a whaaat!?? 'A Habitual Offender.

According to his judge. Ricky ain't even supposed to be behind the wheel of his own burgundy Honda Accord.

That's why he's NOT. His wife humps the Honda bringing him to work, every morning. Every evening, after 3:30, she picks him up, every afternoon. All the way from Smithfield. All the way somewhere out there, across the James River Bridge, from Newport News. So when she drives up today after 3:30, he says,

"Hey Babe, he wants me to show him how to drive a stick, for $75."

"Fo what!?"

"Fo $75." Like we all say it at the same time, right.

"Give it here."

I pay her the $75. And she get up out the driver's seat, and get in the back. I get in the driver's seat, wit Ricky ridin shotgun. The Honda already running.

And he say, "Alright, put yo foot on the clutch...

Take it outta neutral, put it in 1st gear. 1st gear is all the way up, on the top left...

Tap the gas. Ride it in 1st, til you get to 15 miles per hour... Alright, now, put it in 2nd. 2nd gear straight back, on the left..."

And when it got to 25, I put it in 3rd gear. I choked

the clutch a few times. When I got to 35, I was in 4th gear, in the middle, straight down to the bottom. And 5th gear was all the way up to the right, when I got it to 45.

After I was humpin the Honda for 20 minutes. I drove myself home. His wife got back up front, and they drove 'on off, all the way somewhere out there. Perhaps deep into the wilderness. That same night, I was at Casey Chevrolet. THE LARGEST CHEVROLET DEALERSHIP ON THE EAST COAST. Well, Hey! That's what they say.

My most favorite General Motors car of all- time is a Corvette. I never had one, but HEY! I think it's the greatest American machine that was ever made.

I stood eyeball to eyeball, with the beautiful heartthrob of every living automobile and sports car magazine cover since 1953. The blood of her soul, beat as the bust of a bull against the shaled shalloped showroom floor. She just melted me down to the wax of her tile. OHHHHH!!

"I want the RED one."

I wish I could say. But my bank account hasn't made it to $75,000 yet. Mr. Nance ain't paying me that much. I got to find a 5- speed ride in my price range. It didn't absolutely matter to me about it being a brand new car, but that's what I ended up checking out.

Only one problem.: I don't got no damn credit, man.

I got a job. But I don't got no bills. And that means

what!? Yes, I gotta getta co- signer.

For real, I didn't expect my father to do it. He had already tricked a $100 Pontiac Grand Prix up for me a year ago.

This is how it happened.:

After I had came back from Job Corps, wit my $700. I wanted a car. I searched the Classified section of The Daily Press Newspaper, and there it was.:

A Pontiac Grand Prix. The owners only wanted one-hundred dollars for it. I show it to my Pops.

"Hey, Daddy, come on... let's go."

But he... was repulsive; "Aww, man. 'A hu'ned dollars!? Man, that car ain't gon be nothing, fo no hundred dollars."

He procrastinated.

By the time we drive out near Fox Hill (That's primarily a low rich and white middle class area out in Hampton), the owners were telling us,

"You're too late. The car's already been sold."

Then he ain't even get straight back in his truck. He standing there looking at it, talkin bout, "That's nice right there."

The body. The paint. The upholstery. All look good from the outside. I'on know about the mechanical.

We never got to it. But he was looking like he wish he could've bought it for himself.

I think that day never left him.

I had saw a Grand Torino after that, like the one they drove in Starsky and Hutch. But this was like a 2 or 3 years later body style. This one was green. I liked it better, and like it packed more muscle, than the Starsky and Hutch model. It was AS IS on Oyster Point's Used Car Dealership. All they wanted was $500, to whip it to the crib.

I was used to these kinds of cars all my life. It's what my father was used to. It's what he bought. He'll change cars, like 'a poor man change Pic- n- Pay shoes, every 1 to 3 months. Some cars was only good for a week. Or how about the used AMC he had bought, that one time; that shit broke down on the same day. Once you drive em, and get yo lil wear- n- tear out of em, it was time to throw them in the trash. Probably over there in Suffolk. The thousands of dollars it would cost for mechanical repairs, is more than half a year of a poor person's whole salary.

But I already knew what to expect out this Torino. I didn't have a clue what my Dad was gon do. I just left him alone. I didn't disturb him.

But now, here both of my parents was sittin up wit me at Casey Chevrolet, and without any argument, my father was co- signing for me to get a BRAND NEW 5- speed, GEO Metro.

I didn't need no money down. I had proof of employment.

It was, "Sign here...

Sign here...

Sign here...

Sign here...

Sign here..."

For hours, and hours, and hours, and hours. Crestar Bank approved the loan, and we got the insurance. I couldn't even leave the lot, til the insurance got through. Once that got processed, I wassa full- time driving man at 12 o' clock midnight.

I felt so GOOD! This shit was betta than 'a Big Wheel. I wanted to drive all the way to California. But I didn't. I just stopped at my homeboy's, Shawn's house out Warwick Mobile Homes. I picked him up, and we went riding out. I was tryin to see if he knew some hoes. He ain't know none, so I dropped him back off at the house.

I ain't feel like fuckin wit Lynn tonight. That shit can wait-- for Tomorrow. I went on back home. I had to be to work at 7:30 in the morning.

My Dad taught me, not to drive my Brand NEW car to work. The boss man might get jealous and might fire me. I listened to my father for a while. I hadda BRAND NEW car sittin at home, and I was still catching rides wit the guys, back and forth to work. They ain't know, cause they'd always pick me up and drop me off on Briarfield Road.

That's like a 2 minute walk from my house.

At work.: I would think about my car, ALLLL day!! I couldn't wait to get home! I get home, take a shower; and I was GONE!

I was neglecting T- Bone.

My all-black licorice car was parked like a scratch across my momma's front yard. When I be backin out, I look and see T- Bone standing at the fence, wit his head cocked sideways, like he was tryin to understand why I was leaving him.

I did start taking him.

The backseat folds down. So I started riding him in the back of the hatch back. Then I'd put his dog bowls in the trunk, and ride him up front, on the passenger side floor. I wanted to see what he would do. He wouldn't chew the seats, the doors, or the shifter. He would sit there civilized, nearby the vent, panting with his tongue hanging out; and I'd ride him out to Buckroe Beach. He'd walk and run so much, he'd run to the first water puddle he find, and lick it, to let me know he was thirsty. I think him kept sniffin the grass and sand, was gettin him dehydrated.

I think he liked the car too. He seemed sad, when I'd take and lock him back in the backyard. Lynn and all my homies, was glad I hadda car now too. And of course, you know who.:

"Hey..."

Oh yeah. Yeah. You know who.:

"I heard you gotta car now..."

Maybe she "heard;" maybe she saw it for herself.
Either way. I ain't surprised.

"Come round here. I wanna see you. I miss
you... I love you..."

And what happen? I'm round there. What
else supposed to happen? Her and Chavez; that's
the other guy's name, they done broke up. Now, she
back to givin me the pussy. We end up... back
together.

I'm spending nights at Ericka's house now.
So I gotta drive my car to work in the mornings.
And everybody find out I gotta Brand NEW car. I
had already told Ricky, so he already knew.

He said, "Damn, the same day?"

"Yep. The same day."

This time when me and Ericka gets back
together, she hassa new girlfriend named Patrice. I
suspect that this might be how she met Chavez,
because Chavez and Patrice don't stay far from each
other. Patrice is RED too, and lives near the corner
of Shell Road and La Salle, out in Hampton. I take
Ericka to go see her friend, and that's how I meet
PATRICE.

Patrice likes me. I can tell. I see the signs.
I'm not gon lie, I wanted to fuck her too. But I
couldn't. Ericka is here. Ericka will talk shit about

she is open to givin me 'a threesome, with her and another woman, but Ericka is very territorial. She'll patrol other bitches being around me. That's why I don't really feel that she mean it.

Plus, I'm not really trying to swing that door. I can already imagine what she gon say. She might let me get a threesome in, wit her and another girl, or maybe even wit (2) different women, but that shit gon wrap back around.

She gon wanna fuck me and another man, or maybe she want two other men. I have a very darkskin friend, named Tracy. She already told me how she feels about Tracy. She wanna fuck him. She jus can't catch him. And I keep the two of em apart. On purpose.

But I'on know.: I might let her fuck Tracy. If she let me fuck her friend. Not Patrice. But Paula and Missy. That's her baddest two friends.

Paula eat pussy. I'on know how long she been lick'in it. Maybe since we all went to Warwick. But she doin it now. Wit'er sexy light brown pussy eatin ass.

Then, it's Missy. Missy is chocolate. Not jus chocolate, but 'a dirty Hershey chocolate. I'on know exactly what it is about Missy. But she be rock'n me up! The fact she got 'a phaaat ass butt, this bitch can kill'a tight pair of blue jeans. Oh my goodness! Like 'a chocolate cherry on top! But, I jus be keepin all this to myself. I'on lose my composure around her.

Ericka wanna fuck my friends; shit bitch, I wanna

fuck yours too!

Ericka do good though. She don't expose too much. When she do tell me what she want- -

For real, Ericka is not jus sexually advanced. She is very sexually mature. She has her way of being smart and figuring things out on her own. But she'll read almost any kind of information that got to deal with sex.

Even when we was kids in high school. One day I'm at her house, and we jus chillin; I think we was watchin tv. Picture that. And outta no where she just says, "I wanna suck yo dick."

WHA!? WHA!? WHA!? WHA!? WHAT!? I let her go and do it. And you know what she gon say to me?

"Yaaugghh! You taste salty. You got too much salt..."

She told me,

"You need to drink you some pineapple juice. Fo real. Pineapple juice'll make yo cum taste sweet... Here look..."

Then she laid there and read me the article out the fuckin newspaper.

Man, after that shit, I went to Food Lion. I bought (5) cans of Pineapple Juice for $5 and 5 cents. I still remember that to this day. Drank the pineapple juice, went back to see her, and she was,

"Mmmmmmmmmm!!!!"

Hunh. That's all about that. And back then, she was like that at 16/ 17. So now when she wassa grown woman and a mother; sex wit Ericka was on 'a whole nother planet. I know everything she do wit me, so I couldn't jus willingly surrender all that over to another man to get to enjoy. Especially not Tracy. That was my homie. Too close to home.

Now, what she do, and I'on know about. I leave it like that. Told you bout pokin that damn bear! I jus hate it when she move sloppy. I do what I do. But I don't bring it back to her. 9 times outta 10, she'll never even know. I told her about Shiakema; that was kinda sloppy, but I needed to know where she was standing. Was she gon be wit me or was she gon go be wit Leon. When she chose me OVER the father of her child...

It's too much to tell you how I felt.

In order for Ericka to really catch me movin sloppy; if that's what you wanna call it- - she really had to go lookin for it.

After I got the Metro, she would wait for me to fall asleep, then she would get my key and go searching through my car. She caught me- - sloppy.

I hadda lil red phone book in my glove compartment. Inside this book, I only wrote down female names and phone numbers. No man's name was in there. Not even friends. I never wrote a man's number down; only women. So this book had every woman's name and number that I knew. And none of them is family.

At the back of the book, I keep a journal of every woman I have sex with. Even if I don't know they name. It'll be an entry. Generally it was the girl's name, and the date. If I didn't know her name, I still had the system set up, so if I get burned by one of these bitches, or if a girl come tell me she pregnant, I can go back and pinpoint with virtual accuracy, where I might of got it from, or whether or not I might be the father.

I had the book in the car, cause I be on the move. Wit havin a car, now I'm gon run into random women anywhere. If I have sex with 2 or 3 different women, IN A DAY, then I need to be able to jot this information down, not just rely on my mind to remember. Even if I used rubbas; it didn't matter. I still gotta document and keep up wit who I'm havin sex with. Me and Ericka was having sex TOO MUCH; I stopped writing her down. But she was the only one. Anybody else, is goin in this damn book.

So she found the book. She was mad and she brought it straight to my attention. Won't nothing I could say to refute it. It's still not. If anything, I was thinking if they sell chains and padlocks, to keep this bitch out my shit, when I'm sleep. Ericka got terrible. I couldn't even get a shower, wit out her goin through my pants, or flyin out to my car. But it is what it is.

That's what you go through, I guess, when you got someone really in love wit you, and really do care. That's apart of it. I jus felt like this must be what women go through.: cause my momma was the same way. She ain't do it to her husband

414

though. She'll do it to me. Even after I got grown, and graduated high school, I had to be mindful of what I leave in my room. Hiding it ain't mean nothing. Sis Miles got a nose like a bloodhound; she goes through everything. So when Ericka was actin like this, the crazy part about it.: I was kinda used to it.

If I kept it in my car, my momma couldn't get to it, if I kept it in my car, then Ericka would get to it. This shit is crazy.

Patrice was gettin horny bein around me and Ericka. I could see she felt left out. I didn't present them wit a threesome, cause I was layin back, see would they bring it to me. Instead, I did something stupid. Real, real, real Stupid. I wanted to see how far this stupid shit could go.

I went to go get KANE.

Chapter 21.

So, I bring Kane around there. I knew that Ericka wanted Tracy, but I wanted to see how she would act. Jus see how she would do, being around an old flame, and what he would do seeing her. And how Ericka would respond seeing I brought Kane for her friend, Patrice.

Ericka was, "Gaa- gaa- gaa- gaa- gaa." She was clappin her hands and kept laughing at all his lil stupid ass jokes. This shit was annoying me.

Patrice wasn't as humored, but she was still entertained by him. She kept pattin and rubbin on her hair. Then that shit started annoying me. So I say,

"Aye! Look Kane; I'm out, bro. I'll be back tomorrow to get you bro."

"Alllight," he dap me up.

I leave out the door. Ericka follow me outside,

"Uh- uh. Where you going!? No! Come back here...

Come back here."

She follow me to my driver's side door.

It was another reason to me bringing Kane. I knew that Patrice might wanna fuck him, but if he do, and if Ericka still got 'a sexual attraction for him; then maybe we could switch off. And I fuck Patrice and I let him fuck Ericka.

I tried. I tried to see if I could do it. But I couldn't do it. These bitches fucked around and got me mad.

Which I really was. I won't lying. Fuck it; let him get the threesome. I won't gon hate on him. But for real, we coulda pulled it off. I jus won't ready for that level.: not when it come to Ericka. I can't jus stay there and watch her takin 'a dick that won't mine. And the way she kept doin all that stupid ass giggling, like she was real excited to see him...

It was too much.

I went back in, and yeah, Patrice took Kane in her bedroom, and gave him the pussy, and I fucked Ericka in 'a different room. So that half of it did happen.

After I had got my car, and had regular employment, Nations Bank had sent me a Master Card in the mail with a $1000 credit limit. All I gotta do is tear this sticka off the back, and dial this toll free one- eight hundred number... and...

I got that bitch activated. And that mean... It's time to go... SHOP- PING!!

My Metro wassa BRAND NEW car. It had heat. It had A/C. It wassa stick. But one thing my lil black baby was missing... it ain't got no radio. I need to get me some tunes up in da whip!

So, that's what I went and I did.: I went and bought me 'a fuckin system!!

I went to Audio Sound, on Mercury Boulevard. I picked out a deck, some speakers, a woofer box and dual 10 inch speakers, and I picked up (2) AMPS!! One to push my regular speakers, and one to push my 10 inch twin woofers.

The guy at Audio Sound said to me, they was backed up on installation. I didn't feel like waitin a coupla weeks. I'll put all this shit back on the shelf. The guy must be makin 'a commission off this shit. He won't tryin to see me do that.

"Aye, look I gotta guy, he doesn't work at this shop, but he can do it. He's real professional. His name is Sterling...

I'll call him and... uhh... and... uhh..."

"Ok, you go head and call him. Otherwise, all this shit goin back on the shelf."

He made contact with Sterling, Sterling told him to tell me, he couldn't get to it tonight, but to come to his shop first thing in the morning, and gave me the number and address. That wassa Friday night.

Man, I went home, and laid down in my room. I had my system set up in my room. Still in the box. That shit look like Christmas presents. I tossed and turned for Saturday morning to hurry up and get here.

I was supposed to be there like 8 o' clock. Some shit like that. I fucked around and beat Sterling to the shop.

It took all day, into that evening. This brother did a whole open car surgery. I thought he was gon pop out the engine, to nook and cranny all them pieces and get it installed. I hadda amp under each front seat. And Huh. Now, that's how the fuck you BLOW!! 'a thousand dollars!!

I beat the block up!! People in downtown Newport News can hear me, before I even get there. I was getting pulled over by the police, or they'll ride beside me, and twitch they fingers for me to turn my system down. Sitting up in that bitch, was like sittin up in a room wit surround sound.

Crazy part about it, this was past the 80s era. But if you really wanna beat down the block- - the all-time classic joint is Nobody Beats The Biz, by Biz Markie.

Man, I put that shit on... that shit go stupid bananas on 'a system. Niggas used to ride wit me, jus to hear how they music sound in my system.

And the crazy part about it.: having the car brought Ericka closer to me, and havin the system brought her even closer to me. We started havin more sex in the car, before we even get to the house. We was rollin up, and she was lettin me hit it anywhere. And ain't care who was lookin.

One stand out day.: I had rode her and Tori up to Colonial Williamsburg. I did that cause, my father was also a cook by trade. He used to work at a restaurant called, The Kings Tavern, when we lived on 30th Street, and we first moved to Paula Maria.

He used to take me to Colonial Williamsburg, when I was small. They got buggies, of horse drawn carriages. I used to keep pictures of all that stuff. I wasn't a baseball fan, but I hadda Philadelphia Phillies batter's helmet. It's a picture of me holdin the helmet, smiling, in the seats of one of these buggies, up in Williamsburg.

Tori is a lil younger than what I was. But it ain't matter. It's never too early to start havin FUN! But they wasn't doing the buggies. Maybe too much time passed between my generation and Tori's generation. I'on know. But, it turned into a date for me and Ericka. Shopping in Williamsburg is expensive. They have Men's Shoppes. They have ties for like $250.00.

Even the food is expensive. But somehow, I managed to show Ericka 'a good time. Hunh. 'A real good time. She couldn't wait to get it home. She ain't pull her panties down. I had to wait to get her home to do that; but let's just say HEY! she was poppin da top off da Pineapple. The Metro ain't got no tint. This bitch had drew a crowd of white people walkin all round the car, and shit. Men and women. It was one white man who stopped and just stood there, lookin at her through the window. Crazy part.: she ain't even care he was there. He got in close to watch this thickkkk lipped RED bitch put in dat work! Them lips felt like 'a damn pineapple, if anything else.

Whooo!

I ain't gon stop her. Fuck I look like!? I think Ericka was goin for 'a Ring!! Snu, you worked that muthafucka that day. I ain't even mad at you. I just was tryin to get the fuck up outta here before the cops cum. Ain't it.

Ericka didn't even have a license. I know she can ride, but I don't know if she can drive. I taught her how to drive; and on a manual transmission. For real, I was scared how she was gon do. Ericka is quietly intellectual for real. She pays attention and she listens, extremely well.

When she sat in the seat, she adjusted it from the slumping position, I like to have it in. She sat straight up on the wheel, and kept her posture straight. She checked to make sure she could see out all the windows and mirrors.

Her mindset was to be a conscious driver.

And I took her out on the road. I gave it too her, the same way Ricky gave it to me. And she kilt it.

She kilt it.

One day, she wanted to take her son to go see his father. I drove her to Bell Street so Tori could see his father. Bell Street is off Shell Road. Between Shell Road and Pembroke Avenue, out Hampton. Jus up from the W and W. I sat in the car just to see what would happen.

Ericka was maturing as a woman, she wasn't on all that dumb ass giddy ass shit, like she was that day around Kane. That's one of the things I was lookin to see. And she didn't even go in the house wit him. She stayed outside on the sidewalk. It was mature, because I didn't even have to say nothin to her about it, before or after. She administered everything on her own.

And Leon didn't say, or do nothing disrespectful. He ain't try to grab her ass; kiss her, or nothin like that. That was my first time seeing him. His first time seeing me. We ain't talk. We jus spent more time learning each other face. It wouldn't be the last time we see each other.

It's a lot of overlapping parts. Let me get this part out the way first.:

We wasn't officially living together, but me and Ericka was spending every night together. We made love every night. Somethin like that. Ericka don't really like to make love. More like long, deep, fast, and HARD!! That's why I think she keep comin back. I ain't really into it like that; but that's what she like. HEY! I'm here for the customers. And the other part she like is,

"Damn, yo shit never go down."

Yep, it take a lotta dynamite to blow down 'a mountain. And that's what got me up all night. Even on the weeknights. She got me gettin up on 2-3 hours of sleep. EVERY NIGHT. Eventually this shit caught up to me.

I'm supposed to be at work at 7:00- - I'm wakin up at 9: 00. I look at the clock and look at her, she still tapped out. I got to scramble in to work. Mr. Nance let me get away with it the first time. He gave me a warning. The second time he was even more angry at me. I can't just drive and go to work in the Shipyard. The vans and trucks got to get a clearance, so I'm costing him money. Cause he gotta call Chad or Kenny to come out the field, all the way back to the shop, and pick me up.

The third time.: I lied to him and told him I was in a car accident. I had to say something. It was my third strike. I knew he was gon fire me. I won't trying to hear them words. I heard some other words, he said,

"Where's your doctor's note?"

"I don't got one."

"You get a doctor's note, I'll let you back. I'm not gon let you get out here..."

I know I ain't got no damn doctors note. I knew that was it. I had lost my job.

In Virginia, it's always a demand for construction workers. Construction workers, laborers, and helpers. I went searching the Classifieds for a new job. I was searching for a job as an Electrician. I worked around electricians in the Shipyard. I worked around an Asian brother in there, named Egg Roll. And Egg Roll used to always tell me,

"You need to get on through the apprenticeship..."

He said that Electricians can make as much as $50

an hour.

When I was lookin for a new job, I thought about what Egg Roll had said, involving being an Electrician. So when I was looking for my next job, I was trying to get on as an Electrician's Helper.

There was a Haverty's Furniture store being built and Developed, close by where I used to live; up near Oyster Point. I cold stopped at the site. Meaning, I didn't respond to an ad in the paper, or set an appointment. And pulled up, straight looking for the Electricians. It wassa white guy, who keep walking around and following me around with his eyes. I thought he was gon try to kick me off the site. So I keep avoiding him. Crazy part about it.: I saw framers, finishers... plumbers. Everybody but Electricians.

So finally the guy stops me, "HEY! What are you looking for?"

I said, "I'm here to find a job. Where's the Electricians at?"

"Are you an Electrician?"

"No. I'm trying to learn. If I can be a helper, apprentice; something!?"

"They're on break."

On break!?? At 9 o' clock in the morning??

"Ok. Thank you," I turn and start walking away.

"Hey! Wait 'a minute! You say you lookin for 'a job right?"

"Um. Yeah. But I'm trying to be... trying to do electrical work."

"You got tools?"

"Yeah. I got tools." Which I did, because Nance was still a construction company. He supplied company tools, but I was still responsible for buying certain personal tools. I hadda tool belt, tape measure, hard hat; a lil basic shit to get started.

"Be here 7 in the morning," he told me. "My name is Lynwood by the way." And we shook hands.

Just like that. I had me 'a BRAND-NEW job.

Not just a BRAND NEW job, but workin the same hours. Still gettin paid EVERY week, and $7 an hour. Which means, I was makin $.50 MORE an hour, than what I was makin at Nance. Man, I was dancin like Deion Sanders in this bitch!!

Alright, Ericka, we can't fuck this up. I made $280 a week before taxes. After taxes, my check was $222. A WEEK. Ericka saw that and said,

"DAMN!"

I was gettin almost as much money 'a week, as what she made in 'a month, for her and her son. And Ericka caught on Quick! I think that's what motivated her to start workin herself up offa welfare.

She went and got her a job working at the
Wendy's, across from the Patrick Henry Mall. But
even when Ericka was on welfare, only getting like
$238 a month to care for her and Tori, she always
had a good heart for me, and she never was selfish.
When she get her food stamps, and we out grocery
shopping, she'll drop something like bread and
bologna in her cart. Just to let me know, she
thinkin about me eating lunch. Not just bread and
bologna, but she'll fix my lunch box for the week
I'm going to work. And she ain't have to do that. It's
just what was in her heart.

I hadda good girl. And now Ericka was
finally doing EVERYTHING right. And being the
woman I needed the whole time. But for me.: she
came too late. I was ready to move on.

Chapter 22.

Me and Patrice started getting close. So close. We became best friends. I used to see her EVERY day. I'll get off work. Go home and take a shower, and before I go see Ericka, I went to see Patrice.

I didn't see her in a sexual light. After she had sex with Kane, on the first night, I lost that interest. Not that I think something was bad about her givin the pussy up that quick; but I could feel that she did like me, so when she gave the pussy to him, I was kinda disappointed. A part of me was kind of hoping she would reject him.

That night.: if Ericka had let me fuck Patrice, I probably woulda let her fuck Kane, but in a separate room, so I ain't gotta look at it. But that bitch kept doing all that stupid ass giggling. She was too elated. That shit was blowing me.

Patrice is married.

I already knew that. Even before I brought Kane round there. I never met her husband, not during that time. He is locked up on Indian Creek, a prison, in Chesapeake, Virginia. Right beside Saint Brides. They got (2) Virginia prisons, side- by- side each other, in Chesapeake.

After, the her and Kane incident, was when me and Ericka used to take her to see her husband. At first Ericka was going. Then she stopped. And I would take Patrice... by myself.

Her husband's name is Chase. At first, he used to thank me for bringing his wife up there to see him. Then, he started think I was fuckin her.

Ericka thought the same thing.

Every time she go see her husband, and father of her two sons, she'll dress like she going to church service. When she leave from seeing him, Patrice is very quiet. Then when we get closer to the Newport News portion of the Merrimack Bay Bridge Tunnel, she'll start loosening back up. Get it livin...

"Turn that shit off!"

She mad at me because all I listen to is rap music.

"Play some r and b."

Fo what!? Bitch, I'on even own no r and b. Not now. Music ain't what it used to be. Before all the talent was all spread out, now it's all monopolized. All the artist on ONE label. You either Death Row or Bad Boy. The hottest r and b singers, R Kelly ran the male side, and Mary J ran the female side.

And Mary J, she won't on Bad Boy, but Sean Combs was her manager. So she hadda Bad Boy sound. And R Kelly, his style developed from the Teddy Riley New Jack design. R Kelly just

innovated it. And Sean Combs and a lot of the
hardware that ended up on Bad Boy, started as 'a
New Jack on Uptown Records.

So I hear it. But I wasn't necessarily
BUYING it. I liked it better when the artists were
spread out across the field, on different labels.
When the music didn't wear a uniform.

"Put on somethin slowwww."

"Fo what!?"

She'll jus smack her lips. She wouldn't answer that
question.

But my relationship with Patrice proved I
could be around a sexually attractive woman, and
still not have sex. When I wasn't around Ericka, I
wasn't with Ericka. I carried like I was single. Like
we was broke up. I told Patrice,

"Me and Ericka is broke up," one day on her
living room couch. And she said,

"Nuh- uh."

"Yes we are. I ain't wit her." And she said,

"I got somebody for you." And I asked,

"Who?"

For real I thought she was gon say herself, but that
ain't what she said;

"Hold on..."

She ended up putting me on the phone wit her cousin, named Tonya. One problem.:

Tonya live all the way in Charlotte, North Carolina.

Come on. Come on, Patrice. You gotta do betta than this. I talked to her though. I plugged her number into my lil red book. But right now, this wasn't a reality.

"Alright, I got somebody else for you."

"Who?" Again, she ain't say herself. She put me on wit a girl name Crystal.

For real, Crystal was super- beautiful. This bitch was slim. No body fat. She look like she stepped off the page of a magazine. We kissed. But, we ain't really hit it off. She had moved in wit Patrice for a little while, got pregnant, and left. Probably to go be wit her baby daddy. But she was gone.

After that, I didn't think about giving Patrice no more chances.

Alright listen.: I gotta get this part out the way first, before I can flow the story.

I was still spending every night wit Ericka, and fuckin Ericka. I was workin commercial framing and hangin sheetrock for Lamb and Robinson Construction. That's what Lynwood hired me to. Lynwood left.

The construction industry is a very racist

industry. It's dominated by white men. Maybe this is what Mr. Padgett was preparing me for. It was only (4) black guys at most on the site.: me, James Bell, Alvin, and John. And me, Bell, and Alvin all framed and slang rock. Sheetrock. John was the "Electrician."

Alvin was the only Mechanic out our crew. Me and Bell won't but helpers. Alvin is a Deacon in his church, and very spiritual. And a real good Big Brother. He has a new model 5 speed Chevrolet truck. After he saw I could drive a stick, he would give me the keys to his truck, to go get lunch. I had experience driving trucks and vans from working at Nance.

After Lynwood left, we gotta new supervisor named Larry. He brought his (2) sons wit him. Every time he show up, it's like I be standin there alone. The raven in his heart'll be down on me.

"HEY! You!..."

He was mad at me. He told me I "made too much money."

"For all that money, you should be a mechanic. Hell, you make more money than my (2) sons. Every time I see you... you better be working. Don't let me come here and see you sittin down."

He ain't even want to see me pickin up the trash, to clean up after myself. This cracker must not know where the fuck he at. This ain't Ku Klux Klan County, Bitch!

Alvin wasn't there, but was somewhere listening to the conversation. So he was talking to me to calm me down and get my head back into the job. I did. For him. I didn't want to leave him stuck out here by himself. Cause if I leave, Bell gotta leave too, cause shit, I gotta drop him off at Walker Village.

We generally have (90) days to complete these projects. Which means 10 hour shifts. Which means, when I go to work on Friday, my whole Friday is OVERTIME! Time and a half, which is $10.50 an Hour. And still getting paid EVERY week!

We finished Haverty's and moved on to the MCI call center in Newport News. We converted it to a call center, from a former Lowes Warehouse. Where they use to keep a whole lotta paint, plants and store lumber.

Larry was still my supervisor. But MCI was more square feet than Haverty's. I had more space to stay out the way. But even when I avoid Larry, I would walk right up into, "Hey buddy, do you got any drugs?" right there in the bathroom.

It looked like I had ran up on 'a Ku Klux Klan meeting.

They automatically presumed because I was Black and being in the city, that I knew where all the drugs was at. But they wasn't playing. This was serious. These were Mechanics getting paid 20s and 30s of dollars an hour, all across the construction field. Gettin paid EVERY week. And they was white men who wanted to get HIGH. They'll smoke reefa, but they wanted more than reefa. And they was willing to spend THOUSANDS of dollars for it. They thought that by me being Black, I could save them some money, cause the Black drug dealers was charging them higher prices. They wasn't trying to pay the white crack head price.

"Umm, naw. I don't know where any drugs are..." And I just turn around and haul ass up outta there, and I gotta take my chances running into Larry.

I wasn't into the streets or into drugs. They came to the wrong one for that.

After we finished, MCI, we moved on to doing a library out in Toano County. That's just above Williamsburg. I noticed that the General Contractor, which was Lamb and Robinson, generally maintained the same companies of framers, finishers, plumbers, roofers, carpet guys, and electricians rotating around to the same sites, for continuous employment.

Lamb and Robinson was a small building out of Portsmouth in Virginia. I only saw the actual company, maybe like twice. I never been inside. I never had to. All my business was takin care of in the field. Lamb and Robinson kept all of us eating. Those 50 hour a week paychecks. And I was gettin my paycheck in my hand, EVERY week.

Outside of the internal racism, Lamb and Robinson, in and of itself, is an excellent company. I never had any complaints. And it was the best job I had up until this point.

433

In Toano, Larry was still down on my top. He was threatening to deduct my pay. Not just him, but he found an alliance in another white head supervisor, named West. And West was subtly just as bad as Larry. He might do it, wit a smirk on his face.

Me and Ericka had calmed down on the sex. It was still every night, but she at least started lettin me get to bed by 2 in the morning. And I gotta wake up, get myself together, and pick Bell up from Walker Village. Work start at 7 o' clock. I'm at work exactly at 7 o' clock.

And West says, "You're late."

"I'm late!? It's 7 o' clock."

"No, work starts at 7 o' clock. Not you rolling up in here at 7 o' clock."

Nobody was even started yet. I can grab my tools, the same time they still walking tools. It's guys standing around drinking mugs of coffee. Sometimes I was pulling up the same time as his red Chevy truck. But, he'll always come at me,

"You're late," and be tappin his watch.

Afterwhile, his dorky smile evaporated. Which was his implication, he was setting to fire me. Even if I pulled up at 6:45 or 6:50, he'll still tell me I was late, and be tapping his watch. That's when Bell was like,

"You gotta tighten up. He serious now."

434

For what!? What was I doing different from anybody else? I was learning the trade, on the job. I was commercial framing, hangin insulation, and slangin sheetrock. Then one cold December morning; it was cold as hell, and snow and ice was on the ground. Yes, we still had to work in the heat of the sun, even in the rain, in the cold, in the freezing cold, and even in the snow and ice. Maybe unless it's a thunderstorm. That's why they lay that foundation and set that frame and roof up first. So when the weather outside be fucked up, we'll still be working, INSIDE. But I didn't mind that; you dress a certain way, and after while, yo body get used to it.

On this one December day, Larry come up to me, he say, "Go move that scaffold down out there."

When I get outside. I'm there by myself. I start trying to move pieces of the scaffold by myself; next thing I know

"Snnaaaa."

My back had went out. It felt like my spinal cord snapped, like it was just two loose ends danglin in the middle of my back.

"UUUGGHHH!" I hollered out in pain.

It took awhile before anybody came out there. I couldn't walk. I couldn't put any weight on my heels. I thought I was finished.

I think Alvin was the first one to find me. Him and Bell held me up under each of my arms and brought me back inside.

435

"Flip em on that sheetrock," I heard Larry say to them.

"UUUGGHHH!" I hollered. Cause they did what he said.

I laid on top of a fresh stack of sheetrock until the ambulance came. And they flipped me up on a hardboard, and carried me to a local hospital. As they was taking me, I caught a glimpse of Alvin. He had taken off his glasses. His head was in his hand. He was crying. The hospital gave me X- rays, and gave me ibuprofen. Next thing I know...

"Jamie... Jamie..." my mother and father was there to pick me up.

West had contacted them. Wit his fake racist ass. Oh, he is a racist. But he is a passive racist. Not a blatant one. A passive racist will kill you while he smiling and shakin yo hand.

"Theresa goin to pick up your car," my momma told me. And it was FRIDAY which meant, "I got your paycheck," my momma told me.

That was healing me up right then and there. I was riding in the backseat of my father's Cadillac. This was my first time riding in his Caddy, since he bought it. After I got my own car, I didn't ride in his cars or truck no more. He actually had TWO Caddy's at the same time, and still the same ol' Ford pick up truck.

He rode my backseat up to the bank window. I pushed the auto button down on the backseat window, and after I cashed my check, my momma said,

"Where you wanna go?"

It was December 22nd. THREE DAYS BEFORE CHRISTMAS. Where you think I wanna go...

I Wanna Go... SHOP- PING!!!!

We ended up in Super K Mart up Kiln Creek. If it sound rich. It probably is. Kiln Creek is a rich white/ middle class section, in between Newport News and Ku Klux Klan County. They're known for having golf courses out there.

Anyway, I'on play golf. I'm at Super K Mart, SHOPPING!!

But not really for me. For Ericka. This girl been wit me fo real, since I was 17. Since she was 16. But back then, I was broke. We was poor. We really ain't have the money to do nothing real nice for each other for Birthdays and Holidays, for Christmas. So this was going to be THE FIRST TIME, I could really afford to do that.

I was round Super K Mart, shopping, on my tippy- toes. Cause I still couldn't put weight on my heels. I leaned my weight forward on the shopping cart, pushin all around.

I bought my Snu a stereo, because her apartment didn't have no music. The stereo even had a remote. I bought her the Waiting To Exhale soundtrack. Cause that was what was out then. And I bought Tori his first BIG Wheel.

But his BIG Wheel was different than ones I used to ride. This one he could drive. It was black. You put the stickas on it. He could open the door, climb into it, and peddle off. I didn't leave him out. I bought him that.

I didn't hold it against Tori that he wasn't my son. He was innocent. He didn't have nothing to do with what me and his mother was involved with and had going on. I learned that from Lucky. I wasn't Lucky's son. But the same love, acceptance, and appreciation for- - I was crossing those same principles over, that I saw Lucky give to me, and I was applying them to Tori. Making them active in his life.

When I got back home and told Ericka what happened. She said,

"Well you get your rest."

I think it was the 24th. The day before Christmas. She caught a cab to my house. I was SHOCKED!! my momma let her in the room. She came back there, AND closed the door. What!? What the world is goin on!??

I couldn't believe it.

I showed Snu, her NEW stereo. I knew she liked it. Cause she was quiet. I showed her Tori's Big Wheel. It was still in the box. I hadn't put it together yet. She laughed,

"You bought Tori a Metro."

It did look like 'a lil Metro. I didn't think about it like that, til she said something. She started wettin me up wit kisses. That's when I really knew she had liked it. I made her happy.

"Degggg!" she looked down and saw my erection. Part of it was from seeing her wear them TIGHHHT assss black jeans, up in my house. The other part was due to my muscle relaxers, the doctor had put me on. I guess it's 'a side effect.: poppin these pills made me horny as hell.

It went there.

I had to get on top. It's the only position I could hit her in. "Hhhuugghh..."

Alright Ericka, don't get to makin all that dumb ass noise. My MOMMA and My DADDY at home, in the other room. I think the pills had me 'a lil more amped up, and seeing her peel like 'a banana out them tight ass jeans, but come on now, you gettin this dick like every day. You should be used to it by now. She did calm down, so we could finish.

For real, I wasn't supposed to be jus out leaving the house, cause I was on workman's comp. But I had to go get some more of this action. Ericka put the WET! in wet- wet. I popped me a pain killa, muscle relaxer, grabbed my ice pack, and back brace, and rode Ericka back home to her crib.

I had got some mobility back. I was able to put weight on my heels, and I started going back to Patrice's house. And I was going to Dwight's house.:

Dwight was still Dwight. Doin what Dwight do. He was down on them bitches. Can't be mad about that. But he was down on a girl I practically had forgot about.:

"Aye yo, Tara asked about you."

"Tara who??" I was serious. I was genuine when I said that.

"Man you know... Tara. Lynn old girl."

Oh yeah. Yeah. Right. That was her new name, "Lynn old girl."

I told you we was gon get back to this. Didn't I?

I had hooked Lynn up wit the girl that was down at me, so both of us could fuck her, and I keep it a secret from Joy. Lynn ended up falling in love wit the girl and made the girl his girl. Fucked the whole damn play up. But I ain't trip. I ain't trip. I got over it. I let it be.

They was all boo'd up. Then the unthinkable happened...

Tara got pregnant. Huh. And it won't by Lynn. Umm, umm, umm.

It was by a nigga named David. The same nigga who used to drop her off ova to see Lynn. Crazy part about it.: Dwight used to always call it. He would say,

"That nigga fuckin that bitch."

Lynn won't tryin to hear it either. Dwight called that shit, PERFECT. And yep, that's what she was doin. She ended up pregnant, by the other nigga. Lynn was CRUSHED!! A lot of that led to a falling out between Lynn and Dwight. It won't Dwight's fault. Lynn ain't have his own spot, so he'll bring her over Dwight's so he could fuck 'er.

It's his own fault he got CRUSHED!! Hey! You shoulda followed my game plan. Stick to da script nigga.

Lynn don't know how to pick pussy. He'll fuck and fall in love wit any girl that'll give it to him. I'm tryin to at least break him in to fuckin a more elite class of bitches. And bitches that actually look like something. I was just breaking him in wit Tara, cause she hadda phaat ass. But it's bitches way badder than that. He couldn't even get past the first level.

But I gave Tara a chance. To at least hear what she was talkin about. The same thing. She was still tryin to give me some pussy. But I think she was tryin to sucka me in, like she got ol Lynnie-Lynn. We hadda conversation.

I found out she was from 44th Street. That's Tisdale Lane.

"I used to go to Tisdale, wit my homie Damon. He hadda girlfriend named Simone."

"I know Simone. I lived across the street..."

"The only girl I know across the street, was this girl named Poo- Poo..."

441

One night she hadda Birthday party. It was out in her back yard. It was this nigga named Peugeot there. And Glen Garden niggas had showed up...

And they did show up. Wit Eric Harris. Walking wit that nigga, was like walkin 'a Pitbull off the chain. That lil dark skin nigga was solid and love to fight!

Personally, he never gave me no problems though. He ain't never kick it wit me or no shit like that. For real, he never even touched me, not even when we played football against Glen Gardens. If he by himself, and I speak to him, he'll throw his head back. But when he wit his homies, that's when he'll grill me. When he was wit them, he was dangerous. That's when it's likely, somebody was gon get stole 'on.

And that night, that's what Peugeot found out; the hard way, when niggas from Glen Gardens grabbed him, pinned his back up against the fence, and Glen Garden niggas jumped him.

"Poo- Poo? That's me," she laughed.

We talked a few more times, then went upstairs. Cause HEY! I was poppin dat Poo- Poo.

Then, the next time, I was soapin her up in the shower, and I made love to her. I wanted to see how makin love to her would feel. And she was talkin like no man had never did that to her before.

Come on now Poo- Poo. Why the hell is you talkin like a virgin?

Then she got on the phone wit Patrice. And she was over the phone tellin Patrice, "I got him now. Yeah, he my man now. Da, da, da, da, da, da," referring to the misfact that she thought she had took me from Ericka.

What!? Bitch, you gotta learn how to fuck first. This bitch was cryin bout gettin fucked from the back. I went to go get some head from this bitch, and at first she was acting like she don't do that, then she told me I gotta wear 'a blindfold, so I can't see her doin it. WHAT!? WHAT!? WHAT!?

We had sex one more time, and I was DONE. Tara had chased me all these years, ever since we was in 10th grade; I had finally started fuckin the bitch. I gave Tara like (3) chances. (3) chances, and this bitch pussy game was WACK!!

WACK!!

WACK!!

WACK!!

WACK!!

WACK!!

WACK!!

WACK!!

It got back to Lynn that I had fucked Tara, but I didn't care. Since we was playin this game about fuckin each other girls or ex- girls. Let's play.

443

After Tara, my mind was offa Tara. My focus was on this other girl, I met through Dwight named Cindy. Cindy wassa twin. 'A fraternal twin. Wendy was RED. But Cindy was brown. Brown wit green eyes. I liked Cindy, a lot. I was hoping she was gon be my next girl. But she showed me she was too immature to do all that. We did end up having sex; but this shit was worse than Tara. Not even worth talking about. After that that shit was DONE.

I had went to Lynn's Grandmother's house one day, and she said, "Lynn's not here. Lynn don't live here no more."

'Say what!? Lynn don't live here no more!??'

Then she came back to the door, and said, "Lynn moved to Aqua Vista. He livin wit his momma," and she gave me the address.

I went straight over there. He had moved in with his mother and her boyfriend, down on 6th Street, off of Ivy Avenue. I don't know why they call it 6th Street. 5th, 4th, 3rd, 2nd, and 1st Street must all be up under the water, because the James River is immediately behind the Aqua Vista apartments. It's right on the waterfront area of property.

But I went down there to see him, and ended up seeing Kema. But she ain't live out there. When I saw Kema. She told me

I HAD A SON.

Chapter 23.

Kema had moved with her mother out Stuart Gardens. I had went to see her out Stuart Gardens. I already knew where she was. I had been catching the bus over here a year ago. But then that stopped. Now, she was telling me, she had a son. She did have a son. I was lookin at him. But I doubted if he was mine. The timeline won't adding up. I didn't even have to go to the lil red book to figure that out.

I played fair wit Kema though. I ain't come out and say, "Naw, he ain't mine."

I never would do that.

I put the baby in the car and took him around to my Aunt Dottie's house. My momma's big sister; cause she is a Registered Nurse. I know she done seen a lotta babies, dealing with her line of profession.

I held him on her couch and I asked her, "Do he look like my son?"

And she looked me in my eyes, and she told me straight up, "Uh- huh."

"Alright. Thank you."

And I came back to the car. I was gon bring him

445

and show him to my mother. But I didn't do that. Because I wanted to nip all this is in the bud real fast.:

I say to Shiakema that I wanted a paternity test.

"NOOOOO!" she said.

"Why not!? If you so sure I'm the father... Shit, I'll pay for it."

"NOOOOO!" she wasn't wit it.

I know for fact, I wasn't the only one fuckin Shiakema. She hadda boyfriend named Jeff. This nigga was older than me. For some reason, she always wanted me over this nigga. Even if he come to her house, and I was there, she'd send that nigga back home.

This was a anotha of them strange ass girls from Menchville. That was down on me in the halls. Kema did have good pussy though; and she is super sweet to me. I'll give her that. She ain't fuckin wit Ericka, but she about'a notch up under that. Just like Ericka, she 'a go. She do it all!

If this is my son, I'll take care of my son. But Kema want more. She wanna be together. I think she wanna get married. But I can't commit myself to this. It's no way. Her and Lynn woulda got along together real good. But I never showed her to my homies. I do end up having sex with her again during this time, but I can't give her none of that other stuff she looking for.

I had my doubts that this was my son. The

timeline wasn't matching up. I felt like this girl was just obsessed with fuckin me and giving me babies. Ain't nothing absolutely wrong with that. But without that paternity test; I'm out.

Dwight came to me one day. He want us to go to the 103 Jamz radio station over in Norfolk, and spit over a live mic wit the Buddha Brothas. That's the colorful brand of radio DJ personalities that work our local area's radio station. This shit was gonna be So Fuckin HUGE!! Cause it'll give me a chance to broadcast my talent LIVE over the local waves.

Dwight meets me at Ericka's house. And when he meets me, I get in the car with him and we start off. He starts sayin,

"Man, we should take your car. Your car got the system."

"Naw." I didn't feel like takin my car. After I started driving- - I was always driving. I wanted to lay back. I wanted to chill. Dwight can't drive a stick. I was the only one of my immediate homies that knew how to drive a stick.

Then he bother me again, "Man, we need to get yo car. That way I can get in my zone, before we get over there."

Who am I to deny this Bad Newz Legend? This Bad Newz Hip- Hop Royalty?

"Alright, alright," I finally say, "Go head back around."

He circles back around to Ericka's apartments. We pull up. We busy talkin. And he say, "Where yo car at?"

"Where my car at? It's right..."

and my car was gone.

I jumped out his car, and run through Ericka's apartment. I had a key to her house. When I ran through, her and Tori was gone! I check my key ring, and all my keys are there, just the Metro key is gone!

I ran back out the house. As soon as Dwight pull up to Marshall, here Ericka come ZOOMING!! She doing like 50 in a 25. She parks the car in front of her BACK door, and she gets out and runs to open her BACK door. I run up on her. We get in an argument, and I snatch my key out her hand. Tori was still locked inside the car. Me and Dwight take back off. We get to about the same place we did the first time, and he say,

"Man, you need to go back, and get that boy out the car."

He pull back around. We ain't even go two blocks, as soon as he stop the car back at Ericka's, we see a fire truck roll up. Stop on Marshall. A fire fighter jump out, like 'a little GI Joe action figure, wit a fuckin axe blazing in his hands like a soviet sickle, and he about to chop my lil itty-bitty Metro into too many tiny pieces.

"Whoa! Whoa! Whoa!" I ran up on him. "I got the key right here."

"Huh!?" he pulled the axe up above his head. He bout to turn my coupe into charcoal and firewood.

I told him again, "I got the key right here." I kept showing him the key. He put the axe down.

I opened the door. Tori came straight into my arms. He ain't know what was going on. Ericka snatched him out my arms,

"Give me my son."

She took Tori, I grabbed the car seat, locked and closed the door, the police was standing right there. Me, Ericka, and Tori, walk past them and go in the house. The police follow us in the house. They keep asking, "Is everything Ok...

What happened?"

"Oh everything ok. We alright," I answer.

"Well, let's check over the baby, to make sure he ok."

"Yeah, yeah, yeah, he alright," I answer real quick.

"Let's look over him. Make sure he alright."

Ok. Fuck it. So, I leave Tori wit the police. Me and Ericka still arguing all the way upstairs. We go into her bedroom, and she said something slick out the mouth, I don't remember what she said. But then I...

I don't even like talkin about this; but if I'm gon tell the truth; I gotta tell the whole story. I had put my hand on Ericka. I had slapped her, and she fell down.

Damn!

When we came back down, the police was still in there, and they was still asking, "What happened?"

I had answered, in regards to Tori being locked in the car. And that's when they said, "Put your hands up against the wall...

you're Under Arrest."

It was white male cops. One black woman cop. The black woman cop kept saying,

"I got him... I got him."

She took me and put me in her squad car, and rode me over town, to the Newport News Police Station. On the ride over there, she said,

"I got you with me. If you had went with the white officers, they would've beat you."

When I heard her say that, my mind flashed to thinking about my Uncle Johnnie.

When we got over town, she vouched for me before the magistrate, and I got released on my own recognizes.

She drove me back to my car and said, "Ok now, get in your car and you go straight home. Don't let me have to come back out here tonight."

I got out her car, got in my car and went home. When I get home, what I didn't want to happen happened.

"Jamie, what you doing in jail?"

Ericka had called my momma and told her I was locked up. I never wanted my mother to worry about stuff like this. She often told me, but especially when I started going out in my own car, she would say,

"Watch those friends."

After I had gotten arrested, this was the straw that broke the camel's back. I was definitely through wit Ericka. But first, I had to go see my lawyer, Jeffrey Roundtree, over out Thimble Shoals. That's an Industrial Park out Newport News, in between J Clyde Morris Boulevard and Oyster Point Road.

I felt like this was gon be The Lord manifesting my 19 year old dream to reality. When I went to court, I had Ericka and I had Tori with me. I was facing Felony Child Neglect/ Reckless Endangerment. My first criminal charge, in all my life.

Then they discussed dropping it to a misdemeanor, if I plead guilty.

What!?

Then they went back in, they talked some more,

and dropped the charges. Ericka and Tori stayed outside, while I went in and appeared before the court. The court dropped the charges and I was released.

After leaving court, I dropped Ericka and Tori off at home, and I kept rolling. I went to Buckroe to see my momma, so she could see I was FREE. It would've upset her, to see her only surviving son, get arrested and put in jail. Then, I went back home to see my Father.

During all this time, I wasn't working. I was still out of work, on workman's comp. I was too fucked up psychologically and physically to go back to Lamb and Robinson. I wanted a new job. I wanted a career change.

It was a classified ad in The Daily Press for a position at the Real Estate mogul, Greg Garrett's Century 21, out Thimble Shoals Plaza, the same Industrial Park where Jeffrey Roundtree's office is located. I went in- - and I got hired.

They wanted me to come in and talk over the phone. As a telemarketer. I would cold call customers out the phone book. I would sales pitch them on getting a FREE estimate done to their home. A real estate agent would give them the estimate and pitch them on selling their house. If they agree to it, and Century 21 sells the home, then I get a commission. I get paid ON COMMISSION ONLY. I just gotta get the agent inside the house. I try it.

But for real, I saw something more. What if I could get into Real Estate? The money-making potential in real estate is unlimited. I could use this telemarketing as an opportunity to get my foot in the door.

Greg Garrett came out to shake my hand, and meet me in person. When I saw Greg Garrett, it's like I was looking at a real- life Ric Flair. He just didn't wear blonde hair and dress in Rolex watches. Actually, he looks more like a Kennedy. He is about 6 foot 1 or 6 foot 2, and he looks like he could be a son of President John F Kennedy. He was Young, Rich, and Wealthy. This man was God BLESSED, a millionaire, and extremely successful. How many Black kids outta poverty actually knew a millionaire, first hand. I was so mesmerized, I wanted to shake hands again wit the epitome of the American Dream. He'd tell me,

"If you have any questions, my door is always open."

I had stopped seeing Ericka. She would call, but I wasn't there when she called, and I never returned her call. I was horny. I wanted some pussy. I started thumbing through my lil red book. I wish I had Chocolate's number. I had tried to get up wit Chocolate several times. The phone book I had her number in, somebody stole when I was in Job Corps. Even when I got my car, I tried to find people she knew, and nobody knew where she was at. I had lost contact.

I kept thumbing through.

I get to a name.

Miya. Pronounced as Me- ya. Not My- ya.

I had met Miya through Dwight. All the way back, when he was on 41st Street. Next to the cab stand. He put me on the phone wit her. I even used to call Miya all the way from Maryland, when I was in Job Corps. Miya could carry a conversation and has a real good phone voice.

But, I had never seen her in person. She was a mystery to me. She had her own car, but never came to see me in it. Dwight had been out wit Tee, over at Black Mac. That's the Mc Donald's over on La Salle off of Pembroke, out in Hampton. It was near Hampton University, an Historically BLACK University, and it was in a BLACK neighborhood, and predominantly BLACK people live near and go there; so it just fit right in.

Dwight hollas at Miya at Black Mac, and get her number. He wanna fuck her. He can't fuck her. He puts her on the phone wit me, and despite the fact that we had never seen each other, we develop a friendship that expands 3 years!

But now, "I gotta car. Fuck it! I'm coming to see you." That's what I tell her.

At first she's like, "Noooo!" Then she's like, "Fuck it! Come on." She gives me the address.

I leave work IMMEDIATELY. Because I can. I set my own schedule. On the ride over there, I think about, what I'm gon see when I get there. I used to ask Dwight,

"Do she gotta phaat ass?"

454

And he would say, "She got some big titties."

That's all I really had to go off of. I knew she had a pretty voice. I could sense she had to be pretty. But just how much?

When I get there. I can't really see her body. She is plain. She has on a long pink t- shirt. I sit on the couch. She's sitting in a distant chair. I'on know if she got panties on or what. Her hair ain't done. It's just hand swept to the back. Nails ain't done. Toes ain't done. She do got some big titties. And she is RED.

And she keep sittin up watching tv. Oh lord, not this again.

I was thinkin like, if we did have sex, this was gon be somethin I hit, maybe like (5) times. In person, she didn't give me no conversation. I said,

"What's up!?"

She usually has a special ability to stimulate conversation, and it was never stale. We might talk for minutes. We might talk for hours. But now, she was too quiet. I give up. I'm thinking this shit ain't gon be nothing. I abandon it to leave out her door...

she follow me out to my car.

When she get to my car, I can see she got real beautiful RED legs. You know how I feel about these RED girls. First, I hugged her. Then, she let me kiss her. We talk. She let me kiss her again. We talk. She say I said, "I'm not afraid of commitment."

IIIIIIII don't remember saying that.

But I leave and go home. I really didn't think no more about it. My phone rings at 7:30. I plan to be to work at 9.

At the same time I had started working in the real estate field, I started going to real estate school. So, I could be a licensed Real Estate Agent. The college was only 2 weeks. I paid a little under $200 for it.

I just was confused. Carlton Sheets has an infomercial on tv talking about flipping houses. Buying houses for cheap and at government auctions, and flippin it for HUGE!! profits. I'm thinking, if that is real, then how is Greg Garrett in business? Why is all these agents sitting up in here, waiting on commission checks from Greg Garrett?

His office is "always open." But I never approached him, I didn't want to disrespect him with my concern. And at the same time, I didn't want him to pop my bubble, by telling me, that Carlton Sheets was make believe. What he was saying wasn't true. So I just left it alone, and paid $200 or something like that, then I'd learn it through Real Estate College.

But now I had Miya at 7:30 calling me saying, "I wanna see you...

Come through."

So instead of going to work, I went to Miya's. When I get there, when she comes out, she has her hair done, lipstick done, skirt, heels. I'm recompositing this whole situation now. I was seeing Miya just for sex, like (5) times.

Now, I was seeing Miya like.: either I'm gon knock a baby in her, or we gon get married; but either way, I knew I wanted to put her in my life, for the rest of my life.

Me and Miya ended up being together. EVERYDAY. From early in the morning, at like 8 o' clock, I was at her house. She'll have me out with her,

"Take me here...

Take me there..."

The crazy part about it.: she would put money in my gas tank. And I ain't talkin about payin $5 or $10. Hell naw! She would fill my tank ALL THE WAY UP!!

We would go out to eat. And she would say, "I got the bill."

I won't used to no shit like this.

Who the fuck was this bitch?

Miya was a senior at Hampton University; and a bout to be Psychology major. Ain't that somethin?

And this girl wasn't poor. She wasn't rich either. But she came from a thriving, yet silent Black history that is suppressed, or not exploited enough in tv, in movies, and in history books. She is Black middle- class.

On one of the next times I see Miya, we was on a double date with Dwight and his live- in girlfriend, named Deanne. At this time, Dwight was renting a house over on Cherry Avenue, out Hampton; and Deanne is originally from Suffolk. In Virginia.

Miya was looking very healthy and extremely good. Hair done. Nails done. Toes done. Miya is naturally pretty. She doesn't need make-up. But she has it on anyway. Miya's smile was so pretty, she could melt a snowman down, or even make the sun take the day off. She made the whole outside look brighter.

It was during this time, I didn't get another major credit card, but what I did get was jewelry credit cards, every time I shop in the mall. I would apply, and they'll give me a credit line. One of the first pieces of jewelry I bought, was I bought my mother a diamond ring.

My mother is a Saint, by her faith. So she doesn't really wear jewelry. She doesn't wear chains. She doesn't wear necklaces. She doesn't wear bracelets. She doesn't wear earrings. The only jewelry she might wear is a zirconia broche. On her hat, on her coat, or on blouse. And that's only when she goes to church.

And she'll wear her wedding ring. When I looked at my mother's wedding finger, I don't think my mother was wearing her natural wedding ring. I didn't know what happened to it.

It might've gotten lost over the almost quarter of a

century she was married to my father. I'on know.
But when I look at her ring, I see charred cubic
zirconia's. And a broche she doesn't wear everyday.
But her symbol of love, faithfulness, and respect to
her husband is what she wears everyday. So I
decided to buy her a diamond wedding ring.

I know what you're thinking.: it is her
husband's job to be doing this for her. But when he
closed his eyes, smiled, and shook his head. That
means, he didn't have a problem with it.

And you have to understand.: it's not the
mansion I always wanted her to receive. Or the
house I thought I'd build for her by hand. But it's
the least I could do for the woman who gave me so
much of herself, since I been born.

My momma had started showing off her
NEW diamond ring EVERYWHERE. Even when
she went to church. They won't lying when they say
'a DIAMOND is 'a girl's best friend. These women
are smart, her sisters in church was a magnet for
this kind of stuff.

I didn't know what her actual ring size was.
So the ring was a little to big. It used to slip around
on her finger, so we took it back to Reed's Jewelers,
so she could be fitted. And the man behind the
counter had to take her ring off her hand, for (7)
days to get it adjusted. As soon as he was pulling it
off, I heard my momma's heart slowly purr in
disappointment,

"Awwww," her eyes and lips melted off in
the luster of her departing diamond.

When she went back to church, the first thing her sisters would say is, "Where's your ring?"

It's crazy.: how one single diamond had transformed my momma into a whole different style of conversation piece. And she wouldn't say nothing, but I think she was counting those (7) days down to the ground.

I went to pick her up on that 7th day, from where she "worked," and I took her to go to receive her ring. She was real good and quiet on the ride up over there. But when she got there, she couldn't stop smiling. I saw her whip her hand over top of that counter so fast, for that man to get that diamond back on her finger. I never seen her move that fast, to go get a belt. She put it on.

And it fit.

She was so happy! She rubbed that ring. And rubbed that ring. And rubbed that ring. Like 'a genie su'posed to pop out.

The next time I picked up my momma up from work. She was sitting good and quiet again. But this time, still, in her boss' Mrs. Smith's office. And the whole conversation was about that ring. Mrs. Smith looked up from behind her desk at me and she said,

"Oh Jamie, this is a very nice thing you've done for your mother..."

And I look over at momma, and she's just sitting there, quiet. Not making any eye contact with either one of us. Her eyes are opals to the windows of wonder. And she just keeps rubbing, rubbing... rubbing on that ring.

And when she went back to church, I'd hear the sisters say,

"Sister Miles, you got back your ring."

When my mother was young, she always wanted to be a model. And she was attractive enough to be. But despite the fact what she wanted to be; God wanted her to be something different. Even greater. And now for her to model this diamond, was a symbol of the sacrifice of what she is to God, before God's eyes.

My mother ended up being the first woman I'd bought a piece of jewelry for my whole life. A diamond. And a diamond ring. She had diamonds before I even had diamonds.

Ericka was the 2nd. But she ain't get the diamonds part, or the ring. What she did get was some golden earrings. But by this time, Ericka wassa fanning flame.

My heart was churning for more.

When I met Miya. We was spending everyday together, and not having sex. But I saw the potential. Before one of our dates; Miya popped the box. And I had her some 14 karat golden earrings too. But her earrings had a heart danglin down at the bottom. Symbolic to how she make me feel, every time I see into her eyes.

Miya was the Shit!

When we went out to the stores, she'd say to me,

"I don't window shop...

I don't do window shopping."

Uh. Excuse me Ms. Momma Miya. But she meant every word of that. Back then, Coach bag purses was the fashion. And I'd see this young girl in the store, up in the boutique, BLOW!! $200, $300, $450 just on ONE leather Coach purse. Where I came from, I seen women splurging just to set up 'a Avon order. And sometimes they gotta borrow money just to do that. So, I wasn't used to this.

Miya was That Bitch!

It's like I was on dates witta Clueless Stacey Dash. Miya was turning me on to a higher brand of lifestyle.

But we still wasn't having sex.

It wassa lotta kissin, touchin, rubbin, grindin. Every time I see Dwight, he'd pull me to the side and ask,

"Yo, is you hittin that yet?"

The answer was always, No. It almost killed me to admit that, while staring over at Miya wearing that very tight mini- skirt and heels, or deep black spandex pants, stuffed inside her lil red pointy leather boots.

Miya would call me early in the morning. Every

morning and ask me,

"What you doin?"

Of course, Nothing. Just waitin to go to work.

"Well..." and she would start telling me to come to her house.

She always had something for us to do. She had her own car. She had money and she was graduating from Hampton University with a degree in Psychology. Miya and I was spending so much time together that my hours at Century 21 went from 8 hours to 4 hours, to 2 hours, to 0 hours. I didn't even want to work no more.

One night she called me to come pick her up. I did and brought her back over Dwight's house; wit Dwight and Deanne. Dwight asked me the question again,

"Yo, is you fuckin her yet?"

Of course, the answer is still, No. He just slump and shake his head to me.

After we leave his house, this is going to make this story sound real dated, but it's ok, one day your stories will be dated too.: my pager was going off. It wassa nother girl. Miya sensed it; and she was right. Me and Miya was a couple but only in name.

I didn't go back to Dwight's house to make the call. I stopped at 7- 11, on Kecoughtan Road. And when I called, I kept looking at Miya through the windshield. After I finished the call, I got back in the car, and started driving off. Miya said,

"J, I'm ready."

"Ready? Ready for what?"

"I think I'm ready to have sex."

WHA!? WHA!? WHA!? WHA!? WHAT!? Man, I couldn't shift the gears in the Metro fast enough. This was special. And I wanted this to be special. I drove her out Hampton, all the way straight back down Fox Hill Road. They was doing construction, but only some of the homes were built. They had some fly ass 3 story houses out here! I seen plenty of 2 story houses, but I never seen 3 story houses before now. So that's what fascinated me. And there's a near lil field, that has the red blinking airplane lights, towering up into the sky. I liked it. I think it was real romantic.

Perhaps more romantic than the Ghostface IRONMAN album that was in my deck. But HEY! I'm romantic. My dick lickin HARDER!! than an R and B song. We fucked off Ghostface.

The thing I'll always remember is, Miya was CLEAN. Oh, my goodness. Miya was so CLEAN! She couldn't walk. She thought I used an old rubba. Shit, that won't no old rubba. That was me burnin yo ass up, BITCH!

Tore da skin off tha pussy that night. Shouldn't na took so long to get them panties down, BITCH!

Anyway, after this, I was still in Real Estate school,

but I couldn't focus. Miya, would be with me, til I go to class. I'd drop myself off, and tell her to be back at 9 to pick me up. She already knew how to drive a stick. I ain't gon poke the bear to ask where she got it from.

Jus leave it lone bruh. Jus leave it alone.

I'm thinkin about Miya. I wanna lock her all the way in. So the second time, I get us a hotel room. I get us pizza. All da good stuff. Take Miya there, after I get outta class. Plus, this'll be our first time, stayin wit each other all night. Get the room. Bring Miya in the room. Cause the first was in a small dark setting, this time I had more light and space, to really look at Miya. And getta eatin dat pussy!

Miya, was lookin soooo GOOD!! She had dropped down her BOOTY Bag; and why did she have on a short pair of white coochie cutta shorts? Now, how did she know I hadda fetish for thiccckk women in white coochie cutta shorts? When she got up on the bed, and she showed me that RED cheek fall up out the bottom of them little ass shorts; that was it- - I boxed that pussy in, like I was IRON MIKE TYSON!!!!

Miya couldn't even last ONE ROUND!!

"Uh- uh. Alright that's good. That's good. Lay down and go to sleep."

What!? What the fuck is this!? And she was serious too. In that ONE ROUND she came like 4 times. And was through. She ain't give me no more pussy the whole rest of the time. I won't used to no shit like this, from fuckin wit Ericka. Other bitches jus won't built like My Snu.

But, I ain't give up on Miya.

Miya bought the next room, at the Quality Inn. So when she bought the room, I'm thinkin she ready. She know what to expect. And here she go again,

"Aaaaagghhh!" This bitch would run, run, run, run, run, run, more than 'a fuckin Road Runner. She was jumpin like a squirrel; flyin all across the room. I need to get me somma this ACME dynamite, to see if I can't BLOW!! this bitch to stay in place.

This shit is crazy!

Then she bought the next series of rooms, including, she even bought us a room on the Virginia Beach strip. We not tourists, that's our local area. So if you buy a room on the waterfront, that means, you really tryin ta get it in. But instead,

"Aaaaagghhh!"

Here we go again.

You know how it is when you young.: and you go to catch the lightning bugs to put them in a jar. Miya was that lightning bug that jus wouldn't get her ass up in the damn jar. That would keep happening, but there were other facets to our relationship that made me look past the sex. I had to.

After we consummated our relationship,

that's when I started bringing Miya around my friends. I had lost one TTL girl. But now God had BLESSED me with a NEW one. So I definitely ain't have no problem introducing her to my friends. I took Miya to a party at Ms. Yvonne's. That's Lynn's momma's house.

Lynn was happy to see Miya. And Miya and Lynn was dancing. Lynn was doing his world infamous rubba dubb dance all up on Miya's booty. I seen him. But he ain't grab or squeeze her wit his hands. I ain't get mad. I saw it the same way Carlito might see it.

It was just Dancing.

Plus that night, everybody was happy and having a good time. I didn't have time to get jealous. I was more enthralled by the fact, I had The Baddest Bitch outta all my friends. None of my friends didn't know Miya, so when I showed Miya off, ALL my friends wanted to fuck Miya. And they was smiling, when they see her, but that was putting the biggest smile on my face.

The good part is I was testing Miya. To see how she could hold up being in the room of Horny and BLACK testosterone, of my friends. And she had passed. Good job Miya!

That's one of the main things I was looking for in my NEW girl, was a woman who could hold her composure being around other men, and a woman who could hold her composure being around my homies. The crazy part about it.: this was Ray Perry's girl. 'A dope boy from out Phoebus. Miya wassa dopeboy's girl. I'on know if he ever had to put up wit Lady Rocky n Bullwinkle. I ain't never ask him. Miya was wit Ray when we first started talking and made friends, 3 years ago.

But Miya and I came out of similar past relationships. That's another part that brought us together. I took her to the mall one day, to pay on my jewelry card bills. While I'm in there, the lady says,

"We can go ahead and increase your credit card limit today."

Hey! Why not. My eyes are already on this silver and gold Seiko watch. I'm not really a fan of Seiko. A Seiko is like a General Motors version of a Rolls Royce. But they had got they shit off on this one particular piece. I liked it. They only wanted $170 for it. And I rung it up.

When I was growing up, my momma used to buy my watches from the Dollar Store. Everything's A Dollar. So you already know how much that cost. Outside of that, my most expensive watches cost between $10 and $20. Poor people ain't really spending money on watches. That money gotta go somewhere else.

But watching Ric Flair on wrestling, is what made me start paying attention to the notoriety that it puts on your wrist, it looks like a championship belt, when you got on a quality time piece. Because of Flair, championships and Rolexes just go together. I always wanted a Rolex.

Ericka had bought me MY FIRST Rolex, just this past Christmas, the same Christmas I had bought her a stereo. And she bought me a Tommy Hilfiger button down shirt, and Tommy khaki pants. See, I told you, we was finally doin nice stuff for each other. I didn't mind that the Rolie said Made In China stickered on the back. I appreciate Ericka. Believe me I do. But, it's shit surrounding that, that jus came too late.

I wassa long ways from lookin like Ric Flair, but I put my first Real gold luxury watch in the case. No need to gift wrap that. Then I heard my mother's voice talking to me,

"You need to get you a wife." My mother almost always smiles when she talks, or she'll frown, and you'll know she's angry. But when she says this, I could see her face turn straight flat. Meaning, that she was pure emotionless when she said those particular words. Like the Lord was speaking through her.

And I felt that. Gettin pussy in and of itself, didn't mean everything to me. Most bitches was running anyway. I wanted a wife. When I look over at Miya, and I see her standing there looking all innocent and her lips bowed like the glaze in 'a honeybun, I saw that she might can be my Wife. And so it started off with somethin like a game. And of all places to try on this experiment- - WE'RE IN A FUCKIN JEWELRY STORE, MAN!!

And GOOD GRACIOUS!! being in a jewelry store, it was glass of cased islands of RINGS, EVERYWHERE!

Wedding RINGS...

Engagement RINGS...

Wet Diamond RINGS...

She can't get onnx stones, sapphires, or rubies. Of course I'm gon get my girl, I wanna be My WIFE, the RING wit the Diamonds. Right. If I'm gon buy a

RING

I gotta buy 'a RING!

I gotta buy 'a Real RING!

I got my momma one, so I got to get her one. So I say,

"Try on that right there."

WHAT!? Miya is going through, tryin on clusters of diamond rings on that's within my NEW $1300 credit budget. She's going through it. I'm fuckin wit her,

"No, no, nope. That's not the one. That's not the one," I'm justa grinning.

Of course the woman behind the counter is boostin this to the max. She's steppin it up, showin Miya more and MORE diamond rings. Then...

she cuts through the chase.:

"How about... this one?"

She pulled out a ring. And Miya put that ring on. And when Miya put that ring on, I saw her whole face light up in the diamond. Miya is already RED. Sometimes she looks Yellow. And if you put her in the sun too long, she turn Brown. Miya has freckles. But you wouldn't know that unless you get all the way up on her. They are real thin. When I saw Miya's face light up in that diamond, I knew THIS WAS IT, SHE WAS THE ONE. And I thought about, I wasn't gon let this opportunity pass me by;

"Put it up!! Put it up!!"

"WHAT!?" Miya and the sales woman behind the counter said at the same time.

"Put it up! Put that shit back! Put that shit back!" I shouted out.

"Awwwww!!" Miya and the sales woman behind the counter both said at the same time, as she retrieved the diamond ring from Miya's finger, and returned it to it's glass showcase.

The next day, the Coliseum Mall opens at 9 o' clock in the morning. I was in the parking lot before that shit even opened. They opened the back door to the Food Court, and I was at Lundstrom's when the steel cage was still closed down to the floor. But, it wasn't too long after that, the same Sales Woman came and opened up the store. And I told her,

"I'm tryin to get that ring from yesterday."

At first she had to think about it, cause she deals with a barrage of customers all day, but she finally said,

"I think this was it."

She pulled it up, but it didn't look like the right ring. It wasn't glowing. It didn't shine. But, it looked like it might be the right one. I took my chances.

"Is this the one you want?" she asked to me.

"Yeah. That's the one I want," but inside I was unsure if it was the right one.

"Would you like me to gift wrap it for you?-- Yeah, let me gift wrap it."

And that's what she did. In gold wrapping paper, and bowed it with a Lundstrom Jewelers seal.

Now for the next step.: it's time to go pick up da Momma Miya.

I get to Miya's house, and we get into a fight about something stupid. I'on even remember what it is. When she get in the car, she says,

"Take me to Sally's."

Sally's is the beauty supply store out Hampton, on Pembroke Avenue. When we get to Sally's she says,

"You just stay in the car..." Man, this girl really mad at me bout somethin. Ain't it.

She gets back out, and get in the car, and she still tryin to pick up right where it left off.

"Miya, look in the glove compartment."

472

She say, "What is it Jamie? What you got in here a snake? So it can bite me?"

"Just look in the glove compartment."

She opens it.

"What is it a book?" She grabs the Owner's Manual Handbook out the glove compartment. "Is this what you tryin to show me, Jamie?" She's tryin to be funny.

"Uh- uh," my eyes lean over into her eyes.

And she goes back in. It came inside a plastic bag. But I already disposed of the bag, so I can do it wit Class. And the box is sittin right there on top. She reaches for it and pulls it out. She holds it to her ear,

"What is it Jamie? A bomb? You wanna blow me up?"

"Will you jus open the damn box," she got me laughing. Trippin off her.

She listening to the box beside her ear. Shakin the box. The box doesn't rattle. I think she thinks it's some earrings. She finally opens the box and the ring box, and she sees the DIAMOND. Her face LIT UP in the DIAMOND! And that's how I knew I had the right ring. I take the ring and I put it on Miya's left ring finger, and I say,

"Miya, will you marry me?"

Miya melted into me, hunh, like chocolate grapes drippin on sorbetto.

And she said, "Yes."

And that was it. I was getting married.

I BLEW!! $1200 of practically my whole $1300 bonus to buy Miya a 14 karat 7/16ths of a karat diamond ring. Just 'a hair less than half 'a karat.

If you think my momma was pickin up attention, everywhere she go, from the diamond ring I bought for her. Just wait til you see Miya...

Miya was gettin asked questions by all her girlfriends. Her friends. People she ain't even know. And then... by her mother. One day Miya was busy moving round the kitchen, and her mother was sitting at the bar stool. When,

"Miya, what is that on your hand?"

"Huh?"

"What is that ring? What is that ring for on your finger?"

"Jamie gave it to me."

"JAMIE!? Jamie WHO!?"

See, Miya's momma still don't really know me yet. The first time I went to see Miya, Miya was at home alone. Her father and mother were gone out of town to Atlanta. And all these mornings when I was pickin Miya up, I just roll up, and she comes out. I seen her mother. But we was never FORMALLY introduced. The whole time she was thinking in general.: like me and her daughter was just friends.

Plus, Miya is a college student. She ain't got no damn money. So all the money she was spending, was mostly coming from her mom, or from her momma's credit account. So when she say,

"Miya, what is that on your hand?"

or

"What is that ring? What is that ring for on your finger?"

Then Miya betta have'a pretty good explanation. Cause her mother wants to know how much "this thing," is costing HER, or how much it did cost her, when she get a receipt for the bill. On the other hand, she wants to be sure it didn't come from Ray.

"Jamie, gave it to me," she humbly said to her mother.

Her mother is not very tall. But with all respect, her authority towers in the room. So, you betta be humble when you start talking to her. So when Miya goes,

"Jamie gave it to me."

WOW!!

So, you already know what happens next, right.

Come on now. Put 1 and 1 together. Equals... I get the call.

"Hello?"

"Hey."

"What's up!?"

"You need to come round here. My mother wants to see you."

Of course. Of course, she does. Right!? Why wouldn't any responsible parent, especially A MOTHER, not want to meet the man or the dummy, who stucka $1200 rock up on they daughter's finger?

I went around there. It's protocol. And this is how I got my FORMAL introduction to Miya's mother.:

"Hello Dr Graham. How you doin today?" I smile on the outside. My fingers are squeezin my knuckles together on the inside.

This shit ain't being humble. I'm scared to death. I'm bout to shit on myself. Man, I'on know what this woman bout to say to me. Especially when... she puts Miya out the room.

Dr Graham was born in the 1920s. She too was a Georgia Peach, just like my Grandmother and my Great Grandmother. But my Grandmother and my Great Grandmother was from a farm. Dr Graham was from da A. All the way back, when it was just Atlanta. Dr Graham is not a Doctor in medicine, but a Doctor in Education. Which is fitting, for her era and Atlanta background. By now, you know about the Blacks of Black Wall Street, who developed and prospered in Tulsa, Oklahoma, up until it was bombed burned down in1921. But what about Blacks that thrived into the prospects of being boosted from poverty, through the Ministry and in taking advantages of opportunities in Education and Entrepreneurship, chiefly in cities like Atlanta? Hunh. And you wonda why today, you call it Chocolate City?

Morehouse and Spellman had to be built for something.

But Blacks have always had a suppressed history in annals of American History. We had Anthony Johnson, who was a Former indentured servant, who owned 200 acres of land, in Northampton County IN VIRGINIA. We have Blacks that invented. Even during crude negro slavery, you had Blacks that never were slaves, you had slaves that were emancipated before 1865, and you had...

And this is crazy.: but Thanks to my friend Dwight, I was now sitting in the clam shell, of a silent piece of Historical Black, and generational economic success that was already being incubated, yet ROARING!! since the end of America's Civil War History. The Black Middle Class Family.

Chapter 24.

"Hello. I'm doing fine, JAMIE."

She really didn't get MAD. She makes and breaks eye contact. Dr Graham speaks in a loud whisper, as though her voice floats into its cadence. And she calmly says,

"That's a real nice ring you bought for Miya."

And then she got to asking me questions. She ain't really grill me, but she was just concerned, and trying to figure out how I was capable of purchasing such an expensive diamonded piece, and how I really feel about her daughter. Not just her daughter. But her Baby child. Dr Graham is the mother of 5 children. 4 daughters and one son; and Miya is her youngest, out of all 5 of her children. And she's the only ONE that lives with her at home, and in Virginia.

Once Dr Graham relaxed into thinking her daughter was with a good guy, I had her Blessing to be with her daughter. And that's about the time, Miya came back downstairs. Later she told me,

"I came to save you from my mom."

Who knows Miya's Mother better than Miya? It wasn't just like they was mother and daughter; they was Best Friends. Miya had been listening to the whole conversation from the top of the steps.

Then, I took my fiancée home, to show her off to my parents. Miya looked so pretty in her ring. My parents were happy. I was happy they liked Miya. T- Bone didn't think that much of her. He just growled and barked, and barked, and barked at her.

Miya deserved that ring.

Before we had got engaged, one day I was out kickin it wit Dwight. We rode around town and out Pine Chapel, these real hood ass apartments out Hampton. I'm bumpin the system. Dwight sees 3 females walking and wants me to slow up so he can holla at them. He was always being the ladies man, but this one backfires on him. When I'm lookin at them, I'm thinkin, 'these girls look too young.'

He was still talkin, when I pull the car off, but it was too late. I was right. Not only was these three girls under 18, one of the young ladies' mother saw my car stop and saw 2 guys in the car. This was not jus one of the mothers that was protective of her child, but her daughter had a mental disability. So she had to make sure her daughter wasn't being taken advantage of. She reported my license plate to the police.

The Hampton Police pull me over in Pine Chapel. She checks my license and registration. My license comes back suspended. The officer calls for back up. When the back up cars get there, they put me in handcuffs, and sit me in the back of a squad car, and take Dwight out the car, and sit him down on the curb. They bring out k- 9 dogs, and they scrubbed my whole car down for weapons and drugs. They did all of that from me driving on a suspended license?

They took me in. The car is in my dad's name, so they didn't impound it. They let him come pick up His car. I went to jail to go before the magistrate, and Dwight went in a separate car after being searched. He wasn't arrested. They just took him down to wait for me until I get out. I call Miya. I got a Personal Recognizance bond and was released.

When I walked outside, the Hampton Police had left Dwight sitting out on the curb. He was regretful that this had happened. I ain't really have time to think about it. Miya was rolling up, then I felt all better. She got in the backseat and let me drive Dwight home. When I got home, my parents wouldn't give me back the key until I got my license straight. I got it straight. Get my key back. Go to court. The judge dismissed the case after I paid the court fine, and upon seeing proof of the DMV record that my license was reinstated.

That was BEFORE we got engaged.

After we got engaged, my cousin Hugh, is graduating from high school in Richmond. And Miya goes along with me for the ride. It's a chance for me to show her off to my family up in Richmond.

I'm on 95 South, in between Richmond and headed towards Petersburg. The Metro is rippin in

5th, I'm burnin 90 in a 55, lookin for Iron Bridge Road, when this State Trooper pulls beside me and tells me to pull over. I turn the system down and pull over. He checks my license and registration. Thank goodness this time, my license is straight. I get the ticket for speeding. I'm so used to driving on a suspended license. My license is more suspended than what it active. After everything up there is finished, we come back home.

So my cousin, Debbie tells me to calculate $5.00 for every mile I was over the speed limit and mail it to the Richmond Court. That's what I do.

Time goes past. When I bought my car, they gave me my FIRST full tank of gas FREE. And, my car was under warranty for a year. So if my car breaks down for any reason, they fix it for FREE. and my First Year of oil changes was absolutely FREE. So one day, I take my car to the shop for an oil change.

The service guy tells me, they gotta keep my car overnight to service it, because it was a long line, and he couldn't get to it tonight. I put my car in the shop. But no worry, cause that means, Casey Chevrolet gives me paperwork, and a ride over to Enterprise Car Rental. When I turn in my paperwork; they give me the keys to way cooler cars and trucks. They call it, Loaner Cars.

So the next time when Miya saw me, I was in 'a iced shark blue Corsica. I felt so good. I told her, "I'm gon take you out to eat..."

I looked over and I saw her sexy RED body snappin HARD!! in this purple top and matchin short set,

and smellin fresha than'a fish in salty river water.
So I told her,

"... I'm gon take you to Red Lobster."

I just had to stop by the house to pick up
some CASH. When I get home, both of my parents
are gone. There's a note on the front door for me.
But it ain't from my momma. This one is from the
Newport News City Jail. So I'm like, 'What the
fuck!?'

I don't know what the hell is goin on.

I go to my room, get a $100, cash. But my
appetite is all fucked up. This must be a mistake. I
got this Capias on my front door. Why is the police
looking for me? I don't do nothing wrong. My mind
flashes to the dream God gave me when I was 19. I
brush it off. I'll just go down here, get this
straightened out, and take my Baby out to Red
Lobster.

Get down there. So I'm talking to the police down at
the station. Another officer walks out. The first
officer says,

"James Mills? Are you James Mills from
Center Avenue?"

I thought about my dream. But then my brain
snapped back to consciousness, so I said,

"No. My name is Jamie Miles. I'm from
Wickham." And I gave her my license.

She looked and said, "We was just checking. James Mills is wanted for some ROBBERIES. We got you on this Capias. You missed your court date in Richmond..."

So I ended up getting locked up for MY THIRD TIME, in the same year. In a rapid succession of months. In like less than 6 months. But I never hit the floor in Newport News City Jail or Hampton City Jail. The first time and second time, I didn't go no further than the bullpen. This time, I went past to bullpen, and into a holding cell. Without a cellie.

They hold me for a few hours. MIYA bonds me out. My bond was a $1,000. And Miya secures the bondsman and pays the $100. Never woulda got that BLESSING wita broke girl. My ass woulda still been sittin up in here.

When I get out and walk through the door, the only person I see, is Miya sitting on the bench happy and smiling to see me. She had never left from the time the police had took me into custody. Since she put up the $100, I paid her her $100 back.

By the time I got out it was 12 o' clock midnight. Red Lobster is closed anyway. I take Miya home. When we get there, Miya's parents are gone. Dr Graham is back home, in Atlanta. One of Miya's sisters is in Virginia, from Atlanta. And that's when I meet Miya's sister named Marian. But nobody calls her that, except for her boyfriend, Love. Everybody else calls her Buttons.

Buttons is light skinned, like Miya. Buttons

and Miya are Dr Graham's only two light skinned children. Buttons might be 'a inch shorter than me, or the same height. Her hairline is trimmed. Her sides are chopped short, and it's a crop of hair poofing at the top.

Buttons is very chill laid back, and a party girl. Some alcohol and a cigarette and she loves to talk,

"I used to be a big girl," she tells me. "I lost all that weight, see..."

She shows me younger photos of herself, from her mother's photo gallery.

"I used to be married..."

She rolls herself some reefa into 'a stick of 'a joint, so she can rock all the way into her conversation. She roll me a joint and pass it to me, so I can smoke, when I hear her say,

"I used to live in Maryland. Yep, In Baltimore...

... I have (3) children..."

Buttons had got so small, she look like she ain't have any children.

"... Troy, Wayne, and Dottie."

She named her children. Her oldest son was Troy. Numerous times she refers to him as Lil Troy, because he's named after Miya's father. She and Miya have different fathers, she is by her mother's first husband. His name is White. But Miya's father was so impactful and influential, in his role as a stepfather, that she named her first child after him.

And probably since he didn't have a son.

Her second son is named Wayne. Cause his daddy is name Wayne. And her daughter is named Dottie. After Dr Graham's sister named Dottie. But my momma also has a sister named Dottie.

Something else me and Miya had in common.

Then her stories got sad. She told me about she was with a boyfriend, after her and her husband divorced, and her boyfriend was molesting and I think raping her daughter. And she told me about they're other sister named Sheila. Sheila lives in Atlanta too. Well, Stone Mountain.

But anyway, that Sheila had been killed by her ex- husband. The Lord BLESSED her though, and she was resuscitated and bought back to life.

I was glad to hear about that.

After that, Miya took me to her room upstairs. She got this queen brass bed. All pretty. She got this clean white comforter. It got all these pretty pink and purple flowers colored all over it. Wit lil green stems and green leaves. And shit. Miya laid down, and pulled them panties off, and mannnn, 'a nigga was HARDER!! than 'a bronco on 'a Ferrari!!

We heard Buttons downstairs. She kept saying, "DAMN!"

And I kept listening to Miya say, "FUCK ME! You jailbird."

I was bout to knock her sexy lil brass bed right on through the wall! The floors, the walls. All that shit was SHAKING!! I thought we was gon end up somewhere out on the front yard, or drippin down her cul de sac.

Miya ain't run tonight though. She ate all that! She went for four rounds on that jun'.

After we came back down, I was glad to see Dr Graham's house was still intact. I prolly woulda been back in jail, cause I couldn't afford to replace none of these pieces.

About 2 weeks later I get the call,

"Hi."

"What's up?"

"I'm pregnant."

Am I mad? Hell no! This is some of the best news of my life. This was from when I spent those few hours in jail,

"You jailbird! You got me pregnant you fuckin jailbird."

All this jailbird shit wasn't really turning me on. For real, I didn't like it. But who knows. Maybe this was her way of talkin dirty.

I went around there. Miya wasn't showing. She still

looked the same. But she was only like 2 weeks. I kiss on her, and rub on her stomach a lil bit and then,

it was all gone. Gone.

"My mother made me have an abortion."

WHAT!?

This immediately led to our first break up. I don't play that abortion shit. You killed my baby. I was so adamant. I went to Miya, and I took back my ring. I left from Miya's house and I went back home. My house to Miya's house is like a 20 minute drive. I didn't even have 5 minutes to lay across my bed when,

"Rrrrrrrrrrrrrrrrrr," the phone is ringing. It's the same phone from Troy Drive. I just changed the ring tone.

"Hello?"

"Hi." You already know who it is. Not her. But the other one.

"I miss you..." Yeah, they kinda sound alike.

"... Come see me..."

I'm listening. I already know what this gon lead to.

"... And bring me back my ring."

From there and even the ride over there, I was thinking like, 'We would still be together. We would have more chances to make babies.' Plus I still needed to get myself together in a career and financially, so I accepted Miya back.

When I get round there, Miya comes out and meets me out on her front lawn. The first thing she do is kiss me and say,

"Where's my ring? Gimme my ring."

I pulled the ring out, and she put out her hand. When I put that ring back on her finger, her face lit up, even outside in the sun. Her mother was inside. After the abortion was when Miya's mother really learned that this ring was an engagement ring.

Everything was moving kind of fast. Miya's ring was the BIGGEST purchase I'd ever made, all at one time. But it ain't bother me. Cause I knew Miya loved me and loved being with me. The same way she made me feel about her. I pick her up. She wants to go to Wal- Mart to pick up a few things. We go. She was focusing on her graduation from Hampton University, which was about a week away.

After Dr Graham had found out that me and her daughter actually was engaged, of course she pulled me to the side for another conversation. She started out a little more angry this time. And it was something else Dr Graham had admitted to me,

"I don't want Miya in the projects."

And that's right where I had her at. I was flexin my fiancée in the projects, all in the slums of Bad Newz, VA. She was shining like 'a diamond cross the crops of poverty. And ALL my homies love when I bring Miya around. Huh. You already know why. I'm tickling inside.

Miya graduated at the Hampton Convocation Center, with a bachelor's degree in Psychology. All three of her sisters were there. I met the other two. Sheila and Cheryl. Of course, I already knew Buttons. Cheryl is married to Hud. Short for Hudson. But we all keep calling him Hut. Hut is The Vice President of Morehouse College.

Man, this Black class clamshell just keep gettin better.

I had heard about Hut already from Dr Graham. She's loves and is very proud of her active son- in- law. Now I was able to meet him and shake hands with him in person. And I met Miya's nieces.: Tara, Chrissy, and Dottie. Chrissy and Dottie are the same age. 9.

Tara is by Cheryl. Chrissy is by Sheila. And Dottie is by Buttons. Buttons is the only one who has boys. Wayne and Lil Troy, but they was away in Baltimore wit they father and stepmother. Miya's brother Teddy couldn't come either. He lives all the way down, somewhere in Mississippi. This is a very good family. A very extraordinary family. And I'm attracted to it because I don't have any sisters or brothers, nieces and nephews. So by Miya, God will give me all that through marriage.

After her graduation, Miya is outside the Convocation Center in her cap and gown, and she is flexin her ring off for her friends, her graduating peers. Miya is a very popular girl. But she's not loud. Not even when she gets excited, and in her highest emotional state. She don't make a lot of noise. And I like that.

Me and Miya had made it to having sex, getting engaged, and getting pregnant one time. And me seeing her graduate. But she still won't givin up the head. I'on know if somethin was wrong or what. I was puttin pressure on her. And generally I'm not even about gettin it. I usually wait, until she ready. But I Miya made me feel a certain way. I couldn't wait to get my dick sucked by this jun'. I bring it up. And she would say,

"Nooooo." That was her way of sayin she won't ready.

Not long after Miya graduated from Hampton University, she had TWO girlfriends graduating from the prestigious University of Virginia. Miya get us a room, on a strip of 95, in between Richmond and Petersburg. The room is NICE. Air Condition. Cable. Cozy and Clean. Miya gets back to running again. I thought we was past this stage.

She only goes one round.

Then I'm tryin to get some head. She ain't want to do that either. Go to sleep. Get up. Go to UVa to see Lauren and Patsy graduate.

This ain't my first time on UVa campus. I'd been here on field trips in high school. Even an ROTC field trip when I was at Warwick. But when I'm looking at UVa now, I'm looking at it differently. I'm not even mad at Miya no more. This done turned to a Romance Trip, cause UVa has a whole lotta lawns. It's a lot of walking around you get to do. Lauren and Patsy are two smart women. Not just smart. But just like Miya.: young, Black, and Middle Class successful.

Not only are these TWO Black women graduating today from the University of Virginia, one of the most prominent colleges in the United States of America, but they are graduating as TWO Architect Majors. Of all the wonders in the world- - what a fascinating subject to have mastered, completed, and majored in.

To my disappointment, the two ladies are not graduating together on the same stage. The University of Virginia has shuffled the graduations apart, so Lauren is over here and Patsy is somewhere out over there. I think they got Lauren in AC. In a building. And they got Patsy up under this tent. Ain't that something, my Hebrew and Jewish friends. So me and Miya attend Patsy's graduation, up under a tent.

Patsy is even more beautiful and unique, because of her history. Not just because she is middle class, or smart, or because she's graduating from UVa, or because she's an Architect Major. No. But because she's Haitian. Her family migrated to the United States from Haiti. So the Bielas' are even more proud, that their Patricia was 'a Patsy of 'a petal.

The more I sit here. The more I'm compelled to think about how I need to be in college. I think about how I BLEW!! Job Corps. Then how I BLEW!! Job Corps and Union BOTH in the same summer; and how now I might be too far to get back.

After Miya saw Patsy, we never did see Lauren and her boyfriend, Justin. The campus is very packed in with students, administration, and visitors. After Miya see Patsy, we head on back home.

One night I'm with some friends out Hampton, I had met through Miya. These are her male friends. Yeah, she got man friends. But when I met them, I never saw signs that any of them was having sex with her or anything like it. They welcomed me into their circle.

One of them names is Wayne. Wayne is like six- two; six- three. Kinda pretty boy type. He's light skin and got smooth curly hair. He rocks it kinda short on the side, a box up top. But Wayne has a lot of class. Especially for 'a Hampton nigga that's from off Shell Road.

Wayne loves to wear a lot of Polo. Everyday. He'll Polo everything. Polo shirt, Polo shorts; if it ain't shorts, it's Polo jeans; if it ain't jeans, it's Polo sweats. Polo socks. I'm shocked his shoes ain't even Polo. And he keeps a Polo Basketball souvenir'd in his living room. Wayne has his own spot off Aberdeen Road. And this is the hang out spot.

He likes to listen to a lot of Mobb Deep. Wu- Tang. Ol' Dirty Bastard. Music I can listen to all day.

Miya has another friend, that I know from church, name Paul. I ran into somebody else I used to see from church. And just like me, Paul comes out of one of the most formidable families in church. But he was from a more elite class. He is a Smith. People talk about keepin up with the Smiths and Joneses. In the church where we came from, it was The Smiths and The Haltiwangers.

I'on know exactly why. It jus always been like that ever since Best Momma was alive. The saints just always paid attention to The Smiths and The Haltiwangers. Whatever they was doing. Whatever they had on. I guess stuff like that.

But as far as a population.: my Best Momma went there. She bought Mottie and Esther. My father. My mother. Me. My Best Momma's nephew and my father's cousin, Howard. Then Howard has a family. His wife Brenda. His children Tibbs, Bruh, Charlissa, and Othea.

Even Bobby was in church for a lil while.

But when Best Momma passed it changed things a lot. My cousin Tibbs was a special needs child. He never did walk or talk his whole life. But he did know how to be happy. He always kept a smile on his face and in his heart. He had passed as a child. Then his mother Brenda, had passed behind him, from cancer.

After Best Momma passed, Mottie and Esther stopped going. And I was growing up. I stopped going. I did go. I just wasn't regular. I had joined the church after I had my dream, but then I slipped back. I didn't know what this meant. I was still trying to find that out.

In church everyone was tryin to keep up wit

Paul, but out here, Paul was tryin to keep up wit Wayne. He did everything Wayne did, he just do it in a different brand. He rocks Nautica down.

But I fuck wit him too. I feel like he got good class.

One night we was chillin at Wayne's house, when Wayne say, "We about to head to Wipe Out Eddie's."

Wipe Out Eddie's is a Karaoke Bar up from J Clyde Morris Blvd in Newport News. It's just before you hit Oyster Point. It's in a real upscale area. So we head out there. Not for the Karaoke part. But for drinks. Jus guys hangin out. Right.

Get there. And Miya is there. With her girls. I think Wayne did this shit on purpose. But I'on say nothin. I pull up on Miya like I'm seein her for the first time. I'm spittin,

"Yo... What's up shawty?"

Miya's laughin at my lil corny pick up line, while I invite her over to a table. I had to sit her down. Miya is killin me tonight! She is RED. In a tight ass RED dress. RED heels. And RED lipstick! Yo, any woman can kill it in a red dress, red heels, red lipstick. But 'a pretty ass RED bitch doin it- - whole notha planet!

Miya took it there.

She is very classy. Very sexy. I buy us drinks. I forget what she have. I'm drinking Heineken, smokin Blacks. She smoke Newport's. She keep lookin at me. I think she was timing me to finish this beer. Then she say,

"Go home."

"Say What!?" Shit, we jus got here. I'm bout
to buy us another round of drinks. She say it again,

"Go home... I'm gon hit you (on yo pager).
Don't call me back. Jus come straight through."

I'on even make it home. I'on even make it to
Wickham. My pager is goin off on Mercury Blvd.
006. That's her code. When I see that, that mean
My Baby want me to come through. I go through.
Mommy and Daddy upstairs.

She take me on the living room. On the couch. I
squeeze her out that tight ass red dress. She ask me,

"Whose the best bitch you ever had suck yo
dick?"

I was gon say Ericka. But I ain't wanna fuck this
shit up. So I went wit Shiakema.

"Tell me how she used to suck yo dick?"

Is she serious? She really want me to sit here, and
tell her a story about another bitch suckin my dick!?
Let's see how this go.

I told her a Kema story. And while I told her
that story, Miya went to "work." I came. She rocked
it back up. Sucked. I came again. And she
swallowed. I said,

"BITCH WE GETTIN MARRIED!!"

495

It won't long after that, I took Miya for a trip to the Pottery. Out Williamsburg. Before we even get there; she grab that muthafucka out on the interstate.

I pull up in the Pottery. The Pottery is packed too. Buses, vans, cars, tourists out everywhere. I'm surprised I found a parkin space. I find a spot between a van and a car. Miya still suckin. I say,

"Miya. It's people. It's white people right here..." Aye! I did my part. That's the best I can do.

And she say, "So!? You my man."

And the whole time I'm thinkin.: Hey! why the hell you ain't just been bring this bitch out to Williamsburg, a whole lot sooner.

I'on know what it is about Black women and suckin dick in Williamsburg. But Aye! fellas. You in 'a drought. The bitch ain't suckin yo dick right. Aye! jus take that bitch 'on up to Williamsburg. Change yo love life Forever.

And I shouldn't be sayin this.: but um, Miya's head is better than her pussy. If I could switch these two around...

Not sayin she don't got good pussy. But the head is...

Let's jus say, she can write Super Head 'a book.

Once we got to this level, I was definitely

comfortable wit Miya bein my wife. The only thing is, she jus wasn't consistent. Miya might go like once a week. Once every two weeks. One- two nuts, shit, for me that's four play. Miya wassa good girl. In time, I felt like she'll wrap around. At least by the time we get married. I'on know.

But as of right now, it was time for me to put Ms Ericka's promise to the test.

Let's see what happen

Chapter 25.

"Hel- lo?"

"What's up Snu?" Yeah. I called her. "I'm tryin to see you."

"Fo what!?"

"Stop actin crazy. I need to see you."

And I went around there and started stretchin Ericka back out. EVERYDAY! I'll leave Ericka's house, then go see Miya. But Ericka couldn't take that. She couldn't keep her promise. She was tryin to break me and Miya up. When I saw her movin like that, I left her alone to go be back wit Miya.

Miya was mad but we got back together.

When I couldn't take Miya to my house. And she couldn't take me to her house. We didn't have any money for hotels. We used to park the car a block from her house, have sex, then fall asleep in the car all night. We wake up in the sun. I drive her home. Drop her off. Go home. By the time I take my shower. Change clothes. Miya was callin me to come back through.

I was spendin so much time wit Miya, I saw

my parents less and less. When I'm gettin in 7 in the morning, my father done drove my momma to her job. And I'm spending less and less time wit T-Bone.

One day, I went to get an oil change at Casey Chevrolet, and they was backed up, so they gave me a Loaner Truck. A Chevrolet Silverado.

I went to pick Miya up in it. To have some fun. And I took her on a special date out in the truck.

Down on Buckroe Beach, when you drive all the way back, it's waterfront property up out there. On the left side of the parking lot, it's condo rises, and a club house. To the right side is the tennis courts. Behind the tennis courts, is more of those fancy 3 rise story houses. But when you walk straight back from the parking lot, it's a wooden wrap around deck.

It's a wooden course. You can walk out over top of the water. When you look to the right, you'll see the wild animals, like a crane. She's standing in the shallows of water hunting for fish. But when you look to the left, it's a marina of boats and yachts that's sitting out on the water.

It's people on they yachts and boats, like they kicked back at the living room at the crib. They be watching tv. Listening to music. White people bathing out in the sun. People grilling hot dogs, hamburgers, steaks, cheeseburgers...

Some of the yachts are like 3- 4 stories. Most of the boats and yachts might be empty, just resting out on the scrapple of the Chesapeake Bay.

And that's where I got Miya. Pressed in between the colorful magnificent quiet of yachts and salt water, and a rock hard penis. When you look out across the water, Fox Hill is right there. There's the same red airplane lights lighting up, that me and Miya were under the first time we had sex.

That trip made Miya wet as 'a pond.

We went back to the truck and got it in in the parking lot. All right there on the front seat of the truck. Miya was eatin. Too good. We passed out on the seat of the truck, with no clothes on. Butt ass naked.

I woke up to a mag light shining in my face.

"What the fuu..." I thought we was gettin robbed. I see this light. I'm thinking it's chrome from a gun.

Then I see a uniform. I think it's the police. I'm thinking I'm bout to go to jail. But it won't the police. It was a security guard.

He told me to,

"Roll down the window."

I roll the window down, I'm butt ass naked. I gotta BIIIIG tittie RED bitch butt ass in the passenger seat. I just know I'm goin to jail.

He say,

"Put your clothes on."

"Huh?" I'm not drunk but I been drinking. We done smoked reefa. I'm high. And I just got some pussy,

"HUH?"

He say it again,

"Put your clothes on," he holler again.

"Oh yeah. Yeah right." I'm scrambling, scrambling to grab my draws. I hear Miya's keep sayin,

"Those are mine... Those are mine... Those are mine."

Man, I was so fucked up, and thinking I'm about to go to jail, I kept snatchin fo my girl's panties.

It took me like 3 minutes to find my own draws in the cab of that truck. We start putting our clothes back on. He asked me who Miya was to me. I said,

"She's my fiancée." And we showed him her ring.

I think he thought she wassa hoe. If I told him that, he prolly would've tried to hop in on that action. He kept watching Miya take a long ass time to get them great BIIIIG ass titties set back up in her bra. He ain't rush her to get dressed.

But after I told him we was gettin married. He let us go. He jus told us not to let him catch us out there

501

again.

"Yes sir." I can imagine so. Me and Miya was the only two visible Black people out, and we out here fuckin like two loose dogs on these rich wholesome white people property. So I drove off. We left.

Through Dwight not only did he bring me Miya, but I had just got a new job telemarketing for Commercial Roofing, out Riverdale Plaza, out Hampton. Both me and Dwight worked the same spot. I had a split schedule. I go to work from 9 am-1. Then 5- 9 at night. I wasn't even three weeks into the job, when.:

One morning, I'm at home. Restin before about 8 o' clock come. My momma comes in my room;

"Jamie, T- Bone died."

"WHAT!?" This can't be real. This gotta be a lie. I jus saw him, when I pulled up the other day. That Nas and Lauren Hill song was still in my head. I was jus playin wit him the other day. I race to the backyard.

I saw T- Bone in his bed, with his tongue wagging out. Man, T- Bone ain't DIED. I called him,

"T- Bone."

He ain't move. He ain't respond. But he sitting up in his bed lookin right at me. I didn't believe it because my momma came to me way too calm.

"T- Bone. Come here boy. Come here. Shewwww. Shewwww," I whistled. I called to him. I snapped my fingers. And to all this, he still wouldn't respond.

I got closer. It was a gloss in his eye. One eye was red. One eye was green. T- Bone had been poisoned.

My momma knew the whole time. She had called his veterinarian. My mother's yard has a small ditch in the front, but a larger ditch in the back. A poisonous snake had came into the yard. The crazy part about it.: Since we had that house, I'd been all over that yard. I done worked out. I done played wit T- Bone. I done cut the grass. Raked the leaves. My Dad has scrap iron and old tires over in the yard.

There's a garage. The back of the garage has a side door. That's where T- Bone's bed is. And it's an aluminum and wood shed right behind the garage. It's dark in here. No natural light and no electricity. This where my father keeps his old chicken coups. And T- Bone's old dog house from Troy Drive sits behind that. If anything, I'd expect to come across a snake, in all this stuff. I never seen a snake.

And by our house having a ditch in the front and the back, our house has mice. I never seen mice in the yard, the garage or shed, but they run straight for the house. They're only in the kitchen, living room, and front bathroom of the house. I never seen them in any of the three bedrooms. If anything, I'd expect to see snakes hunting for them. I never seen it.

Plus my momma's clothesline is in the back yard. After she washes clothes, she'll bring them out to dry in the sun. T- Bone is a HERO for protecting me and my family from a poisonous snake bite.

They killed each other. The snake bit T- Bone, but T- Bone ate the snake. When T- Bone was sitting up in his bed, I could see a small snake head laying in his stool.

Now it made some sense to me. The past couple of days, when I go to run and throw the football to T- Bone, he would run then stop running. It's like his legs would lock up. And he would stop running. He wouldn't fall over. He just would stop running. But I ain't know what was wrong. And strut on his hind legs. He would do that, then he'll walk a little bit like his legs was lockin up, then he'd go back to normal. I thought he was just sick. Like he was working a cold out his system.

After he died, my mother said she'd contacted his veterinarian. The veterinarian said it was nothing they could do. T- Bone had been poisoned. All we could do is enjoy him as much as we can, before he die.

T- Bone DIED. When we buried him, we buried him with his football, and my old dark blue Sedgefield Mustangs sports jacket. T- Bone loved my old 5th grade jacket more than I did. He loved chewing on it. When I throw it on his head, and he'll snap his head back and forth, until he jus work it down to his teeth. He didn't do that to anything like he did to that Sedgefield jacket. That's how we knew he liked that jacket.

And when I'd put him in the shed, in the cold of February, when he was a puppy, the only way he would sleep, after I rock him to sleep, is I lay him down with his blue Sedgefield jacket. But this time, when I threw it over the crown of his furry black domain, he didn't snap. He didn't bite back.

I had known T- Bone all the way from when I was 16. I had lost my friend, and at the exact same time, I had lost my child.

Miya didn't have any pets, so she couldn't understand. But Ericka could understand. The same woman who helped me get through the loss of my Grandfather, was helping me get through the loss of T- Bone.

This time Ericka hadda new man, named Tony. It ain't matter. She would put him out, so her Boo- Bear could come, cum, and claw that pussy down to 'a honeycomb. Miya only wanted to fuck like 2 to 3 times in two weeks. I won't used to no shit like that. I needed Ericka for sex, but I wanted Miya for love.

Ericka went a while. But she is too territorial. She couldn't keep her promise. She went back to tryin to break me and Miya apart again. That's when I went back to Miya.

The last time me and Ericka had sex, it happened like a month after that. Usually, I plan for it. But this one, I didn't plan for. I had got fired from Commercial Roofing. I didn't get enough leads. So I went back to Reliance, and I got a new temp job, out in Poquoson.

On break, I'm supposed to be changing my oil. I put too much oil in the engine, and now the engine is sputtering when I get off work. I drive straight to Casey Chevrolet. My car is a little out of warranty, but they still hook me up anyway. The car gotta go in the shop so they can service it.

They still give me a Loaner Car. I trade in a black Metro wit a manual transmission. They give me a red Metro wit an automatic transmission. I usually have these loaner cars like for (5) days. I think this was on the first day or second day. I'on know what made me go get Ericka, but I show up at her job, at Wendy's. I knew she got off at 4 o' clock.

I show up by 3: 59.

Her brown ass sittin out in the day room. She ain't even red no more. That sun done got 'a hold to her. And she musta been standin out, waitin for the bus, cause them lil heat bumps done got to her. And she got them lil red cherry heat bumps in two places.

When I see her, I see her sittin at the table wit one of her co- workers. So he tryin to holla at her. But her seein me bust that play all to pieces. They watchin me walk up. So I tell her,

"Yo, I'm here to pick you up."

She say, "Alright, let me go get my things." And she go in the back to get her purse, log out, and whatever else she gotta do. While she gone, dude walk over to me and say,

"Yo. You the man. We was jus here talkin bout you," and I nodded as he dapped me up.

Ericka came out right after that and said, "Ok. I'm ready."

We went out to the car. She thought I traded in my black Metro for this red one. I asked her if we needed to go get Tori, she said,

"Nuh- uh. Tony got him." Referring to her new man.

And I drove her to the spot. The same spot I took Miya. But across the street. I ain't park right in the same spot. I couldn't do it anyway. Somebody had moved into that 3 story home. I couldn't park on somebody's property. So I had to park her across the street.

We kissed. And I didn't have to say no more after that.

Ericka climbed all that PHAAAAT JUICCCCY ASSSS up in the back seat. That bitch ASSSS was so damn PHAAAAT up in that Wendy's uniform. I pulled all that shit off. Ericka's ASSSS was bent ova and spread out cross that back seat. Her pussy was so PHAAAAT, I can see it drop down and hang open from the back. That pussy look wet and crispy, like it still had French fry sweat drippin on it.

I grabbed that bitch by the back of her head, and punished that bitch in the back of that lil ass Metro. That lil car was swingin by the axles. So was she. By the time we finished, it was so much steam on the windows, I had to use the defrost and the windshield wipers, before I could put the car back in drive.

I drove Ericka home. I couldn't pull right up. I had to drop her off from the house. But somehow her man still saw it, and by the time I get home, she was calling me, sayin Tony put his hands on her.

"I'll be right there." I went back round there. I ain't even have time to get in the shower. I was back round there. This time I parked my car, so he can know I was up in there.

He was gone.

Just Ericka and Tori was there. We went somewhere, came back. He still won't there. I went in the room wit Ericka, that bitch pulled 'a pussy out on me PHAAAATA than 'a fist.

What you think I'm gon do to this?

I tore her BIIIIG ass up in that bedroom. I tore alllll that BIIIIG shit up! Pull'a ASSSS and 'a pussy out on me that PHAAAAT. I'm gon BUST!! alllll that shit up!! And Ericka don't run from no dick!

But, yeah, we collapsed each other. I fell asleep beside my Snu. This go on for the next few days. All the way until I turn the loaner back in, and get my regular car back.

Then early one morning, I was in her bed. I was

sleep. But I keep hearing a noise. I can hear this car keep,

"Rruuuuuuu! Uuuuur! Zzzz! Rruuuuuuu! Uuuuur! Zzzz! Rruuuuuuu! Uuuuur!"

I knew who it was. I jus wish it wasn't. Not right now. I'm too tired.

When I go to my car; she left me a note. I'm in some like Thin Love Between Love and Hate type shit.

I jumped in my car, and went after Miya.

I had to. When I caught up to her, back at her house. Miya was crying. She was upset. She threw my ring at me. It landed in the grass. The sun hit the diamond, and that shit BLINGED!! right up. Couldn't miss it. I picked it up.

It won't even 5 minutes I returned home, Miya was calling me to bring back her ring. I took it back. I did have to lie a little bit back then about me and Ericka, to get Miya back. I knew that Miya was the one I ultimately wanted to be with Forever.

Ericka had kept tryin to force it. To make me choose between her and Miya. And Miya was doing the same thing. I wanted to bring these two together, but Ericka woulda been tryin to fight the girl, and assert her dominance. I couldn't let Miya get hurt, cause I woulda been responsible for that to her family. So that's why I had to keep these two women apart and separate from each other.

And it did hurt. But when it come to this... I had to kiss Ericka's pussy Good bye.

Chapter 26.

In October tragedy rocked my family when my cousin Monty died in California. He died from a Grandma Seizure at the age of 18. I knew that Hugh has seizures. Well, I heard. He never had one around me. He been on medication since we were children. But Monty was a surprise. He was never known for having seizures or being on medication.

Before he went to California, Monty was always a cool quiet kid. I met him through my Uncle Pernell. My Uncle Pernell was dating his mother, Sandra. They got together and even before they started having April and Michael, I had already seen Monty as family. He is my cousin.

After Pernell lost his job in the Shipyard, he was down on his luck in unemployment being in Virginia. He wanted a change. And so he packed up and headed with his girlfriend and three children, and they left to go be with Charles and Johnnie in Carlsbad, California. Then eventually around San Diego and Oceanside, in Southern California.

So by Charles being stationed in the Marines, that's what put pieces of my former Virginia family on the West Coast, in California.

And now, you can't tell them they ain't West Coastin.

When Monty died, they came back home. My cousin was a star basketball player in high school, and when he left, he was the same height as me, now he had shot to well OVER SIX FEET TALL.

They sent Monty's body back to Virginia, by train. My cousin was so tall, they didn't have a casket to fit him. They had to bend him at the knees, and twist him at the waist, the fit him in a casket. When he made it to Newport News, Franklin Funeral Home, over on Madison Avenue, took possession of his body.

He had a wake scheduled for Franklin Funeral Home, and my family was still up the street, at my Grandma's house getting ready.

So I drove over to the funeral home by myself. When I get there, Monty's casket is opened, and they have him laying out in the chapel.

This is The First Time I've seen my cousin in maybe like 4 Years. I can still hear his little soft voice following me around, and saying,

"Haime...

Hello Haime...

Hey Haime..."

That was his kind and friendly way of saying Jamie, in Spanish. But now, he is lifeless. He is without the breath of God in him. I can see him as close as I can. Standing back a little bit, in front of the first pew.

They went a little too heavy on his make-up. His skin is dark, at his nose. I could go all the way up. But I'm not. That FEAR from the Spirit of God is still in me. This is the first time I been at a wake or funeral since our Grandfather DIED, when I was 17.

It was other people that DIED. I didn't go to none of those wakes or funerals. It's not no disrespect. I just couldn't do it. You had to REALLY be close for me to show up to your wake or your funeral. It's just the way it is.

I'm watching Monty. But I can't go but so far. I can't bring myself to touch him. It was sad to see so much potential leave away from us at such an early age. I leave. I got to go.

I still come back for his wake. I go to his funeral. I even go to Pleasant Shade to see where he's buried. But I never touch his body. As close as I go is to view his body with the rest of my family. And my feet don't stop moving when I do that.

While my family was home from California, I got to introduce them to Miya. But the best part for me, was seeing my Uncle Johnnie. When he left for Cali, I was still a young kid, now, I wassa 21-year-old man. I hadda car. I put Unc up in my car. I hadda system. I let Unc hear my system.

I know he like George Clinton. Parliament/Funkadelic. And that's what I got. That's what I put on. Me, him, and one of his homies. We went around.: smokin, drinkin, bangin the system. The Metro jumpin like 'a treehouse.

But Unc is his own man. He grown too. And in to what he in to. He wanna do more than drink and smoke Blacks and bud. Unc was on drugs rougha than reefa. So I had to drop him off. Plus he want 'a shot of pussy. This his chance to catch up wit some ol school hoes.

I can't deny him that.

I drop him off where he wanna go. We'on catch up to Johnnie to maybe like 3 days later. The family didn't even really get a chance to see him. His sisters down on me about where I dropped him off at. I dropped him off a lil bit into Hampton. He ain't there. I had to end up catching up to him in Newport News. 2 blocks from his momma house.

When I got Johnnie back, he was BENT!! But I see he had a good time. So I ain't fuck wit him. He was alive and he was safe, that's all that mattered to me.

They came by Greyhound. They say it take 3 days to go from California to Virginia, and Virginia back to California. So we packed up my family from California, and rolled them off to the bus station. It was sad it took losing Monty to bring us all together.

They say Joy Comes In The Morning.

Miya had set our wedding date for December 28th. Three days after Christmas. So we're planning for that. She goes to Register at Target and JC Penny's.

Miya's father.: His name is Troy. He is from Mullins. In South Carolina. One of the very first times he talked to me he said,

"I paid $75,000 CASH..."

He was referring to Miya's Hampton University education. If 'a Black man tell you he paid $75,000 CASH for anything, and it's all legal... you better pay attention.

So he had my undivided attention.

By the time I meet him, Troy is retired from the Newport News Shipyard. But he owns his own Heating and Cooling business from out the garage of his home. Almost everything this man does he do it In CASH.

That's his favorite words.

He bought Miya a car In CASH. He sent Miya to college, In CASH. He bought his own Oldsmobile In CASH. He probably bought Dr Graham's 929 In CASH. He paid off his house. And he even got his own BOAT. He paid for that too. That's right. In CASH!

This the first Black man I ever met with his own damn BOAT. He got this big ass shit backed up in the driveway, like it's a Cadillac.

By the way, Yep. He got one of those too. And a Ford pick up truck.

I have Black middle class in my family too. I already told you about Lucky and Audrey. They had their house built from the ground out in Chesterfield. And excuse me, Chesterfield is on the east side of Richmond, not the West Side. I wanna make that correction.

And one 'of my mother's other seven sisters, Paulette. Paulette is a Registered Nurse. And her husband is Hugh Sr. The family calls him Big Hugh. He is a supervisor for Phillip Morris. The Largest Tobacco Manufacturer ON THE EAST COAST.

Well Hey! That's what they say. Everybody gotta say somethin. But who cares. They was payin my Uncle Hugh 'a fuckin fortune. Somethin like that. He was the first one in our family to build his house from the ground up. Out here, you hardly ever see the white neighbors, and HEY! they hardly ever see us either. Cause on the inside, it's a split level 2 story, super luxurious 3 bedroom home in Chesterfield County.

Well, it is split level, so it's 3 bedrooms and the living room, 2 bathrooms, a kitchen and a dining room, upstairs. Downstairs, is two more guest bedrooms, a bathroom, a den, a washer/dryer, and a back door. So that means yo ass ain't gotta step down off they HIGH ASS deck.

The dining room upstairs has a slide door, and when you walk out on the deck, the deck is ALL WOOD. They got a grill and a picnic table already set up out there. And when you walk down about 25 damn FEET, it's a swing set waiting for Hugh and his sister Kiana, to play on in the backyard.

The house has AC. But it also has ceiling fans and skylights up in the ceilings. I used to always think a house supposed to come wit roaches, until I came into this house. Man, this house was so nice, it ain't even have a roach in it. I ain't never even see NOT ONE roach up in this house. That shit fucked me up!

Air and heat blow through all the rooms. Man, that shit is NICE. A whole lotta class. Wall to wall carpet. When you take off yo shoes, the carpet'll rub you in- between your toes.

I seen two good examples in my family, and wit Miya's family, I was seein this whole Black middle class thing had levels to being in it. At Miya's house, I never saw so much FOOD before in my life. They had FOOD. It was FOOD every damn where. They had FOOD in the cabinets. They had so much FOOD, the FOOD in the cabinet had kicked out FOOD. And it was FOOD that was homeless, and out sittin on the flo, beside the cabinet do'. They had FOOD in the refrigerator, that was in the kitchen. And FOOD still needed to go somewhere, so that's when you go in the garage, and they had TWO MORE refrigerators crammed with FOOD. AND a deep freezer plunged wit ice cream and frozen FOOD. Man, this shit was crazy!

And the tv had ALLLL the cable channels in the world. Any cable channel you wanna see. Even pay per view. I can watch all that shit at Miya house.: the fight, Luke Peep Show that came on BET Starz. All I gotta do is flic to the channel.

The middle class in my family were former military and hard working class people, but when I got wit Miya, it UPGRADED my whole family. The middle class in my family won't on this level. Her mother is A DOCTOR in Education. Her father is retired, got his own business, and buying up

516

everything in Cold CASH; her brother- in- law is the Vice President of Morehouse College. And her Godmother is a long lasting Delegate in the Virginia General Assembly.

For Thanksgiving, Miya's momma fed MY WHOLE FAMILY in Newport News and in Hampton. And I'm not talking about just cooking a dinner and inviting everybody to come through. Nawww. She was literally sending individual whole Thanksgiving Dinners out to my family. She sent one to my momma house. She sent one to her momma house. She sent one to my momma's sister, Theresa's house. I think she sent one to Shanda's house too. But I do know, she did feed my whole Bad Newz and Hampton family. They ain't even have to come out the house to go get it.

It was about a week and a half before Thanksgiving, that Mr. Graham found a cute and cozy one and a half bedroom house for me and Miya, on Atlantic Avenue. It's about 2 blocks away from Buckroe Beach.

Me and Miya moved into our first house together.

I am excited, because I never officially lived with any one who wasn't my parents or room mates in Job Corps. I never was a fan of bachelor pads. I thought about it for a minute, but I didn't want to live with another man. Being with Miya was good. We finally had our own place. We ain't have to go to Wayne's house, or stay the night out in the car no more, to be together.

We finally had our own spot.

It's crazy.: cause Atlantic Avenue is a high drug infested area. But we never had no break- ins, or had to duck down from gun shots being fired. Glory be to God for that.

We got houses beside us and across the street, but right across the street is also a small trailer park. And when you roll straight to the back, it's a gated community of waterfront Condo property. And all the way back left of the stop sign, is the spot where me and Miya got caught in that truck. And right cross the pond from there, is the first time me and Miya had sex.

It's crazy how our life jus wrapped right back around, and it involved Buckroe Beach. Now, we was right back. Out here and living in it! But Miya still didn't give in to sex every night like I thought she would.

"We got the rest of our lives together." I guess she had her reason.

I ain't trip. I still felt like after this wedding, she would change.

Miya was selecting who she would have as her bridesmaids. She had her girlfriend Kat, who was also the mother of Miya's (2) Godsons. Of course she picked Lauren and Patsy, and she had her girlfriend Shawnna. And she had TWO Maids of Honor.: her best friend, Patsy and her niece, Tara.

When I was pickin the 5 guys to be on my groom side, this is one of the hardest decisions I made in my life. Even if you shuffle FIVE of the most important guys in your life that's around your same age, it's still one of the most hardest decisions you'll make in your life.

The first FIVE guys I think about is.: Lynn came first.

But I couldn't put him in it. Why? Because I still didn't forgive him for his role he played in Kane fuckin Ericka. Even through everything; it all won't his fault; but I did still hold it against him.

So, not only was he not my Best Man, or even my Groomsman; but he wasn't even invited to my wedding- - PERIOD.

Next, is Kane. I didn't put him in it, because he was the one who fucked Ericka.

I had loved Ericka but, I didn't have no brothers. All I had is homies. And certain homies I gravitate towards, I see them physically like brothers. So if I gotta girl that's fuckin my homies; I see that like a bitch that'll fuck my brother, if I had a brother. And to me... that's 'a dirty bitch.

At the same time, if you gotta homie that'll fuck yo girl; and fuck your girl behind yo back, then how much do he really value you as a friend? or see you as a brother?

I saw it like, I was seeing more for these niggas than what they saw for they self. These niggas that we went; we grew from high school kids, to grown men. It's special to me to bring and to invite niggas I came up wit to my wedding. I was the first one outta all my homies to get married. And wit Miya, in some regards, setting a high standard. I was subconscious of that, even back then. I wasn't just going to marry any ol woman. Because that's not what I would want for them.

For real, I woulda married Ericka. But if anything, they exposed Ericka to me. I appreciate it from that regard. But it shouldn't have to take homies to do that. When I had Miya, I felt like I hadda solid girl. I'm not that insecure.

I like to be the one that got the girl that light up a room, that can make 'a nigga crash up a few cars tryin to get to her. BUT CAN'T. That's the bitch that make my dick hard.

My mindstate was.: I wanna woman that's 'a Wife. Not 'a wife that's 'a hoe. I didn't want a Wife that any man can have. That's what they make hoes fo.

I thought about Dwight. I did think about Dwight, because of him, me and Miya was together anyway. The shit wit him, Tee, and Ericka had something to do wit it, for the same reasons as above. But the other reason is because he didn't have a car at the time. It's my wedding day. I didn't have time to be pickin niggas up, drivin niggas around, and bringing them back home. This my day to be wit my bride.

I didn't plan on driving myself.

I had to put a little more thought into who my Best Man was going to be. Sometimes you gotta go backwards to go forwards, so I just had to start off with selecting my Groomsmen first. Miya's whole line up had class. All of her bridesmaids were beautiful, sexy, intellectual and extraordinary powerful Black women. So to some degree, I had to match that. If anything, I had to put class on my side of the line up as well. That's why my very first two picks was Wayne and Paul.

And I fleshed my line out from there.

I got (3) more spots, I was gon go with Ed. Ed got class, like a Wayne and Paul. Ed lives in Bad Newz but is from Chicago. But if I put Ed, then I gotta put his roommate Manny in. I can't leave Manny out. Manny is 'a fly Hispanic pretty boy. That woulda made an interesting line, but Wayne, Paul, Ed, and Manny; I had met all them from fuckin wit Miya. It's all too much of the same circle. The same people seein each other every time we hang out together at Wayne's house, or when we go out to clubs and restaurants. I really wasn't a big social person. I didn't have the homie from the sandbox, or the homie that we both go back to runnin around wit the lil tight dick n ball shorts, wit the 3 stripes. Over the years, I didn't maintain those kinds friendships.

The closest one to that woulda been my friend Anthony. And I saw him too. Me and Miya ran into him one day out Patrick Henry Mall, just a few months ago. And he came, dapped me up, and was happy to see me. I coulda instantly got his number and address right then and there, and plugged him or him and his brother Shawn in for my wedding. And my mother woulda been happy to see them and their mother. Because we didn't see them since we left Paula Maria. I coulda set the play. But I didn't do it. I had dropped everyone from my Paula Maria childhood. I didn't consciously plan it out like that; it's just how it played out.

If I gotta go wit family- - I won't ready for
that yet either. I gotta put the hood up in here. I
can't be the only one. I didn't look at Wayne and
Paul like hood niggas. They cool ass niggas, but
they ain't have that kinda cut to them. Lynn was
out. Kane was out. Dwight was out. Tracy didn't
have a car. He was out. Next... it was EZ.

EZ Mc.

I kinda hadda flash or anotha homie named
Roscelle and his brother name Buff. But neither one
of them ain't have no car. They was out. My mind
went back to EZ.

Yep, that same cool ass kid, wit his NIKES
up on Commander Wheeler's desk, I had met all the
way back when I wassa ninth grader in ROTC. It's
crazy.: but through Lynn, me and EZ ended up
growing into being close friends. Ain't that crazy.
And now, he was about to be In MY Wedding. Not
just in my wedding, but he almost even made it up
to being my Best Man. Why?

Well because we was two hood ass niggas.
Both from Bad Newz. Both went to Warwick. Knew
him since Warwick. I always admired his swag, and
in a lotta regards he supplanted Lynn and Kane not
being there. Him, Lynn and Kane is from the same
hood. But Lynn and EZ is REAL Official 13th Street
niggas. Kane is from 14th.

It did make sense. Didn't it?

EZ woulda been my Best Man, but only one thing was standing in his way. Ahhh, HUGH! Family. Family man. I had to put the family in here. Hugh is my flesh and blood. He is my cousin, we grew all the way up, a year apart, as snotty nose babies. And Hugh was like a brother. We went crabbin. We went to Disney World. TWICE. Went to The Y. Went to see Wrestling. Went to see Union basketball and football games. Shot basketball...

And my whole family thought I would go wit Hugh as my Best Man. Especially my family from Richmond. After all we did come up from the sandbox, but from two different cities...

Me and Hugh are cultured different.

Hugh can be in my line, but I needed a family piece that was young, fresh, HARD!! and hood. If this man was gonna be my Best Man, then like, we gotta be flesh from the same cloth. He gotta come wit that grit and grind of bein in THE STRUGGLE!! And that's jus how I saw it...

I went wit my cousin Sabrina's husband. Tony. He wasn't from Bad Newz, he was from Roanoke, but it didn't matter. He was hood and he reflected each of all the other elements I needed and- - he was family. He was married into it. And he was living in Bad Newz now. And all of this was good enough for me to choose him. Not just to choose him, but to set him in place, as being my Best Man.

So it was Wayne, it was Paul, EZ, Hugh, and it was TONY. That's how I got my line. I didn't pick TWO Best Men, because I didn't want to copycat what

Miya was doing.

So me and my Groomsmen get to the
Tuxedo place, up in the Coliseum Mall. This is only
the second tux I had in my whole life. The first one,
was when I was the ringbearer, all the way back in
Audrey's wedding.

The tuxedos from Menchville, Senior Year
school pictures, wasn't even whole tuxedos. It
wassa tuxedo jacket, then they give you a flap shirt,
with a made- in bow tie at the top. But Today.:
HEY! I'm a grown man. This is real deal. My first
real tuxedo I'll pick as a man. I'm up in the store,
and they got a room stuffed with ties and
cummerbunds in GREEN, DARK GREEN, LIGHT
GREEN, in TURQUOISE, in BLUE, DARK BLUE,
NAVY BLUE, SKY BLUE, in YELLOW, GOLD,
RED, PINK, BLACK, PURPLE, WHITE, in
LAVENDER, TWO- TONE, STRIPES, and
POLKADOTS...

Hhhh, and RED- - did I say RED?

Why of course I did. And that's the hue I
went wit. Why? Cause it was in homage of my most
favorite Uncle. It's what he wore in that picture.
Johnnie couldn't be here, cause he was just here 2
months ago. 'A funeral cost 'a fortune. So he didn't
have enough to get back to see me get married. But
it's all good. He was represented.

On my wedding day, me and ALL (5) of my
line up was flex'd and dipp'd in black tuxes. They
had black ties and black cummerbunds, and I was
the groom, so I was red tied and bunnin it up, like
my most favorite Uncle.

Me and Miya's wedding was on December 28th. Just (3) days after Christmas. Let me just say this.: Miya had her Bridal Shower at her precious Godmother's house. So I personally got introduced to Virginia Delegate, Mary T Christensen. Alright, just to put that in there, because it's overlapping parts. Alright, now back to the Wedding.:

Except for my Groomsmen, I didn't have anything to do with who got invited. I left that into the hands of the women.: Miya, Dr Graham, and my Mother. And Miya and Dr Graham know more people, it's like I was marrying a Princess from the City of Hampton. That's why they had like two-thirds of the chapel filled up. My family and people my momma invited ain't even fill up a tenth of the third section of the chapel, and so, they just slid on over to the middle, to look like they was part of the same audience.

I and Miya were joined together at the Chapel on Hampton University by Rev Duck before as the saying goes, both before God and man. I walked down the isle with Dr Graham. Just like we rehearsed it. But the part that came as an unexpected fruition was that my family was joining to a family that was not famous, that was not greatly influential, but was still one of the greatest African- American families not only in African-American History, but in American History- - PERIOD.

And when My RED Rabbit walked down that isle...

I didn't see her last night. I don't think I seen her the past coupla days before the Wedding. I was staying at my momma's house, wit Hugh. Back in my old room.

Mr. Graham had moved us into our own house a month earlier, with the promise that me and his daughter would be getting married NOW. And here she was. When Miya walked inside that chapel, it's like God had set the sunshine in between her teeth. Miya is as pretty as a DIAMOND on 'a petal. Her presence literally LIGHTENED the whole room. Everything all pushed up, squeezin, and rubbin all together. Her white dress is strapless. I was lookin- - thinkin man, them BIG ass titties bout to flop right up out this dress.

I looked across the room to how many men's mouths was gaping open. It looked like Rev Duck's mouth was even hanging open. Miya is about to be DA CHERRY ON TOP of my life!! We was so HIGH. I needed it from the pressure of being in front of a large crowd. We had to concentrate to light those candles. Then we stood back in front of each other and finished exchanging our wedding vows.

Then Rev Duck said those magical words to me, "You may kiss your Bride."

And I went in, and I held Miya as close as I can. It felt good to hold, to rub, and to squeeze on that butt. I kissed on her lips and swallowed on her tongue. Umm, I could tell from her kiss, Miya was soft and wet. Then, that's when Rev Duck had to break us apart,

"Alright. Alright. I said, "Kiss your Bride." I ain't say, Start your Honeymoon."

The audience laughed. But they won't mad.

I looked at my momma. I see her and Ms. Lois sittin there like they lookin at a soap opera. Well Mrs. Lois. She was married herself by this time.

Following the Wedding, we had to take like 'a thousand PICTURES! PICTURES! PICTURES! PICTURES! PICTURES! It was so many PICTURES. PICTURES in COMBINATIONS. PICTURES wit the Bride's Family. PICTURES wit the Groom's Family. PICTURES wit the Groom's men. PICTURES wit the Bride's maids. PICTURES wit the Groom's men and wit the Bride's maids. PICTURES wit the Groom's parents. PICTURES wit the Bride's parents. PICTURES wit the Best Man. PICTURES wit the Best Man and the Bride's maids. PICTURES wit the Best Man and The Maids of Honor. PICTURES with me and Miya. Of course we had to go back and reenact scenes from our Wedding.

PICTURES of me walking with Dr Graham. PICTURES of Miya walking with Mr. Graham. PICTURES of me and Miya lighting the candles. PICTURES of me and Miya exchanging rings. PICTURES of me and Miya praying at the altar.

We're taking pictures for so long, that our limousine driver gives up; and ups and leaves. I was finally happy to be able to be out the chapel.

Then when I get out the chapel, I take pictures outside the chapel. Pictures with Miya. But I got one wit Tony, my Best Man. To this day I'll never forget it. Both us fresh in tuxes. And I got the

14kt gold and silver Seiko FLEXIN!! on my left wrist. That picture is HARD!! as 'a bitch!! To this day, it holds up. I'll never forget it.

Our wedding reception was held on Hampton University's campus as well. And I had one 'of the illest DJs in the 757, DJ DESTROY!! aka Kevin Rogers. That's the father of Kat's (2) sons. Well Hey! I woulda had one 'of the illest DJs in the 757, but he ain't get to perform and flip this whole Hall into a party, because Sis Miles had a lot of influence over our wedding reception. Sis Miles don't play no loud music at her parties. And if it is too loud, you gon be clappin yo hands. Cause it's gon be 'a Holy Ghost party up in here. That's the only parties that get allowed round Sis Miles. She'on play it. She'on play it.

And you come to her house, she ain't got but ONE bathroom. Yeah. So a lotta people don't stay long at Sis Miles' parties. But HEY! it's gon be what you end up wit.

The Hall was supposed to have Champagne. Somma that Bubbly. But messin round wit Sis Miles, I couldn't even get Champagne to show up for my guest. So they ended up with Sparkling Cider. And after we threw the garter belt and bouquet, and throw everything else it was to get throw. I was tired. Miya was tired. I was praying that that damn picture man wouldn't show back up again. He didn't. Not even when we cut the cake. When we get outside, we ain't have any limousine. Our limousine was gone. I didn't drive. Miya didn't drive. Wayne's car is full. I got to find a way to get My Bride back to the crib. Then there was

Nate.

Nate. Of course, it was. My brother from church.

    And that's who drove me and Miya home and dropped us off at the crib. I opened the door. I lifted My Bride and took her all the way cross the threshold. I took her straight to bed and laid her down on top of the bed. And I looked her into her eyes and I said to her,

    "I love you Mrs. Miya Miles."

    She just laughed so tickled. I unwrapped and unbuttoned her out that long white dress, and took her out ALL her clothes. Miya got me hypnotized. And I eat it and beat it. I'on know what Ms. Miya thought she was doin, walkin all around the church like that. All around me, wit everything all pushed up, squeezin, and rubbin all together. Huh. Look at her now.

I eat it and I beat it.

    All up against that mattress. Lick that Booty. And tilt that pussy, like it's 'a juice box, and eat all the girl cum up out that pussy, like it's soft sweet peach granola CRUNCHED wit TRIPLE STUFF'D cheese cookie dough and iced creamed. My dick had to lap it up!! where my tongue left it off. Ain't it.

    My Wedding came to $7500 Cold CASH!! After our wedding, Mr. Graham owns time share property. So he let us use one of his weeks, so we can go down and take our honeymoon, in a Condo on Myrtle Beach.

On the way down there, I was sitting up listening to Miya give me driving directions. The first stop we make is to JRs Cigarette and Cigar Factory, down North Carolina. They say that they THE LARGEST CIGARETTE AND CIGAR WHOLESALER ON THE EAST COAST. But HEY! Who knows?

All I know is they got crates of Blacks for under $10. I'on get greedy. I get like (2) crates. They got Philly cigars I never seen before. Miya pick up a few boxes of that. I didn't see the chocolate Titans. They had Garcias. Got 'a few of those. Miya gotta cute lil weed pipe.

I forgot if she got cigarettes. I'on think they had her brand. When I first start chillin wit her, she smoked Newport's. But you know how that go.: when niggas see you smokin Newport's, errybody try to bum one off you. So she stopped smokin Newport's and started smokin Virginia Slims.

Matter of fact, nope, they didn't have Virginia Slims, cause after we left JRs, I had to stop for gas, and she went in there and got her Virginia Slims.

We kept beatin down 95 South. Now I'm grown, wit my Bride, and going back and forth between Iron Man, Reasonable Doubt, and The Purple Tape.

Ready to Die and All Eyez On Me.

We stop at South of the Border. In South Carolina. This the first time I been here, since I was maybe like 12. I was grown up. And it was built up. They had casinos out here now. Me and Miya spent more time in The Glass Slipper, than we did touring through the shops.

And Aye! I was nabbin 'a fuckin fortune!

Well, I tried to. But I couldn't do it. Miya had to get me to go. One thing I notice bout being out here in South Carolina.: the culture is different down here. It's more chill. Laid back.

You might see a Burger King joined to a KFC, and 'a gas station. And when you go to buy you some gas, they gotta big ass or little ass slot machine grinnin up in there wit it. It was numbers, it was scratch tickets, it was slot machines; it was FUN!! It was gambling everywhere!!

When we left from South of the Border, we rode past Florence, and went to see Miya's Grandma in Mullins. The Metro scooted just right up next to her clothes line. She was happy to see us.

Miya stood outside tryin to explain it to me, that her father and her Uncle Johnnie, had they momma's house turned around. So it'll do somethin like face the road. So I was standin out here lookin at that. Miya has an uncle named Johnnie too, something else we got in common.

We was havin 'a grand good time at Miya's Grandma's house. Her Grandma had started makin a place for us to spend the night. I had thought we was stayin the night.

"No. We just came to visit," Miya said to her.

"Oh. Ok." Now we all understand.

We said, "Good bye," to Grandmomma, and me and Miya was boppin back down the road B. Til she said,

"J, it's gettin late."

Now, she wanna say somethin. I thought I hadda wife that wassa Road Dawg. 'A, Uuuu!! Uhh! Uuuu!! Uhh! Uuuu!! Uhh! Uuuuuuuuu!!!! 'A Road Dawwwggg.

But naw. She just stayed more asleep than what she was awake. She left me to handle the road by myself. But she always seem to wake up on time, when it was time to tell me where the hell I should go.

She went into telling me about her father's brother Frank, just as we was crossing over an overpass. He had lost his life in a trucking accident. It was very sad to hear about that. And I never got to meet him.

It won't too long after that, we saw some civilization. We saw Wal- Mart. You jus don't know how good you got it, til you see that blue sign. But we kept on ridin past it. And I was seein, this lil 2 door hatch back Metro is turnin out to be a very decent luxury cross country road car.

We was on the strip.

And it's stores. But it's Burger Kings. Mc Donald's. Wendy's. KFC. The strip is FLOODED!! wit more

FOOD than Dr Graham's kitchen cabinet. It's Casinos. All you need is 'a slot machine, and HEY! CASINO lights GO UP EVERYWHERE!!!!

We rolled past The Hard Rock Cafe. It was made like'a pyramid. That shit looked HARD!! Especially at night when it's all litttted up! I wanted to go up in there. I kept lookin at it, but Miya wanted me to keep on goin straight. It won't too many stoplights after that when I heard her say to me,

"Turn RIGHT here."

As I made the right turn, we passed through a shy residential neighborhood. We get ALL the way straight to the back. It's a big ass litttt up! Sands Dunes Hotel on the left. That shit look like a Christmas Tree, how much light was lightin that shit up. And it was a Resort Escape on the right. And that's right where our Condo was. We go right. We park right up in the parking lot. We check right in. Miya get the right key. We shoot right up three flights of grey wood steps. To get to the right room.

When we first open the door, it's an inline kitchen. When we go back to the left, it's the master bedroom. When we go back to the right, it's the living room, dining room, and a 2nd bedroom. The dining room is a round table, circled up under a matching round ceiling light. The 2nd bedroom don't got no door. It gotta an accordion slide petition. You can lock the petition from the inside for privacy.

And it has a balcony.

When you slide the glass door and go stand out on the balcony, it's a pool up under the balcony. And just right behind the pool, is beautiful white sand beaches. Well HEY! It look like white sand beaches from standing up here.

But who cares? I WAS HAVIN THE TIME OF MY LIFE!!

And it's crazy. It's crazy how our lives came to this. Cause Miya ran from me for 3 years. Now we was MARRIED, and she was running again.

Miya wasn't wanting to have sex. And I felt like, I wasn't gon let this girl destroy this honeymoon. Because everything else around us was going good. The next day we went to the mall and caught a movie. For dinner, I wanted to go to that Hard Rock Cafe. But Miya wanted to go to The Original Benjamin's. It's unique to us, because we never seen one 'of these before in Virginia.

Inside of The Original Benjamin's, the bar is wall- to- wall seafood. ALL fresh FISH, CRABS, CRAB LEGS, KING CRAB LEGS, SHRIMP, LOBSTER, CLAMS, OYSTERS... they probably even hadda crayfish and 'a octopus. They had damn near anything 'a hook and 'a harpoon can pull up outta an ocean.

It cost us $21 a person, for ALL YOU CAN EAT SEAFOOD. And that's what we paid, for the time and experience of a Honeymoon lifetime! Then they had sex shops on the strip. We stopped up in there, but I won't really into it. I didn't want to see porn. I wanted to see my Wife.

534

I think she kinda felt that. Cause we ain't leave out with nothing. Of course, we would went to Black people best friend. WAL- MART. And then everything changed...

My sister-in-law, Sheila and my niece Chrissy stopped by the Condo, on their way back to Atlanta, following Christmas, our Wedding, and The New Years. They stayed in the 2nd bedroom. And that's when me and Miya stopped by the liquor store to celebrate The Holidays and being married. Some E and J, some Bacardi, 'a lil Christian Brothers. We stop, pick up some groceries, head back to the Condo.

And that was when Miya got loose.

We make love that night. Sheila and Chrissy leave in the morning. And I thought Miya was gon stop. I think it was breakfast first. Then it was a Black and Mild. Then it was Miya was on the couch watching me clean and vacuum the carpet. Then we smoke.

Then, Miya comes and straddles over me on the couch. I put the blunt out. I cuff my hands up under her thighs to bring her in closer. She lean back. Unbuttoned her blouse. It hit the floor. I had to do something, huh. I unfastened her bra. That shit hit the floor.

I filled my mouth with suckin on those nipples and areoles. She stepped out her shoes, socks, jeans, and panties. She pushed me back down on the couch. Miya can suck wit no hands.

Where she get all that from? I think somethin more to it than suckin on a soda bottle. But HEY! Don't poke that bear. Don't poke tha muthafuckin bear.

Cause we went from the couch to the floor, to the table, to sliding open the glass to that sliding door, to the balcony...

To Miya was on the balcony. RED Ass and BUTT ASS! First she was down on her hands and knees. Then when she got up, she threw her right leg over across the rail.

"Miya, what if somebody comes out...

What if the neighbors come out?...

Somebody can see us..."

She just kept laughing at me. At first. Then, she was takin it. Good. Tooo good. And deep. Toooo deep. The whole balcony was shakin up under us, like it's bout to break way! Miya was holding for the banister, wit one left hand and one right leg. She kept tryin to wrap around it, wit her left arm, but she kept skipping her balance. I just saw it like Miya was bout to go flyin out through this air.

Maybe she might land in the pool.

I'on know. But what if she miss the pool? or The pool is five feet too shallow? She was scarin me. I'on got time to be goin to jail. In South Carolina.

"Naw. Fuck that. Fuck that. Get down. Get down. Get yo ass down ," I hysterically said to her.

We just had to finish this wit her face down. On her knees.

Miya stayed in the room. I went for a walk. I wanted to see the grounds a little bit more. The Sand Dunes is right next to the Condo, I walk through the lobby of The Sand Dunes. It's a wide Hotel. A whole lotta floors and room. It's about 4 or 5 stories, including the lobby, but it's spread out. The whole Hotel is in more than one building. It's at least 3 buildings.
I walk out the back door of the lobby, to the white sand beaches. It's crazy, this is January, and it felt like summertime. The sand starts where the concrete patio ends. Just 6 feet out the door. I had bread on me. I ain't come out here for swimming.

I ain't swimming out in that damn water. I'm the only one out here too. Shit, I'm in South Carolina. I'on know where this water go. I look, and all I see is RoLLiNg tides of WATER. I'on see 'a bridge. It's a small island of land. But I don't see people. I see piles of crumpled up sand, trees, and grass. And that's a long swim away. And to the left, you need a big boat to swim out there. It's nothing but WATER. Nothin but Roaring RoLLinG dinosaur tunnels of WATER. It look like it was waiting to drown me. Ain't no lifeguards and rescue team out here. What is out here?

A bird.

Not just a bird. A seagull. A hungry seagull. I take out my bread and start feeding him. Then I look up. It's another seagull soaring up over the water and the shore. She twists her body around,

"HRRRRRR! HRRRRRR! HRRRRRR! HRRRRRR!... HRRRRRR!" I look up at her, and she's lookin straight down, making face to face, eye to eye contact with me, and she keep screeching at me.

Then I'm feeding (3) seagulls. Then (3) seagulls turn to 30 seagulls. Then 30 seagulls turn to (300) seagulls. I felt like I was in a scene from THE SEAGULLS. All these birds was piling up and flying up to me, and let me feed them like a dog.

I would break the bread into crumbs, and I'd toss the crumb of bread, and they would catch it in they mouth and fly up and off. Then more seagulls would come, or the seagulls that just ate, would turn and come back at me. They kept coming in closer, closer, closer,

closer and closer.

Next thing I knew, I was staring at seagulls face to face. One had swooped right down, right in front of me. I had to step back; the gault of his wings almost hit me in my face, and

"HRRHHHHHH!!" he screeched out at me.

When he opened his mouth, I could see his beak open up, like in slow motion. And I could see straight down his throat. I could see the dirt on his tongue. His throat hanging wide and opened. Everything. His stomach was pink and it looked empty as a ghoulish gorge. And that's it. Aye! I threw all the bread I had at that bird! And I got the hell up outta there. One thing about it.: feedin a wild seagull, ain't nothin like feedin my momma's

parakeets. I walked back through the lobby, and
went back in the room to go be back wit Miya.

It was almost sad to leave Myrtle Beach behind. I
think both of us felt like, we would be back.

On the way back, we stopped back by Miya's
Grandma's house. But, we ain't stay overnight.
Then, we went back to The Glass Slipper. So I can
trick some money up. My gambling luck is just bad.
Miya won like $10 or $20. Ain't that nice? That
prolly was $10; $20 of my money. But it turned into
an amazing Honeymoon. Then, we was back in Va.

It felt good to come back and already have a place
to stay. Miya and I were in love with each other.

I would go into my yard and think about
going to get T- Bone. Then I would catch myself.
When I went out to play with him those days before
he died, he would run then he would slow down and
rotate his rear legs like he was locking up. Like he
might've had pain from sleeping wrong. Then I
thought he might be sick. I would look at him and
ask him what was wrong, as if he could actually
respond. But I thought it was something he'd get
over, because he never really been sick, and because
he'd go right back to doing something regular, so it
slipped past me that it was something that serious
and severe.

I had lost one tremendous friend, but then I found
a new friend in the form of a Wife.

I have a landlord, named Luz, who is Latina. She's
probably Puerto Rican. She can be very strict. But
that comes with the territory of Bein 'A Boss.

Typically, she is friendly and plays really fair.

In front of my house, is a tree. Where T-Bone would go sometimes, if only he was here. Behind my house, is a white wooden shed, that I don't get to use. All Luz's stuff is in there. Fastened. Bolted. And Master Locked away, to keep me and Miya up out of her personal storage property. And to the right of my house lives Luz's Puerto Rican daughter, Natacia. Natacia lives at home with her Mexican Husband. Juan.

And to the left of me lives Luz's other daughter, Michelle. Michelle has her Puerto Rican side from her mother, but Michelle is Black; a developing Sunni Muslim, and a single mother, raising two sons.

Before me and Miya had went on our Honeymoon, I wasn't working a permanent stationary job. I was working at the temp service. That helped me make it easy to go on our Honeymoon vacation, because I didn't have no vacation time, or stored up sick days.

When I came back, I had got my job back with Reliance. I did temp service work for a while, until I ended up finding a job on my own. I worked for Reliance, and made about minimum wage, at $4.50 an hour. When I got a job at Rick Thomasson's Heating and Cooling, I made $5 bucks. $5 an hour.

It was an interesting job. Bending up sheet metal for a living. I would have to insulate pieces, then we'd roll up to the house, and set everything up in between the floor and ceiling joist of the

house. The scariest part is when you have to get up
under the house. You crawling around; working in
sand or dirt. Anything can be up under that house.
My first fear was snakes. But it might be spiders
too. I didn't have any fear of spiders. I wasn't
educated on recluse and poisonous spiders back
then, so I didn't have no fear of them. I saw all
spiders just as insects. If I wanted to kill em, jus kill
em and keep it movin.

One day me and Miya was fuckin around.
And she told me she hadda sexual attraction for
Tracy. And that's where she fucked up!

She laughed when she said it, like this shit was
supposed to be funny. But to me, it wasn't a joke.

This is the same girl who told me when we
was dating, how her and her girls don't share men.
Well she did have one. But that was something else
that attracted me to Miya, is because I saw her as a
girl of some principle. But now.: she was just like
Ericka. When did these girls even have the time to
formulate a sexual attraction for Tracy?

Ericka, I can understand- - cause we all went to
Warwick. But Miya? She mighta saw Tracy one or
two times. I thought. I guess that's all it takes, huh?

But I ain't never push up on her about
wanting to fuck her friends.: Lauren, Shawna,
Kelley, or Patsy. I never revealed it, and she would
never know it. That's jus something I would have
take to the grave. But when she said what she said
about Tracy, I never forgot it. I never forgot it.
That's the day she fucked up.

One day I went around Aqua Vista to see Lynn. Him, his mother Yvonne, and her boyfriend Bobby. But when I get there, Bobby's niece, Gwen, is there. Gwen is here with her young adorable son named Ja' Quan. Ja' Quan is just a baby.

A few more days, I go back around there looking for Lynn. Yvonne comes to the door,

"Lynn ain't here."

But she let me in. Ja' Quan is on the couch. So I say, "Where is Gwen?"

That's when I learn that Gwen has drug and addiction problems. This girl'll be gone for days at a time, down on that dope. And it's crazy. Cause she don't even look like it. Gwen gotta ass that's Stupid THICKKKK like Cherokee. This girl is Crazy PHAAAAT, even in 'a pair of sweatpants!

Ja' Quan keep smiling at me. Like he happy to see me. Maybe he remember who I am. He keep smiling. Then I go to lift him up.:

"Aaugghh! Yvonne why you ain't change this boy diaper? This baby shitty ass hell."

"I can't. I don't got nothing. His momma didn't leave nothing."

What the!? The Lucky Principle came outta me. That's when you lift a kid in a lowly disadvantaged situation.

"Alright. I got him."

542

"Wait. Where you going?"

"I got him... I got him."

Ja' Quan didn't have a bottle. A diaper. A diaper bag. Nothing. He had nothing but his one lonely dingy white onesie, and his precious baby smile. And I picked him and I carried with me to my car.

I probably won't even there five minutes.

My key was already in my hand, to get the door open for him. I put him in in the passenger seat. And I put the seatbelt on him, around his neck. I checked it to make sure it wasn't choking him. It wasn't. And when I got in, I checked it again.

I turn the Metro on. Cut the system on, and Hey! Then me and Ja' Quan been boppin down da block B.

I drive straight back home. I didn't know what Miya's reaction was going to be...

As soon as I showed her Ja' Quan- - she has a natural mother nurturing principle,

"Ohhh!" she said. And she just took him out my hands.

I told her his story, and the next thing I know.: we was at Target shopping for Ja' Quan.

Miya bought him diapers, a pacifier, a diaper bag, baby lotion, baby shampoo... she bought him

543

clothes. We didn't know what he can eat. He just a baby. He can't even talk. We don't know if he got allergies. We took chances. We bought Similac. And boxes of cereal. And we had to buy bottles.

We get him back home. He never cry one time. Not even from being hungry. And when we get back home, Miya jus kept sayin,

"I got him... I got him." She wouldn't let me do nothing else for him.

She took him in the bathroom, washed him, soaped him, and cleaned him up. The baby lotion had him all shining. The lotion in his hair, gave his whole head a sheen. And he was just grinning and sucking on his bottle. He can hold his own bottle.

He had on a NEW diaper, and NEW clothes. Miya had me throw his old diaper and dusty onesie away in the outside trash.

When I get back in, Miya sat him down on the carpet, and he finished off his bottle. Then he started doing something I didn't even know he could do...

he started CRAWLING around on the floor.

"Miya, I didn't know he could crawl," my eyes and mouth is popped open in AMAZEMENT!

"Yeah, it's probably cause he got food in him now. He got energy," she said.

We laughed. We was happy for him. Ja' Quan was a real good baby. He never fuss. I never heard him cry. He wouldn't even wake us up in the middle of the night. Nothing. And I would leave him and Miya in the mornings and go to work. When I get back, her and Ja' Quan be there waitin for me.

He go wit us, where we go. We showed him to Dr Graham and Miya's father. Miya told them his story, and they loved him and accepted him. How could anybody not love Ja' Quan? Ain't it. Miya even showed him to Michelle, when she would come over and kick it wit Miya.

Me and Miya had had Ja' Quan with us for like A WEEK, and I get in from work one day and Miya says,

Yvonne is on the phone."

"Hello?" Miya had passed me the phone.

"Hey," Yvonne had said. "Gwen want her baby."

"Say What!?"

"Gwen want her baby," she said it again.

"Ok." I hung up the phone.

I never told Miya, but I was afraid for Ja' Quan, because I didn't know what would happen next. It was literally like 7 DAYS, by the time I had taken him from when he was at Yvonne's house, then me and Miya had had him A WHOLE NOTHER 7 DAYS. So what if this happens again, somewhere else? Will this baby even be alive?

Me and Miya was waiting. We was thinking about adopting Ja' Quan. We both were sad to see him go. Miya didn't go with me. I took him myself. I packed his diaper bag, bottles, food, and clothes. He had his pacifier in his mouth. When Miya waved bye to him. He waved bye back to Miya.

I snaggled him back in the car, the same way I brought him over there. The seat belt wasn't choking him, so we pulled off. When I get him back to Aqua Vista,

"HEY! Ja' Quan..." Yvonne's mouth drops all the way open on seeing Bobby's nephew.

So she bring him in.

Bobby see him and his momma see him. When Gwen see him, her mouth did the same thing Yvonne's mouth did. I didn't think nothing that big of it. It was just The Lucky Principle. And I felt like, it was just what I was supposed to do. Gwen look at me, she happy and she smiling, she say to me,

"You, his Godfather."

And just like that. It happened. I HAD ME 'A GODSON.

And it was the next day that I came to check on Ja' Quan again. I saw Gwen. She was lookin kinda rough. Probably comin down off that dope. She had her WIC and her food stamps, she wanted me to take her to Wal- Mart to get somethings for her and her baby. And I did. I don't got no problem wit that.

When I go check on Ja' Quan again, like (2) days later, by this time, Gwen IS BACK! Gwen done cleaned up. I take her to the store.

Gwen gotta BIIIG PHAAAT JUICCCCY ASSSS, like Tiny. Her momma. Tiny is Bobby's sister. Tiny might be 'a little bit PHAAATA, but Gwen look better than her momma. She not dark skin, but she got that beautiful flowing chocolate milk skinned body. This girl don't need no makeup. That's why it's crazy she was into gettin high real bad, and fuckin wit that dope and crack. You see this girl sober; you wouldn't even guess it.

All my homies wanted to fuck her. This girl's body was BADDD! Stupid Bananas! She had EVERY nigga out Aqua Vista wanted to fuck this girl. Every time I get over there, all the way from the first day she came around, all I hear these niggas say was,

"Gwen..

Gwen...

Boy, you seen Gwen?"

I was almost jealous. Cause I ain't hear them make this much noise about Miya. So, I had to go eyeball Miya's competition, personally myself. Why these nigga's won't doin all this shit for Miya? Who was it so special that was makin these nigga's tongues roll like'a fluffy red carpet that won't MY Bitch?

And I saw her.

I already explained her to you. She is 'a BAD BITCH! I can't take that from her. And she is PHAAAT. I can see why she got these whole jects JUMPIN!! This bitch gotta asss that make a pair of sweatpants look like 'a pair of tights. That's WORD! I seen it wit my own eyes. Then I went round the Vista a few days later to check back up on Ja' Quan, and he and Gwen was GONE. Not DIED. Thank God for that, but they both had left Bob's house out the Vista. And nobody know where they went. So I went back into worry for Ja' Quan.

After Ja' Quan had left us, it sparked me and Miya to try for another baby. So we was having sex more. Even if financially we wasn't ready to afford having a child. Truthfully, financially me and Miya struggled in our marriage. Somewhat. I was the only one working. It ain't bother me. I never complained about it. I liked coming home everyday, and Miya be waitin for me at home.

I came home one day, and Miya was upset, like she was crying. I asked her what was wrong. She hadda phone conversation wit my mom, and my mother told her she was putting too much burden on me by being the only one working.

A BURDEN. What!? BURDEN!? Why did she do that? She upset Miya. I tried to get her over it. But Miya wouldn't get over it. And

so Miya went to go get a job.

Miya is a Psychology MAJOR from Hampton University. Even when she don't get into her field- - it doesn't matter

When Miya goes and gets A Job-- Miya don't make what I make. Miya gets THREE TIMES What I Make. First Off!!

Miya gotta NEW Job. And wit her NEW Job means NEW Money. And Fresh NEW Money means, Miya done outgrown the Metro.

Now, she wants her own car. She wants a NEW car. I thought she would go back to Oyster Point Dodge, like she did a year ago.:

O, I didn't tell you about that yet. Did I?

Well, Oyster Point had a special, that they'll sell you a Brand NEW Dodge for just $5 Down. Of course that's all pending upon your job, your income, and if you got good credit. But Miya was tired of whippin that 323 her father had paid his Cold Hard CASH!! for. And she was lookin for a NEW way to make him spend dat dough. Especially since his only child and daughter. His Boo. Was graduating college from Hampton University.

And so I went wit Miya out Oyster Point Dodge to at least, you know.: see what they was talking about. And low and behold, I run into one of my homies all the back from Paula Maria. No. NOT Damon. Not Barry either. I did run into Barry and Damon; but it won't this day. It was another one of my childhood homies. Called Corey Mc George.

Corey was a lil bit older than me. He grew up under my first neighborhood bully, Terrence. It was Terrence, Eric Steele, and Corey Mc George. That was they team. But Eric and Corey never gave me no problems. Not for real. They won't on

Terrence's type time.

     I use to always look up to Corey for real. Cause he was always clean, he always dress nice, and hadda smooth style to him. When I used to get sick, wit the flu, or flu like symptoms, my father used to pay his mother, Ms. Sherry to watch after me.

     His momma was real nice and sweet. But she loves her (2) children.: Corey and Jimmy. On them, she'll come down strict when she got to. She was a stereotypical disciplinarian. Meaning.: she is what I was used to seeing as a Black Woman and as A Mother. I saw her the same way I would any one of my Grandmothers, or as I would my own Mother. That's why I always had respect for her.

     As we got older, I ain't never really rock wit Corey. Cause we was from two different age brackets. But he'll pull me to the side from time to time and pull me up on "shit." And when I say "shit," I mean that literally. He was the first one I ever used profanity around, one day out on the monkey bars, that we use to use for a basketball court. And we was out there one on one, shooting around, and I missed the shot and I said,

     "Shit!"

He say, "What?"

And I said, "I said, "Shit!"

     And he laughed. He was surprised to hear me say it, cause that was the first time I ever used a curse word. He knew I didn't use curse words.

Neither of us did; originally. It's not how we was raised.

When we got to Warwick; I'm not saying this to embarrass him, but I was a Freshman and Corey was a fifth year senior, because he had to stay back and repeat the 12th grade. We like 4 or 5 years apart. Anyway, we was up in the bathroom, pissing in the urinals. And I used to walk all the way up on the urinal, and piss in the urinal. And Corey was the one who taught me not to piss like that, so the piss wouldn't splash back on my clothes. I feel like that was some man shit. An older man teaching a younger man. And from that day, I always kept that wit me.

And two last things about Corey.: Cause earlier I had said that Damon was the most advanced out Paula Maria. Which he was- - until Corey was the First one with a car. Not just any car, but an all- white Audi. It hadda diesel engine. So every time he cranked it up, it sounded like a big rig was sitting up outside. But Hey! He had a car. Maybe that's how he met this number 1 thing I'm about to tell you about.

The day I see him on the lot of the Oyster Point dealership, he has this bad ass shorty wit him. This girl was PHAAAAT. Her and Miya spoke. But I ain't say nothing about her. He ain't introduce to me who she was. And I ain't introduce Miya to him either.

We just left it at that.

Now that Miya had slapped her résumé all together, she was showin all off, cause she ain't wanna let me just pick her up and drop her off; or she take the Metro when I ain't using it. So, I get the call.

To make'a long story go fast.: She was out with her mother, shopping for a NEW car at Mercury Nissan. On the corner of Aberdeen and Merc. She was calling me to come meet her at the dealership. When I get there, Dr Graham had co-signed for Miya to get this green Nissan Altima. It wasn't NEW, but it was nice.

It had 4 doors. Automatic windows, locks, and transmission. A moon roof, 2 factory Bose amps, speakers and music system. Factory five star rims, fog lights that hit like headlights, wit a wing on the back. The bottom line.: it was more advanced than 'a Metro.

We got it back and left the Metro at home. We went out in Miya's new Altima, and she was letting me drive it.

Miya was a girl who had a high school diploma from Peninsula Catholic, and a bachelor's degree from Hampton University in Psychology. And her extra income enabled us to buy a better car. But I was STUPID!!

I was supposed to be more supportive of Miya and work together with her as a team. Instead, I took her BOOSTED income, as a blow to my ego. I started feeling like, I wasn't supposed to trust her. For no reason, I started thinking she was cheating, or the possibility that she could cheat; or that she could leave. And that's what I let start to corrode our relationship.

I was thinking that I'm supposed to be The Breadwinner and take care of her. I wasn't looking at it like I was supposed to combine incomes and I still could've taken care of her. I didn't know nothing about that.

My Grandmother was a housewife. My Best Momma worked, but her income was nothing like what Miya was making. Even my own mother, made less than $12,000 a year.

Subconsciously, I started rejecting Miya, and then, that's what would cross over into our real life.

Chapter 27

I started to not bring my money home and share it with my wife. I was getting more and more into drinking and my marijuana habits. I stopped paying bills, or helping to pay bills. Like Miya and her momma supposed to pay all the bills.

I was wrong. That's how I carried it.

But me and Miya ain't always have beef, or internal beef. One day me and Miya was getting along. You know, like we was Cold Chillin, kicked back and coolin at the crib. When she admitted to me she was sexually attracted to one of her friends. Of course you know what that mean.:

"Who?"

Shawnna?...

Lauren?...

Patsy?...

maybe it's Kelley?

One day she showed me a BACKSHOT of

Shawnna bending over on a bed witta tight ass pair of bluejeans. I gotta fetish for BIG BOOTY BITCHES in tiggght asss jeans. Especially BIG BOOTY REDD ASSS BITCHES in tiggght asss jeans. Gettin married didn't change that. But it did tame it. I wasn't ready to cheat on my wife. But if she wanted to have sex with Shawnna, I damn sure couldn't blame her for that. And I wasn't going to be mad. I didn't see it as cheating.

But...

Shhhh, it wasn't Shawnna.

It wasn't Lauren neither.

It wasn't her Maid of Honor and Best Friend. Nope... it wasn't Patsy.

And Kelly. She is RED wit Green Eyes, and she look like she tryin ta get 'a phaat lil butt.

But, no. It wasn't Kelley either.

Well HEY! all my Top Four is dead.

Then, I thought it might be Kat, the mother of her (2) godsons. But nope. It won't Kat neither.

Who it was? Who could I be? Come on... come on and tell me...

Remember that line all the way back in Chapter 26, from when I said, "Well she did have one."? Well, that's was the ONE. The same ONE that got the exception to her rule, about fuckin each other's man. It was her friend. Named,

"Tiffany."

"TIFFANY!?" Don't that sound like I'm shocked?

She's the one you'd absolutely MOST LEAST expect. So MOST LEAST likely to expect, that's why I ain't even talk about her yet. I'll do it now. First, I gotta give you some background.:

Before Miya went to Hampton, she and Tiffany went to Mary Washington. That's a college that's out there somewhere in Virginia. Miya had this boyfriend out there. This brownskinned dude, named Elgin. Yeah, yeah, yeah. Like the watch. Anyway, he started out being Miya's boyfriend, then HER FRIEND, Tiffany starts liking him. So Miya breaks up wit Elgin, so him and Tiffany can be together. And one night Miya was turned on hearing Tiffany and Elgin have sex.

I'm not all the way clear about what she saw or what she heard.

But it go something where she said, "I'on know. I just wanted to do something. I wanted to get involved."

And when she say she, "wanted to do something. [She] wanted to get involved." She don't mean that how most women might mean, in a violent or in an aggressive way. But in the alternative. The more she kinda talked about it- - maybe it was the reefa we was smokin, but she sounded less interested in Elgin. She talked more and more about Tiffany. She felt some type of way about Tiffany. The same girl who BROKE her lil girlfriend golden rule. Jus crumbled it all to lil pieces.

I'on know what it was. I ain't gon lie.: at the time; I didn't see it. Except that Tiffany is dark skinned. So that's what led me to think that, 'Well, maybe Miya has a secret hidden sexual attraction for dark skinned people.'

But Hey! We'on know. What I do know.: I like pussy that eat pussy. So I wasn't gon break this shit apart. She ask me for permission for her to talk to Tiffany. If she can you know.: bring Tiffany 'on up round here.

"Yeah. Yes. Sure. Of course."

So, it don't happen that night. 'A few nights go by, and she ask me,

"Do you mind if I call Tiffany?"

"Naw. No. Sure don't. Of course not." I'm real SUPPORTIVE now. Right.

Tiffany gets over here.

I'm not gon lie.: I don't see it. As a man, I just don't see ANY sexual attraction. Tiffany is a dark-skinned girl, but she look...

Let me see.:

She dress...

How best to explain?

She don't...

Alright...

Alright...

Alright...

Alright...

I'm jus gon come out and jus say it.:

She don't look like nothing. That's not to say she's ugly. I'm not saying that. But she's just...

Plain.

Plain. It's 'a good way to say it. She don't got no ass. She don't got no titties. She don't dress in any sexually seductive way. I mean, I'on know... just 'a Plain. Just 'a Plain Jane. I'll just... leave it like that. For real.: I most expected her to say Lauren, Shawnna, Patsy. Somethin like that. So, I'm kinda judging her on her taste in women. But umm...

So Miya feel some type of way about this girl, name Tiffany. I'on stand in her way. I'm just gon sit here in this chair, smoke this blunt, and drink down this Heineken. Ok, and listen to her go at Tiffany.

And yes...

Miya's pussy talkin game is Wack! So bad, it'll fuck up the pattern of my book, for me to play it back in print. She sound worse than me tryin to get 'a piece of pussy.

This shit was so wack, I fell asleep in the chair watchin these two bitches sittin there, tryin to cherry chop.

I keep falling asleep. Waking up. They still there sittin and talking. So finally, I give up tryin to watch this fake ass in- person porn pic. I go get in my bed and go fall asleep. I'll jus find out what happened later on; in the morning or something, or just catch em on the next round.

A few HOURS go by. I guess. I feel something wet around my dick. Of course, the first thing I think.: man this bitch done cut my dick off. Cause I feel something kinda wet. I been real fuck'd up over this, ever since that Lorraine Bobbitt shit happened.

I'on open my eyes. I kinda feel something scrapin. I feel teeth. I wake up. It's Miya. And she is ALONE.

So the first thing come to my head.: "Where's Tiffany?" I'm looking all around, or thinking she bout to come in the room.

"She went home."

"HOME. Home for WHAT!? What Happened?"

"She wanted you to be involved..."

Aww, now forget everything bad I said about Tiffany. My fault. My bad. I apologize. This 'a girl witta Heart of Gold. I love you Tiffany.

"... She said she wouldn't do it, unless she can fuck you too."

DAMN! WHAT!? Where is she at? Go... Go call her back!

But Miya is on her bullshit. She is subtly very territorial. She don't want me fuckin no other bitches. She don't want other bitches fuckin me. Well bitch, you need to pull these panties down more than three times in two weeks. But, I was kinda sad for Miya. Cause she failed at her first attempt at tryin to eat some pussy. At least now she can see for herself.: this going at pussy stuff, was just as hard for ladies as what it is for men.

Afterwhile, eventhough I was gettin paid EVERY week, I got tired of making $5 an hour. I sought a job where I can make more money. I hadda chance to get hired back in the Shipyard. But not working for the Shipyard itself, or for Nance. But working for it's Security subcontractor. Wackenhut, which they say is the #1 Security company IN THE NATION. Well, HEY! I say it's what they say.

Dr Graham was actually the one who got me set up for the job. She knows alot of people in alotta places. So I go in for the job, this job woulda paid me like $15 an hour. I put in my application. But basically, because this was Dr Graham's connect, I already had the job. I guess I kinda took that for granted. And I went in, and they piss test me. Of course, my urine comes back positive for THC.

I didn't get the job.

It was CONFIDENTIAL information. So Dr Graham never knew the reason why I didn't get the job. If they didn't tell her, I sure as hell ain't gon tell her. Of course Miya knew. I told her. But she ain't get mad about it. We just picked up on trying to get me a better job. In the future, when I tried for a better job, I used to use the herbal teas to try to detox my body, before I go in there and piss test.

I was hoping that job would wrap back around, cause it could of changed my whole future. My whole life now. But it never came back around. Dr Graham never set the play back up again. I had to move on.

I went through odd jobs back with Reliance Temp Service. And I was just trying to hustle to make it. That's when I started putting my check into reefa, and trying to flip it to make money. I didn't want to get into crack, cocaine, or dope.

Cause those was FELONIES.

I ain't feel like getting myself into something that could put me in prison for YEARS. For 10, 20, 30 YEARS. I was conscious that that is what I was trying to avoid. And trying to prevent God's prison plan for me from coming true.

It's crazy. But I was working to defeat God. Like what HE said-- HE ain't really mean it. One thing about it.: I could tell that dream, but it was no one around me to interpret it.

The only closest one.: of all people, was a Psychic.

When Me and Miya was dating. They have palm reading spots set up all over the place. Shops in the mall and in various places. They charge $5 to do a palm reading. A quick $5 bucks. I don't do it. I never do it. I just watch Miya do it. For real, I'on believe in it. I think it's just entertainment, to rip people off from they money. Cause the way I see it, if they really was so Psychic, shit, they'll be HITTING!! the Big Lottery Numbers on every Friday, and every night. Right.

So I don't take this shit serious.

One day, me and Miya was out Waterside. In Norfolk. And it's a shop set up out there. The Psychic is standing outside the shop. She prolly got all kinds of Tarot Cards, incense, and witchcraft shit inside. Right. So it's this 30ish, stringy brown hair white woman. She's the Psychic.

And Miya asks her, "Do you mind giving me a psychic reading?"

And the woman is, "Sure," she's really real cool and laid back.

So she finished reading Miya. Giving HER some good news. And she looks over at me- - and she predicts I would be going to prison and doing a long time. I didn't pay this woman NOTHING to tell me this.

I was expecting to hear her say for MURDER, like it was in the dream. But she says... she keeps saying,

"I don't know... I don't know what it is. I just know it's going to be for something REAL REAL BAD...

And I see you in an orange jumpsuit, and I see handcuffs and something on your feet." That probably was the shackles.

After we left, Miya never did another palm reading ever again. But after leaving, and being in the car, she kept saying,

"I don't believe that. She just saw you being a Black Man and..."

I heard what Miya was saying. For real, I wanted to believe her. But it's crazy how that Psychic was lining up with that dream, I had at 19. I didn't tell the Psychic about the dream. Not even after she gave me her prediction. I NEVER even told Miya about that dream. Cause I was tryin to side swipe it. Her reading this, is her First Time even knowing about it. EVER.

I got into hustlin. Wit the reefa business. I used to

stop at the store, over on Mallory. Not far from my house. This store was EXCLUSIVE. Cause they sold High Times magazines. Back then, you couldn't go to just any store and getta High Times. It was very select stores. And this was one of those very select stores.

I purchased the High Times magazine. When I get it home. To the back of the book, they selling ounces of this stuff that look like bud. So I order 'a ounce. I'm thinking; at these prices- - if this stuff look like what it do in the magazine, I can sell this shit, or mix it with the real weed. Shit, it's like adding cut. YO! I can BOOST!! da sack B. That way, I can hustle, hustle, hustle, and get more money.

I didn't order it in my name. Cause I just knew the ATF gon pop up, soon as this UPS man peel off. THIS SHIT GOTTA BE A SETUP.

But, the sack show up. It's no feds. I hurry up. Get it inside. It's in 'a red, white, and blue box, like this shit the American Dream or somethin. The ends of the box is wrapped witta whole lotta box tape. I gotta whip out the utility knife to get this shit open up, befo the feds show up. I get open the sack. It don't look nothing like it do in the magazine

This shit just loose spirals that krinkle. It ain't even bud. It's not budded. See what I'm saying?

It's green. And it stink. But not like skunk. It stink

like- - like some shit you'll feed to 'a goldfish. This shit like goldfish food. Mannn... no wonder the feds ain't on toppa this bullshit.

So I roll it up. And me and Miya, we go head and smoke it. I ain't high. She ain't high. We don't get a buzz. Nothing. It's just pure, what they call, "Alternative Smoke." They right about that, cause this shit ain't got no THC in it.

We smoke that shit one time, and put that shit up on the shelf in the computer room. That shit start getting some dust. Won't nothing I could do with it. I lost money. I couldn't even blend that shit wit real weed. I took the loss.

They had more shit in there for more money, but I won't gon keep trickin my paychecks up for that shit. I left it alone. Plus, I ain't tryin to bait the feds. I just kept looking for better jobs. I had to get up out that Rick Thomasson bullshit. One day, one of my greatest fears had happened.:

We has working on these apartments, up North King Street. Just before you get to Langley Air Force Base. It's this lil swampy lookin pond out posting up; out in between these apartments and Langley Air Force Base. This part of America is popular for water moccasins. A water moccasin is a very dangerous and poisonous snake. It's what they say. I ain't never seen nobody get bit by one, but I ain't tryin to be THE ONE who get bit by one either.

One day I'm out working. I'm under the crawl space to these apartments. That means, I'm all the way up under the first floor. I'm down wit tha foundation. And this foundation is in the sand. I hate that. I rather have dirt than sand. Cause if something is hiding to get you, up under some dirt, you gotta better chance to see him. Cause you'll see bulges or whatever, in the dirt surface. You'll see the dirt is uneven.

You can't do that in sand. All sand is uneven. And the whole ground is soft. So you might put yo hand or feet, right down on top of it. And this is just not a real good space. I'm high. I been drinking. I just left the strip club, at lunch.

They gotta lil strip club like 'a block and 'a half; two blocks down the street. It ain't Moonlight, Solid Gold, or Magic City. Nothin like that. It's jus all lil skinny ass white girls up in there. But I jus getta few dances from these lil thin ass bitches, guzzle me a drink, eat and smoke 'a stick in the car, and get it back to work. All in 'a hour.

So when I get back to work, I'm HIGH!! as gas! Crawling around in the sand, up under these apartments, and The Spirit of the Lord talk to me and tell me to get from under there. It was a still small voice. But I listen. And I leave from up under there.

I go to a different section of the apartments. But I don't go up underneath it, I go inside it. The sheetrock ain't even up yet. It's still being framed. I climb up the frame to the second story. The second story is a frame. It's just all wooden two by fours. And it's a plank. That's a wooden beam of board, that's just stretched across air space. It's a fly over, from one section over to another. I coulda walked around on the frame, but I get up and, I walk the plank. I'm FUCK'D UP!! Like 'a ECW wrestler. Up 25 feet. Like I'm in 'a ol school NWA scaffold match.

I easily could've fell. I coulda dropped. When I look down to the first floor, all I see is tools, nails, circular saws. If I fall. I'm done. It's no way for me to catch myself.

I make it through. I make it cross the other side. It won't too long after that, I heard, they found a water moccasin snake. Crazy part about it.: it was right from where I just left from. But it won't down in the sand. It was up, in the floor boards. So I usually look down at the ground, I never think about the fact, it might be UP. But The Lord saved my life. I was impaired. I coulda got bit B.

And they say it was a pregnant female. So her bite woulda been all the way tee'd off! They had to call animal control out to seize the snake. And they did. I stayed in the building. I didn't even go out there to watch it.

But after that.: this job is done! I didn't just go up and quit. I completed the job, but I never went back up under that house again. After those apartments was done, I hauled ass to go look for a NEW job.

I saw the Classifieds section of the Daily Press newspaper, and I saw they had SALES positions open. Earning between $50 thousand-$80 thousand a year. I was attracted to those kinda numbers. For real, I wanted to be in auto sales. I was filling out applications for Auto Sales jobs both NEW and USED, all over the place. From The Casey Auto Group, where I got my car, all the way down to the lil rinky dink AS IS car dealerships. Like where my daddy used to buy all his lemons. Ain't none of these bastards hire me.

Then one day I was out wit my homies.: Lynn, EZ, and AJ. I'm bumpin tha system. We rolling up on that little street, leading up to Parks Inn on 27th Street, when I see her.

Yes Her. Like, really really, it was HER. NO. Not the singer, H.E.R. It is the other HER. It is the Joy Jackson. HER.

I saw JOY!! I was driving up one way. She was driving down the other. And we stopped, right there in the middle of the road. And, I jumped out!! And I ran for Joy. She still looked the same. This girl was BADDD as 'a Bitch! And I was high. I been drinkin. They call it Liquid Courage. Cause I won't scared no more.

I was talking to her.

"Man, get out the car. So I can see you." I did wanna see her. But at the same time, I was showing off in fronna my homies. They never knew about Joy Jackson. I never told them about her. So, I wanted them to see. I see them keep lookin.

Joy is hesitating. At the same time, cars are now starting to blow!! cause we holdin up traffic. Joy pull off to the side of the road. But the cars won't just go around my car. They want me to MOVE my car too. Lynn sittin there, lookin crazy. He can't drive a stick. Man, this one time I wish I had taught it to him. EZ can't drive a stick either. I shoulda let AJ. But my mind ain't all the way into it. Plus AJ one 'a the most fucked up out all of us.

Joy won't by herself. She was driving, but she was in the car with a car full of women. All of them was beautiful. But to me, ain't nothing fuckin wit Joy! I was tryin to see if I could see Joy's younger sister, or other girls from Menchville. They coulda been, or girls from Howard. I'on know. But I know, I want Joy out this car.

She wouldn't get out. I think she was surprised, all

of a sudden, I could do all this talking. And cars keep blowing. When I go to move my car... Joy is GONE!

I was hurt. But for real, it was nothing much I could do. I had already spent my ring. I was already married.

But it's just something to Joy, that I felt that day. Just from me just seeing her. Just LOOKING at her made me wanna do better. Wanna be better. I ain't never SEEN no girl make me feel like that before. JOY was the only one.

I LOOK at her, and she was driving me. Just LOOKIN at her, I feel like, I can go out and go GETTA BILLION DOLLARS. And all legal. Everything legal. You can't getta girl like Joy on trees. It was nothing matching to her.

But, I shoulda just got her number over, and got up wit her later. It probably would've worked like that; or I shoulda tore my momma house up for that old year book. Just to try and see if the number was the same. But if that had materialized.: then what about Me and Miya?

But, it didn't work like that. So, I was back to looking for a regular job. I was putting in for SALES. I was putting in applications, but NONE of them would hire me. But I did finally get me a job in SALES. I was hired by a man, named Mr Melvin

Artis, to work for his small warehouse business called BTN Distribution. Melvin kinda looked like Gwen's boyfriend. That's who he reminded me of.

But Melvin hired me. He gave me a chance, to go from business to business and offer to sell, basically I was selling toys at $5 each. I would load my Metro up with at least (3) different kinds of toys, that you might find similar look- a- likes in stores, and marked dollars BELOW the retail price. I might have a total of 100 toys, or units or pieces. For every unit or piece I sold, I'd make $1 or $1.25 on every $5 piece. I was getting COMMISSION. And with this job, I got paid in CASH!! EVERYDAY. I didn't have to wait on a paycheck.

If I could move 100 pieces, then I could easily earn $100 or more A DAY! The downfalls were.: I didn't always sell every piece,

#2.:) Deals get made COLD in the field, which means people like DEALS. Which means I might give a piece away for FREE, just so I can move units, or I was taking shorts in the field. Which means, I lose money. Cause Melvin gon get his, and

For #3.:) If I have a partner, then I gotta split money with him. If I was taking a new person out into the field, then I was encouraged to give the new person perhaps more than half of what was made, in order to stimulate the morale of that new person. To motivate them to keep coming back, and to keep up the hard work.

But the part I liked.: I was like my own boss working in the field. I always had money for gas. I always had money for food. I always had beer money. All that FUN and party shit, I was used to, from working in construction, I was doing it. And that means, by the time I finished all my deductions, I might be taking Miya home like $20 or $30.

But the experience I was getting in the field. PRICELESS. I was on the road everyday. Going to different cities. All over the place. Norfolk, Battlefield Boulevard, Campostella, Tidewater Drive, Princess Anne, Virginia Beach Boulevard, Military Highway, Newtown Road, Independence, Lynnhaven, Airline Boulevard, Chesapeake, Portsmouth, Suffolk, Newport News, Hampton, Washington Street, Wythe Street, Broad Street, Hull Street, Chamberlain, Chesterfield, Mechanicsville, Laburnum, 9 Mile Road, Henrico, Tappahannock ...

all over the place.

When I HIT!! Petersburg, over by the Church's Chicken. You know what it is. People don't pull up on me. I gotta go pull up to people. And pitch them my pitch,

"Hi, my name is Jamie. Hey! I got this...

ONLY 5 BUCKS!...

I tell you what-- give me $5 for this, $3 on this, and I'll THROW this in for FREE!!"

HEY! for the price, you can't beat it!

It was times, I got my haircut in the field. I usually had a spot out Petersburg and Capital Cuts out Norfolk. That's if I won't gettin my hair cut into a smooth bald fade by Big Walt and Tino, out Peddlers. In Bad News. By this time I was off Esquire. Ain't shit but old ass men cut up in there. I gotta be where it's poppin at.

And sometimes the products were ice breaking mechanisms to draw me into conversations with some interesting people. Even wit people that ain't got no money. I could be in the thick and thin of everyday sights, sounds, and the stone cold art of the Hustle and Bustle. I wasn't just in barber shops, but I was in beauty salons, local area restaurants, furniture stores, repair shops, retail stores, I was even up in funeral homes, pitching to employees.

After I had left Rick Thomasson's Heating and Air, I went back to the temp services. I went back to Reliance. What a name, cause they truly are. I get a job, of all places, working at a jail. I'm helping doing construction work at the Virginia Peninsula Regional Jail. It's a jail that will house inmates awaiting trial from Williamsburg, York County, Poquoson, and Gloucester County. In other words, Ku Klux Klan County Jail.

But my job in the jail. Mostly I'm doing labor, and I'm doing floors. For like a whole summer that I stayed at Dwight's, I watched Menace II Society and Boyz N The Hood EVERYDAY. I'd play em back to back. And it was nothing on tv, so I watched them EVERYDAY. In combination, that all I really listened to was gangsta rap. Gangsta music. So my mind became desensitized, through what I programmed my mind to through entertainment. Through entertaining thoughts. Today, it's video games. It's Fort Nite. At one time, it's Grand Theft Auto. But at my time, it was tv, music, and movies. I was gon off that gangsta thug lifestyle.

I'm just telling you my truth.

And one day, while I was working. They had a cell in there. It was on the top tier. I don't know what drew me to this cell. But I went. And I went inside this particular one. Usually when I go in cells, I'll just do my work, and come out. But this cell. I started reenacting in character,

"Hey, what's crackin homie? What you got on my 40?"

Duh- duh- duh- duh- duh. And I got myself like yeah. Yeah. I can do this. Subconsciously, I was programming myself to do time in prison. And I was "acting out," like I was doing time in prison.

I sat on the bed. It was the first time I had ever sat on the bed, in any of the cells. And that's when the Spirit of God rolled up, and stood beside me. It was a still small voice, but I heard it as clear as day. HE said,

"I'm gon give you 10 years."

And I said, "10 years. I can do 10 years." Because I thinking how young I was. I was 22. So if I go at 22, I'll be out at 32. I'll still be young. That's what's in my mind.

And HE said, "You right. I'm gon give you 20 years."

And when he said that. That's when I shut up. I didn't do no more talking. I just sat there thinking like, 'Is that real? Did that really just happen?"

And I saw the door CLOSE. But it didn't physically close. It metaphysically closed. I was trapped inside the cell. Then the door opened. And when it opened, I ran out!

But I didn't leave my job. I stayed at the job. But I never went in THAT cell ever again after that. And when I got off work, I hauled ass home. I didn't say nothing to Miya. I just kept trying to live a normal life. As normal as I could get it. The Spirit of God was chasing me, but HE was still keeping me alive.

It wasn't too long after that, that one night I was round my homie's Lynn's crib. And I was smoking. Drinking. Gettin high. It got late. Like 2 in the morning. I got to get home to Miya. And I left. What fucked me up is, I had to take AJ and EZ home, then take myself home; and I was up on the interstate. And, I Blacked Out. I BLACKED OUT behind the wheel, on the interstate.

When I woke up, I saw the concrete wall. The concrete wall that separates east bound traffic from west bound traffic. I threw my hands out. I braced myself to be thrown from my car. To be ejected through my windshield.

All of a sudden... I HIT THE WALL.

But when I hit the wall, I wasn't thrown from my car, nor was I ejected through my windshield. The car was riding up next to the wall. I heard a low murmuring sound. I pulled the car over to the shoulder of the road. I thought I had smashed my little Metro all too pieces. When I got out the car, and looked at it.

There wasn't any significant damage.

I had scraped the bumper on the left side, blew out the front left tire, and crumpled the rim. That's all that happened.

I was close to home, but still far from home. I put the car in first gear and drove it for the 249 exit. That's the last Hampton interstate exit, before you head into Norfolk. I parked the car at Hardee's, and I walked home the rest of the way. It's a straight shot down to my house on 202 Atlantic Avenue.

When I get home, it's 6 in the morning.

Miya in the bed sleep. When she wake up at 9, and look out the door, the first thing she come and say,

"J, where's your car?"

And I explain to her what happened. I called my Father. My Father came through for me. He bought my rim and replacement tire, so I wouldn't have to ride around on a donut. It cost him a hundred and some change. And my momma had him change the tire.

So wit BTN, I was heavy in the streets. But in 'a whole nother sense. I had to talk to people. I love to talk to people. I'll talk to everyone. Anyone. I

had to push my products. I didn't wanna take
nothing back. I'on give 'a fuck! I'll even pitch to
other vendors, and other street vendors. I even
hadda few of them tell me,

"You're good. You're very good."

Then try to offer me a job doing what they
was doing, or working for their company. But I do
this shit, like I do rapping. I do it for the thrill!
Man, I Love It! for the THRILL!! Sometimes they
had what I wanted, and I had what they wanted.
And we'll make it all exchange like,

"Say WHAT!? You got that NEW Makavelli
13!??"

Hip- Hop. Humidifiers. Hair cuts. Incense.
Oils. Fake gold chains. T- shirts... The art of the
deal is in the Pitch. Pitch. Pitch. Pitch. Pitch. Pitch.
Pitch. Pitch. The whole damn baseball game; it's all
in the Pitch, man. I'd Pitch to ANYBODY.
ANYPLACE. ANYTIME. At ANYWHERE. It wasn't
all about the money. I had the heart. I had the
passion. I fell in love with my job. I fell in love with
my job, because the field, it soothe me. It made me
relax. It took my mind off things. Like, my last (2)
jobs, and like me crashing my car. I was going.

But with no prosperity.

No matter how much I work. No matter how much I hustle. All the work of my hands was futile. I couldn't even sell reefa. And reefa can sell itself.

I was crumbling apart. My life was crumbling apart. Everything that God promise, HE was working it, into fruition. Why? Cause The Word of God CANNOT be made into a lie.

Everything that God was doing in my life, HE was chasing me. But HE was bringing me through.

And during this time, I was cheating on Miya. But not with who she expected. She thought I was having sex with Luz's daughter, Michelle. But I wasn't.

It wasn't easy for me to have sex with other women. I hadda wife at home. Even when I was in the field, working for BTN, when it's women that used to give me their phone numbers. But I never called them. I always tore the numbers up, and threw them away. Cause Miya wassa woman, she'll go through my pants, through the closet, through my drawer, through my car. But she never found nothing. I never let her find nothing. Never no numbers. My lil red book, I think was locked at my momma's house. Cause after I got Miya, I didn't use it. I never called no more of those numbers. I'm not bringing no woman home. And I definitely ain't gon let her catch me wit no condoms.

But I used condoms. For the most part. I buy just enough, and use em up. I ain't gon be wit no 12, 20, 100 condoms. 3 pack, use it; I'm done. Maybe. Sometimes. But I was fuckin street hoes. I don't even know when it started. Because I wasn't comfortable about cheating on my wife. But I know it was more than 3 months. It was maybe about 4 months into the marriage. I was scared with how it would feel to be having sex with another woman, who wasn't my wife. I was conscious of that feeling.

And the first time I did it. It didn't feel like nothing. It didn't mean nothing to me. And I knew it didn't mean nothing to her. I was just gettin 'a nut. But street hoes or not, every now and then, you gon run into bitches that really are that sexually attractive. And one day that's what I did, but without knowing it. I won't trickin on the hoe stroll. Like Jefferson or Shell Road.

I had just got out the field, from after working one day at BTN. I was driving, when I saw (2) girls come outta Farm Fresh. One of the girls was RED. One of the girls was PHAAT as hell. She was swaying. All I saw was asscheeks; her buttcheeks was fallin out the back of her daisy duke shorts. It look like she ain't have no panties on. I'on even know how she got up in Farm Fresh, like this. But they was walking. They wasn't driving. So I pull up at the bus stop to offer them a ride, and they get in. The red one get in the back. But the one I really like get in the front.

I'm talkin to the one in the front. Shoal nuff. The bitch ain't got no panties on. Pussy phat. It look alright. I'm tryin to fuck. Come to find out, these hoes is trick'n. She say to me,

"Well, since you was nice to give us a ride, just give me $5."

I'm thinking she talking about the pussy. She end up giving me head. Then she tell the red girl to give me head. The red girl start giving me head from the backseat. I'm driving. These two girls, taking turns, going back and forth. But it's not doing nothing to me. It's not what I want. I ride these bitches from Phoebus all the way to the crib behind Darling Stadium. Where Hampton high school students play football.

But who I wanna fuck, still won't give me no pussy. Shit, I woulda paid $5 mo dollars Bitch! She put her girlfriend on me. The lil red one. Well, I thought she was little, cause she had on this great big huge baggy grey sweat suit. I'on know why she had on these hot ass clothes, in the summer time. She was dressed tom boyish. But she got up in the front, and when I pulled her sweat pants and panties down, I saw she was phaata than what I thought she was. And the pussy wassa scud!

This was one of them times, I didn't use a rubba. Cause like I said, I don't just keep em around. And I hadn't planned on trickin or hittin pussy. But shorty ended up burning me. By the grace of YAHWEH, it was gonorrhea. It coulda been way more dangerous. I don't think me and Miya had sex, in the days, during that time. But I had to go to see the doctor, and with her being one of my sex partners, and my primary sex partner. They called her ass in too.

They called her from her job. It was CONFIDENTIAL, so they never explained to her exactly what she was there for. I don't think she actually contracted it; but this'll be her first time KNOWING what that was all about. That was my 2nd time getting burned.

YAHWEH may was keeping me alive, but my life was deteriorating. I was slipping. I wasn't even paying on the Metro. They came to get it. It got repossessed. I got it back, the first 2 or 3 times. Then, the last time came. I couldn't get her back this time.

I didn't have the cash.

My father drove me to the auction house over in Suffolk, to take out all my belongings. I got my speaker box. I couldn't get the amps, regular speakers or deck. They was bolted in. I was sad about it. More than anything, cause I fuck'd my father's credit up.

But the other part of me wasn't mad. Cause I had got all my wear and tear out the smalled 1.0 liter engine. I had outgrown it. I wanted something better. I sold my speaker box and (2) 10 inch woofers to Lynn's cousin, Poodie. For $20. Just to get it outta my sight.

After I lost my car, I kinda thought that meant we was gon get Miya's old 323 to get to kickin her wheels. But my father gave me a surprise. He had an 83 Buick Century that he had bought for $900 CASH. As Is. He planned to flip it. But after I lost my car, my father is a very spiritual man. He didn't treat me harsh or come down hard on me for messing his credit up. He gave me the keys to the Buick for FREE.

To this day, that Buick is one of the best cars I ever had. Perhaps missing out on that Pontiac had stuck with him, but my father gave me my first Buick. I'll never forget it as long as I live.

It was a nice, I think about a 4 cylinder, V- 6 engine. All burgundy exterior. All burgundy interior. Electric. Automatic. And the Century is luxury. I loved it better than driving any of his Cadillacs.

I'm just saying.

When I drive them, they float. Like a boat. It's automatic. All electric. It don't even take much, to turn a curve, or bend the corner. It feel like the Caddy driving itself. But I'on know what it is about Cadillacs. I just can't get into them. If I had to put the money into one, I'd never buy it. But it was my father's car. His dream car. The Lord had BLESSED him. He had TWO of them.

I was grateful for this Buick. It was 4 door. But Miya ain't never ride wit me up in it. It's ok. I drove it to BTN. I had it on the rode a little while. Then, like all the rest of my daddy's lemons; it broke down.

I drove it to the side of the interstate, on my way to BTN. They say the piston, shot through the engine block. I'on know. I ain't see it. I didn't go lookin for it. I just know I was driving, in the opposite direction I'd crashed the Metro, not far, right up under that overpass. And my foot was on the accelerator. But the Buick wasn't pickin up speed. It was descending. I drove it to the shoulder, and parked it. Til the tow truck come.

Now wit no car, it wasn't long, I had no job. And with no job, means no money. And it wasn't long after that. I had no wife.

Miya had left me.

Chapter 28

Miya had moved out. She moved to an apartment on Spanish Trail. Out Cordoba. Off King Street. In between Cherry Acres. She was living by herself. I was living by myself on Atlantic. This wasn't a happy time. I was fuck'd up.

I was embarrassed.

All my homies loved Miya. I wouldn't let them in the house. When they called, they say, "Where's Miya?...

Where's Miya at?"

Cause they was so used to us being together. I was used to us being together. After me and Miya had broken up, my settlement from my Lamb and Robinson injury came through. It was for $7500.

I had got lump sum payments periodically. Which basically, off workman's comp, I was supposed to get two- thirds of my paycheck. But they'll skip MONTHS. It was times, I didn't get nothing for 3 to 6 MONTHS. Then they'll lumpsum the payments, all at one time. Generally around

$3800. But, I coulda got more, if I had did what I was supposed to do. I was supposed to be going to therapy. That was my job. It was from 9 to 1.

It was Mon- Fri. Then (4) days a week. Then (3) days a week. The part that was throwing me off, is the man they had kept rubbing down my back. Giving me massages. The feeling was weird. I didn't like no man greasing my back. But if I would've completed my whole therapy, my lawyer, Leon Sarfan, probably would've cleared me for about 'a whole fuckin fortune! of at least $20 grand. $20 grand coulda been a permanent life changing experience.

But I still had $7500 at the backend.

When I went to the bank to cash my PHAAAT ASSS check, I was dealin wit 'a large summa money. So the bank didn't cash my check in the same day. I had to WAIT (5) business days. Which counting the weekend, is the equivalent of ONE WEEK, I had to wait.

But after that, when I went back to the bank (7) days later, the little lady at the teller window, pointed me to walk over to the cubicle. Back over there. To the right. When I get back to the cubicle, it was a Representative waiting there on me. No. Not 'a congressional politician. But a bank representative. And he asked me,

"How would you like your money?"

Meaning he was askin me how many in 1s, 5s, 10s, 20s, 50s, and 100s. I said to him,

"I want it in all 100s."

Didn't have to say it twice. He left and came back, and when he came back, I hadda sack filled with (75) FRESH!! crispy shining 100s. We was both smiling when he gave it to me. I walked back out, past the check cashing line, witta FUCKIN FORTUNE!! look'n like I HAD JUS ROBB'D DA BANK!!

It was probably a month too late to rescue the old trusty Metro. I went for my new young lady. The 83 Buick my daddy gave me. Something about it.: from the disappearing dye of the burgundy exterior, all the way down to the faded Buick emblem on the hubcaps. But I really really liked this car. I went to go rescue my Betsy. It cost me a fortune just on towing and $15 dollars a day of storage fees. Cleared all that. Then I went and got my baby's engine rebuilt, from where that pesky little piston had cracked through her cinder block. But she still kept the same carburetor. Got her tags, title, inspection, and paid for insurance. I got my baby back on the road! I was feeling like one- half my dad's all - time favorite meditations.: "Praise the Lord. I gotta car paid for."

About the same time I put Betsy back together, I got a NEW job doing telemarketing, at the MCI call center. Yep, the same MCI call center I'd helped build, when I worked for Lamb and Robinson. Now I was working for them 6 hours a day, and $6.50 an hour. Plus, commission when I get outta training. Getting hired at MCI was extremely difficult. Dr Graham had helped me get the job, through Hut's brother. Jeff. Jeff was a supervisor there.

I had went to see Miya in her apartment. I told her about the settlement money. I had the Buick, but I used to make Miya come pick me up and take me to work. I used it for some time for us to be together. I whipped out 10 of those FRESH Crispy 100 dolla bills, and I gave Miya $1,000 in her hand. I felt like this money might help to repair our relationship and put us back together. I wanted Miya AT HOME. I needed Miya AT HOME. Our home. TOGETHER.

Plus she had a birthday coming up, November 29th. I wanted to take her out to an EXCLUSIVE restaurant. Even if it cost $200 'a plate. Miya is worth $200 'a plate, and more, and I wanted her to buy something nice for herself, out her money. Whatever she wanted. But Miya took offense to the $1,000 dollars I had put in her hand. Like,

"That's it?"

That's what she said. She felt like being Wifey, she supposed to get HALF! AS IN $37 HUNDRED AND 50 DOLLARS! Hunh. Who the fuck she thought I was? Michael Jordan? Bitch?

"Yeah, you right. What THE FUCK!? was I thinking? Give that shit here..."

She gave me back the thousand dollars. I took out $800, and gave her back jus $200 dollars! And got the fuck up out her car and I went to work.

Later she said.: "Damn, I shouldn't said nothing."

You shoal shouldnt'a bitch! You fuck'd the whole damn play up.

For real. I was playing wit her. I was gon give her the $800 back. But shit happens. Sorry Miya.

I think that was the last day she ever drove me to work. HEY! Time to start humping that Buick. Ain't it. I ain't gotta problem wit it. I paid for it.

Eat'cho pussy out Bitch!

The Buick picked up more attention from the ladies. They really don't care what car you drive. Long as it work. But the Buick was doing something special to dese hoes. Me and Miya, we was married.

But we wasn't together. We was broke up. We was separated. We wasn't even having sex. She didn't give me no signs like she was trying to get back together. But that still don't mean move on. Cause I loved Miya. We might be ESTRANGED. If that's what you wanna call it. But it'll take a whole lot for just any bitch to come along, and kick her throne.

I wasn't even trying to kick her throne, but one day, when I was out Cruisin- - that's what it is when you hand pushin the steering wheel of that Big Boy Buick. But like I was sayin, uh- umm, but one day I was out Cruisin... and I see this THICCCKK JUICCCCY!! ass'd bitch, in 'a pair of blue jeans. The jeans wasn't even tight. But she is PHAAAT and LoOse. Both at the same time. She walkin and all I see is ASSSS just juMPIN. It's soft and it's LOoSe. All up and down her legs and all up and down her back. Betsy musta like girls too, cause she pulled to 'a complete stop. So I can SqUEeZe this big booty bitch in for 'a ride.

She let me take her home. All the way home.

Just met her. She tell me to stop a block over, in front of her house, cause her husband was up in there. I can't even tell you this girl name. I can't even tell you the first initial. The Metro had smalled bucket booty seats. But this Buick, stretch out like 'a couch in the front, and like 'a bed in da

591

back. I ain't even have ta tell it to her. She figured this shit out all on her own. Cause she got up in my backseat. And 'a block from the spot. But she became the first bitch I fuck'd in tha Buick. She was just as PHAAAT and soft, wit her jeans and panties off, as she was wit em on. Nutt'd off in that pussy and errythang.

She told me to come back see her again. But I never did.

After that, since me and Miya was on 'a lil hiatus. Was this girl name Santa. I know her name, cause she Tracy girl.

Santa had chased me for 'a coupla YEARS. Every since Tracy started postin her up round the homies. I knew she had liked me. But I ain't never push back at her. Even when I had times to fuck Santa, I still didn't do it.

Then one night.;)

I went to see Lynn round Santa's apartment. Lynn's girl and Santa are like BEST FRIENDS. So, umm... it started out like a hang out fo friends. We round Terrytown. Smokinnn... Drannnkin... Talkin shit. Playin spades. And Santa wanna give me some pussy.

Tracy won't here. Probably out hustling. This ain't one of his trap spots. This where he lay low, near the streets, but out the streets. You know.: lay low. Near the streets. Out the streets. Get some pussy. Fuck Santa... Shit like that.

I don't fuck her at her house. Tracy can BUST!! up in here at any minute. I'm not comfortable wit that. I take her back to Lynn's house. It's 10 minutes up the street. I get her to Lynn's house, in the dark. She in the living room. Sitting on the couch.

For real, I was having 2nd thoughts. I didn't wanna do it. I didn't want to do to Tracy the same thing Kane and Lynn had did to me. I thought like that. Plus, it was times Tracy saved my life. Tracy from Glen Gardens. But he from a different era of Glen Gardens. He GGP. But he ain't from the GGP, that was chasing after us at Huntington. Running us home, everyday. They hadda nigga BUSTING!! OUT the backfield like Walter Payton, tryin ta get to da crib. Haulin ass from the bus stop. None of them could catch me.

They had calmed down somewhat by the time Tracy came through there though. But they was still fuckin niggas up, and probably even shooting at niggas. One of the first guns I saw my whole life, was out Glen Gardens. I'm just BLESSED it won't pointed at me. Them niggas get crazy!

I had met Tracy for real, because of Lynn. Lynn the

reason how we got close. A few times, it was Tracy who saved my life, around his GGP homies. When his homies start circling, before they even get started, he'll say,

"Now Jamie, gon 'on home now."

He ain't have to say it twice. And he'll stand and look to make sure I get back to Paula Maria safe. So I never forgot that. It's hard to cross that. On the other end, I had (2) of my girls that wanted to fuck Tracy. Even my own Wife. He just ain't know it though.

I'een gon tell him.

It's 'a dirty game. That's the part that made me feel justified for me to gon 'on head and say when I said,

"Santa, come here."

She ain't just come. She RAN up to me. Damn, the bitch almost knocked me down. I pulled off Santa's clothes. This bitch has some HUGE ass breasts. HUMONGOUS!! Like you can lay on top of her; suck her titties, and still make love to her, all at the same time. But, we didn't make love. I fucked her on Lynn's living room carpet.

I'm not gon lie. I slept on Santa. I did. I ain't know this bitch pussy was gon be this wettt. And that bitch soooo deeep. I probably lasted like two minutes. My sex game was gettin WACK! I haven't had a bitch to stretch out and roll up in ALL NIGHT, in over a year. Miya won't fuck like that. And street hoes don't fuck like that. That $5/ $10 only get you one nut, then you get up. 'Care yo ass. So on Santa, I gave her a WACK ass fuck game. After we had sex, we left Lynn's house. I was driving her back home. A half of me was still feeling fucked up, about what happened. Another part of me wanted to take Santa home wit me. Give her a shower, and start this back over again. I can drop her off before I go to work tomorrow at 2 o' clock. I thought about it.

But I wasn't ready for that. I couldn't bring myself to that. Miya is the only woman I ever had sex with in that house. That was the house for me and my Wife. I know it was lines crossed, but I wasn't trying to desecrate that one. I had to save something that was just Me and Miya. Me and Miya had had sex in that house, before we even had any furniture. All we had was a box tv on top of a dark brown woodened end table. And our bed was sheets, comforters, pillows, and each other's bodies.

We got our furniture. And the very next night, we started seeing mice run round on the floor. Ain't that crazy? About the same spot we used to sleep. So, I never had sex with no other woman in my home. That house was just me and Miya.

For real, I still wanted to get back wit Miya. That's who I was in love with. I was missin her. But how much. How crazy was I for really in love, for this girl? I came to her house. But, when I showed up, I ain't go the normal way. To the door, like regular people. I went the other way. I went through her bedroom window, like lunatic people. Why?

Cause I was trying to catch her fuckin. That's why. I went through her bedroom window. There's her bed. But she won't in there FUCKIN. It was made. She won't even in there. I go to her living room. There she is.

She is sleep.

On her couch. But she is on one end of the couch. And Steph is on the other end. I know Steph. Steph is her "friend." He's also friends wit Wayne and Paul. Look at them...

They been smokin.

But, I don't see nothing sensual or sexual goin on. She ain't like layin on him. He ain't on toppa her. They ain't kissing. Her hand ain't in between his legs. His hand ain't in between her legs. They not holdin hands. They both got all of their clothes on. It's no signs of sexual or sensual contact. They not even touching. So when I was calming down, Miya wakes up. She always has a way to know when I'm in the room.

"What are you doing here?" She even still got her glasses on.

I didn't answer her question. For what!? I was just standing there, lookin like Sting. If he was 'a crow. I walk back to her bedroom, I knock her whole rack of CDs all on the floor. She had em stacked all neat up by her bedroom door. I'm looking back over her bed. I'm looking for any signs she was in here doing what? FUC- KING! But I ain't see it. She come follow me in her bedroom,

"J?..."

"J? What are you doing?"

She was scared. She ain't know what I was gon do. But I couldn't get what I came here for. So my anger went away. I heard her front door slam shut. Steph was gone.

One thing about it.: I'm not a woman beater. I'm not gon hit my wife. No matter how angry I might get. She don't know that. But I know that. I still want her to respect it.

The same way she don't wanna see me fuckin other women... that's the same way I feel. I don't wanna see her fuckin other men either. Even if she is doing it; just don't let me see it. O, I'm gonna snap. I got every right to go off. I put that $1200 rock on her finga. So, eat'cho pussy out Bitch!

I'll fuck 'a nigga up fo Miya. I just will. Steph ain't fuckin wit me anyway. Steph from Hampton. I'm from Bad Newz. I'm from that grimeball. Plus, I got that Big W on my Wu- Tang sweater. It's 'a whole lotta shit that can come outta this. I can flip Ol Dirty Bastard UP IN THIS BITCH!!

After Miya saw I was calm, she still wanted me to leave. It's just fucked up. We haven't even been married for a year, and to be going through this. Our marriage had inspired so many of our friends. EZ Mc, the same FRESH cool kid, I'd met all the way back as a freshman at Warwick. We was strangers back then. Now we grew into friends as young men. He was a Groomsman in my wedding. Then, he ended up getting married to his wife Tawanna. I ended up being at attendance at his wedding.

Then, Lauren, who was Miya's Bridesmaid in our wedding, she ended up getting married to her boyfriend, Justin. They had a beautiful wedding and reception over at the Chamberlain Hotel. It felt like their wedding was a continuation of me and Miya's union.

And here it is. We was falling apart.

MCI had a Christmas party, over at my Supervisor's, Michelle Berrian's house. I gotta say that, cause it's two Michelles. Not my next-door neighbor. But two. Two MORE Michelles out here at this party.

My boss, Jeff. He's at the party. Michelle is my supervisor. But Jeff is the supervisor of all of us. We all work at the same big cubicle, hustlin long distance. We on the same team.

Jeff is in the living room. He keeps fiddling wit a deck of cards. Shufflin and cuttin. But Jeff is mad. He also cheats on his wife. The word is that he's fuckin Michelle. Berrian. It's another girl here too that he's fuckin. His other supervisor under him. I forget her name. But she is very attractive.

But who Jeff wants is the other Michelle. The one who is standing. Up here in this kitchen. Up at the counter. Across from the refrigerator. Carving her a drink. It ain't all she's carving. The eyeballs outta niggas heads.

She ain't at work. So, it ain't 'a dress code out here in these streets, or at Michelle Berrian's house either. This brown Puerto Rican bitch got on a tiggght ass leopard print cat suit. And the way Michelle is shaped, it look like this shit is painted on. Her phat lil coochie- booty pokin out at me. Pussylips look as hard as two cheetah nipples.

I got her mad at me right now though, cause I keep calling her Lil Kim. That's the style. That's who she reminded me of. Her name is Michelle Alize. But we keep calling her Alize. So both Michelles won't look at you at the same time. Although, it wouldn't hurt.

But um, if I could hit her Alize wit this tangerey; maybe it'll make it some Thug Passion. Right. I love Pac, but B.I.G. is my most favorite rapper of all time, with all respect to HOV. But tonight, we doin Bailey's. I bring the Irish Cream to the party. This 'a dedication. I'm doing this for BIG, cause this the first Christmas he won't be here. It won't be no Fresh NEW B.I.G. tracks this holiday season. But I'm gon keep his memory alive, cause sippin on Bailey's is something he rapped about.

So I'm bringing this Bailey's in honor of B.I.G.; now if I can just get this Lil Kim...

With me being out in the streets at BTN, one of the things I picked up in the process, is this 20-track Best of Biggie mixtape. So when this shit go on, this shit got EVERYBODY at the party UP!! UP!! and dancin!! Bitches dancin. Booties Bouncing!! It's bout to be some sweaty blackmen all up on Alize.

Apparently Michelle can feel it. The other Michelle.

Then on toppa that, shit don't always go as

planned. Jeff is mad at me, cause he down on
Michelle. But she won't give him attention. I got her
over there fuckin wit me. And of course, that mean.:
he think I'm tryin to fuck her.

I'on know.

Michelle did gravitate more towards me. But shit
was in the way.

"Alright that's it. That's it! Party Over!

We bout to go to the club," that's all what the other
Michelle said. She too probably sensed Jeff won't
happy. She knew him better than I did.

Before the music started, I saw him kept
putting his head down. But overall, I was ignoring
the nigga. It was pussy in here. Shit, Alize was in
here! Fuck, I'm gon be worried about this nigga fo.
These MCI bitches be ho'ing. But on 'a whole
nother level. They ain't like the crusty ass
crackheads and dopefiend bitches, I be fuckin in the
streets. Even though, some of them be smokin
crack too, or toot that nose.

These bitches wanna nigga to pay TOP
DOLLA to getta piece 'a dat pussy. They wanna
nigga to pay THE RENT. They wanna nigga to buy
em a car. Car note. Insurance. Something. You
wanna fuck these bitches, you gon pay fo
something.

That's why I think Alize keep swishin round here, in that tiggght asss suit. Lookin like 'a heated animal. Lettin me see how phaaat that asss and pussy is. This bitch tryin ta get up at somma that $7500. Ain't it.

All of them end up going to the Mirage. I can't get in, cause I got sneakers 'on. It worked out good for me. I was drunk. Soon as I got back behind the wheel, my head start twinnin. I had to keep stopping at lights and stop signs, to pop the door to throw up. I stopped at Burger King. I tried to get some food on my stomach. Once that grease hit wit that alcohol. Aww man. I'on know how I made it home. Only by the grace of God. I won't tryin to crash another car, or kill myself behind the wheel. But YAHWEH bought me home, from the top of Newport News, all the way back to Atlantic Avenue, out Buckroe Beach. I had made it home.

Me and Miya spent Christmas together. I like the way Miya do Christmas. Miya's Christmas means, we exchange ONE gift at Christmas. At 12 o' clock. Just ONE gift, in between the end of Christmas Eve and the start of Christmas Day. The rest of the gifts we open later that morning. But just to hear Miya say,

"Merry Christmas."

Nobody says Merry Christmas sweeter than Miya. Then I'm unwrapping her greatest gift and made love to my wife...

Then we was having sex straight through to our anniversary. I thought this was it. This gotta be it! But it wasn't IT. And she ain't wanna come back home. She ain't wanna come back to Atlantic Avenue. She never wanted to step foot back in that house no more.

I woulda moved in where she was at. But she...

she won't ready for that either. I had to go back to Atlantic alone.

I went on back home. Just me and my AMEX money. I had some AMEX dollars. Which is travellers checks issued by American Express. I got it from working at MCI. It was some commission money, from getting sales, and extra little bonuses for the Holiday Season. These AMEX dollars spend just like Real CASH. Sometimes, the manager gotta come out to explain to their subordinate employee what it is. But HEY! it all cheques out. And then, it's time to go...

SHOP- PING!!!!

But I went and bought a NEW bucket, mop, broom and dust pan, spray and scrub and cleaning stuff. Why? Because the new year had came in, and I was preparing to make the house into a bachelor pad. Just 3 months out, I was preparing for a new permanent life. A life without Miya. I didn't think we was gon get back together. Just having sex...

That shit won't...

I mean, if that's what it's gonna be, then let's call it that, and just move on. My mindset now was focusing on moving on, and living my life on Atlantic as a single man.

Then one day, I take somebody out Courthouse Green. That's these apartments all the way up Warwick. Near the top of Newport News. That shit just Newport News. That shit ain't even Bad Newz all up here. Anything past Denbigh Boulevard, anything past J Clyde Morris for real; all that shit is just Newport News.

The grimeball that's down, from Briarfield Road all the way down to like 6th, Aqua Vista. The Towers. For real. By the time you hit up Mercury, that shit change, man. Merc is too commercial. All the restaurants and stores on Merc. Then it change again by the time you hit Main Street. Then J Clyde. Then Oyster Point. It's 'a big ass industrial park between J Clyde and Oyster Point. Then Denbigh. And Ft Eustis, that's the army base. That's the military. Them niggas ain't Bad Newz. You got to feel this. Errybody from that city know what I'm talking about. Newport News 'a small city. But it's so diverse.

But that's what make us so GREAT!! and Special.
Bad Newz, Newport News, Newport Nam. Aye! We
On Top!

So one day, I'm out Courthouse Green; now
don't get it twisted. Niggas do put it in out here.
This is a high drug infested area. And anywhere it's
drugs, it's subject to crime violence. So, that's
where I'm at wit it. Of all people, guess who I see?

"Jamie."

NO. It's not Joy. Wish it was. It's not Ericka
or Miya either. It's Patrice. Ericka's ol friend. They
ain't friends by now, Ericka think I was fuckin
Patrice, and Patrice moved on from being friends
wit Ericka. I almost ain't recognize Patrice. She got
a poofy curly mushroomed hair style and she put on
'a lil weight. But once she got closer, and I saw her
face, I knew it was her.

"Hey," I bounced up out the Buick and went
to go meet her and hug her. "What's up?"

I was happy to see Patrice. I asked her the first
obvious question,

"How's Chase?"

She explained to me that he came home. But
the two of them didn't work out. He had left, and
she was now living out here wit her two boys. For

real, I thought the conversation was gon go into us fuckin round and doing something. But it didn't. It never do. Do it? It went into,

"Tonya is coming here."

"When?"

"She on her way here from North Carolina right now."

Word!? This got me curious now. I wanna see how this girl look. I keep hearing how PHAAAT her BOoOoTY is. All this good shit. Let me see for myself.:

Tonya gets here. I went and brought Lynnie-Lynn wit me. I'm gon fuck Tonya. I brought Lynn to fuck Patrice. So she don't be lonely. That's the play. Got it. HUT! Hhhh, why this shit never go to plan?

When we get here. Patrice ain't payin Lynn no attention. This ain't the first time she done this. She did the same thing wit Kenny. My co- worker from Nance. And Kenny stayed in the apartments, right behind her house on La Salle. She ain't even wanna meet Kenny.

Where the hell was this Patrice at when I brought Canaan over that time?

I'on know. But she givin ol Lynnie- Lynn the cold

shoulder. Crazy part about it.: Tonya doing the same thing to me. Alright.: first off, she not as pretty as I thought. As what Patrice portrayed her to me, and what she made herself out to be on the phone. But she is still attractive. She got some sex appeal. I'on see myself doing nothing extreme... like MAKING HER MY NEXT WIFE.

She is dark skin. But that don't got nothing to do wit it. She got that lil dirty Hershey Bunny look to her. It ain't that milky, creamy, smooth. But it's chocolate nevertheless. Maybe, it's 'a lil crunchy. But she ain't as PHAAAAT as what they tried to make her out to be neither. But she does have 'a phat shape. Maybe. You know, sometimes women's weight fluctuate. I'on know.

Cause she keep makin all this LOUD!! dumb ass noise. This shit is throwing me off. She ain't even drunk. She ain't act like this, 2 years ago, on the phone.

And she keep draggin me. So in my head, I'm done wit this shit.

Somehow, she calls me the next day, she want me to come through, for My Birthday. February 19th. I did go to see her. When I get there, I'm looking for my friend, Patrice. Patrice ain't here. The kids ain't here either. Only Tonya is here. Without even saying too much. She take me upstairs, in Patrice's room, into Patrice's bed. And I don't do too much suckin no titties. I don't eat the pussy. Nothing. I just grudge fuck the shit out this bitch! Just straight grudge fuck! Cause she made me mad how she dragg'd me last night, and in fronna my homie.

But she like it. Some reason, this bitch keep nuttin like every 15- 30 seconds. Then she cream like 1 to 2 minutes apart. After that. I had this bitch curled round my dick, like'a lil puppy dawg. She was in love and wanted to bring me home with her back to Charlotte.

I had to think about it at first. Tonya used to be married, and she got (5) kids by her ex- husband. But I thought about

CHARLOTTE.

Charlotte is a major southern city. They have the Carolina Panthers there, and The Charlotte Hornets. It's way more advanced than any city in Virginia. Even Alexandria. This would be a fun new experience, and perhaps a chance for me to get a better job, or a new career making more money. I didn't tell Tonya, but I was agreeing to go. Just one thing. First...

I gotta run all this past Miya.

Cause Legally, she is still my wife. I can't just leave and not tell her where I'm going. Especially,

WITHOUT her. I get there. I get there. February 20th. The day after my 23rd Birthday. I'm standing in her living room, and it's,

"Miya, this is it. I'm leaving. I'm moving to Charlotte, in North Carolina..."

Something to that effect. I didn't tell her about Tonya. That would make it look like I was leaving her for Tonya. Which I wasn't. I wasn't leaving Miya for Tonya. I was leaving Miya for OPPORTUNITY. If I was gon go back to being a single man, then I had greater opportunity in North Carolina, than what I had had it in Virginia. With my wife gone; there was nothing left for me in Virginia.

My Uncle Bruce had always talked to me about moving to a bigger city. But he was referring to coming to Richmond. What's bigger than Richmond? CHARLOTTE is bigger than Richmond. Like I explained before. And one thing about it.: Charlotte is 'a whole lot closer to dat 305. I was done. Just one more paycheck. I'm gon take my whole check, and drive Tonya back to Charlotte; and be in Charlotte.

Then as I was going to put my hand on Miya's doorknob, I heard her say,

"J... Wait."

And when I turn around, Miya was in my arms, soft as 'a pillow case. We was kissin then,

"Come on. Let's go to the room," my wife cherry churly churrled to me.

I went in Miya's room. And we fuck'd and we made love. And I got up. For real my mind was still focused on leaving. I see Miya on the bed, and she keep holding her legs up. Her legs are open to her shoulders. So, I think she telling me she want some more. But this ain't like Miya. I know my wife. So I say,

"Miya, what are you doing," I was pulling my pants up and buckling my belt, when she say,

"I saw this on Roseanne. This how you get the sperm to the egg. This how you get pregnant. I'm bout to get pregnant."

"Ha, ha, ha," I laugh. I think this bitch is silly.

I end up spending EVERY night at Miya's house. So called, waiting on 2 weeks for my paycheck, to happen. I was gon stack 2 paychecks. By now I had BLEW!! through the $7500. Man, Miya came one day and she said,

"J," she hesitate slightly gripping her stomach, then say, "I think I'm pregnant."

Say WHAT!?

Miya had missed her period for the month, and the way her body feel. She went and she bought and she took her pregnancy test; and she came out the bathroom, and that's when she said,

"I'm pregnant."

Say WHAT!?

"I'm going to schedule an appointment with the doctor."

And that's what she did. And when we went to see the doctor, he confirmed the same thing. He confirmed that Miya's date of conception was FEBRUARY 20TH. That date after my birthday. The same date that my Best Momma passed away on. Well I wasn't going nowhere near Charlotte now.

Cause I done popped up da Momma Miya, and she was having my Baby!!!!

From Poverty, To Prison, To Prosperity.

The last (20) Chapters of this book were censored from email transmission, due to interference by The Virginia Department of Corrections and JPay Inc.

The Author's contact information is.: Tekur Dalga Anbessa #1006204; Keen Mountain Correctional Center; 3402 Kennel Gap Road; Oakwood, Virginia 24631. Email.: TEKUR ANBESSA #1006204@jpay.com.

PLEASE support Author's Tekur Delga
Anbessa's petition for clemency to Virginia
Governor, Glen Youngkin, by signing your
support at; www.change.org/freetekurnow

& Add him on twitter: twitter.com/freetekur

**Thank you, and Anbessa thanks you in
advance for all your support.**

A loving wife, mother, sister, aunt, teacher, and friend.

REST IN BLESSED PEACE Evelyn Miles.

Made in the USA
Middletown, DE
02 April 2023

28123349R00345